THE ETHICS OF WAR

Included here are authoritative commentaries addressed to the principled grounds of war. The editors have chosen topics and contributors with skill, acutely aware of the timely and the timeless in this grave subject.

Daniel N. Robinson, Philosophy Faculty Oxford University and Distinguished Research Professor, Emeritus, Georgetown University

This book will be a strong contribution to the international debate on the ethics of war.

David Blankenhorn, President of the Institute of American Values, New York

9/11 and the subsequent invasions of Afghanistan and Iraq have left many people baffled and concerned. This interdisciplinary study of the ethics of war provides an excellent orientation not only to present, but also to future conflicts. It looks both back at historical traditions of ethical thought and forward to contemporary and emerging issues.

The Ethics of War traces how different cultures involved in present conflicts have addressed similar problems over the centuries. Distinguished authors reflect how the Graeco-Roman world, Byzantium, the Christian just war tradition, Islam, Judaism, Hinduism and the Geneva Conventions have addressed recurrent ethical problems of war. Cutting-edge essays by prominent modern theorists address vital contemporary issues including asymmetric war, preventive war, human rights and humanitarian intervention.

Distinguished academics, ethical leaders, and public policy figures have collaborated in this innovative and accessible guide to ethical issues in war.

Dedicated to Wolfson College, Oxford

The Ethics of War

Shared Problems in Different Traditions

Edited by

RICHARD SORABJI
Wolfson College, Oxford, UK

and

DAVID RODIN
Oxford University, UK

ASHGATE

Reprinted 2007

Published by
Ashgate Publishing Limited
Gower House
Croft Road
Aldershot
Hants GU11 3HR
England

Ashgate Publishing Company
Suite 420
101 Cherry Street
Burlington, VT 05401-4405
USA

Ashgate website: http://www.ashgate.com

British Library Cataloguing in Publication Data
The ethics of war : shared problems in different traditions
   1. War – Moral and ethical aspects – Cross-cultural studies
   2. Just war doctrine – Cross-cultural studies
   I. Sorabji, Richard II. Rodin, David
   172'.42

Library of Congress Cataloging-in-Publication Data
The ethics of war : shared problems in different traditions / [edited by] Richard Sorabji and David Rodin.
   p. cm.
  Includes index.
  ISBN 0-7546-5448-6 (hardcover : alk. paper) – ISBN 0-7546-5449-4 (pbk. : alk. paper) 1. War – Moral and ethical aspects. I. Sorabji, Richard. II. Rodin, David.
  B105.W3E86 2005
  172'.42–dc22

2005006171

ISBN-13: 978 0 7546 5448 3 (Hbk); 978 0 7546 5449 0 (Pbk)

Typeset by IML Typographers, Birkenhead, Merseyside
Printed in Great Britain by TJ International Ltd, Padstow, Cornwall.

Contents

List of Contributors

Nick Allen was for twenty-five years Lecturer/Reader in the Social Anthropology of South Asia at the Institute of Social and Cultural Anthropology at Oxford University, and a Fellow of Wolfson College, Oxford, until his retirement in 2001. His DPhil., based on twenty months' fieldwork in east Nepal, focused on the mythology and oral traditions of a Tibeto-Burman 'tribal' community. His main research interest in recent years has been Indo-European cultural comparativism, and in particular the common origins of the Sanskrit and ancient Greek epic traditions, on which he has published a number of academic articles.

Anthony Coates is Lecturer in Politics and International Relations at the University of Reading. His research interests and publications are in the areas of international political theory and international ethics. He is the author of *The Ethics of War* (Manchester University Press, 1997) and editor of *International Justice* (Ashgate, 2000). He is currently writing a book entitled *War and the Virtues* for Routledge.

Noah Feldman is Associate Professor of Law at the New York University School of Law. Formerly a Junior Fellow of the Harvard University Society of Fellows, he is the author of *What We Owe Iraq: War and the Ethics of Nation Building* (2004) and *After Jihad: America and the Struggle for Islamic Democracy* (2003). In 2003 he served as senior constitutional adviser to the Coalition Provisional Authority in Baghdad. His work focuses on the relation between religion and political authority.

The Right Reverend Richard Harries has been Bishop of Oxford since 1987. Prior to this he was Dean of King's College, London. He has written extensively on modern military conflicts. His earlier books on the subject include *Christianity and War in a Nuclear Age* (Mowbray, 1986) and *Should a Christian Support Guerrillas?* (Lutterworth, 1981). His more recent writings include *After the Evil: Christianity and Judaism in the Shadow of the Holocaust* (Oxford University Press, 2003) and *The Passion in Art* (Ashgate, 2004). He was elected a Fellow of The Royal Society of Literature in 1996. He is active in the House of Lords, and a long-standing contributor to BBC Radio 4's *Today* programme.

John Kelsay is Richard L. Rubenstein Professor of Religion at Florida State University, where he teaches courses in ethics and in Islamic Studies. Professor Kelsay's publications include *Islam and War: A Study in Comparative Ethics*

(Westminster/John Knox, 1993) and a number of articles discussing the just war and jihad traditions. He is co-editor with James Turner Johnson of *Just War and Jihad* (Greenwood, 1991), and *Cross, Crescent, and Sword* (Greenwood, 1990). Professor Kelsay's recent work, supported in part by fellowships from the John Simon Guggenheim Foundation and by the Princeton University Center for Human Values, focuses on the Islamic law of war and peace.

Angeliki Laiou is Dumbarton Oaks Professor of Byzantine History at Harvard University. She is a Member of the American Academy of Arts and Sciences, and Permanent Member of the Academy of Athens, and was formerly Director of Dumbarton Oaks, Washington DC. Her research interests include Byzantine social and economic history, the history of the Mediterranean in the later Middle Ages, and the history of Modern Greece. She is co-editor of *The Crusades from the Perspective of Byzantium and the Muslim World* (Dumbarton Oaks, 2002).

Jeff McMahan is Professor of Philosophy at Rutgers University. He is the author of *The Ethics of Killing: Problems at the Margins of Life* (Oxford University Press, 2002), and is presently working on a sequel provisionally called *The Ethics of Killing: Self-defence, War, and Punishment*. This too will be published by Oxford University Press, in the Oxford Ethics Series, edited by Derek Parfit.

Karma Nabulsi is Research Fellow at Nuffield College, Fellow-elect in Politics at St Edmund Hall, and University Lecturer in International Relations at Oxford University. Her DPhil. was a study of the foundations of the laws of war in Europe, and was published as *Traditions of War: Occupation, Resistance, and the Law* (Oxford University Press, 1999). She continues to publish articles and other writings on the laws of war. She is currently researching her book on the nineteenth century for W. W. Norton, entitled *Conspirators for Liberty: The Underground Struggle to Create Democracies in 19th Century Europe*.

Richard Norman was formerly Professor of Moral Philosophy at the University of Kent, and now works part-time at the University. His publications include *The Moral Philosophers* (Oxford University Press, 1998) and *On Humanism* (Routledge, 2004). His previous work on the ethics of war includes *Ethics, Killing and War* (Cambridge University Press, 1995). He is co-editor of *Human Rights and Military Intervention* (Ashgate, 2002).

Sir Michael Quinlan was a United Kingdom Civil Servant from 1954 to 1992, working mostly in the Ministry of Defence; he was Policy Director from 1977 to 1981 and Permanent Under-Secretary of State from 1988 to 1992. From 1992 to 1999 he was Director of the Ditchley Foundation. He has written many articles on international security issues, especially nuclear weapons, and on ethical questions raised by these issues. He is a Roman Catholic.

David Rodin is Director of the war programme at the Oxford Uehiro Centre for Practical Ethics, Oxford University, and Senior Research Fellow at the Centre for Applied Philosophy and Public Ethics, the Australian National University. He is the author of *Self-defence and War* (Oxford University Press, 2002), which received the American Philosophical Association Frank Chapman Sharp Award. He is currently researching the ethics of pre-emptive war, terrorism and a range of issues in international justice with the support of the Leverhulme Trust programme on the Changing Character of War.

Norman Solomon retired in 2001 from the Oxford Centre for Hebrew and Jewish Studies, where he was Fellow in Modern Jewish Thought. He remains a member of Wolfson College, Oxford, and of the Oxford University Teaching and Research Unit in Hebrew and Jewish Studies. He was previously Director of the Centre for the Study of Judaism and Jewish/Christian Relations at the Selly Oak Colleges, Birmingham, and before that rabbi to a number of Orthodox Jewish congregations in England. He has published several books on Judaism including *Judaism: A Very Short Introduction* (Oxford University Press, 2000).

Richard Sorabji CBE, FBA is Emeritus Professor of Ancient Philosophy at King's College, London, former Director of the Institute of Classical Studies, University of London, former Gresham Professor of Rhetoric, and currently Fellow of Wolfson College, Oxford. He is general editor of 60 volumes so far of translation of the Ancient Commentators on Aristotle, and editor of the accompanying *Philoponus and the Rejection of Aristotelian Science: Aristotle Transformed*, and a three-volume Sourcebook on the Commentators. His other books include *Aristotle on Memory*; *Necessity, Cause and Blame*; *Time, Creation and the Continuum; Animal Minds and Human Morals*; *Emotion and Peace of Mind*, and he is currently writing a book on the Self.

Introduction

Richard Sorabji and David Rodin

This is an interdisciplinary book. Each of the cultures involved in the main conflicts current today has a tradition of thought about the ethics of war. In the Christian tradition, the idea of just war is the most influential. But it is important for each party in a dispute, and equally for those who intervene, to understand the traditions of other parties, not just their own. Our authors will consider the Islamic, Jewish and Indian traditions, and the Graeco-Roman antecedents of Christian ideas. The traditions are relevant to some of the most pressing ethical problems we are currently facing. The first seven chapters consider historical and religious traditions on the ethics of war. The second six consider some of the most important contemporary problems in war in the light of modern just war thinking and practice.

The book is interdisciplinary both in terms of its themes and its contributors. It ranges over religious and historical traditions of thought, and delves into issues arising both from philosophical theory and from concrete cases. The contributors are prominent figures in the fields of philosophy, history, anthropology, religious studies and politics. A number have played an important part in public life relating to war. Sir Michael Quinlan was head of the Ministry of Defence in Britain at the time of the 1991 Gulf War and the intervention in Kosovo. He argues that the invasion of Iraq in 2003 has significantly violated just war principles. Richard Harries, as Bishop of Oxford, argued in the House of Lords against that invasion for the same reason. Noah Feldman, an expert in Islamic law, has had responsibility for *post bellum* reconstruction as Senior Advisor to the US Government on the new constitution for Iraq.

We should say a few words about why we think this kind of interdisciplinary approach is so important to the ethics of war. The reasons are tied up with three themes which we hope will emerge clearly from the essays. The first is that there is a considerable recurrence of ethical issues, both through different periods of time and across different traditions of thought. Questions of regime change, of humanitarian intervention, of indiscriminate weaponry and collateral damage, of whether it is ever permissible to engage in deliberate attacks on civilians, and the rights and responsibilities of occupiers and occupied have all been faced before. Rich traditions of religious, philosophical and legal thought exist on them. Although the experience of war – its cultural and technological context – changes, the basic nature and the form of the ethical challenges it gives rise to remain in many ways the same. Even such paradigmatically 'modern' issues as asymmetric war have long historical precedents.

The second theme is that different traditions are not hermetically sealed from each other, and neither is modern just war thinking independent of its historical foundations. For example, we will see in these essays how Jewish, Christian and Islamic thought on the ethics of war has been influenced by ancient Greek and Roman precursors. Noah Feldman shows how medieval Jewish and Islamic thinking, in the forms of Maimonides and Averroes, interpenetrated each other.

In our own age, it is just war thinking that has become the dominant discourse on the ethics of war (partly through its process of transformation into modern international law, charted by Karma Nabulsi in Chapter 3). Just war thinking is still deeply indebted to its medieval Christian foundations, even though its modern form is now substantially secular, expressed in a philosophical and legal rather than religious idiom. It draws resources not only from the Christian tradition, but also from political philosophy, legal theory and modern moral ideals such as human rights. The six chapters in Part II of this volume cover some of the most difficult and pressing contemporary problems in the ethics of war, and represent the 'state of the art' of modern just war thinking.

The final theme is the interaction between ethical thought and political action, and the considerable influence the former is capable of exerting on the latter. For example, Angeliki Laiou, in her essay on the crusades, argues that a failure to understand different conceptions of the ethics of war – a 'just war' paradigm on the part of the Byzantines and a 'holy war' ideology on the part of Western Crusaders – contributed to the breakdown of the alliance and the sack of Byzantium during the Fourth Crusade. Richard Sorabji discusses how the Spain of Charles V halted the conquest of the American Indians for a year to enable thinkers such as Vitoria and las Casas to debate its ethical status. John Kelsay shows how manifesto statements by Usama bin Ladin and representatives of Hamas fit into a long tradition of Islamic Shari'a reasoning, and may be engaged with and challenged on these terms.

These connections are important because they show the sterility of the often asserted division between 'ethics' and the supposedly 'realist' world of international politics and war. In fact, war leaders and politicians are often motivated by moral ideals, and they justify their actions in ethical terms. Similarly, as democratic citizens we must reflect on and debate our leaders' decisions, using moral arguments and concepts. Michael Quinlan demonstrates how the British Government and Civil Service have been substantially, though by no means perfectly, guided by just war principles. Anthony Coates emphasises that the character of war is inescapably moral, and shows how moral zeal can inflame and brutalise war as much as it can restrain it.

All chapters are meant to help one think about present day problems in the ethics of war. As has already been suggested, it will emerge that many of these problems are old and recurrent. But even where our problems are new, it helps us to think about them to see what has been said by past traditions and, equally important, to see how our opponents may think about them.

The aim of providing tools to think with is explicit in Sorabji, Laiou and Kelsay's contributions in the first seven chapters that trace traditions. Conversely, the guidance of Augustine or Thomas Aquinas is explicitly considered by Harries, Quinlan and Coates in the last six chapters on contemporary problems.

The ethics of war can be discussed in connection with two different questions: the question of when it is just to go to war (called in the just war tradition the *ad bellum* question), and the question of how it is just to behave in the course of a war (the *in bello* question). To start with the Christian tradition, five criteria are now commonly emphasised for justice in going to war, the *ad bellum* question:

1 There should be a just cause.
2 Reasonable attempts at peaceful resolution should have been exhausted (the war should be a 'last resort').
3 The right authority should authorise the war.
4 War should not make things even worse than they were already (proportionality).
5 War aims should be achievable.

These criteria seem reasonable to many people regardless of their original justifications, such as the appeal to divine or natural law. Anthony Coates in Chapter 11 advocates return to a sixth ancient requirement, the right attitude towards the enemy, and Michael Quinlan in Chapter 13 discusses a seventh criterion, that of obligations after a military conquest, (the *post bellum* question), which was also recognised in the sixteenth century.

Sorabji traces the development of these criteria, and emphasises that it started not with Christians, but with pagan antiquity in Plato, Aristotle and Cicero. They discussed the right cause, the right attitude of mind, and in Cicero's case, the need to make an advance declaration which gives peace a chance. The early Christian Church went in another direction, being faced with an apparent conflict between Old Testament approval of war and Christ's talk of turning the other cheek. As a result, some major Church Fathers in the early centuries thought that Christians should be pacifist. Around 400 CE, Augustine rejected pacifism and therefore had to return to the question when war would be just. He advocates, first, having the right attitude to the enemy, with the corollary that the war must be one of necessity not of choice; secondly, having a just cause and, thirdly, having the right authority. As Richard Harries points out in Chapter 12, these three criteria are found also in Thomas Aquinas in the thirteenth century. Both Augustine and Aquinas also discuss the need not to do more harm than good, though they discuss it in the different contexts of punishment and tyrannicide. Augustine and Aquinas contributed in addition to discussion of requirements for justice *in bello*. Aquinas benefited from the systematisation of Augustine's ideas by the canon lawyer Gratian and his successors in the twelfth century. Gratian, besides requiring a just cause and the right authority, also returned to the need for a proper declaration of war. The requirement of war aims being achievable was debated by Cajetan and Súarez in the sixteenth century.

Angeliki Laiou shows how important differences of conception can be, as between holy war and just war. Problems are not always shared, and she argues that misunderstandings on this help between Western crusaders and their Byzantine allies to explain the Westerners' subsequent sack of the Byzantine capital, Constantinople. Once at cross purposes, the Westerners took the attitude that he who is not for me is against me, and it finished up splitting the Christian side – a lesson, she has suggested, for our times.

Sorabji picks up the story again when, in the mid-sixteenth century, Europe's most powerful sovereign, Charles V of Spain, halted the Spaniards' conquest of the American Indians for a year while his thinkers debated the very issues that confront us now: the justice of regime change, preventive killing, invading another country to protect the victims of its regime and *post bellum* obligations. The great thinker Vitoria and the passionate defender of the Indians Las Casas strongly developed European thinking on justice in war. In the process, the extent of Augustine's influence becomes clearer from the number of Augustine texts cited.

Karma Nabulsi analyses the development of these ideas into the modern period, with the contrast between Grotius in the seventeenth century and Rousseau in the eighteenth, who denied that war was natural, and the subsequent legislation drawn up in Geneva, Brussels and the Hague, starting in 1864. She argues that war has always been asymmetric between the strong and the weak, so that the problem made central by David Rodin in Chapter 8 is not a new one. What was new was the principal question addressed, or rather the reason for addressing it. The old question of which side was just, which unjust, in going to war was not so central, and what was central can have undesirable consequences, as Anthony Coates argues in Chapter 11. Nor was the new question of which individuals should be exempt from attack. It was rather which individuals should be allowed to fight. This question had been much addressed for an entirely different purpose by Maimonides, as Norman Solomon brings out in Chapter 6, and by Gratian and Thomas Aquinas, whose interest was in exempting clerics from military service. But now the purpose of the question was entirely different. How long should individuals in an unequal war be allowed to resist the stronger invader, particularly after occupation? The stronger powers have wanted resistance to occupation made illegal as soon as possible, while weaker powers have wanted it recognised as legitimate. Two traditions have favoured the strong: those of Martialism (the glorification of war) and of Grotius, which has been the dominant influence. He sought to limit the right to fight to soldiers controlled by a state, whereas the citizens of the occupied country are required to obey the occupiers, if they wish to be protected. The rival republican view encouraged by Rousseau insisted on the legitimacy of civilian defence.

Turning to the Jewish and Islamic traditions, we find them both starting from warrior contexts. The Book of Deuteronomy already considers, from a rather warlike perspective, questions of justice *in bello*. As regards justice *ad bellum*, Norman Solomon tells us, later rabbis often discussed when war was obligatory or optional, rather than just or unjust. The rabbis and the philosophers, starting with Philo in the first century CE and continuing with Maimonides in the twelfth, introduced important modifications into their interpretations of Deuteronomy. But in Maimonides, at least, the discussion had a somewhat theoretical character, since Jews had no state or army of their own for much of the time from Philo in the first century CE until the foundation of modern Israel.

Islam, like Judaism, starts from its earliest history to develop restrictions on conduct in war. These *in bello* restrictions are already well advanced in the eighth century CE. Around 1200, the great philosopher ibn Rushd, or Averroes, in Cordoba reports the jurists' attempts to resolve apparent differences of viewpoint in the Qur'an about whether the aim should be to kill all polytheists. Should the verses advocating peace be given precedence, or should the verses that seem more bellicose be applied only to the historical situation at the time, and not generalised? Noah Feldman shows us that Averroes borrows from Aristotle an idea about the nature of judicial discretion, to draw a moderate conclusion. He also argues that Averroes' contemporary born in the same city of Cordoba, Maimonides, modifies the ethics of war in the Book of Deuteronomy by interpreting it in the light of the moderate Islamic regime in Spain which Averroes represented. Solomon does not see the Islamic influence on Maimonides as being so benign in other contexts.

We learn from Noah Feldman how Averroes and Maimonides, and from Norman Solomon how Philo, modified their original warrior traditions. Early Christians, we have seen, were drawn instead to pacifism, but we have also seen how the possibility of war was opened up by Augustine. Thus from opposite directions, Augustine, Averroes, Philo and Maimonides were leading their respective religions towards greater convergence on the rights and wrongs of war.

With the crusades starting in 1099, and with the sack of Baghdad by the Mongols in 1258, thought was increasingly given by Islamic thinkers to defence and resistance, which had not originally been a relevant problem. John Kelsay distinguishes two Islamic strategies for justifying resistance against an occupier. On one view, the occupying government is not a just and legitimate one. This may have been argued by Ibn Taymiyya (died 1328) against the Mongols, even though the Mongols had converted to Islam, and was argued against the British in India in 1824, when it was seen that they were replacing the Islamic regime of the Mughals. It is particularly important for us to understand Ibn Taymiyya, because his complaint that illegitimate governments have been imposed has been used to justify modern Muslim terrorist resistance, and Ibn Taymiyya has been much cited. But it involves the difficulty that resistance cannot be called 'jihad' unless it is declared by a just and legitimate government. This constraint of legitimate authority affects also the liberation movements discussed by Richard Harries in Chapter 12. The other line of argument is that the war has been imposed as a matter of necessity, as it was by the Crusaders, and this argument too has been used to justify modern terrorist resistance. It is also important to understand the modern Muslim reply to this case *ad bellum* for terrorist resistance. The reply often appeals to considerations *in bello*. Even though increasingly many may think that there is a real injustice being suffered by many Muslims, an honourable, that is to say morally acceptable, war cannot be fought if it involves so much killing of non-combatants.

The great Indian epic the *Mahābhārata* is about a war between two branches of the same family. It presents a different society again, one in which chivalry introduces rather different restrictions on conduct *in bello*. Subject to these restrictions, one's station determines whether one must or must not fight. Nick Allen shows that most of the *ad bellum* requirements about going to war are respected, even if this was not the central interest of the epic. One sobering outcome was that the two warring families almost wiped each other out in spite of their rather chivalrous attitude to warfare, which suggests that the respect for the enemy which Anthony Coates advocates in Chapter 11 as a safeguard is not an absolute guarantee that slaughter will be kept within bounds. The Indian epics are not appealed to in the same spirit as in Islam, in which medieval jurists are accepted as authoritative interpreters of divine law. But they are very much part of public consciousness, and I would expect that modern appeals to them would carry weight.

We now pass to the second part of the book, which addresses some of the most pressing contemporary issues in the ethics of war: the ethical issues raised by asymmetric war, the legitimacy of pre-emptive war, humanitarian intervention, nuclear weapons, guerrilla conflict, and finally a discussion of the justice of recent conflicts including the intervention in Kosovo and the wars in Afghanistan and Iraq. David Rodin addresses a subject that arises in our authors more frequently than any other, namely asymmetric war and the closely related dilemma already mentioned created by the disparity between strong invaders and weak victims of invasion. The problem of asymmetric war is raised in one form in Richard Harries's discussion of Aquinas on rebellion, in another by the Islamic search for a justification of resistance. It is argued by Karma Nabulsi to have defeated twentieth-century attempts at war legislation. How long and by what means are the weak entitled to resist? Their very weakness prevents them using the same kind of weaponry as the invaders, but that encourages resort to guerrilla tactics which are likely to kill non-combatants. Are the strong powers entitled to define their own weapons as legitimate and the methods of the weak powers as illegitimate? Nabulsi's point that the strong powers do not want resistance to remain legitimate beyond a short window of opportunity makes it unsurprising that Geneva legislation about guerrillas was delayed as late as the protocols of 1974–7, and that the strong powers have not been willing to concede much to the weak.

What Rodin brings out is that asymmetric war creates a conflict between considerations *ad bellum* and *in bello*. The weak and oppressed may have just cause to embark on war, but they lack the overpowering force of the stronger. So their only method of making an impact may be to harm non-combatants deliberately, in violation of the requirements of justice *in bello*. The standard understanding of just war disallows this, and makes the *in bello* requirements override the considerations *ad bellum*. This connects with John Kelsay's report, already mentioned, that many Muslims agree, against the arguments of terrorist groups, that although there is just cause for fighting back against repression, this is in practice ruled out by the illicit killing of non-combatants that would be involved. Rodin's proposal is that although the rules *in bello* cannot be waived, a more scrupulous observance should be required of the overwhelmingly stronger side. Quinlan disagrees, and proposes instead a more moderate constraint that the rules of engagement used by the strong should not make the non-combatants among the weak take all the risks.

Jeff McMahan criticises the recent advocacy of pre-emptive war. The term 'pre-emptive' lends a certain respectability, since a pre-emptive war forestalls imminent attack, whereas what is really being advocated is preventive war which attacks people on the basis of speculation about what they might do, when they have not in fact done anything. Like Vitoria in the sixteenth century, McMahan draws a parallel with civil law and with preventive detention before anything wrong has been done, which cannot be regarded as a punishment, and does not purport to offer justice to the detainee. He argues that a preventive war against a state is similarly not supported by considerations of justice.

Richard Norman argues that wars of humanitarian intervention are not justified. This is not because of any inherent right of a state to be free of interference, but because it creates international disorder and worsens human rights. Quinlan does not agree in his discussion of the air strikes in Kosovo in 1999. This was designed to prevent an immediate humanitarian disaster, when hundreds of thousands had already been driven from their homes with widespread torture, murder and home-destruction, and the policy already in existence was being sharply accelerated, also creating problems for the neighbouring countries who were receiving the refugees.

Norman considers that the idea of human rights has an important role to play. Western societies tend to impose the idea of human rights as part of any *post bellum* settlement. But there are questions, which have been discussed elsewhere, of how the idea fits into societies which, without necessarily violating human rights, have been used to settling disputes in a different way, for example in terms of how different parties can best get on with each other in the future, given their rather different levels of rights and expectations, or in terms of character rather than of rights.[1] This supplies a warning that the idea of human rights will not everywhere be found so intelligible as it was in *post bellum* Kosovo.

Anthony Coates addresses the complaint that the idea of just war can arouse an undesirable moral fervour. So, he warns, can the realist approach, which insists that might, not right, is the only thing that counts. In fact, he argues, both parties need to consider the possibility that they are being driven by a cultural contempt. He gives the example of Plato's belief that more savage treatment of the vanquished is appropriate when they are non-Greeks. Aristotle, as Sorabji points out in Chapter 1, had already rebuked his teacher, Plato, for this. The idea that savagery may be due to culturally based contempt contrasts with the suggestion by Laiou in Chapter 2 that in the sack of Constantinople by the Crusaders, it was due to a mis-understanding concerning the difference between holy war and just war.

Coates advocates a return to the requirement, which he draws from Augustine and Aquinas, of the cultivation of a charitable attitude to one's enemies, as a safeguard against cultural contempt. Given the right inner attitude, he argues, many other requirements of just war will look after themselves, since people will not go to war precipitately, nor conduct war in violation of *in bello* requirements. It might also be said that open adherence to a code of law such as the Geneva Convention helps to create the right attitude so that the influence goes in both directions. Although Coates is surely right to warn that the insistence on going to war justly can lead to a blind self-righteousness, it has to be said that every position has its dangers. For scholarship referred to by Sorabji in Chapter 1 finds Sepúlveda, and even to some extent Vitoria, justifying the Spanish conquest of American Indians on the grounds that the war is carried out with charitable intentions, or in a charitable manner.

The final two chapters continue Coates' appeal to the just war tradition, addressing concrete cases in the ethics of war, and are authored by two figures who have significant experience beyond academic circles in 'practice'. Richard Harries, Bishop of Oxford and member of Britain's upper house of government, the House of Lords, argues that, contrary to what many believe, the tenets of just war theory apply to two recent issues: the liberation movements of the 1960s and nuclear weapons. In both cases, the application requires careful thought about the new context. Sir Michael Quinlan's subject is complementary: Britain's wars since 1945. His application of just war principles is hard-headed, or as he says, 'pragmatic'. It can and should take into account costs to one's own side, the duration of the war and, of course, the probability of success of various methods of pursuing it. None the less, he argues that it clearly rules out certain wars, and certain (though not all) uses of nuclear weapons. In addition, he considers it wrong that all risk should be unloaded onto the country attacked. Rather, one must strike a balance between protecting one's own troops and protecting non-combatants in the invaded country.

The book is extremely relevant to present wars, but we intend it to be relevant to other times as well, to other wars, and to the avoidance of war. We want it to be readable by the ordinary citizen troubled by present conflicts and seeking to understand them. Such people formed much of the audience at the two-day conference at Wolfson College, Oxford, in June 2003, from which we have drawn 8 of the 13 chapters. All the chapters are new, although a version of Norman Solomon's will appear in a work in preparation: Torkel Brekke (ed.), *The Ethics of War in Asian Civilisations*. We should like to thank Wolfson College, Oxford, where David Rodin was and Richard Sorabji is a fellow, and we have great pleasure in dedicating the book to Wolfson, which does so much to facilitate the interchange of ideas. In particular, we wish to thank the College Secretary, Jan Scriven, for all the work put into making the conference a success, and we should also like to thank Clive Marks, who urged publication and arranged for preparation for press to be supported by the Ashdown Trust. In addition, we would like to thank the Oxford Leverhulme Programme on the Changing Character of War, whose generous support has enabled David Rodin to work on this project.

Note

1   Rosen, Lawrence (2002), *The Justice of Islam*, Oxford, and 'The Islamic idea of justice revisited', paper to conference, 'Islamic Law and Human Rights: An Ethnographic Approach', held at Wolfson College, Oxford, 5 December 2003.

PART I
TRADITIONS

Just War from Ancient Origins to the Conquistadors Debate and its Modern Relevance

Richard Sorabji

The issues about war that face us today have been thought about for up to two-and-a-half thousand years in all the cultures that are involved in the main present conflicts: Christianity, Judaism, Islam and India. So we need not think that we are facing them for the first time without guidance. What I want to spotlight above all is a sixteenth-century debate about the conquest by Spaniards of the American Indians, because by that time the Christian tradition on just war was considering in detail many of the issues that confront us today, and I think knowledge of that debate will give us tools to think with in our very different context. Some readers may wish to skip ahead to that debate. But first I want to trace its historical background, which started more than two thousand years earlier in Graeco-Roman antiquity, and then passed through Christianity. The role of the Christians Augustine around 400 CE and Thomas Aquinas in the thirteenth century is often mentioned. But I want to show that the issues were being discussed up to 700 years before Augustine in pagan antiquity, and that Augustine and Thomas represent important steps in a longer history, a history which begins to look closer to our concerns by the time it reaches the sixteenth century.

The two following chapters will extend the picture to the medieval Western crusaders and the idea of holy war, and to Grotius in the seventeenth century and modern legislation. We shall then pass to Jewish, Islamic and Indian approaches, because we need to be aware of how different parties think. Tools to think with are useful, even though people may come to different conclusions about our current predicaments.

Historical Background

First, a preliminary: the Christian tradition formulated a useful distinction between when it would be just to go to war (*jus ad bellum*), and how to conduct a war justly, whether it has been justly entered into or not (*jus in bello*). As the Introduction has explained, the first five criteria for justly engaging in war are fairly widely agreed:

1   There should be a just cause.
2   Attempts at peaceful resolution should have been exhausted.
3   The war should be decided on by an appropriate authority, and it needs to be clear which that authority is.
4   War will not make the situation even worse than it is already.
5   There should be a reasonable prospect of achieving the aims of the war.

In Chapter 11, Anthony Coates recommends returning to a sixth ancient criterion, that of having the right attitude of benevolence. In Chapter 13, Michael Quinlan considers a particular criterion, that of commitment to obligations to the conquered after the war (*post bellum*). Other criteria are sometimes treated separately and sometimes subsumed under the above: for example, an obligation to declare war, and the requirement that war should be a matter of necessity, not of choice.

As regards the question of justice in the *conduct* of war (*jus in bello*), the Christian tradition did not develop so quickly perhaps as some other traditions. The Greeks and Romans, especially Cicero, already had plenty to say.[1] From the eighth to twelfth centuries CE, there are discussions in Islam about not intentionally killing women or children, even the children of polytheists, about what to do if there are women and children in a fort you propose to attack, or if Muslims are used as human shields, about cheating, treachery and mutilation, and rejecting suicide or hopeless attacks.[2] In the Jewish tradition, the sparing of fruit trees, already mentioned in Deuteronomy 20, is expanded by Maimonides in the twelfth century, so as to ban other destructive acts. And earlier than that there are rules about the treatment of women in war and about allowing civilians to escape from a siege.[3] In the earliest Indian epic, the *Mahābhārata*, there are ethical constraints of chivalry which forbid or allow attack, partly on the basis of the role allotted to the individual by his dharma.[4] The actual conduct of war was thus from early on the subject of ethical reflection in all these cultures at least as much as it was in Christianity. It is only with the Hague and Geneva legislation since the late nineteenth century that Western focus has switched from *jus ad bellum* to *jus in bello*.

Ancient Origins of the Ad Bellum *Requirements*

As regards the *ad bellum* constraints, the first requirement of just cause was already discussed by the Greek philosophers Plato and Aristotle in the fourth century BCE, and by the Roman Cicero in the first century BCE.[5] The second requirement of attempts at peaceful resolution was, as Cicero says, embedded in the fetial code of ancient Rome.[6] This code required that no war was just (*bellum justum*), unless 33 days' notice had been given, with a warning or demand for restitution, and a formal declaration. As regards the sixth requirement of right attitude, relevant considerations, though not described as such, were already introduced by Aristotle when in *Politics* 7.7,1328a7–8 he criticised Plato *Republic* 5, 470C–D, as does Anthony Coates in Chapter 11 in this volume, saying that destroying the land and houses of non-Greeks is not appropriate. Only the unjust should be treated harshly, and closer kin more than the distant. Cicero criticises the razing of Corinth, bids us spare those who are not cruel, protect those who surrender, punish only the guilty and keep promises to the enemy. He further forbids selling back prisoners, destroying, or plundering: *On Duties* 1.35; 1.38; 1.39; 1.80.

Pacifist Interlude

Cicero was influenced by the Stoics, who, as we shall see, believed in the unity of all mankind. It may have been in this spirit that the Stoic Chrysippus and the Cynic Diogenes wrote their treatises *On the Uselessness of Weapons*.[7]

Christianity started with a pacifist tendency for quite different reasons.[8] There was a tension between the Old Testament with its bloodthirsty wars and the New Testament with Christ's injunction, if someone takes your coat, to offer your cloak also, and if struck on one cheek, to turn the other (Matthew 5:39–40, Luke 6:29). In the Old Testament, such advice is given only once, to young men in Lamentations 3:30. Such early Christians as Tertullian, the contemporary of Ulpian at the beginning of the third century CE, and Origen in the middle of that century held that Christians should not fight. Tertullian says that a Christian cannot forsake all for Christ if he is a soldier, and he takes the injunction to turn the other cheek as reinterpreting the ancient Judaic law of an eye for an eye and a tooth for a tooth.[9] This means only that you should not take someone's eye, because if you were to, he would take yours.[10] Origen explains that war was necessary for the ancient Jews, but now would be forbidden them by Rome.[11] Elsewhere, commenting on the particularly bloodthirsty wars of Joshua, he gives spiritual reinterpretations of the Old Testament wars.[12] Vitoria still has to open *On the Law of War* by asking at Question 1, Article 1, whether a Christian may fight, and in Chapter 3 below, Grotius is shown as complaining in the seventeenth century of the opposite view.

Augustine's Return to War and Just War

Augustine in the early fifth century made a huge difference. He too was pressed, in this case by the Manichaeans, on the discrepancy between Old and New Testaments. Augustine responded that Christians are allowed to fight, and the injunction to turn the other cheek is not against fighting, but only against having the wrong inward disposition. The need to turn the other cheek can only be revealed along with the revelation of the Kingdom of Heaven in the New Testament.[13] This immediately introduces what came to be seen as a criterion for just war, namely the right inward disposition, whose importance is argued by Anthony Coates in Chapter 11. It is also applied to just punishment. Even if severe, the just executor of war or punishment must act with the benevolent intention of correcting those who have done wrong. This is the sort of context in which it is said that the just warrior must fight from necessity, not from choice, which some took up as an extra criterion. In this spirit, he will keep faith with the enemy, seek peace and teach him to seek peace.[14] Talking of punishment, Augustine points out that St Paul thinks one person's sin should cause grief (*luctus*) to all the Church, but the punishment must seek to save the sinner's spirit (1 Cor. 5:2 and 5)[15]. The sinner in Paul 2 Thess. 3:14–15 is not to be treated as an enemy. Nor in 2 Cor. 2:6–11 is his punishment to be too great, or as Augustine interprets Paul, that would break the bond of peace and charity. This seemingly benevolent criterion has its dangerous side. For it has been pointed out that Sepúlveda was able to cite one of these same texts of Augustine, *Letter* 189, to cover up a move from an 'ought' to an 'is', and argue that the Spanish conquest is acceptable because it aims at peace and pities the conquered. Even Vitoria, it has been pointed out, concedes that the conquerors would have a just title to protect converts by arms, because they could plead friendship for the converts.[16]

As regards just conditions for entering on war, Augustine discusses what would later fall under the heading of just cause. And here, living in the period of ancient Greek and Roman philosophy, he drew on it. The aim of war is said, as in Cicero, and before that Plato and Aristotle, to be peace.[17] In a striking passage, Augustine refers to the customary definitions of just war as avenging (*ulcisci*) injuries, and specifies in particular the refusal to return what was unjustly taken away or to punish transgressions. This echoes Cicero's definition of just war – he coined the phrase – at *Republic* 3. 23, 34–5, according to which one first demands the return of goods, and then avenges (*ulcisci*) or repels the enemy. Unfortunately, in the same passage, Augustine opens the door to holy war by saying that a war is just if commanded by God.[18] Elsewhere he says that it is legitimate to go to war for violation of the right of passage across territory, which is granted by the law (*jus*) of human society.[19] Again, the law allows killing in defence of oneself or another, but there may be a stronger secret law which will punish the individual who so kills, and it would be wrong on the part of an official who had discretion.[20] Elsewhere approval is given only to killing by a soldier or official in defence of *others*.[21] The saying in Luke 14:23, 'Compel them to come in', justifies violence only against heretics.[22]

Augustine also discussed the right authority, recognising in a passage already discussed[23] that it is not open to everyone to wage even a just war. The right authority is here treated as a separate requirement from the justice of the war. Augustine also expressed the idea, so ambiguously debated in Shakespeare's *Henry V*, that the ruler has the authority to undertake war, and it is not for the ordinary soldier to decide on whether the war is just,[24] a view which is also reflected in Vitoria[25] and, as Chapter 3 in this volume shows, in Grotius.

The requirement that a just war must not do more harm than good is not formulated in general terms, but particular examples are given at least in the sphere of punishment. One we have noticed is that punishment must not be so severe as to break the bond of peace and charity in the Christian community. Another example is Christ's much cited parable of the tares or weeds (Matthew 13:29–30). One must not uproot the weeds, for fear of uprooting the wheat as well. Similarly, sinners should be left unpunished if one cannot distinguish them from the good. The point was made before Augustine by John Chrysostom (died 407 CE), and is repeated by Thomas Aquinas and Las Casas, among others.[26]

As regards the conduct of war after it has been undertaken, Augustine, like Cicero, requires one to keep faith with the enemy and show mercy to prisoners and the defeated.[27] Joshua's ambush (*insidiae*) is declared acceptable, but only given the justice of the war. This is in the passage which defines just war and requires the right authority, and it covers so much in a short space as to be worth quoting.

> From the fact that God, in speaking to Joshua, orders him to prepare ambushes in his rear (that is, fighters in an ambush to ambush the enemy), we are alerted that this is not an unjust thing to do for those who are waging a just war. So a just man should think of nothing specially in these matters except undertaking a just war, if he is allowed to wage war, for not everyone is allowed. But when he has undertaken a just war, it makes no difference to its justice whether he wins by an open fight or by ambush.
>
> Just wars are customarily defined as those which avenge injustices, if a nation or state that is to be attacked has neglected to punish transgressions by its side, or to return what has been unjustly taken away.
>
> But undoubtedly that type of war is also just which God orders, in whom there is no iniquity and who knows what ought to happen to each person. In such a war, the commander of the army or the populace itself should be judged not so much the author of the war, as the agent of it.[28]

The importance of Augustine becomes clearer from the number of references back to him in subsequent literature.

Gratian and Thomas Aquinas

Augustine's views on war were not crystallised by him into criteria. But they were collected in Gratian's compilation of canon law, the *Decretum* of 1140. Gratian required that for a just war, there should be an injustice to be avenged and the right authority which must pronounce an edict – in other words a type of declaration of war. Canon lawyers thereafter built on Gratian's *Decretum*, so that in the next century Thomas Aquinas had much extra material available, as well as Augustine and other sources. His treatment of just war is, however, very succinct. Three requirements must be met in order for a war to be just, all of them mentioned by Augustine. There must be the right authority, just cause, and just intention, or attitude of mind.[29] Later in the same work, he discusses self-defence, though not in the context of war, and again insists that the attitude of mind must not be one of private lust or hatred, or the defender will be guilty of homicide.[30]

Richard Harries in Chapter 12 draws attention to Thomas's treatment of tyrannicide in *Summa Theologiae*, 2.2. Q. 42, Art. 2 ad 3. This uses the principle that tyrannicide is not legitimate if it does the populace more harm than good.

Vitoria, Las Casas, Suárez

I come now to the case which should impress and inspire us. It culminated in the action of King Charles V of Spain, the Holy Roman Emperor and most powerful sovereign in Europe, who in 1550 suspended the ongoing conquest of the American Indians while a jury of theologians and counsellors evaluated a year-long philosophical debate which was held in 1550–51 to discuss its justice. I shall pick out Vitoria and Las Casas, but there were many others involved in the preceding years of controversy. Vitoria's pupil, de Soto, has been highlighted for going beyond Vitoria in his defence of the Indians in 1535, four years before Vitoria's more qualified defence.[31] Three successive professors in the same chair at Salamanca provided defences: Vitoria, Melchor Cano and de Soto.[32] There was also a debate on Indians called much earlier in 1511 by King Ferdinand.[33]

In the debate of 1550–51, the protagonists were Sepúlveda, against the Indians, and Bartolomé de Las Casas for them. Las Casas' surviving *In Defence of the Indians* is a Latin revision, made after the debate, perhaps in 1552, of the Spanish manuscript, which he had written just before the debate. The standard request for permission to publish the original Spanish version was not granted, but the debate was a substitute.

Less impassioned and more theoretical than Las Casas was Francisco de Vitoria. Both Spaniards had been writing on related issues for many years at the time of the debate, and Vitoria too had defended the Indians, even though with more qualifications. His *On the Indians* and his related *On the Law of War*[34] were both delivered at Salamanca in 1539.

Vitoria's two works are beautifully arranged. In *On the Laws of War*, he discusses right authority in Q. 1, Art. 2, and right cause in 1.3. He is there, so far as I know, the first to rule out war for the sake of religion, and he would also exclude a lot of wars in forbidding wars for expanding territory, or for the glory of the ruler. The idea that war must not make things even worse comes up in 2.5, conclusion, and 3.1.

In *On the Indians*, Q. 2, Vitoria considers unjust titles that have been wrongly proposed as providing just cause for the conquest. We shall see below that *On the Indians* also discusses *post bellum* obligations. Q. 3 considers titles which would be just. The first ones permit dwelling, travelling, trading, mining and preaching. But as Vitoria moves on to the right to protect converts, he increasingly does make concessions after all to the conquerors.

Las Casas' *In Defence of the Indians* is not so neatly arranged, because it follows the arguments on the other side of Sepúlveda, but it covers much the same criteria of just war. We shall see him below discussing proposed just causes for war such as rescuing victims among a foreign country's citizens, or an absence of proper government (cf. 'failed states'). Like Vitoria, he rules out the spread of Christian religion as a just cause in Chapters 45–8. We shall find him, in the discussion of rescue, requiring that war should not do more harm than good. Limits to the authority of the Church are discussed extensively in Chapters 7, 9–12, 15–29 and 40.

The remaining *ad bellum* criterion for just war is that there should be a reasonable prospect of achieving the war aims. It was discussed in the same century by Cajetan in Italy (1469–1534), with a reply from Suárez, who, like so many others, was of the school of Salamanca, and was born later in the century (1548–1617).[35] Cajetan had required that a ruler must be morally certain of victory before engaging in war. Suárez objects that such certainty is often impossible, and especially so for the weaker party, and in any case time-consuming. What the ruler does have to do is to weigh harm against good, if he should succeed. He should also take into account whether the war is defensive, and so of necessity, or aggressive, and so of choice. If it is aggressive, he should have at least an equal balance of probability of success. If it is defensive, he can have less. Here we see a subtle interplay of many of the considerations earlier raised by Augustine, but now put to work in new combinations for new purposes.

So far in speaking of Vitoria and Las Casas, I have discussed only their treatment of the *ad bellum* criteria for just war. But taking the earlier just war literature as background, they go far beyond the ideas I have cited above and address many of the issues which face us today. Several of the relevant works of Vitoria are commentaries on Thomas Aquinas, one of which will be cited below, but Daniel Deckers is of the opinion that Vitoria owes more to the twelfth-century canon lawyers after Gratian than he does to the succinct statements of Thomas Aquinas.[36] All parties cite Augustine extensively, and this is true of the Indians' enemy, Sepúlveda, as well as of their defenders. I shall now take some examples of present-day issues which have been thoughtfully handled by Vitoria and Las Casas.

Ideas Relevant to Modern Issues

Innocent Non-combatants in a Just War

First, building on their predecessors, they both prohibit the killing of innocents, and offer lists of types of innocent non-combatant.[37] They would be far from condoning the modern bombing of civilian populations. But would they even allow collateral deaths of civilians? They concede certain exceptions. Sometimes killing is accidental, as when there are civilians along with soldiers in a fort, or as when one cannot distinguish a foreign merchant visitor from one of the enemy. But even so, in the case of the fort, the exception is allowed only with heavy restrictions. The war must be just in the first place, taking the fort must be necessary for victory in the war, and the evil effects of proceeding must not outweigh the good. This last is the proportionality rule, which we have noticed as governing one's embarking on war in the first place. So if the only means to victory are too costly of innocent life, one should presumably re-evaluate one's decision to fight at all. This is a high standard. But both refer to the even higher standard of St Paul, who in Romans 3:8 rejects saying 'Let us do evil, that good may come.' This would not even allow calculations of proportionality.

There is no reference to sending conscripts to their death, because the Spanish Conquistadors were not conscripts, but adventurers, and in any case conscripts cannot be viewed as innocents. Rather, we rob conscripts of their innocence and make them legitimate targets when we place them in the role of threatening the enemy. Questions here should be about our having sufficient grounds to make them legitimate targets, rather than about their innocence.

Intervening in Another Country to Rescue Some Members of It

Both writers had to face the suggestion that it would be just to declare war on the Indians to protect the victims of human sacrifice. This is parallel to the cause pleaded in justification of the recent invasion of Iraq: rescuing the victims of a tyrant. Vitoria allows this as a just cause in one brief paragraph, which he had elaborated further in his *Relection on Dietary Laws* or *Self-restraint* of 1537, and in *On the Evangelisation of Unbelievers* in 1534–5.[38] One cannot intervene on the ground that human sacrifice violates the law of nature, but one can do so on the basis that victims who have the right of self-defence also have the right to be defended, and that even if they do not wish to be.

Las Casas, by contrast with Vitoria, opposes at 12 chapters' length the idea of rescuing the victims of another regime, and gives a number of reasons.[39] First, it is wrong to kill even one innocent, but further, it is against natural law to bring about more evil than good (proportionality again), and in rescuing the victims of sacrifice, we would kill more people than were victims, and more than were sacrificers. This point is equally relevant to modern advocacy of intervention, that we need to consider whether the bad effects would outweigh the good.

Second, Las Casas also cites Christ's parable of the wheat and the tares (or weeds) from Matthew 13:29, which had been cited for a related purpose long before by Augustine's older contemporary, John Chrysostom (died 409 CE).[40] In rooting out the weeds, one can damage the corn. Equally, attacking the Indians because of those guilty of sacrifice will put off the innocent, and make them hate Christianity, thereby preventing the conversion that was so important to Las Casas. Although we may not share his interest in conversion, we should take note of his concern with psychology. In modern predicaments too, the right psychology may achieve one's objectives more effectively than military force.

Finally, Las Casas draws a contrast. Sacrificing to God is prompted by natural law, which turns into the law of nations. But *what* to sacrifice is, as Aristotle says in *Politics* 1.1, a matter of *human* law, and open to honest error. It is not obvious by the light of natural reason that human sacrifice is wrong. God prompted Abraham to sacrifice his son, and Christ himself was in a way offered as a sacrifice. What language would the Spaniards use to explain to the Indians their error on so difficult a point?

Preventive Execution or Detention in a Just War

Vitoria, in *On the Law of War*, [41] rules out the preventive killing of non-combatants even in a just war, with the convincing argument, similar to that used by Jeff McMahan in Chapter 11 below, that we do not execute individuals in civil society because of sins that lie in the *future*. He does not consider exactly the doctrine that McMahan is opposing, the recently revived idea that it is acceptable to fight a whole war on a preventive basis, before any wrong has been done or prepared. But he does, a little later,[42] turn from ordinary non-combatants to the case of non-combatant hostages and combatant prisoners, and he allows that one might execute non-combatant hostages, if the enemy have broken their promises, and if the hostages would otherwise become combatants, and that one might execute combatant prisoners after the war, if the war was just and if they impose an implacable danger, as would only be plausible, in his view, in the case of infidels. Vitoria reveals the inferior status he accords to the law of nations, when he says that it is all that protects combatant prisoners.[43] If the motive, however, is not security but vengeance, then one may not execute a whole population as guilty, which would not be for the public good, but one must take account of the scale of injuries done. We ourselves have to face a similar question about enemy prisoners currently transported from Afghanistan to Cuba and subject to execution by US military authorities. Their very treatment there might make them implacable. Would that make it just never to release them, or to execute them?

Preventive imprisonment is even more common. The British practised pre-emptive internment in the Second World War, and more recently in Northern Ireland. To combat terrorism after September 2001, the USA introduced the so-called 'Patriot Laws', reportedly permitting the indefinite imprisonment of non-citizen suspects without charge, trial, legal representation or notification of family, and it is further reported that the UK's anti-terrorism crime and security Act introduced somewhat similar legislation, and that the UK subsequently agreed to extradite UK citizens to the USA for such imprisonment on demand. If this is true, and if it is for possible *future* crimes, it would presumably be rejected by Vitoria – all the more so, given that prisoners in the USA are liable to execution by US military authorities.

Regime Change

In *On the Law of War*, Q. 3, Art. 9, Vitoria also asks whether one is entitled to depose the enemy government at the end of a war. His answer, 'not normally', contrasts with proposals concerning Iraq, where regime change was proffered by some parties as one of the objectives of the war, providing it with a just cause. However, Vitoria does allow two exceptions. One is the case in which the injuries done by the former government are great enough, not inflicted in good faith and likely to recur. The other is that in which regime change is needed for the security of the conquered nation itself. Regime change raises questions of legitimate authority for fighting, both when the change is imposed by external invaders and when it is sought by resistance movements, as discussed by Kelsay and Harries in Chapters 4 and 12.

Post Bellum *Obligations*

In the last example, regime change is presented not as offering a just cause, but as a *post bellum* obligation to protect the conquered nation. In *On the Law of War*, Vitoria recognises other *post bellum* obligations. According to the third and final rule in his Conclusion, the victor in a just war must think of himself not as prosecutor, but as judge between the two warring commonwealths, and must give satisfaction to the injured. More than that, according to Q. 2, Art. 5, if the victor discovers that his war was not just after all, he must make restitution to the conquered nation.

Can Ideas be Detached from Their Ancient Background?

All these issues were addressed in the sixteenth century, despite the difference of contextual background: the theories of the law of nature and of nations and the idea of *dominium*. And this brings me to the subject of the detachability of ideas from their original context. I shall pick out half-a-dozen aspects of the ancient background to the discussion of the Conquistadors, which will further reveal the difference of intellectual context. None the less, I do not believe that the difference of context makes the foregoing insights inapplicable to our own predicaments. The considerations borrowed from the past are human ones which do not depend on our first accepting the original background. They have their own intuitive appeal which is stronger than that of the background, and I shall not be offering a new theoretical background in place of the old one. Such detachability from the original background is common in the history of philosophy.

Return to the Ancient Background

I shall now return to the ancient background, to fill it out further. Some of the ancient concepts will crop up in other chapters below.

Natural Slaves and the Roman model

The first issue discussed by Vitoria in *On the Indians*, and Las Casas in *Defence*, was the charge that the Indians were, in Aristotle's sense, natural slaves. The charge had been made by the Scotsman John Major in 1510, by Gregorio in Spain in 1512 and by Sepúlveda in his *Democrates Secundus*, composed in support of the conquest of the Indians around 1542. Aristotle in the fourth century BCE justified the universal Greek practice of slavery by saying that some people needed a master, because they lack the deliberative power (*to bouleutikon*) to plan their own lives (*Politics* 1.13, 1260a12–15), and so are natural slaves. They can listen to someone else's reason, but this means that they only *share* in reason (*Politics* 1.5,1254b21–3), or possess reason only in a secondary sense (*Nicomachean Ethics* 1.13, 1103a1–3). It is to the credit of Aristotle's near contemporary the orator Alcidamas (to be mentioned below) and the Stoic Chrysippus, in the following century, that they denied that any human is a slave by nature, Chrysippus adding that irrational animals take the place of slaves.[44] I believe Aristotle's mistake is not, as Leibniz says, that there are no such people as Aristotle describes. Some people may feel that some of their best friends or colleagues cannot plan their own lives, although they may not meet Aristotle's further criterion of being physically strong. The mistake is to say that any such people should be enslaved.

Sepúlveda justifies the conquest of the Indians as natural slaves on pp. 19–22 of his *Democrates Secundus*, citing Augustine as agreeing with Aristotle when the latter says that people can be compelled to justice. He emphasises that there are different types of rule, but that in all it is natural for the better to rule over the worse by natural law, soul over body, reason over appetite, husbands over wives, fathers over children (p. 21). On pp. 31–2, he cites Augustine as if in *City of God* Book 5, he supported Roman rule.

It looks to me as if Sepúlveda must be influenced, directly or indirectly, by a passage in Augustine, *City of God* Book 19, Ch. 21, which points back even further, because it records a lost part of Cicero's *Republic* as making nearly all these points. The Augustine passage is used by editors of Cicero as a guide to reconstructing the Cicero passage from fragments. Cicero seeks to justify Rome's dominion through the idea that Rome is ruling over slave peoples. Augustine speaks of Cicero's *Republic* as follows.

> It is replied on the part of justice that [rule over provinces] is just because servitude is helpful (*utilis*) to people of that kind, and is brought about to help them, when it is rightly brought about, that is, when the license to injure them is removed from bad men and those subjected will be better off, because they were worse off when not subjected. A noble example is added, so as to confirm that reasoning, as if drawn from nature, and it is said: 'Why therefore does God rule over men, the mind over the body, reason over appetite, and the other vicious parts of the mind?' By this example it is shown clearly enough that servitude is useful to some people, and indeed that serving God is useful to everyone.[45]

How do Las Casas and Vitoria, in reply to Sepúlveda, treat the claim that the Indians are natural slaves? Las Casas, in *Defence*, Ch. 2, takes Aristotle to mean by natural slaves a much rarer category, the totally solitary outsider discussed by Aristotle in *Politics*, 1.2.[46] Las Casas can easily say that the Indians are not like that. Vitoria has a different defence. In *On the Indians*, Q. 1, he takes the question to be whether the Indians have *dominium*, that is, the right to property and self-governance. In Q. 1, Art. 1, he says that even natural slaves have *dominium*. So do children (Q. 1, Art. 5). As for the claim that the Indians lack *dominium* because they are mad, madness is disproved by their elaborate institutions (Q. 1, Art. 6). Vitoria does not decide on a further claim (Q. 3, Art. 8) that they may be uneducated like abandoned orphans, but he says that if so, that would only justify ruling them for their own benefit.

Dominium

The idea of dominion appears in the Book of Genesis 1:26, which says that dominion was given to humans over the animals by God. Cicero in the first century BCE, knowing nothing of this, writes in a passage already discussed that *dominium* is supplied by *nature* for certain kinds of rule, that of God, mind and reason over lower things. This is a prelude to his defence of Rome's empire.[47] Augustine returns to the subject after 400 CE. Although human *dominium* was at first granted by God only over *animals*, Adam's sin and Fall resulted in *dominium* being extended over human slaves as well as animals.[48] Augustine would have sympathised with the view of the Stoic Chrysippus that it would have been natural for animals only to fulfil the role of slaves.

Natural Law

The idea of divine law appears early in Greek philosophy in the fifth century BCE, and that of natural law in the fourth. Heraclitus in the fifth century says that all human laws are nourished by a divine law which is sufficient for all.[49] Socrates is represented as persuading the sophist Hippias that there are unwritten laws made by the gods.[50] The idea of a common law in accordance with *nature*, and a common *natural* justice independent of community and contract, is said by Aristotle in the fourth century BCE to be the theme of two fifth-century texts and a fourth-century one, although Aristotle's appeal to *nature* is not explicit in the first two.[51] Thus Antigone in Sophocles' play knows that the king's law forbids her to bury her brother, but appeals at line 456 to the ever-living unwritten laws of the gods. Again, the philosopher Empedocles regards the ban on killing animals as a law (*nomimon*) for all, not as something only for some people. As Aristotle's third example, the orator Alcidamas, already mentioned, declared that *nature* had made nobody a slave. The Stoic school, which started in 300 BCE, is reported as speaking of natural law and identifying it with reason,[52] and this will have influenced Cicero's extensive references in the first century BCE. Cicero says that the true law is right reason in accordance with *nature*, but it comes from God, even though it is also described as being received from nature.[53] He also makes the law internal to one, saying that one must follow the Delphic precept, 'Know thyself', because the law is in oneself (*in se*) as so many shadowy understandings (*adumbratae intelligentiae*).[54]

Augustine was able to draw both on Cicero and on St Paul, who wrote[55] of gentiles without the law, who none the less have what the law requires 'written in their hearts' – a phrase borrowed from the Book of Jeremiah. Augustine uses the phrase when he tells of his stealing pears just for the pleasure of stealing. He had a law against theft written in his heart.[56]

Law of Nations

The first explicit references to the law of nations (*jus gentium*) are in Cicero's *On Duties*. But he does not yet distinguish the law of nations from the law of nature that is within us.[57] His examples are of not injuring people and not cheating them, for example in the sale of your house if you know it has rot. Tony Honoré has a theory about how the law of nature and the law of nations came to be distinguished well over two hundred years later. In 212 CE, Roman citizenship was extended throughout the Empire. So the law of nations could no longer be seen as a natural unwritten law superior to the written laws applying to Roman citizens. It was downgraded for this reason, and also because it accepted slavery, which some felt was contrary to natural law. The jurist Ulpian at this time both distinguishes the law of nations from natural law and makes natural law give some protection to slaves. The protection is extremely modest, but what matters is that it is based on wider principles. Honoré entitles the second edition of his book (Oxford, 2002) *Ulpian, Pioneer of Human Rights*, and reports in Chapter 3 Ulpian's saying that by natural law humans are equal, and so the master should enforce debts owed by others to the slave's purse. Humans are by natural law born free, so the practice of freeing them can only be based on the (inferior) law of nations. Slaves are by nature entitled to injure themselves to avoid work, without loss of purse.[58]

Individual Human Rights Based on Laws of Nature and of Nations

A suggestion was made in the mid-nineteenth century about the origin of the idea of human rights, namely that it arose out of the ideas of natural law and of the law of nations.[59] If Honoré's suggestions are right, it will have arisen out of the idea of natural law in Ulpian's time, when natural law was being distinguished from the law of nations – a distinction which did not always remain firm, however.

The founding of individual human rights on ideas of natural law and/or the law of nations is much clearer in Vitoria and Las Casas, judging from recent discussions. It has been pointed out that Vitoria says in his commentary of 1535 on Thomas Aquinas' *Summa Theologiae* that originally, after the creation of the world, anyone (*quilibet*) was *dominus*, that is, had dominion, over all created things, but only to *use* them, not to own them. The reference to common use may go back to Ulpian, *Digest* 1.1.5. The reference to 'anyone' has been seen as representing an individual human right. When, as Genesis 13:9 tells us, Abraham and Lot agreed to divide up the land, then there was ownership, but it was due to the law of nations, not to natural law. [60] Las Casas treats the matter differently in a very late work, *On the Treasures of Peru*.[61] The Indians, he claims, have *dominia* and *principatus*, rights of property and self-rule, by *both* natural law and the law of nations. Moreover, the rights of rule are individualised. Individuals (*singuli*), or even one vote, can invalidate rule by the Spaniards.

In an earlier book, I sided too quickly with those who dismissed Voigt's claims.[62] I still hold that the admirable Stoic theory of universal human justice was not at all like a theory of human rights, so the Stoic influence suggested by Voigt could at best be, as he said, that of precursors. But Ulpian, as well as Las Casas and Vitoria, do seem to exemplify in different degrees a connection between the law of nature or nations and the idea of individual human rights.

Natural Unity of Mankind

A final piece of background to be noticed is the dispute between the schools of the Stoics and Epicureans, which were founded in Athens just after Aristotle's death, in 307 and 300 BCE respectively. They disagreed on the natural relation of humans to each other. According to the Stoics, it is natural to feel attachment (*oikeiosis*) to one's fellow human beings, and hence justice is natural, which is not to say that it is *easy* to achieve, but that it would be in accordance with nature if one could achieve it. It was this sort of Stoic view that Augustine borrowed in *City of God* 19, to describe the humans and angels who belong to the City of God, and to describe the Church in the account of just punishment in *Against the Letter of Parmenianus* 3.1.3, described above. According to the rival Epicurean view, it is natural for everyone to seek his or her own pleasure, and hence justice is a *faute de mieux*, which depends on a self-interested contract. The philosopher Thomas Hobbes was to cite the Epicureans in support of his idea that the state of nature for humans was nasty, brutish and short, and hence that a sovereign was agreed on by contract to keep the peace. This ought to have some bearing on international relations, for nations do not have a sovereign over them, and so are in the position of individual humans who have not, or not yet, made a contract. What, then, is the natural relation of nations? A Stoic might expect it to be naturally one of amity. But a Hobbesian or Epicurean will not only expect it to be one of competition, but also will think that the very idea of Justice has no application in the absence of a contract.

There is little doubt that Vitoria and Las Casas sided with the Stoics. Vitoria, echoing Cicero, *On Laws* 1.23, says in his *On Civil Power* of 1528 that the world is a single republic. That is why it enacts the law of nations. He also cites the natural society, intercommunication and friendship of mankind in specifying just titles open to the Spaniards, in *On the Indians*, Question 3, articles 1–3, but these allow force to be used against the Indians, when it is to their benefit, as he sees it.[63] Las Casas interrupts the Spanish of his *Apologetic History of the Indians* to quote at length the Latin of Cicero *On Laws* 1.29–33, and to emphasise that all humans are alike, and that the only definition of the human is rationality.

This is only a small part of the background that historians may keep in mind in understanding the ideas of another period.[64] But it is a feature of history that ideas are often wrenched by philosophers from their original background and applied to new situations. It has to be admitted that I have been speaking of theory, not practice. After the one-year halt in the Spanish conquest, no verdict was ever delivered and the conquest of the American Indians resumed. None the less, I think it would raise the standard in making the case for war, if we applied the Spaniards' ideas to new situations as they arise, even though their original background was so different.

Notes

1 See below for all three discussing the right cause for war, for Aristotle and Cicero discussing the right attitude of mind in warfare, and for Cicero discussing making a declaration which gives a chance for peace.

2 See, for references, Wensinck, *Handbook of the Early Muhammedan Tradition*, and for specimen translations, Peters, Rudolph (1996), *Jihad in Classical and Modern Islam*, Princeton, NJ: Marcus Wiener. Some of the issues were discussed by Al-Shaybani, the Islamic jurist who died as early as 805 CE: see Kelsay, John, 'Islamic tradition and the justice of war', in Brekke, Torkel (ed.), *The Ethics of War in Asian Civilisations*, forthcoming; Kelsay, John (2003), 'Al-Shaybani and the Islamic law of war', *Journal of Military Ethics*, Vol. 2, 63–75.

3 Maimonides, *Kings, Their Wars and the Messiah*: from the *Mishneh Torah* of Maimonides, trans. from the Hebrew by H. M. Russell and J. Weinberg, Ch. 6, Royal College of Physicians, Edinburgh 1986. Norman Solomon ascribes allowing civilian escape to the Rabbi Nathan in *Sifré* on Numbers 31:7: 'The ethics of war in Judaism', in Brekke (ed.), *The Ethics of War in Asian Civilisations*. In Chapter 6 of this volume, he discusses the treatment of women by Philo in the first century CE.

4 See Nick Allen in Chapter 7 of this volume.

5 Plato and Aristotle agree that war should be for the sake of peace, and, Aristotle adds, leisure, but many nations, including some admired by Plato, are said by Aristotle wrongly to take war as an end in itself: Plato, *Laws* 1, 628C–D; Aristotle, *Nicomachean Ethics* 10.7, 1177b5–10; *Politics* 7.2, esp. 1325a5–7; 7.14–15, 1333a35; 1334a14–15. Aristotle allows as justifications for war capturing natural slaves for one's use, avoiding being enslaved, and the good of the governed, *Politics* 7.14, 1333b39–1334a5. Cicero recognises as just purposes of war securing peace, protection promised to others (*fides*), security (*salus*), repelling attack, revenge, survival, but also glory, and Rome's dominion over what, developing Aristotle, he calls slave peoples, an idea commented on by Augustine: see Cicero, *On Duties* 1.35; 1.36; 1.38; 1.80; *Republic* 3.23.34–5; 3.25.37, the last with subsequent comments by Augustine, *City of God* 19.12. Cicero, *On Duties* 1 is influenced by the Stoic Panaetius. The *actual* cause of war, by contrast, so Socrates is made to say in Plato's *Phaedo* 66C, is money, but Platonist commentators questioned whether this was the only motive: Harpocration, Dillon, John (ed.), *California Studies in Classical Antiquity* 4, 1971, 125–46; Olympiodorus, *Lecture 6 on Phaedo*, sec. 8, Westerink. Aristotle described one type of war as the art of acquiring slaves: *Politics* 1.8, 1256b21ff, cf. 1.7, 1255b37.

6 Cicero *On Duties* 1.36; *Republic* 3.23.34–5.

7   According to Philodemus, *On the Stoics*, col. 14, Cronert = col. XV 31–XVI 4 Dorandi.

8   For the Christian period through Augustine up to Thomas Aquinas, I am guided by the standard works, especially Russell, Frederick (1965), *The Just War in the Middle Ages*, Cambridge: Cambridge University Press. See also, for example, the succinct summary by Barnes, Jonathan, 'The just war' in Kretzmann Norman, *et al* (eds) (1982), *The Cambridge History of Later Medieval Philosophy*, Cambridge: Cambridge University Press, 771–84.

9   Tertullian, *On the Crown* 11.

10   Tertullian, *Against Marcion* 4.16.

11   Origen, *Against Celsus* 7.26.

12   Origen, *Homilies on Joshua* 15,1.

13   Augustine, *Against Faustus* 22.74–9; *Letter* 138, 2 and 13–15; *On the Sermon on the Mount*, 1.19.59.

14   Augustine, *Letter* 189, in agreement with Cicero, *On Duties* 1.35; 1. 80, who agrees with Plato, *Laws* 1, 628C–D; Aristotle, *Nicomachean Ethics* 10.7, 1177b5–10; *Politics* 7.2, esp. 1325a5–7; 7.14–15, 1333a35; 1334a14–15.

15   Augustine, *Against the Letter of Parmenianus* 3.1.3.

16   Vitoria, *On the Indians* Q. 3, Art. 3, cited by David A. Lupher (2003), *Romans in a New World*, Ann Arbor, MI: University of Michigan, 75–6; 121.

17   Augustine, *City of God* 19. 12; *Letter* 189.6.

18   Augustine, *Questions on the Heptateuch*. 6.10.

19   Ibid., 4.44.

20   Augustine, *On Free Choice of the Will* 1.5.

21   Augustine, *Letter* 47.

22   Augustine, *Letter* 220 to Count Boniface.

23   Augustine, *Questions on the Heptateuch*. 6.10.

24   Augustine *Against Faustus* 22.75.

25   Vitoria, Francisco de, *On the Law of War* Q. 2, Art. 2, 3 and 5.

26   John Chrysostom, *On Matthew, Homily* 47; Augustine, *Against the Letter of Parmenianus* 3.2.14; Thomas Aquinas *Summa Theologiae* 2. 2. Q. 64, Art. 2, ad 1; Las Casas, Bartholomé de (1992), *In Defense of the Indians*, trans. Stafford Poole, DeKalb, IL: Northern Illinois University, Ch. 32.

27   Augustine, *Letter* 189.6.

28   Augustine, *Questions on the Heptateuch* 6.10.

29   Thomas Aquinas, *Summa Theologiae* 2.2. Q. 40, Art. 1, answer.

30   Ibid. Q. 64, Art. 7, answer.

31   Lupher, *Romans in a New World*, 73-6.

32   Ibid., 98.

33   Ibid., 59.

34   Translated from Latin in Pagden, Anthony and Lawrence, Jeremy (eds) (1991) *Vitoria, Political Writings*, Cambridge: Cambridge University Press.

35   Cajetan, in his commentary on a passage of Aquinas on self-defence, *commentaria in secundum secundae*, Q. 96, Art. 4. Suárez's reply is in *De triplici virtute theologica: de caritate*, disp. 13, sec. 4.10. I owe this information to Martin Stone, 'Moral Philosophy and the conditions of certainty: Descartes's *morale* in context', in Salles, Ricardo (ed.) (2005), *Metaphysics, Soul and Ethics: Themes from the work of Richard Sorabji*, Oxford: Oxford University Press 507–50.

36   Deckers, Daniel (1991), *Gerechtigkeit und Recht*, Freiburg 1991.

37   Vitoria, *On the Law of War*, Q. 3, Art. 1; Las Casas, *Defence*, Chs 28–39, esp. Ch. 30.

Norman Solomon in Chapter 6 of this volume ascribes the exemption in Judaism of religious devotees to Maimonides and in Christian canon law of clerics to Gratian, both in the twelfth century. He ascribes the exemption of merchants to Pope Urban II in 1095, with incorporation into canon law under Gregory IX, whose decretals became official in 1234.

38 Vitoria, *On the Indians*, Q. 3, Art. 5; *Relection on Dietary Laws* or *Self-restraint* of 1537, Q. 1, Art. 5, conclusions 4 and 5. I thank Annabel Brett for the first reference; the second is given by Lupher, *Romans in a New World*, 70. Both are translated in Pagden and Lawrence (eds), *Vitoria, Political Writings*, 205ff and 339 ff.

39 Las Casas, *In Defence of the Indians*, Chs 28–39.

40 John Chrysostom, *On Matthew, Homily* 47.

41 Vitoria, *On the Law of War*, Q. 3, Art. 1.

42 Ibid., Art. 4 and 5.

43 Ibid., Art. 6.

44 For Chrysippus, see Philo, *On the Special Laws*, 69 (= SVF 3.253) – at least the part about animals is ascribed to Chrysippus by Cicero, *On Ends* 3.67. For Alcidamas, see below.

45 Cicero, *Republic* 3.25.37; Augustine, *City of God* 1921.

46 Aristotle *Politics* 1.2, 1253a3–10.

47 Cicero *Republic* 3.25.37.

48 Augustine, *City of God* 19.,14–15.

49 Heraclitus, frag. 114, Diels-Kranz.

50 Xenophon, *Recollections of Socrates* 4.4.19–25.

51 Aristotle, *Rhetoric* 1.13, with scholiast's gloss on Alcidamas.

52 Arius Didymus, reported by Eusebius, *Preparation for the Gospel* 15.15.

53 Cicero, *Republic* 3.22.33–4; *On Laws* 1.33.

54 Cicero, *On Laws* 1.22.58.

55 Romans 2:14–15.

56 Augustine, *Confessions* 2.4.

57 Cicero, *On Duties*, 3.23 and 3.68–9. The law is described as the reason of nature.

58 These judgements from different works of Ulpian are incorporated in Justinian's later legal *Digest* at 50.17.32; 1.1.4; 15.1.9.7.

59 Voigt, Moritz, *Das ius naturale, aequum et bonum, und ius gentium der Romer,* Vol. 1, Leipzig 1865, 267–344.

60 Deckers, *Gerechtigkeit und Recht*, discussing Vitoria's commentary on Thomas Aquinas, *Summa Theologiae* 2.2., Q. 62, Art. 1; 2.2, Q. 32, Art. 5, n. 5.

61 Tierney, Brian (1999), 'Aristotle and the American Indians – again', *Cristianesimo nella storia* 12, 1991, 295–322, citing the Spanish edition of A. Losanda, Madrid.

62 Sorabji, Richard (1993), *Animal Minds and Human Morals: The Origins of The Western Debate*, London and Ithaca, NY. Ch. 11, esp. 150–55.

63 Lupher, *Romans in a New World*, pp 75, 78.

64 For more on regime change, see summary of my lecture in *Proceedings of the Royal Society of Edinburgh*, 2005.

Chapter 2

The Just War of Eastern Christians and the Holy War of the Crusaders

Angeliki Laiou

On 27 November 1095, Pope Urban II, after having held a Church council in the small French town of Clermont, went outside the town walls and there gave what must be considered one of the most effective speeches in human history. He appealed to the fighting men of Western Europe to stop warring against each other, and instead to turn their arms from fratricidal war to war with a holy purpose: the liberation of the Eastern, that is, the Byzantine, church and of Jerusalem itself from the Seljuk Turks. Their reward was to be a remission of penance, a promise quickly re-interpreted as a remission of sin. The act of fighting a war with avowedly religious purpose against enemies of the Christian faith would bring eternal salvation. This speech launched the First Crusade, and therefore the entire crusading movement, a movement which has captivated the imagination of historians as well as popular writers from that time onwards. From the start, a basic functional element of the crusade, whether it was directed toward the Muslims or, eventually, against the pagan Slavs, the heretics or others, was that this was a holy war for the true faith, declared by the Church as the sole competent authority, whose fighters were rewarded with spiritual rewards.

Urban II's appeal was cast in terms of the brotherhood of Christians Eastern and Western, and of the help that the West should bring to the Byzantines who were the victims of the rapid expansion of the Seljuk Turks. The report of Foucher of Chartres will serve as an example: 'You must hurry to help your brothers living in the Orient, who need your aid for which they have already cried out many times. For the Turks, a race of Persians, have invaded their lands even to the Mediterranean to that point, that is, which is called the Arm of St George, are occupying more and more the land of the Christians within the boundaries of the Romania ... and have killed and captured them, have overthrown churches, and have laid waste God's kingdom. If you permit this for very long, God's faithful ones will be still further subjected.'[1] These are statements of support to the Christians of Byzantine Asia Minor, and are imbued by the spirit of fraternity between Christians in East and West. It was their brother Christians whom the Pope asked the Western knights to help against the Muslims. It was also from brother Christians that Alexios I, the Byzantine Emperor, had sought aid against the advancing Turks.[2] And yet, in a little more than a hundred years, the Christian brethren of the East had become heretical enemies, and the Byzantine Empire was destroyed by the crusaders. Why did this development occur? The question, often asked in the past, still requires answers.

As the armies of the First Crusade set out for the Holy Land, they passed through the Byzantine Empire – the largest Christian state of its day, until a few years earlier and again in the near future the most powerful, a land of virtually legendary wealth, and, according to some scholars, pre-eminently the land to whose aid Urban II had called the knights of Western Europe. The crusades resulted in massive, if periodic, contact between Byzantines and Western Europeans. The armies that went through Byzantine territories on their way to the Holy Land, that is, those of the First and Second Crusades and that of Frederick Barbarossa in the Third Crusade, took anything from two to six months to traverse the Balkans, although Frederick Barbarossa stayed in southern Bulgaria and Thrace for nine long months. Relatively brief as the contact was, it was intense. It was also attended with acute problems of a practical nature.[3] The presence of 60 000–100 000 people, many of them soldiers, on the soil of a pre-industrial state could not but tax the resources of the area. Provisioning was very difficult. Prices soared. Inevitably, the crusader armies plundered Byzantine territories, and thus the problem was compounded. Connected intimately with the problem of provisioning was that of currency exchange. The crusaders complained, not unjustly, that they lost considerably in the exchange. All of this proved to some of them that the Byzantine Emperor was duplicitous, making promises which he had no intention of keeping.[4] Thus, practical problems formed a solid foundation to the image of the Greek as untrustworthy, an image which has its origins in the Roman period, and which was broadcast in Western Europe during the period of the crusades and to a large extent because of them. Soon enough, untrustworthiness became elevated to treachery – and things became much more difficult and far more dangerous.

Surely, however, practical problems alone could have been overcome, indeed *were* overcome time and again, albeit leaving a bitter aftertaste in the historiography, and perhaps traces in the collective memory of crusading families. The excessive weight that practical problems acquire in Western sources must, I think, be ascribed to a fundamental problem which lies at the heart of the relations between crusaders and Byzantines.

The fundamental problem was ideological. The crusaders considered themselves to be the army of God, carrying out the highest duty of a Christian, fighting for the Christian religion. They were the *pugnatores Dei*, the *milites Christi* fighting under Jesus Christ.[5] They expected and almost demanded that other Christians share this view and give them every assistance, with enthusiasm. But the Byzantines did not see them primarily as soldiers of Christ, a term which in any case in Byzantium designated a monk or an ascetic.[6] They considered the crusading armies from a practical, political and statist viewpoint. At best, they saw an army to be used to recover some Byzantine territories lost to the Turks, certainly a potentially dangerous army to be ferried to Asia Minor as soon as possible, and at worst, a grave threat, which could easily divert its activities toward the Empire itself and its capital, Constantinople, and that long before this threat was realised with the Fourth Crusade, in 1204. To a very considerable extent the fear and suspicion went back to Bohemond's crusade against the Byzantine Empire, the third stage of the First Crusade. But at the heart of the matter lies the fact that the crusaders and the Byzantines had two very different conceptions of Christian warfare.

During the eleventh century, Western Europe elaborated older ideas regarding war and gave them the specific form of holy war, that heady brew of warfare and religion. The crusade was launched as a holy war, 'the struggle of good men against wicked men', as St Augustine had put it long before. It was a war for the faith, with spiritual benefits for the warriors, the spiritual and salvationist aspects becoming stronger in the course of the twelfth century. This holy war, on behalf of the Christian religion, was one which was proclaimed by the Church. But the Christian brethren whom the warriors of Western Europe were asked to help in the first instance failed miserably to embrace and even quite to understand the principles of holy war. Indeed, they were the only post-Old Testament people in the Mediterranean and in Europe never to develop the basic principles of holy war ideology. This came to be a fundamental difference between them and the Western Europeans, and one which formed the ideological foundations of the growing mistrust between brothers. There was, I argue, a conflict of ideologies, indeed of cultures. The Byzantines understood very well the concept of Christian brotherhood and Christian community, but not very well at all the novel idea of a Christian holy war.[7]

The fact that the Byzantines neither developed nor embraced the concepts of holy war is in some ways remarkable. They had fought both defensive and aggressive wars against the Muslims for centuries – first the Arabs, then, in the eleventh century, the Seljuk Turks. In some respects, Byzantine society was profoundly religious; its armies certainly prayed before battle and often marched with religious symbols at their head, as they had done since the days of Constantine the Great, the first Christian emperor, and his war against non-Christian Roman armies. There were times in the long history of the Byzantine Empire when its leaders would have been quite comfortable with some of the rhetoric employed by Westerners at the time of the crusades. In the days of the great wars against the Persians in the seventh century, against the Arabs in the tenth, Byzantine rhetoricians and exhortation manuals used statements comparable to those attributed to Urban II. 'On whom,' he had asked the Frankish knights 'is the labor of avenging the wrongs [wrought by the Turks in the Byzantine territories of the East] and of recovering this territory incumbent if not upon you? You, upon whom above other nations God has conferred remarkable glory in arms, great courage, bodily activity, and strength to humble the hairy scalp of those who resist you'.[8] A tenth-century circular letter from the Byzantine Emperor Constantine VII to the army commanders of the East, which was meant as a harangue before an important battle against the Arabs, had proclaimed, 'You shall avenge and defend not only the Christian people, but Christ himself against those who have harmed him.'[9] Baldric of Dol's Urban says: 'Under

Jesus Christ our Leader may you struggle for your Jerusalem, in Christian battle-line, most invincible line, even more successfully than did the sons of Jacob of old'.[10] And Constantine VII: 'He, oh men, He will be your aid, He who alone is mighty in battle, whose glittering sword is whetted and whose arrows are drunk with the blood of those who resist him, who breaks bows and reduces fortified cities to dust, He who humbles the eyes of the proud while to those who have hope in Him He teaches their arms to fight; He places a brazen bow in their hands; He gives them the shield of His salvation [that is, He protects them so they will not be killed].'[11] The examples could be multiplied. There are thus some clear rhetorical parallels between the exhorting decree (*exhortans decretum*) of the Pope in 1095 and the exhorting circular of a Byzantine emperor issued almost a hundred and fifty years earlier.

Yet the rhetoric should not be allowed to obscure the fundamentals of the perception of Christian warfare in Byzantium and Western Europe. Even at the time of the epic struggles against Persians or Arabs, in which some historians have seen a Byzantine crusade, mistakenly in my view, at the very most we find elements of holy war, not the full-blown ideology.[12] The Byzantines were talking about the recovery of their own territories from the infidel invaders, so that behind the emotional religious symbolism there lurked the old Roman concept of just war: the recovery of things lost, the defence of the territory and the subjects of the state. In the case of the Western call for the crusade, the emotional appeal was on behalf of Christians far away; the redressing of injustice is conceivable only if the lands of the East are established as lands which belong by rights to the Christians – an idea that was, indeed, propounded by the Pope at Clermont. Most importantly, in the crusade it is the Church that proclaims the injustice, the brotherhood of Christians, the duty to redress injustice. The basis for the justification of the war that is being declared, the community which is being asked to do the redressing, and the authority which declares the war, are all religious. In Byzantium, the basis for the justification of war is to a large extent secular; the community addressed consists of the subjects and soldiers of the Byzantine state, and the person who proclaims all this is at all times the Emperor, a secular, not an ecclesiastical, authority.

The Byzantine concept of war was not holy war. It was, pre-eminently, that of just war. In the tenth century, as in the eleventh or the twelfth, the concept of just war is rather more indebted to Aristotelian and Roman ideas regarding war than to religious ones. War, according to those Byzantines who wrote about it, and one was a tenth-century emperor, is a measure of last resort, to be undertaken when all else has failed. The war has to be just, and has to be seen to be just. All must strive for the state of peace. Each people, including the 'barbarians', is entitled to inhabit its own territory, and as long as it remains within its own frontiers, it is to be left in peace. The infidels, the Muslims, are subsumed in the larger category of barbarians. War is justified only when the barbarians breach the peace and invade the Empire. At that point, war becomes necessary; it is a just war, and its purpose is the restoration of peace – a good Aristotelian concept. At that point, too, one seeks God's help, tells the soldiers that the fight is for God, 'for our kin and the rest of our Christian brethren', and against the enemies of God.[13] Thus a just war is a defensive war, and by extension, its objectives are limited: they are not the eradication of the enemy.

In texts of the twelfth century, the reasons clearly emerge for which a just war may be waged: for self-defence, for the recovery of territory, for averting a greater evil such as the destruction of the state and its inhabitants; war is also just when the enemy has broken treaties or solemn oaths. This is a secular concept of war.[14] Its most important aspect is that the authority competent to declare war is and always remains a secular one, namely the state. The Church in the Byzantine Empire never declared war, never became engaged in war and rarely issued warlike statements.

The Byzantines and Western Europeans were, to some degree, heirs to the same religious traditions regarding war against peoples of a different religion. They shared both the Old and the New Testament: both the image of the avenging God of Hosts and that of Christ the Prince of Peace. Both cultures could draw on texts such as Deuteronomy 20:16–17 'In the cities of these peoples that the Lord your God gives you for an inheritance, you shall leave nothing alive that breathes, but you shall utterly destroy them … as the Lord commanded you', but also on texts such as Matthew 26:52: 'Put up again thy sword into its place; for all that take the sword shall perish with the sword.' Both religious communities received mixed messages from the fathers of the early Church. There had been some in the west (Tertullian, Lactantius) who condemned war in powerful terms. The most influential teaching, however, had been that of St Augustine, who had seen war both as a consequence of sin and as a remedy for it: war was a way of punishing sin and sinners, and it was a labour of love, for it prevents the sinner from sinning further. The notion of redressing injustice, a moral idea and thus quite open-ended, is important in St Augustine's thought. In the Eastern Church too, there had been some fourth-century Church Fathers like St Athanasios of Alexandria who had considered the killing of the enemy in war as lawful and praiseworthy.[15] However, the most influential figure in the Eastern tradition was St Basil of Caesarea, who punished the soldiers who killed in war with a three-year abstention from communion: 'Our fathers have not included the murders committed in time of war in the category of murder, pardoning, I think, those who defend prudence and piety. But it seems to me that it is proper to advise them to abstain from communion for three years, for their hands are unclean.'[16] The Byzantines also had retained from the Roman past the idea that wars have to be just, and the idea that a defensive war, and a war for recovery of things lost, was a just war; this was incorporated in their legal system, as was the maxim that only the public authority, namely, the Emperor, may declare war. They also had the corpus of Aristotelian writings, which gave a secular definition of just war.

Common roots, different developments – that is the story of the development of theories of war, as also of the concept of Christian brotherhood. East and West had a mixed heritage in terms of religious approaches; it was social and political conditions that allowed the concept of holy war to develop and spread in Western

Europe. And it was political and social conditions that led to the development in Byzantium of the concept of just war. For the Byzantine Empire was the one state in medieval Europe and the eastern Mediterranean which retained, both in tradition and in reality a strong centralised state that, while very closely connected with the Christian religion, had also a line of descent straight from the Roman Empire. It was therefore normal for them to have had a statist view of war, even against infidels.

Jonathan Riley-Smith has argued that at the time of the First Crusade, members of the fighting elite of Western Europe transferred to Christ the fealty they owed to their overlord.[17] In the matter of warfare, there was no question among Byzantines that the Emperor and the state commanded their loyalty. This was a point of crucial difference at the time. Thus the reaction of Byzantines and Westerners to important events of the crusade was stunningly different. The Byzantine historian whose work covers the First Crusade, Anna Komnene, barely mentions the capture of Jerusalem, that Jerusalem which had so rapidly become the focus and aim of the First Crusade and whose capture, attended by visions and prophecies and ending in the wholesale slaughter of its Muslim and Jewish inhabitants, had brought the crusaders to transports of exultation. 'This day,' wrote Raymond d'Aguilers, 'marks the justification of all Christianity, the humiliation of paganism, and the renewal of our faith.'[18] Anna Komnene's description of the capture of the city is brief, to the point, and with no whiff of exultation in the victory of the Christians: 'The walls were encircled and repeatedly attacked, and after a siege of one lunar month [Jerusalem] fell. Many Saracens and Hebrews in the city were massacred.'[19]

How profound the difference in attitude was with regard to war in general, and more specifically with regard to war against the infidel, in this case the Muslims, can best be seen not in rhetorical statements whose purpose is to incite men to fight, but, rather, in cultural expressions of these attitudes. One litmus test is the treatment of soldiers fighting in war and dying in the course of it. Holy war is a justifying war – the warrior for the faith finds salvation through the very act of war. In Western Europe, the eleventh century saw the evolution of the idea that one who dies fighting for the ideals of the Christian faith deserves the crown of martyrdom. At Clermont, Pope Urban had linked that idea specifically to the war against the Muslims: 'We now hold out to you wars which contain the glorious reward of martyrdom, which will retain praise now and forever.'[20] The first martyrs begin to appear in the sources in 1097.[21]

At the other end of Europe there was, in the late tenth century, a great general and then emperor who had given the most powerful impetus to the Byzantine reconquest of territories lost to the Arabs. Nikephoros II (963–969) is undoubtedly the epitome of the pious warrior fighting for the Christian people. A profoundly religious man, when he became Emperor he called a Church council and asked the prelates to declare that his soldiers who had fallen in war against the Arabs be proclaimed martyrs for the faith. There was much debate, but in the end the prelates refused, on the basis of the teachings of St Basil.[22] Nikephoros Phokas' innovative effort to proclaim his soldiers martyrs was remembered well into the twelfth century. At that point, after a hundred years of being exposed to crusading ideas, and after more than a hundred years of wars against the Seljuks, some canonists argued for an attenuation of the canon of St Basil, saying that it was praiseworthy to fight in defence of piety and prudence. But they did insist that martyrdom is excluded for soldiers dying in battle.[23] In the early thirteenth century, Byzantine theologians still argued against the concept of the remission of the sins of crusaders dying in war.[24] Both before the onset of the crusading movement, and well into the period when it was a cardinal event in the eastern Mediterranean, the crown of martyrdom eluded Byzantine soldiers who fought against the enemy, even if the enemy was an infidel. Thus the 'revolution' of Nikephoros II failed, while that of Urban II had a long life.

The difference in the perception of war, and specifically war against Muslims, can be seen eloquently in the literature of the period. From the time of the First Crusade, a little earlier or a little later, dates the oldest extant version of the great French epic the *Song of Roland*, which, of course, is based on older songs and poems. The *Song of Roland* has long been recognised as a poem which encapsulates the elements of holy war that make up the ideology of the crusades. In the East, the *Song of Digenis* ('The Twyborn') seems to have taken its extant form a few decades later. In both poems, the action takes place in a liminal environment – on the borderlands between Christians and Muslims: on the Spanish march in one case, in eastern Asia Minor in the other. The *Song of Digenis* consists of two parts, of which the second, the story of the Twyborn warrior himself, is really a romance, involving tales of love and adultery, fights against lions, semi-regular soldiers, Arabs and Amazons. He spends a good amount of time engaging in adulterous pursuits and then repenting of them, and dies at a very young age; his funeral is attended by the great rulers of the East, both Christian and Muslim.[25] This is hardly epic stuff. The first part, however, the 'Song of the Emir', the father of Digenis, retains resonances of the Arab–Byzantine wars of the tenth century. It may thus be considered comparable, for our purposes, to the *Song of Roland*, which has the wars of Charlemagne at its core.

The way in which a society perceives and describes its enemy reflects its values. In both poems, Muslim Arabs are the foe. In the *Song of Roland*, the Saracens and Charlemagne's army are depicted in very similar terms. But there is one all-embracing and all-important difference: religion. The verse 'The pagan cause is wrong, the Christian right' encapsulates the morality of the poem. Because they are Muslims, the enemies are always evil, unjust, false and unrighteous. The struggle between Christians and Muslims is a struggle between good and evil. This is most clearly the case at the end of the poem, where Roland, a man surrounded by light, is pitted against the Arab Chernuble:

> the ruler of that land
> men call the Hills of Darkness …
> In that land, they say,

> the sun shines not, nor rain nor gentle dew
> fall from the heavens, and not a grain of corn
> may ripen. No rock is there that isn't solid black;
> some say it is the devil's habitation.[26]

One of the Saracen leaders is a man named Abisme:

> A Paynim black as molten pitch
> no wickeder than *he* in all the swarm;
> spotted with many sins, believing not
> in God the son of Mary; loving more
> treason and murder of his fellow men
> than good Galician gold ...[27]

His shield had been given him by a demon, in contrast to Roland, whose sword (Durandel) had been given to Charlemagne by an angel. Abisme, the personification of evil, is met in the field by the archbishop Turpin, who with a single blow rends him in half. The symbolism is stark. Muslims have two choices: conversion or death. This was, in fact, the choice given by the crusaders to Muslims and Jews as well as to the pagans of northern Europe at various times in the period of the crusades.

The contrast with the 'song of the Emir' is sharp. The very description of the Emir who, objectively, is the equivalent of Abisme, is indicative:

> Was an Emir of breed, exceeding rich,
> of wisdom seized and bravery to the top,
> not black as Aethiops are, but fair and lovely,
> already bloomed with comely curly beard.
> He had a well-grown and rather matted brow;
> his quick and pleasant gaze and full of love
> shone like a rose from out his countenance.[28]

The early part of the poem presents a scene of destruction: a field of war, strewn with the limbs of lovely girls who had not given in to the illicit desires of the victorious Arabs. But when the brothers of the girl who would eventually become the emir's wife meet him, they greet him thus:

> Emir, servant of God, and prince of Syria,
> ...
> [may you]be found worthy to adore the Prophet's tomb;
> so may you hear the consecrated prayer.[29]

The entire story revolves around the Emir's love for the girl, a Byzantine Christian, for whose sake he abandons Islam and converts to Christianity. The almost metaphysical battle between good and evil is absent from this poem. Instead, we find popular motifs such as the brothers of the Christian Byzantine girl running to her rescue, or the motif of the mother who first scolds the Emir for abandoning his heritage and then follows him out of motherly love. The Emir's conversion comes not at swordpoint, but rather through the arrows of Eros: it is the act of reconciliation, which is sealed with the birth of a son: ' To them a child is born, indeed most fair, / who from his very birth was named Basil, / called also Twyborn as from his parents, / a pagan father and a Roman mother.'[30]

A society that can reduce to a love story the centuries-long struggle between Muslims and Christians on the borderlands of Asia Minor, in Syria and the borders of Iraq, is hard put to understand the crusades. The Pope had asked the crusaders to help their fellow Christians against the Muslims. But when the crusaders met with the Byzantines, there was a meeting of two worlds which, although they had a great deal in common, also had much that set them apart: differences which surprised them both. I suggest that the differences were most unwelcome precisely because the Westerners expected to meet fellow Christians, Christian brethren who would share their views of the enemy. The Byzantines, with a centralised state and a good foreign service, held no such views: at the time of the first crusade, they wanted help from the West, but in the shape of a small, professional army under their own control. And they did recall most vividly throughout the twelfth century that it was Christian Normans, members of the First Crusade, who had tried to conquer the Empire.

Thus the Byzantines had very little truck with holy war and, since the state and not the Church was the authority competent to declare war, this is not surprising. In practical terms, this has certain corollaries. It is true that any war has its horrors, and the wars waged by the Byzantines were certainly not exempt from horrors.[31] On the other hand, it is inherent in the theory of just war that the objectives are limited, and that there are rules governing the treatment of civilians and captives – and the purpose is always the re-establishment of peace. Holy war as elaborated in Western Europe had unlimited objectives and an almost unlimited scope: which is why its victims included not only the Muslims against whom it was first preached, but also the Jews, heretics, pagans, political enemies of the Papacy and, eventually, the Byzantine Christians. The unlimited objective is the domination of the Christians over the infidels or the pagans, and the extinction, physical or moral, of the enemy. This is what permitted the massacre of the inhabitants of Jerusalem in 1099, the atrocities of the Albigensian Crusade, the virtual extermination of some pagan populations along the Baltic. When St Bernard of Clairvaux preached the crusade to the German nobles, he promised remission of sins to those who went to war against the pagan Slavs 'for the total destruction or, at least the conversion (moral destruction) of all these peoples'; he forbade peace treaties with the Slavs 'until, with the help of God, this people, or its religion, should be exterminated'.[32]

What explains the differences between Eastern and Western Christians on the subject of Christian warfare? At the socio-political level, these differences stem from attitudes towards war in general, themselves the result of specificities in the makeup of the state, the ruling class and the warrior class. In Western Europe, of course, the aristocracy was a fighting class, the fighting class *par excellence*. So much was this still the case in the eleventh century that scholars in recent years have based their interpretation of the stunning appeal of the call to the First Crusade on the spiritual needs and martial attitudes of this fighting elite, who had imbued the crusading movement with their warrior ethos.[33] When the Byzantines were exposed to certain egregious forms of this ethos, they sometimes saw it as the strange ravings of stranger people.[34] Anna Komnene reports the vain boastings of a crusader in the army of Godfrey of Bouillon to the Emperor Alexios I: 'I am a pure Frank and of noble birth. At a cross-roads in the country where I was born is an ancient shrine; to this anyone who wishes to engage in single combat goes, prepared to fight; there he prays to God for help and there he stays awaiting the man who will dare to answer his challenge. At that crossroads I myself have spent time, waiting and longing for the man who would fight – but there was never one who dared.'[35] What to the Byzantines seemed a simple boast of an imprudent man, was still, in Western Europe, the way to acquire lands and vassals; the elite still acquired wealth mostly, though not exclusively, through war.

In Byzantium, however, individuals had not traditionally achieved wealth, power and social position through warfare as much as through administrative office, given, withheld or recalled by the Emperor. The accuracy of this general statement certainly would vary with locality and chronology – for there is no question that in the period of Byzantine expansion along the eastern frontier, that is, in the ninth and especially in the tenth century, great private fortunes were formed in the newly conquered lands, which in turn gave the great aristocratic families a strong territorial and economic base. But even in these cases, the early accumulation of fortune had come because of administrative office, and in the tenth century the salaries drawn by the high military officials were probably higher than the revenues from their lands. In other words, the system of rewards was very different indeed in Eastern and Western Christendom. To illustrate the point, one may look at the tenth-century Byzantine text to which reference has already been made, and which has been thought to encapsulate the 'aspect of true "crusades"' that the same scholars consider Byzantine military enterprises to have acquired after the eighth century.[36] This harangue, addressed to military officials in the East before an important battle against the Emir of Aleppo Saif ad-Daulah (952–3), speaks of the soldiers' faith in Christ, contrasts the help that can be given by Christ to that offered by Muhammad to his faithful, and calls 'the fight on behalf of Christians' to be the greatest ambition – none of which, in my opinion, is sufficient to qualify the sentiments behind the text or the enunciations in the text as pertaining to 'holy war', much less to a 'crusade'. There is also an oath involved in this text. Not an oath to fight for the Christian God, or the salvation of Christianity, but an oath to the Emperor, by the generals, who promise that they will send him truthful reports regarding the conduct of individuals in battle, so that the Emperor may reward them. The rewards are not, and indeed cannot be, spiritual: the Emperor cannot offer, as the Pope is said to have done, spiritual salvation.[37] The Emperor's promises are of quite a different order:

the generals of small themes (a theme is an administrative unit) will get large themes, and other donations and rewards, and so hierarchically up and down the list of officers.[38] The rewards, as I have indicated, were anything but negligible – they made a difference between glory and wealth on the one hand, and obscurity on the other. What is clearly considered optimum here is not individual bravery resulting in individual acquisition of wealth, but controlled bravery in the service of the state resulting in rewards derived from the state. This would, of course, apply equally to all wars, whether between Christians and Muslims or other non-believers, or among Christians, or even to civil wars – a rather cold climate for profoundly held concepts of 'holy war' to take root and bear fruit.

And then there was the civil service. In its heyday, the Byzantine Empire was a well-administered state, with a command economy. From the point of view of the state, fiscal policies and their results were of paramount importance, and safeguarding the tax-producing assets (specifically, in this period, agriculture) was a stated purpose of the Emperors. From the point of view of the subjects, fiscality was so important that the tax-payer was one of the best-known figures in the countryside; so important also, that justice was often equated to fiscal justice; and significant enough in terms of the rural economy that it influenced, to a varying but considerable degree, its monetisation. It could not have escaped the eyes of the bureaucracy that the seasons for fighting were the same as for agricultural pursuits; nor could the fact have escaped their eagle eye that although successful war could result in windfalls for the Treasury and territory to increase the tax base, wars were not always successful; campaigns were expensive even in terms of cash alone; campaigns on Byzantine soil had destructive effects which could range from the loss of one year's harvest to the destruction of productive capacity. The glory in gore that we find in Western troubadour songs[39] or in chronicles of the crusades are not reproducible in the Byzantine Empire. In war, the Byzantines were capable of great cruelty and destruction of the enemy's resources: the slaughter of men and beasts were tactics advocated by the *Taktika*.[40] But they did not glory in destruction – they were too well aware of its cost. Much more in the Byzantine tradition is a thirteenth-century exhortation to 'avoid human slaughter and the dreadful bloodshed that are the fruits of war'.[41]

Peace, that ever-present cry in Byzantium, which we find in all sorts of very different sources, from manuals on military tactics to the liturgy,[42] made perfect bureaucratic sense, and it was a rare Emperor who bucked it and engaged in unprovoked and pure wars of expansion. To the bureaucratic ethos, and it was a powerful ingredient of state policy, defensive wars, especially to restore peace in territories under attack, were a clear necessity; we do not really know what they thought of unprovoked wars of expansion, except that, in ideological terms, these were accommodated under the general rubric – a Roman idea – of the restoration of things lost, even if they had been lost for a very long time. The point, of course, is that the pious sentiment that the 'aim of war is the restoration of peace', of good Aristotelian pedigree, and found in the *Taktika* of Leo the Wise, is much more than a pious sentiment; it often governed imperial policy, and it made good financial and therefore bureaucratic sense. Again, not a very fertile soil for the fervours of crusades or holy wars.

We have, then, two views of Christian warfare, which developed through a different mix of elements that had very similar origins, a difference which in turn was due to the social and political conditions in East and West respectively. The imperatives of holy war on the one hand and just war on the other clashed and went on clashing during the period when they had to confront each other, that is, during the period of the crusades. The misunderstandings between Western Europe and Byzantium, between the Orthodox and the Latin Churches that occurred during this period owe a great deal to the different concepts of war and the courses of action each vision dictated. In the end, this ideological difference had a victim of some consequence: this was the cause of Christian brotherhood, in whose name Urban II preached the First Crusade, and which began to erode as soon as the crusaders set foot on Byzantine soil. Ultimately, the victim of such differences and misunderstandings was the Byzantine Empire itself, conquered by Westerners in the course of the Fourth Crusade, when the concept of holy war had expanded to include the Byzantines. The Byzantines watched in horror as their churches were defiled, ancient statues melted down, their state dismembered in the name of the God of Peace. And it is no accident that the one time that an Orthodox Patriarch promised eternal salvation and remission of sins to those who died in war was a few years after the fall of Constantinople to the crusaders. The promise was most probably aimed at the Byzantine soldiers who died fighting the Westerners for the salvation of their country: 'Having received the great gift of the grace Jesus Christ our Lord, we give you, who fight on behalf of the Lord's people, forgiveness for the sins committed during your lifetime, if it should happen that you die in defence of your country and the common salvation and rescue of the people.'[43] It is one of the ironies of history that when one of the two great medieval Christian cultures turned towards holy war, it was to defend itself against the successors of those who had, a hundred-odd years earlier, set out to defend it against a perceived common enemy. Different concepts of the war against Muslims in the end divided Christendom more than they harmed Islam.

Notes

1   *RHC Occ.*, III, 323–4. The translation is adapted from that in Peters, E. (1971), *The First Crusade*, Philadelphia, 52–3.

2   Charanis, P. (1949), 'Byzantium, the West and the Origin of the First Crusade', *Byzantion*, 19, 17–36.

3   For a full discussion of the problems of provisioning and exchange, see Laiou, A. E., 'Byzantine Trade with Christians and Muslims and the Crusade', in A. E. Laiou and R. P. Mottahedeh (eds) (2001), *The Crusades from the Perspective of Byzantium and the Muslim World,* Washington, DC, 157–79.

4 Odo of Deuil (1948), V. G. Berry (ed. and trans.) *De profectione Ludovici VII in orientem*, New York, 40–41, 66.

5 Foucher of Chartres, *RHC Occ.*, III, 324; Baldric of Dol, *RHC Occ.*, IV, 14.

6 Dennis, G. T., 'Defenders of the Christian People: Holy War in Byzantium,' in Laiou and Mottahedeh (eds), *The Crusades from the Perspective of Byzantium and the Muslim World*, 36ff.

7 For an incisive argument making similar points specifically in the time of the crusades, see Dagron, G. (1997), 'Byzance entre le djihad et la croisade: quelques remarques', *Le concile de Clermont de 1095 et l'appel à la croisade. Actes du colloque international de Clermont Ferrand, 1995*, École française de Rome, 325–37.

8 Robert the Monk, *RHC Occ.*, III, 728; translation in Peters, *The First Crusade*, 27.

9 Ahrweiler, H. Un discours inédit de Constantin Porphyrogénète,' in *Travaux et Mémoires du centre de recherche d'histoire et civilisation de Byzance*, 2, 1967, 393–404.

10 Baldric of Dol, *RHC Occ.*, IV, 15; translation from Peters, *The First Crusade*, 32.

11 Ahrweiler, 'Un discours inédit', 398; Ps. 23 (24), 8; Deut. 32:41–2; Is. 25:2, Ps. 17 (18): 31, 35–6 in the King James version. See also Pertusi, A., 'Una acolouthia militare inedita del X secolo,' *Aevum*, 22, 1948, 145–68, esp. ll. 22ff, and Kolia-Dermitzaki, A. (1991), *O Vyzantinos ieros polemos: I provoli tou thriskeutikou polemou sto Vyzantio*, Athens.

12 I disagree with Kolia-Dermitzaki, *O Vyzantinos ieros polemos*, who claims that the Byzantines engaged in holy war in the seventh and the tenth centuries. I think that she is misled by rhetoric, and fails to examine the structural and functional elements of holy war.

13 Vari, R. (1917), *Leonis Imperatoris Tactica*, Budapest, II, 44–6.

14 The argument is made in Laiou, A. E., 'On Just War in Byzantium' in (1993), *To Hellenikon: Studies in Honor of Speros Vryonis Jr.*, I, New Rochelle, NY, 153–77.

15 Migne, *Patrologia Graeca*, 26, col. 1175.

16 Canon 13 of St Basil: Ralles, G. and Potles, M. (1854), *Syntagma ton theion kai hieron kanonon*, 4, Athens, 131.

17 Riley-Smith, J. (1980), 'Crusading as an act of love', *History*, 65, 1980, 177–92, esp. 178–80.

18 Raymond of Aguilers, *Historia Francorum qui ceperunt Iherusalem*, *RHC Occ.*, III, 300; Peters, *The First Crusade*, 260.

19 Reifferscheid, A. (ed.) (1884), *Annae Comnenae porphyrogenitae Alexias*, Leipzig, II, XI.6, 123; trans. in Sewter, E. R. A. (1985), *The Alexiad of Anna Comnena*, 352.

20 Baldric of Dol, *ROC Occ.*, IV, 138: *Nunc vobis bella proponimus quae in se habent gloriosum martyrii munus, quibus restat praesentis et eternae laudis titulus.*

21 Flori, J., 'Mort et martyre des guerriers', in *Cahiers de civilisation médiévale* 34, 1991, 120–39.

22 Thurn, Io. (ed.) (1973), *Ioannis Skylitzae Synopsis Historiarum*, Berlin/New York, 274–5.

23 Ralles and Potles, *Syntagma ton theion kai hieron kanonon*, 4, 133.

24 Constantine Stilbes in Darrouzès, J. (1983), 'Le mémoire de Constantin Stilbès contre les Latins,' *REB*, 21, 77; written soon after 1204.

25 The newest edition and translation of the poem is by Jeffreys, E. (1998), *Digenis Akritis: The Grottaferrata and Escorial Versions*, Cambridge. Here, I use the older, poetic translation by Mavrogordato, John (1956), *Digenes Akrites*, Oxford.

26 I have used the most literary translation: Luquiens, F. B. (1952), *The Song of Roland*,

New York, 35. For this quotation, I have also made partial use of Harrison, R. (1970), *The Song of Roland*, New York, 1970, No. 78, 82.

27   Luquiens, *The Song of Roland*, 52.

28   Mavrogordato, *Digenes Akrites*, 5, verses 30–37.

29   Ibid., p. 9, verses 100–105.

30   Mavrogordato, *Digenes Akrites*, p. 69, verses 1028–31. Both Mavrogordato and Jeffreys translate *ethnikos* as 'pagan'. However, by the twelfth century the word meant 'foreigner', which makes more intelligent the juxtaposition with 'Roman'. Thus the verse should be rendered 'a foreign father and a Roman mother'.

31   See below, note 40.

32   Brundage, J. A. (1962) *The Crusades: A Documentary Survey*, Milwaukee, WI, 184–5.

33   Riley-Smith, J. (1987), *The Crusades*, New Haven, CT, xxviii.

34   This statement should be somewhat softened. Some Byzantines were sympathetic to the crusaders' avowed purpose of liberating Jerusalem or bringing aid to it. In the late twelfth century, Niketas Choniates, the most important historian of the period, reports a speech by Conrad III to the German contingent of the second crusade that is reminiscent of crusading rhetoric: Bekker, E. (ed.) (1835), *Nicetae Choniatae Historia*, Bonn, 91–4.

35   Alexias, II, 94–5 (X.10); trans., *The Alexiad*, 326.

36   Ahrweiler, H. (1975), *L'idéologie politique de l'Empire byzantin*, Paris, 35, and Kolia-Dermitzaki, *O Vyzantinos ieros polemos*, 242 ff.

37   Baldric of Dol, *RHC Occ. IV*, 15: '*Tali imperatori militare debetis, cui omnis non deest potentia, cui quae rependat nulla desunt stipendia. Via brevis est, labor permodicus est, qui tamen immarcescibilem vobis rependet coronam.*'

38   Ahrweiler, 'Un discours inédit', 399.

39   See Bertrand de Born: 'When battle is joined, let all men of good lineage think of naught but the breaking of heads and arms, for it is better to die than to be vanquished and live. I tell you, I find no such favour in food, or in wine, or in sleep, as in hearing the shout, 'On, on!' from both sides … in seeing men great and small go down in the grass beyond the fosses; in seeing at last the dead, with pennoned stumps of lances till in their sides', quoted in Miller, T. S. and Nesbitt, J. (1995), *Peace and War in Byzantium: Essays in Honor of George T. Dennis, S.J.*, Washington, DC, 7.

40   There are cases in the historical record where Arab prisoners were tortured horribly: in 874–5: Skylitzes, 153–4, Bekker, E. (ed.) (1838), *Theophanes Continuatus*, Bonn, 300–301. It is true that these were pirates who had engaged in very destructive raids, and the purpose was to punish them by acts similar to their own and deter them from more attacks. Similarly, the capture of Crete was attended by atrocities: Niebuhr, B. G. (ed.) (1828), *Leo Diaconus*, Bonn, 14–15; Attaliota, M. (1853) *Historia* (ed). E. Bekker, Bonn, 227–8. While the atrocity should not be played down, it should also be said that it was not necessarily due to the demonisation of the Muslim other. After all, possibly the worst horror perpetrated by the Byzantines was the blinding of 15 000 Bulgarians by Basil II, and the Bulgarians had been Christianised for one hundred and sixty years.

41   Theognostos, in Munitiz, J. A., SJ, 'War and Peace Reflected in Some Byzantine *Mirrors of Princes*', in Miller and Nesbitt, *Peace and War in Byzantium*, 52, 54.

42   Taft, R. F., SJ, 'War and Peace in the Divine Liturgy', in Miller and Nesbit, *Peace and War in Byzantium*, 17–32.

43   Oikonomides, N. 'Cinq actes inédits du patriarche Michael Autoreianos', *Revue des études byzantines*, 25, 1967, 119, lines 70–75.

Chapter 3

Conceptions of Justice in War: From Grotius to Modern Times

Karma Nabulsi

This chapter will focus on the conflicting views of justice in war, traced through the seventeenth century to the last century, and is an introduction to the modern debate on justice in war in historical context. When exploring recent frameworks and conceptualisations of particular types of modern war, such as 'unequal war' and 'asymmetrical war', scholars claim to be exploring new phenomena and draw their evidence from very recent practices of the late twentieth and early twenty-first centuries. They analyse suicide bombing, acts of terrorism by sub-national and religious groups and other acts that are seen as outside the bounds of national warfare. They also look at the responses to these tactics of modern war, such as the aerial bombardment that was practised during the two Gulf Wars, or in Afghanistan, and Falluja or Gaza. But are these practices of war truly modern phenomena? I will explain here that they are not. By setting out the historical context of those debates, concerning the nature of war and the concepts of justice in war, this chapter will demonstrate that the debate was always about cases of asymmetrical and unequal wars. War, more often than not, is between an army and a people, not between two professional armies.

Just war is not only about the just causes for going to war in the first place, it is also about the just means of fighting it. Accordingly, the main rule to establish in being able to set standards of justice in war is: who is a legitimate combatant. So in these wars, the issue is always: who is just? Or more importantly, who is the just warrior? Equally, who is the criminal? The different answers to this fundamental question actually come from differing philosophical conceptions of political justice. Indeed, the laws of war were created to get around this very problem. It removes itself from the highly political concept of *just war*, where one side is just and one not, and relies upon a modern concept of justice *in* war, which is designed to be ideologically neutral. This latter concept introduced a foundational principle on the modern laws of war: the distinction between combatant and non-combatant. Only by separating classes of those who could and those who could not fight (it was argued) could moderation be introduced into the act of war itself, and important restrictions and restraints introduced. The whole puzzle of the laws of war is there – they never solved this first issue about who these laws applied to.

But first we will explore the modern origins of this just war debate, especially the question as to how one can distinguish between just war and justice in war, given the conditions of unequal war and asymmetrical war, and from there it will set out the ideology of justice in war in such conditions. So we begin with Hugo Grotius, who is answered by Jean-Jacques Rousseau – who associates Thomas Hobbes' vision of war with that of Grotius. We begin in the seventeenth century, and go into the eighteenth with Rousseau's response before coming to the modern debate in the late nineteenth century between just war and justice in war, and the formation of the modern laws of war, the great attempt to regulate war with the Hague Treaties 1899 and 1907 and Geneva Conventions of 1949.

Grotius and the Nature of War

Much like Hobbes' *Leviathan*, the ambition of Grotius' *De Jure Belli ac Pacis* can be found in its title. Grotius' goal was not to establish whether there could be rules that governed war and peace, but what those rules were. He proceeded by first defining war as broadly as possible, in order to include a comprehensive range of permissible activity within the scope of its laws:

> In treating of the rights of war, the first point, that which we have to consider, is, what is war, which is the subject of our enquiry, and what is the right, which we seek to establish … war is the state of contending parties, considered as such. This definition, by its general extent, comprises those wars of every description, that will form the subject of the present treatise.[1]

He also created a system of law which could offer bilateral rights to both belligerents in war, an additional principle to traditional *jus ad bellum*. Writers on the laws of war before Grotius had argued that either there could be bilateral rights in war (that is, each belligerent could have an equal right to make war on the other), or that there was only one just party. Grotius, unsurprisingly, took a position in between these two, and suggested an entirely new legal approach. He argued that although sovereigns could *not* have bilateral rights, their subordinates *could*, so that belligerents in the field of battle could both be lawful and just. This was put forward as a custom of war, sourced in a type of contractual *jus gentium*. It allowed Grotius to put forward a theory which claimed that states had tacitly agreed that, irrespective of the objective justice of their claims, their representatives in battle (commanders and soldiers) could be recognised as having mutual and legitimate rights against each other in war.

Grotius' method of analysis was driven by both principal and subsidiary purposes. The principal goal was to counter what he believed were the two established theories of war and peace, thus advancing his own system in their place. He claimed the alternate philosophies of war and peace were both too excessive and too absolute in the extent and limits they sought to place upon war. In his famous statement in the introduction to his book on the laws of war and peace, the *Prolegomena*, Grotius defined his philosophy as a response to the problems encountered in each extreme view:

> Confronted with such utter ruthlessness, many men who are the very furthest from being bad men, have come to a point of forbidding all use of arms to the Christian, whose rule of conduct above everything else comprises the duty of loving all men. To this opinion sometimes John Ferus and my fellow countrymen Erasmus seem to incline, men who have the utmost devotion to peace in both Church and State; both their purpose, as I take it, is, when things have gone in one direction, to force them in the opposite direction, as we are accustomed to do, that they may come back to a true middle ground. But the very effort at pressing too hard in the opposite direction is often so far from being helpful that it does harm, because in such arguments the detection of what is extreme is easy, and results in weakening the other statements which are well within the bounds of truth. *For both extremes, therefore, a remedy must be found, that men may not believe either that nothing is allowable, or that everything is.*[2]

His secondary purpose was to introduce a concept of 'moderation' into the practice of warfare. His appeal for the application of this virtue formed several chapter headings of Book III of *De Jure Belli ac Pacis*, which was concerned chiefly with the customs and practices of war. The manner in which Grotius introduced the notion of *temperamenta* was typical. After listing a particularly brutal range of customs which he described as acceptable under various types of law, he began: 'I must retrace my steps, and must deprive those who wage war of nearly all the privileges which I seem to grant them.'[3] Indeed, his system of introducing improvement was to illustrate the possibility and limits of change. His method of seeking moderation, *temperamenta*, was crucial, and laid a foundational stone for the nineteenth-century Grotian tradition of the laws of war. Although it was the last phrase in his quotation about finding the middle way which is most remembered, it was his method of introducing change stated earlier which was much more consequential: the search for a *media res* between 'both extremes' which he believed so disastrous.

Here Grotius develops a concept, which was aptly captured in Hirschman's notions of perversity and jeopardy, which posits the idea that any substantive change is dangerous, because it either has the reverse effect to that intended, or endangers the positive values already achieved, endangering some 'previous, precious accomplishment'. (This concept in practice will also be illustrated in more depth later by an illustration of its development in the late nineteenth century.) Further, Grotius maintained this method of seeking change by 'pressing too hard in the opposite direction', actually undermining various customs which ought to be maintained; this amounted to a belief on his part that the more utilitarian and harsh practices of war had a recognised place *within* the law.

Accordingly, Grotius' system defined all customs and practices as legitimate in wartime, but advanced a more normative claim to moderate these customs. Both the normative claim and the customary practices could, according to Grotius, be sourced from divine law, natural law, the law of nations or volitional law. His method in establishing a theory using this eclectic procedure represented his unique contribution to the foundations of a new school of thought on war. There are five features of the Grotian system that are particularly worthy of mention. The first of these concerns his way of defining what were customary practices of war, searching for illustrations of these customs in ancient history and examples from his own century. He explained the reasons for choosing this procedure:

> History in relation to our subject is useful in two ways; it supplies both illustrations and judgements. The illustrations have greater weight in proportion as they are taken from better times and better peoples. Thus we have preferred ancient examples, Greek and Roman, to the rest. And judgements are not to be slighted, especially when they are in agreement with one another; for by such statements the existence of the laws of nature, as we have said, is in a measure proved, *and by no other means, in fact, is it possible to establish the law of nations.*[4]

His selection at first may appear simply arbitrary; on a complete reading of his work, however, it is apparent that the examples used are purposely and selectively chosen. Among the Romans, he had a particular devotion to Livy, Machiavelli's favoured promoter of savage war.

The second theoretical feature concerned the artificial contrivance Grotius deemed necessary to achieve his desired *media res*. As he selected an enormous collection of brutal practices of war, a structural imbalance developed within his system. As the architectural pillar supporting barbaric practices at one end of his scale was so heavily loaded, its weight destabilised the more normative pillar which he had constructed to embody the other end, thus abandoning a true middle ground. The hypothetical *media res* was not merely conjectural, it was not even in the middle. Accordingly, Grotius' work drew more heavily from the conservative view of history than the progressive in constructing this ersatz 'middle'.

A third feature was the moral relativism in Grotius' vision of war which, along with the ideological relativism set out earlier, remained unresolved both in his work and tradition. This was a conflict between procedural and substantive conceptions of pluralism. The normative pillar, which held up one end of Grotius' theoretical edifice, claimed to need the more 'realist' positivist pillar in order to constitute a balanced structure. This was perceived as the only means of finding the just route: the gate at the centre of Grotius' edifice through which one had to pass in order to navigate a true middle path between the absolutist claims of any single ideology. Yet the normative pillar, by its nature, consisted of moral claims which established the absolute virtue of specific values and principles, such as the justness of choosing such a middle path. Likewise, the positivist pillar claimed that the theoretical structure must encompass both extremes of the discourse on war. Yet the pluralistic procedures took precedence over the pluralistic substance. These discourses embodied a mechanism which allowed different moral visions to coexist, making adherence to any one ethical claim near impossible.

The fourth feature lay in his declared attempt to make a moral claim for moderation in warfare, using the techniques of inclusivity. The contradiction between making a moral claim, based on Christian law, the law of nature or any other law, whilst simultaneously maintaining the ability to detach from any ethical scheme whatsoever, created irreconcilable tensions. Yet the uniqueness of this approach had to do with Grotius' ability to cite ethical claims within the same system (and alongside others) which denied other moral claims; these precepts could equally be claimed by the humanitarian, 'normative' Grotian tradition or the more 'realist' Grotian lawyers.

And finally, a notable feature in Grotius' theory of moderation in war was his audience. The appeal for moderation was made specifically to rulers and princes in authority. His entire argument rested on the fact that only by writing for, and about, power and powerful leaders could incremental change be brought about. By sustaining, and indeed constructing, legitimising arguments which endorsed rulers' actions, the entire body of the work assumed an asymmetrical character, seeming to offer an endless range of rights for rulers, and mere obligations for subjects and slaves.

Indeed, this was the essence of the Grotian legacy to the founding of the laws of war. At the heart of the Grotian system was an essential dichotomy between the rights of states and armies on the one hand, and the position of ordinary members of society on the other. Although he devoted some effort to justifying private wars, the thrust of Grotius' writings was to concentrate the legitimate recourse to war in public hands. Within these limits, however, states and armies were given an open field to visit destruction and mayhem upon each other; these actions were justified by the hallowed principles of practice and custom. On the other side of the equation lay the hapless subjects of their respective states, condemned to wallow in the private sphere, enjoying no political or civic rights either in war or peace, and with the peculiar formulation of Grotian charity as their only hope for salvation. Between the public sphere of the state and the private realm of the subject, there was no question in Grotius' mind as to which enjoyed the primary position. Sown by Grotius, the seeds of the distinction between the rights of states and armies and the subordinate position of civilians – expressed in the legal dichotomy between lawful and unlawful combatant – germinated in the later nineteenth century and remains with us today.

Rousseau and The Nature of Asymmetrical War

In his opening paragraphs of *Principes du Droit de La Guerre*, Rousseau descends upon Grotius' and Hobbes' philosophies of war with a remarkable literary force. After attacking their methods, he goes on to address their motives in equally scathing terms:

> What human soul would not be sickened by such sad scenes? But one is no longer considered a man if one pleads the cause of humanity. Justice and truth must be bent in the interests of the strongest. That is now the rule. Since the poor cannot provide pensions or employment, since they do not grant tenure or endow university chairs, why should we protect them?[5]

Finally, he assaults the principles upon which their version of the nature of war is based. His aim is not only to destroy their logic, demonstrate the poverty of their principles or illustrate the viciousness of the ethics of the old world, but also to reveal his own system with as much lucidity as possible. Only by dramatically crushing the opposition could he clear the way for an entirely new formulation. Within his system was a way to guide relations between states with radically different political structures. Accordingly, he needed to juxtapose the new world of his virtuous republic with the old world of power politics, brute force and conquest, and in so doing demonstrate that there was no fatality about the latter phenomena. Unequal wars of occupation did not have to be endured with stoic resignation, but could (and in fact needed to) be met with a firm collective response by the citizenry.

Rousseau illustrates the nature of war by defining it in a wholly original way. As he repeatedly professed in *Principes*, and went on to argue in the *Social Contract* as well, there is a political nature to both just and unjust war. In his *Principes de la Guerre*, he argues that in fact war arises directly from Hobbes' unjust 'peaceful' institutions:

> For a moment, let us put these ideas in opposition to the horrible system of Hobbes. We will find, contrary to his absurd doctrine, that far from the state of war being natural to man, war is born out of peace, or at least out of the precautions men have taken to assure themselves of peace.[6]

He next focuses his attack on Grotius' claims in *De Jure Belli et Pacis*. Grotius' world of unjust war endorses three principles which Rousseau rejects: private war, conquest, and the rights that naturally accrue to conquest – in short, slavery and the principle of might is right. Chapter 3 of the *Social Contract* is actually entitled: 'The Right of the Strongest'. As he explains, 'the "right of the strongest", a right that apparently seems to be ironic, is in reality an established principle', and he asks, rhetorically, 'but will no one ever explain to us this phrase?'. Rousseau argues that force is only a 'physical power, and I cannot see what morality can result by its effects. To yield to force is a necessity and not an act of will; at most it is prudence.' He concludes: 'in what sense can it become a duty? … this so-called right can only produce a bewildering nonsense'.[7] In his next chapter on slavery, he points the finger more directly:

> Grotius and the others claim to find another justification in war for the alleged right of slavery. According to them, the victor's having the right to kill the vanquished implies that the vanquished has the right to purchase his life at the expense of his liberty; a convention thought to be the more legitimate because it proves profitable to both parties.

But it is clear that the so-called right to kill the vanquished cannot be derived from the state of war ... the right of conquest has no other foundation than the law of the stronger. And if war gives the conqueror no right to massacre a conquered people, no such right can be invoked to justify their enslavement ... Hence far from the victor having acquired some further authority besides that of force over the vanquished, the state of war between them continues; their mutual relations is the effect of war, and the continuation of the rights of war implies the absence of a treaty of peace. A convention has been made, but that convention, far from ending the state of war presupposed its continuation.[8]

Hence unjust war, in his definition, emanated from the 'first world' of empire and inequality – the worlds inhabited by Hobbes and Grotius and all those who subscribed to their 'desolate philosophies'. Just war, as derived from the true principles of the nature of man, was a war fought not by the professional soldiers in the pay of kings, but by citizens of the republic, who rallied to its aid in times of crisis. Rousseau explained the difference between the two in no uncertain terms in his advice to Poland: 'Regular troops, the plague and depopulators of Europe, are good for only two purposes, to attack and conquer neighbours, or to shackle and enslave Citizens.' He then added: 'I know that the state should not remain without defenders; but its true defenders are its members. Each citizen ought to be a soldier by duty, none by profession.'[9]

An essential feature of his paradigm, however, is the fact that this republic was not utopian. Unlike the Abbé St Pierre's *Projet*, Rousseau did not believe that total peace was always possible, because within his system these two worlds could coexist simultaneously. A natural consequence of this multi-dimensional vision was that once these two worlds were juxtaposed, wars coming from the old world were unjust wars of conquest, while wars from the new world were just wars of self-defence. Here, in a recommendation to the Polish people on how to preserve their sovereignty, he juxtaposed the old world with their potential new one to illustrate this point:

To look for a means of guaranteeing yourselves against the will of a neighbour stronger than you is to seek a chimera. It would be of an even greater one to try and make conquests and to acquire offensive force; it is incompatible with the form of your government. Whoever wants to be free ought not to want to be a conqueror.[10]

In summary, Rousseau's perception of the nature of war was underpinned by his belief in its political nature. War, he believed, was the result of a particular type of government. He expressly rejected any justification for wars of conquest, but did not imagine they might be banned from existence; rather, they would cease only when corrupt empires transformed themselves into virtuous republics (and he had no illusions about the time this might take). Even so, his belief that republics were less aggressive towards their neighbours was heavily qualified, as he noted the ability of unprincipled leaders to pervert or confuse the general will.

Even more ingeniously, as his system allowed for the past and the future to coexist, he could suggest policies for the republic, and rules which could guide relations between states during different stages of their development, thus allowing for prescriptions to proto-republics such as Poland. Central to this view was that citizens could not be detached from the defence of the state. A just war of self-defence was by its nature a war in which the state was defended by the sovereign citizens, who acted in the very name of public authority under such circumstances. Hence unequal war only occurs if there is an absence of common rules in the international arena of justice and fairness. Commonly used to describe a strategic reality, unequal war for Rousseau meant inadequate laws to deal with the problems that were created by an unjust balance of power.

The Modern Laws of War from 1874 to 1949

By 1874, the European powers had agreed upon two international conventions, the Geneva Convention on Prisoners of War of 1864, inspired by Henri Dunant's book *Un Souvenir de Solférino*, an eye-witness account of extreme suffering endured by wounded soldiers on the field during the Austro-Italian War, and the St Petersburg Declaration of 1868, which contained the famous statement of the principle that the *'only legitimate object which States should endeavour to accomplish during war is to weaken the forces of the enemy state'*.[11] Still unresolved were the lawful practices of armies on land, and the difficulties these caused, notably the distinction between combatant and non-combatant and the rights and duties of occupying powers and occupied inhabitants.[12] The one existing national codification, the Lieber Code, introduced a set of legal guidelines at the time of the civil war in the United States, and provided the basis for a draft text presented to the various delegations which gathered at Brussels in the summer of 1874.[13]

The Brussels conference took place against the express wishes of Bismarck, and in origin was a scheme devised by the heads of two royal families. From European capitals' archives it is clear that very few diplomats wanted it to take place at all. The reasons for their reluctance was this:

> Lesser powers, with Britain and France on their side, had no ambition to see the Prussian army's occupation practices of 1870–1871 codified into international law, while even Bismarck could see little advantage in such a development. German war ambitions were, in fact, more suited to an uncodified customary 'might is right' philosophy, which the Chancellor had no desire to see challenged in a public arena. The smaller power's fears were confirmed by the Russian draft of the convention circulated to delegates in the summer of 1874. The legal norms proposed so obviously favoured occupying forces that this text became known in European ministries as the 'The Code of Conquest'.[14]

It was the Franco-Prussian War of 1870 that fundamentally confirmed the tenet that force equalled law, and so disturbed the French diplomats cited above, and which illustrated that the right of conquest was still a legitimate feature of the international system. International law was seen as an exclusive tool of states, and indeed states were regarded as the only recognised actors in the international system. But the relationship among these states was clearly ordered: empires remained the dominant political norm, and the hierarchical role they enjoyed within the Concert of Europe meant that their interests were always given priority. This strictly hierarchical conception of international society was also in evidence during negotiations, where there was no equality in the decision-making process among the European states invited – lesser powers had little real negotiating ability. Lambermont, the Belgian host, noted how all the diplomats invited were terrified not to 'compromise' themselves with the great powers, but none the less could *not* be absent from the conference: '*Saturday, Sunday and Monday I successively received all the delegations. Except for the Russians and the Germans ... all are vague, all perplexed, all desperate not to compromise themselves.*'[15] In the end, the Brussels Conference broke up after a month of debates without any clear agreement, except for a pretty useless draft 'Brussels Declaration'.

The next set of negotiations on the laws of war took place at the Hague in the summer of 1899. The international atmosphere was radically different (although the underlying fissures remained). The Hague was one of a series of grand international 'peace' treaties envisioned by diplomats and politicians from various corners of the world to resolve such vexing issues as world disarmament and international arbitration. There were also several strands of broadly divergent political ideologies which gave support to the general notions of disarmament and peace; the peace internationalists, organisations promoting the economic values of free trade, institutes such as Nobel's which offered a peace prize as from 1897, and the more rarefied Institute of International Law of 1873.

As at Brussels, it was the Russian Emperor who gave the impetus for the conferences. Although this time it was the growing realisation of the dangers of Europe's rapid over-militarisation which pushed statesmen to the table, rather than the desire to regulate the manner in which wars were fought, a convention entitled The Laws and Customs of War on Land (known as the 'Hague Regulations') emerged from the first round. It omitted the majority of troublesome issues which wrecked the Brussels Conference of 1874.[16]

The period between the Hague conferences and the Geneva Conventions in 1949 saw an acceleration of the pace in international legal codification. The 1929 Geneva Convention on Prisoners of War constituted a great advance from the previous regulations, but still failed to raise the question of civilians who resisted occupation, and whether they should be granted the privileges of belligerency (Prisoner of War status). Equally, the efforts in the 1930s of the International Committee of the Red Cross (ICRC) to persuade the major powers to sign a convention protecting civilians proved fruitless.[17] However, two other international treaties of the era also bore indirectly on the laws of war: the Covenant of the League of Nations and the Kellogg-Briand Pact (1928). Both were informed by the liberal internationalist view that war could be eradicated through enlightened diplomacy and collective action.[18] Also directly influencing the Geneva negotiations in 1949 were the various national and international positions on war crimes during and after the Second World War, in particular the Nuremberg Trials of 1946, and the Universal Declaration of Human Rights of 1948.[19] [One of the most important legal precedents was the 1942 London Declaration of War Crimes, issued at the height of the war by the Allies, which proclaimed hostage-taking and other customary occupying army practices a war crime. This gave an enormous impetus to states to create a legal convention that would actually reflect this politically inspired stance.[20]]

A final set of negotiations resulted in the four Geneva Conventions of 1949, which covered different aspects of the limitations on war. Two of these contained issues which addressed the distinction between lawful and unlawful combatant: the Prisoners of War Convention, and the Civilians Convention, the latter being related to individuals who came under military occupation.[21] However, although comprehensive, these conventions still did not provide a clear solution to the central problem of the distinguishing between lawful and unlawful combatant.

The Legal Controversy

The challenge of formulating a distinction between lawful and unlawful combatant drove most aspects of the legal controversy at conferences between 1874 and 1949.

The first problem was the definition of 'occupation': the precise conditions necessary for its legal commencement. (For invading armies, the sooner an overrun territory was declared occupied, the more rapidly they were recognised as occupying powers, so for them, simply tacking a poster to a tree was sufficient to declare that a military occupation had begun in that area. It was thus the only condition needed by an invading army to require the complete passivity of the population.[22]) Others, however, believed a large number of conditions had to be met; not only did the local population first have to be completely subdued, but also for an occupation to continue, it needed to be maintained by force. The object of stipulating such exacting conditions was tactical: the further a state of occupation could be delayed, the longer citizens had a right to bear arms in defence of the country.[23]

The second problem was the question of legitimate combatants. In the traditional customs of war, only professional soldiers were granted belligerent status. Accordingly, all civilians who participated in hostilities were considered *outlaws*, and were to be 'delivered to justice'.[24] Those contesting this legal norm argued that all citizens who bore arms for the nation were legitimate combatants.[25] On the subject of *prisoners of war*, small countries sought for armed defenders to be protected from reprisals if captured (as professional soldiers already were).

A further debate centred on the concept of *levée en masse*. The larger powers sought to have the conditions for a legitimate uprising restricted in several ways, above all by requiring its necessary organisation under military command. It was also to be limited both temporally and spatially, in that it was to be launched only at the moment of an invasion, and occur only in territories not yet subjected to occupation.[26]

Finally, there was the question of permitted army methods in occupied territories, such as reprisals, levies and requisitions. The first of these, reprisals, was a customary method used by armies to punish illegal acts by the inhabitants of occupied territories. There were three views. The first argued for the rights of armies, and wanted to maintain and consolidate the practice; second were those who campaigned for the rights of resistance, and advocated its complete abolition, and finally, there were those who saw themselves as introducing a degree of 'humanity in warfare' desired to mitigate the practice of reprisals.[27]

Conceptions of Justice Emerging from Distinct Traditions of War

All of the legal controversies were driven by the problem of distinguishing between who was a lawful fighter in wartime, and who was not to be granted this privileged status. The challenge of maintaining this distinction between classes of those who could fight arose in a particular historical and political context in the nineteenth and twentieth centuries. It also emerged under the specific circumstances of this period in Europe, which was replete with wars of foreign rule, invasion and occupation. It was from this crucible that the three distinct articulations of war emerged. Hence the recurrence of such themes as conquest, resistance, obedience, patriotism, sovereignty, and independence in their ideological discourse. These three philosophical traditions of war also held a particular and exclusive view of what political justice ought to consist of. The final sections of this chapter will outline the three traditional conceptions of justice, and demonstrate how the debate set out between the positions of Rousseau, Hobbes and Grotius continued through the nineteenth and twentieth centuries.

The Martial Conception of Justice

The term 'martialism' defines an ideology which glorified war and military conquest, and quite simply can be defined as the view that war is both the supreme instrument and the ultimate realisation of all human endeavour. It was a doctrine which manifested itself most emphatically in the practices of conquest and foreign rule. Indeed, it could be said that martialism constituted the political philosophy of occupying armies. In this sense, its precepts were entirely favourable to the practices of occupation, and strongly hostile to all manifestations of resistance to its moral and political authority. For those that advanced this position, war was seen as natural, and could not (and should not) be codified. At the conferences on the laws of war, various proponents of this ideology set forth this position, and in doing so illustrated the martialist conception of justice, as well as their paradigm and understanding of unequal war.

The official Prussian position on war during the mid- and late nineteenth century represented martial ideology in full. Their response to their own legal expert Bluntschli was paradigmatic. Bluntschli had attempted to write a manual on the laws of war, involving many other international lawyers, but his draft reflected the more conservative view on war in Europe. Major von Hartmann wrote the official reply of the Prussian Ministry of War to Bluntschli's proposal for a 'Codification of the Laws of War' of 1880, entitled *Military Necessities and Humanity*: 'The expression "civilised warfare", used by Bluntschli, seems hardly intelligible; for war destroys this very equilibrium … If military authority recognises duties it is because it imposes them upon itself in full sovereignty. It will never consider itself subject to outside compulsion. Absolute military action in time of war is an indispensable condition of military success.'[28] But there was worse in store for Bluntschli. Von Moltke, the military hero of Prussia, used the opportunity to compose his now infamous exposition on war and peace: 'Perpetual peace', he wrote to Bluntschli, 'is a dream, and it is not even a beautiful dream: war forms part of the universal order constituted by God. In war are displayed the most noble virtues, courage and abnegation, fidelity to duty, and the spirit of sacrifice which will hazard life itself; without war humanity would sink into materialism.'[29]

Some British jurists agreed with this conservative view held by Prussia, and advanced a notion of political justice that claimed almost total rights for the occupying power over the civilian population. Halleck's manual of war, in 1878, took this position. Occupied civilians were: 'virtually in the condition of prisoners of war on parole. No word of honour has been given, but it was implied; for only on that condition would the conqueror have relinquished the *extreme right of war which he held over their lives.*'

In 1949, at the negotiations at Geneva that would create the four Geneva Conventions, the British War Office Delegate William Gardner continued in this tradition. He attempted to have the practice of hostage-taking preserved, behind the back of his own delegation who were seeking to ban it absolutely, and in spite of the fact that his own government had loudly and publicly proclaimed this practice a war crime a few years earlier. In 1941, at the Allies conference in London, President Roosevelt had declared that the 'practice of executing scores of hostages in reprisals for isolated attacks … revolts a world already inured to sufferings and brutality'. Churchill had added: 'the cold blooded executions of innocent people will only recoil upon the savages who order and execute them … the atrocities in Poland, Yugoslavia, in Norway, in Holland, in Belgium, and above all behind the German Fronts in Russia surpass anything … Retribution for these crimes must henceforward take its place among the major purposes of the war.' Four days after his secret meeting with the ICRC official, which was unsuccessful, Gardner publicly set out this position with the rest of the delegation: 'The foundation on which to rest in argument was that the Occupying Power must have certain powers which went beyond the normal peacetime powers of the Government, for example, the right to take hostages and the right to destroy property as a reprisal.' For the martialist, all activity by civilian population was seen as a crime, even passive resistance. In 1949, the War Office directed the position at the international conference to be: '[The] Occupying Power must have powers to take stern measures against passive resistance.'

The Grotian Conception of Justice

The Grotian tradition of war developed in a particular manner from 1874 to 1949 in the context of the framing of the laws of war. It was the most dominant tradition, in that its core principles lay at the heart of the very project of the laws of war. Although Hugo Grotius devoted some effort to justifying private wars, the thrust of writings was to concentrate the legitimate recourse to war in public hands. This was the essence of Grotius' legacy to the founding of the laws of war. At the heart of the Grotian legal system on war was an essential dichotomy between the rights of states and armies on the one hand, and the position of ordinary members of society on the other. Important values were law, order, power and sovereignty of the state. The Grotian tradition was thus 'index-linked' to legitimate power. Accordingly, absolutely central to the Grotian position was the ambition to limit the rights of belligerency to a particular class of participant (the soldier), and to exclude all others from the right to become actively involved in it, no matter if they were being invaded.

Keeping the concept of *jus ad bellum* theoretically separate from that of *jus in bello* made it easier to establish and maintain a legal parity between belligerent parties. An important principle in the Grotian ideology was a pragmatic rule upholding the equality of belligerents: 'International law has no alternative but to accept war, independently of the justice of its origin, as a relation which the parties to it may set up if they choose, and to busy itself only in regulating the effects of the relation. Hence both parties to every war are regarded as being in an identical legal position, and consequently possessed of equal rights.'

The military rulebook at the time of the Hague Conference in 1899 reflected this position: 'The right of the non-combatant population to protection for their persons and property, the limits and extent of which right we have hitherto been discussing, necessarily involves on the part of those who have obtained this protection on the faith of their being non-combatant a corresponding duty of abstaining from all further hostilities against the invaders.'

The Russian delegate at Brussels in 1874 explained, when advancing his draft treaty: 'it has been said that the Russian project paralyses the rights of defence. This reproach is not founded … But war has changed its nature. It was once a sort of drama where strength and personal courage played a great role. Today, individuality has been replaced by a formidable machine which genius and science has put into motion. Therefore it is our imperative duty to regulate inspirations such as patriotism … The great explosions of patriotism that occurred at the start of our century in several countries cannot be reproduced today.'

In order to underscore this normative conception of civilian passivity, Grotian jurists attempted to assert that certain historic forms of resistance by civilians were imaginary. At the Geneva 1949 conference, for example, the existence of the *levée en masse* was dismissed out of hand by the representative of the ICRC, even though the facts on the ground proved otherwise, and were well documented in archives and by eye-witnesses and participants throughout the nineteenth century in Europe. The method was to introduce state practice only, and to deny existence of resistance. This was, of course, much harder in 1949, after the Second World War, and the various uprisings throughout it, such as at Warsaw.

The Republican Conception of Political Justice

Wars of empire and of foreign occupation occurred in Europe throughout the nineteenth and twentieth centuries, and it was the republican response to this predicament which directed the trajectory and development of the tradition's ideology. The tradition emerged as a direct result of the quest for independence, and developed subsequently into a distinct republican doctrine of patriotism. Its main features were liberty and equality, individual and national self-reliance, patriotism and public-spiritedness (and the importance of education to arouse these virtues), and a notion of just war combined with justice in war:

> There can be no patriotism without liberty, no liberty without virtue, no virtue without citizens. You will have all these if you train citizens; without doing so, you will have only wicked slaves, from the rulers of the State downwards. To form citizens is not the work of a day; and in order to have men it is necessary to educate them when they are children.[30]

For republicans, defence by civilians and citizens against an invasion and occupation was always legitimate. Indeed, in republican ideology, there was the duty to disobey the occupying power, and the duty to resist the invasion and occupation. For the republican conception of political justice in war, the cardinal precept was the legitimacy of civilian defence. Unlike the Grotian and Martial traditions, which clearly saw military occupation as the end of formal war and the collapse of legitimate authority of the occupied state, republicans saw military occupation as a continuation of the state of war. Equally important for republicans was that although the formal institutions of their state may have collapsed through the actions of the invading army, the source of their government's legitimacy came from the people. Therefore, the locus of authority and sovereignty reverted to the individual and collective inhabitants of that state, the sovereign citizens, who became its representatives and agents during its suspension.

From the nineteenth century onward, smaller countries consistently asserted that there was no legal obligation of obedience to the occupying power, arguing that citizens' resistance to occupation was a 'sacred duty'. By 1949, some countries re-interpreted their domestic law to reflect this view. At two important post-war trials in Holland in 1946, a judge ruled that the Hague Conventions did not create legal obligations in conscience binding on the inhabitants. The Dutch Court of Cassation ruled that resistance was a 'permissible weapon to use against the occupant'. And Yugoslavia's post-war constitution specifically prohibited the acceptance of foreign occupation by the officials or the population.

Thus, for republicans, there were two types of crime in war. The first was that invasion and aggression itself was criminal. This view was reflected in the development of early twentieth-century international law, such as the Kellog-Briand Pact. For republicans, unlike the Grotian legal position, law came before war, not after it. At the negotiations at Geneva in 1949, the Danish delegation argued that 'all States agreed that wars of aggression constituted an international crime, and it was therefore obvious that resistance by the civilian population should in such a case be considered as an act of legitimate defence'.[31]

The second conception for republicans emerged from their broader notion of political justice: war crimes are acts by an invading or occupying army against its defenders. At Brussels in 1874, the Greek delegate stated the obvious: 'one can punish the population if it is not considered as a belligerent, but if we accept this status then they are in a condition of legal resistance.' There was the attempt, equally, by republicans to resist the codification of reprisals into treaty law. The Belgian representative Lambermont argued this at the first conference on the laws of war in Brussels in 1874; 'There are some things done in wartime that will always be done, and this one must accept. But it is proposed here to convert them in law, into positive prescriptions, and international ones at that. If the citizens are to be taken to the execution posts for having attempted to defend their country at the peril of their lives, they should not have to find, inscribed on the poteau at the foot of which they are to be shot, a treaty signed by their own government that has condemned them to death in advance.'[32]

Conclusion

Throughout the modern era, of which this paper traces just a fraction of the debate, there has always been a sharply contested concept of the nature of war, and the just cause for engaging upon it. Equally, the notions of asymmetrical and unequal wars were predominant concerns of many of the key philosophers, legal jurists and advocates in the past as they are today. Wars have rarely been the chessboard playing field set out by military theorists and strategists, and which the rules set out to codify. The rules introducing humanity in warfare in the late nineteenth century had consistently served the already stronger party of an invading state in unequal wars. Through the gradual increase of introducing humanity in warfare by means of international humanitarian law over the last half of the twentieth century, this imbalance has been addressed. Sadly, it may go some way to showing the reasons why the stronger parties to various conflicts are today refusing to apply these legal constraints to themselves.

Notes

1   Grotius, Hugo (1990), *De Jure Belli ac Pacis*, trans. A. Campbell, London: Hyperion Press, Book I, 17–18.
2   Ibid., 'Prolegomena', 21. Emphasis added.
3   Ibid., 76.
4   Ibid., 'Prolegomena', 30.
5   Rousseau, Jean-Jacques, *Principes du Droit de la Guerre*, in Gagnebin, B. and Raymond, M. (eds) (1979), *Oeuvres Complètes*, Vol. III, Paris: Pléiades, 602.
6   Ibid., 610.
7   Ibid., 354.
8   Ibid., 356, 357.
9   Ibid., 1014.
10 Ibid., 1013.
11 Cited in Roberts, A., and Guelff, R. (1989), *Documents on the Laws of War*, Oxford: Clarendon Press, 30–31.
12 Graber, Doris (1949), *The Development of the Law of Belligerent Occupation*, New York: Columbia University Press, 13–36.
13 'Actes de la Conférence Réunie à Bruxelles, du 27 Juillet au 27 Août 1874 pour régler les lois et les coutumes de la guerre', *Nouveau Recueil général de traités*, 1879–80, Vol. IV, 15.
14 Savile Lumley, note dated 7 July 1874, FO83/481, Foreign Office Archives, Public Record Office (PRO).
15 Baron Lambermont, noted dated 29 July 1874, Dossier B.7484, Archives of the Ministry of Foreign Affairs, Brussels.
16 Roberts, Adam, 'Land Warfare: From The Hague to Nuremberg', in Howard, Michael et al. (eds) (1994), *The Laws of War: Constraints on Warfare in the Western World*, New Haven, CT: Yale University Press, 123.
17 See McCoubray, Hilaire (1990), *International Humanitarian Law: The Regulation of Armed Conflicts*, Aldershot: Dartmouth Publishing, 144.
18 See Draper, G., 'The ethical and juridical status of constraints in war', *Military Law and Law of War Review*, 55, 1972, 169–86.
19 On the legal foundations of the Nuremberg trials, see Paulson, S., 'Classic Legal Positivism at Nuremberg', *Philosophy and Public Affairs*, Vol. 4, No. 2, 1975, 132–58.
20 'Declaration of War Crimes, adopted by the Inter-Allied Conference at St. James's Palace on January 13, 1942', cited in Schwarzenberger, G. (1943), *International Law and Totalitarian Lawlessness*, London: Stevens, 140.
21 The other two conventions covered forces wounded in the field, and also those wounded at sea.
22 On the notion of 'allegiance' to occupying rule, see Birkhimer, W. (1892), *Military Government and Martial Law*, Washington, DC: Chapman, 3.
23 For an in-depth discussion of the legal debate on the accepted conditions for military occupation, see the contributions of the Institute of International Law jurists in *Revue de Droit International et Législation Comparée*, 8, 1875–6.
24 Draft Russian Text at Brussels Conference, 1874. 'Actes', 223–4, and Appendix, 302.
25 See Clarke, M., Glynn, T. and Rogers, A., 'Combatants and Prisoner of War Status', in Meyer, M. (ed.) (1989), *Armed Conflict and the New Law*, London: British Institute of International and Comparative Law, 11.

26   See Meyrowitz, H., 'Le statut des saboteurs dans le droit de guerre', in *Revue de droit pénal et de droit de guerre*, 5, 1966, 144.

27   For an overview of nineteenth- and early twentieth-century practices see Fritz Kalshoven's comprehensive 1971 study, *Belligerent Reprisals*, Leyden: Sijthoff.

28   Von Hartmann, J. (1877–8), *Militärische Notwendigkeit und Humanität – Military Necessities and Humanity*, Bonn: Deutsche Rundschau, xiii, 123.

29   Quoted in Andler, C. (1913), *Frightfulness in Theory and Practice*, London: Fisher Unwin, 23.

30   Rousseau, *Discourse on Political Economy*, in Gagnebin and Raymond (eds) (1979), *Oeuvres Complètes*, Vol. III, 97.

31   The Final Record of the Diplomatic Conference of Geneva of 1949, 3 v., Federal Political Department, Berne, 1949.

32   Baron Lambermont, 10 July 1874. Dossier B.7484, Archives of the Ministry of Foreign Affairs, Brussels.

Chapter 4

Arguments Concerning Resistance in Contemporary Islam

John Kelsay

Introductory Comments[1]

Arguments concerning resistance in contemporary Islam comprise an expansive topic. The ultimate focus of this chapter is on several recent documents, including the 1998 *Declaration Concerning Armed Struggle Against Jews and Crusaders*. This document, produced by Usama bin Ladin and four others styling themselves leaders of the 'World Islamic Front', was quoted with some frequency in news analyses following the attacks of 11 September 2001.[2] Many readers may be familiar with it. For those who are not, I attach a translation (see Appendix to this chapter). As I hope to show, the document is most interesting as a contribution to contemporary discussion among Muslims concerning the justification and conduct of armed resistance. It fits in a context of vigorous debate about the fit, or if one likes, the purchase of long-standing judgements about matters of political ethics, including the justification and conduct of war in Islam, in contemporary settings.

I begin with a description of the particular form of Islamic practical reasoning exemplified by the *Declaration* and related documents. I then provide a brief overview of those precedents that provide the background for contemporary discussions of armed resistance. This leads to some comments on the *Declaration* and related statements, and to some discussion of the ways these have been received in Muslim circles. I conclude with some remarks about what one ought to make of this material, in terms of understanding the career or trajectory of arguments about armed resistance in Islam.

The Form of Islamic Practical Reason

If one asks about the Islamic equivalent to our word 'ethics', the answer is that there isn't one – or, what is much the same, there are several. Native speakers regularly associate the Arabic *akhlaq* ('character') with the academic discipline practised in European and North American departments of philosophy and (sometimes, at least) religion. One can understand why, since it is associated with the discussion of those virtues characteristic of a cultivated person. Similarly, *adab* ('letters') indicates discussion of the manners and morals associated with elite professions: medicine provides one example, politics another. *Falsafa* ('philosophy') certainly includes discussion of matters related to the study of ethics, particularly in terms of political justice. *Kalam* ('dialectical theology') deals with the question of moral foundations, among other concerns.[3]

If one is thinking of ethics in terms of the study of practical justification – that is, as a matter of understanding (and to some extent, evaluating) the judgements people make about right and wrong, or good and evil, and the arguments they advance in support of these – a complete description of Islamic ethics will have to account for all the disciplines listed above. It will also take account of one other, however, and this is the one most relevant to Muslim discussion of the *Declaration.* This discipline focuses on the *Shari'a,* which is usually called Islamic 'law' or 'religious law', neither of which is entirely adequate. For reasons I hope will become clear, I prefer to speak of 'Shari'a reasoning'.

One could describe Shari'a reasoning as a text-based theory of practical reasoning. Its baseline or foundation is the faith that there is a right way to live. This way accords with the nature of human beings as creatures of God. It can be characterised by a variety of images drawn from the Qur'an: the 'limits set by God', the 'approved and well-known,' or most decisively, the 'straight path'. Arabic lexicons connect this last with the term *shari'a,* and suggest it is the 'path' that leads to refreshment. The great al-Shafi'i (died 820), sometimes described as the first to put Shari'a reasoning on a systematic basis, spoke of this as the way of behaviour that leads to felicity, in this life and the next.[4]

For the practitioners of Shari'a reasoning, the fact that there is a right way to live is never in question. The issue is rather the form of that way; in that respect, the question to be resolved is one of discernment. Al-Shafi'i and others took quite different positions with respect to the absolute necessity of special revelation in this task.[5] Practically speaking, however, Shari'a reasoning assigns priority to texts understood as 'sent down' by God as a gift or provision for human beings in need of guidance. These form the basis of the theory indicated by the term *usul al-fiqh,* the 'sources of comprehension' of the approved way. The Qur'an is basic in this regard: it is 'the book wherein is no doubt, a guidance for the watchful'.[6] Similarly, basic is the *sunna,* or exemplary practice of the Prophet Muhammad.[7] Indeed, the Prophet and the Qur'an go together, since the authority of the Prophet is as an exemplar of the meaning of the Qur'anic text, and the Qur'an refers those with questions about its meaning to the 'wisdom' of God, that is, the Prophet.

The Qur'an and sound 'reports' (*ahadith*) of the Prophet's exemplary practice provide the basic texts for Shari'a reasoning. Theoretically, anyone able to read them is on the way to comprehension of the path. 'Able to read' is a more difficult requirement than it seems, however. To cite al-Shafi'i again, the texts are more clear on some matters than on others. Particularly with respect to the latter, proper reading requires people trained in the language of the texts (Arabic, and that in the style common in the Arabian Peninsula at the time of the Prophet). These must have training in grammar; a basic comprehension of the rules of logic is also important. Further, they must be acquainted with a number of problems related to the interpretation of reports concerning Muhammad's practice.

In connection with such necessities, the class of religious specialists known as *al-ulama* developed. Most generally, these were people trained in the reading of the Qur'an and reports of the Prophet's practice. Some developed sub-specialties as exegetes or, in the case of prophetic reports, as students of the biographies of those who transmitted the texts. One could see all such sub-specialties as serving the ultimate goal of the class, which was to enable Muslims to comprehend right guidance. In this way, the rights and responsibilities associated with Shari'a reasoning became less a matter for every Muslim and more a matter of the authority of the learned class. The following pattern emerges early on: a Muslim or a group of Muslims facing a situation in which he/she/they has reason to wonder about the mode of action proper for human beings asks one or more members of the learned class for an opinion (a *fatwa*). The opinion is rendered as an exercise in matching textual precedents with the circumstances of the case. The evidence indicates that the learned described such matching in diverse terms: as *ra'y* ('opinion') or *istihsan* (seeking 'the best') or, for most, as *qiyas* ('analogy'). The last, in particular, involved sifting through texts for precedents understood to share an underlying principle with the current case. The entire process could be described as *ijtihad*, implying 'effort' in the attempt to discern the approved way in particular circumstances.

There is much we do not know about the development of the learned class and its authority in these matters. A story related by al-Tabari (died 935, the standard historical resource for the early period) is interesting in this regard. Here, one finds the Abbasid ruler Harun al-Rashid (died 809, the Caliph of the *Thousand and One Arabian Nights*) calling on several noteworthy scholars of his day. He asks them about a matter pertaining to the most prominent leader of a dissident group. At some point, it appears that Harun gave this leader an *aman*, or a writ of safe passage throughout the territory of the empire. But, as Harun tells it, the man continues to cause trouble. Surely the *aman* is no longer valid, and Harun can have this rebel thrown in prison or place a price on his head? The scholars do as scholars are wont to – they disagree. Harun takes the opinion he likes and declares the *aman* no longer valid.[8]

The other scholars do not simply fade away, however. Indeed, they are two of the most important exemplars of Shari'a reasoning in the history of the tradition. Abu Yusuf (died 795) and al-Shaybani (died 804) continued to advise Harun even after this incident. 'Difference of opinion in my community is a source of blessing' – or so the Prophet is reported to have said. In Shari'a reasoning, the effort is primary: as another report has it, the Prophet said that anyone who tries to find the correct answer to a question receives merit. Anyone who actually finds the right answer receives a double portion. One could say that conscientiousness is the point, rather than rightness.

Nevertheless, if enough of the learned agreed on a particular judgement, their collective judgement came to have the authority of consensus. Practically speaking, such consensus emerged among smaller groups of the learned; these came to be identified with 'schools' or more literally 'directions' of interpretation. Within the schools, the *responsa* of exemplary scholars were collected and used in the training of subsequent generations, who then reasoned by analogy from these as an additional source of precedent. Layer upon layer, generation after generation of the learned practised the art of Shari'a reasoning in the quest to comprehend right guidance for the Muslim community, and indeed (according to the self-understanding of the learned) for the world.

Armed Struggle: Shari'a Precedents[9]

The most important Shari'a judgements pertaining to armed struggle, as to political ethics generally, were set by members of the learned class between 750 and 1350.[10] We can get an idea of these by means of a brief commentary on one of the standard citations in their texts, a report of the orders given by Muhammad to Muslims preparing to fight. The text reads, in part:

> Fight in the name of God and in the path of God. Combat those who refuse to acknowledge God. Do not cheat or commit treachery. Neither should you mutilate anyone or kill children. Whenever you meet your enemies, invite them to adopt Islam. If they do so, accept it, and let them alone. You should then invite them to move from their territory to a place of security … If they refuse the invitation to Islam, then call upon them to pay tribute. If they do, accept it and leave them alone …[11]

'Fight in the name of God and in the path of God …' Classical precedents indicate the importance of establishing a political order taken to embody Islamic values. Individual members of the learned class differed over whether the establishment of this order was a matter of rational necessity, or of obedience to divine commands. In either case, the establishment of an Islamic state is a duty. Once established, this state or its rulers are similarly obligated to seek justice, (1) by extending the area within which Islamic values are established; (2) by protecting the boundaries of Islamic territory; and (3) by maintaining order within the territory of Islam. In fulfilling this charge, it was taken for granted that military force would, at least under certain conditions, be an appropriate means for seeking justice. It is not the only means, of course; one could even say it is not the best, hence the requirement of a formal invitation to accept Islam or to pay tribute, that is, to come under the protection of the Islamic state. Should these offers be refused, however, the enemy is put to the test of the sword.

'Do not cheat or commit treachery. Neither should you mutilate anyone or kill children.' If armed force is required, Muslims are not to shy away from their task. They are, however, to fight according to notions of honourable combat. In this regard, we find a great deal of material (1) restricting targets at which Muslims armies may aim, and (2) discussing various tactics, including the use of particular weapons that raise the possibility of disproportionate force. With respect to the first, classical precedents are quite consistent in stipulating that children, women, the old, the lame, the blind, those whose mental capacity is in doubt and monks are not to be the direct and intentional target of attack. There are ways in which these can forfeit their protected status. For most of the learned, such forfeiture occurs if and when a person takes up arms and fights alongside the enemy soldiers. It thus seems best to read the lists of protected persons as 'non-combatants', in the sense that their protection rests on an assumption that members of these groups do not normally fight. To put it another way, the idea is that honourable combat involves soldiers fighting soldiers. Still following the consistent pattern of judgements by the learned, it should be said that a certain realism comes into play with respect to the protected status of non-combatants. There are military situations in which non-combatants are killed, even though they are not the direct targets of action. Thus in a famous report, the Prophet is made aware that enemy women and children died in the course of a night attack. He comments that 'they are not from us'.[12] The most straightforward reading of this text, in my opinion, is that the night attack was a legitimate tactic, and that the non-combatant deaths are to be considered accidental or, to use a modern phrase, 'collateral damage'. In other texts, such killings are dealt with in ways that suggest a kind of double effect reasoning: a commander authorises an attack on the enemy's military capacity. *Prima facie*, the attack is thus legitimate. The commander knows there is a strong likelihood that non-combatants will be killed as the result of the attack. He nevertheless deems this attack necessary, in the military sense. The deaths of non-combatants are thus foreseen, but not intended. The attack is justified, and with respect to non-combatant deaths, the Muslim fighters are excused from blame. Judgements differ as to whether the Muslims owe reparations to the families of non-combatant victims in such a case, as well as to whether Muslim soldiers engaged in such an attack must perform acts of expiation.

Honourable combat also seems to require consideration of weaponry. In classical texts one finds, for example, extensive evidence of concern about mangonels or hurling machines, of water (in the sense of causing flooding), and of fire. The reasons for concern generally have to do with the likelihood of harm to non-combatants. In that sense, the Muslim discussion of weaponry is analogous to the *jus in bello* criterion of proportionality, where the worry is that the harm inflicted by certain tactics may cause civilian deaths in numbers disproportionate to the evil against which troops are fighting.[13] Such excess would be blameworthy, although there is no direct attack on civilians. I hasten to say that many of the learned are utterly realistic when it comes to weaponry, suggesting that in the end, military necessity (understood in the sense of 'that which is necessary in the conduct of a just campaign') trumps other considerations. However, there are those who judge that, if the necessities of war require large-scale violations of the rules of honourable combat, the Muslim troops must simply negotiate for the best settlement possible and wait for another day to pursue a more complete justice.

In many if not most of the texts we have, judgements about honourable combat are made in connection with what one might call 'wars of opening'.[14] Here, the idea is that the ruler of the Muslims organises a force in an attempt to extend the boundaries of Islamic territory. This fits well with the Prophet's orders, particularly in connection with the requirement that the enemy is described as 'unbelievers', and also with the requirement of an invitation (1) to accept Islam or (2) to pay tribute. In either case, the goal is political: either to extend the blessings of Islamic governance into heretofore 'uncivilised' regions, or to make the Islamic state more secure, or some combination of the two. The learned are nearly unanimous in the judgement that the ruler of Islam is obligated to work at this goal, and there developed early on a notion that the normal course should be a yearly incursion into non-Islamic territory in this regard. Such fighting is described as a 'collective duty', indicating that it falls on the Muslim community as a whole. In order to fulfil it, the ruler maintains a standing army and levies taxes sufficient for its support. So long as sufficient numbers of people volunteer and there is sufficient funding available, ordinary Muslims have met their obligations.

Other judgements deal with fighting aimed at maintaining order in the Islamic state. Here, the texts divide potential enemies into several categories. There are the 'protected' peoples, indicating non-Muslims who live within the territory of Islam. These have a kind of contract with the Islamic state, by which their security is guaranteed, so long as they respect the Islamic establishment. In accord with this, they are not to be fought, until and unless they violate their contract – say, by lending aid and comfort to a foreign enemy, or by acting in ways that offend the integrity of Islam (for example, by blaspheming the Prophet, though even this would usually involve punishment of one or a small group of offenders rather than an entire community).

Other groups include 'brigands', 'apostates' and 'rebels'. Brigands or 'highwaymen' are criminals. Typically, they are depicted as small groups operating in less populated areas and preying on travellers. The texts seem to assume they are Muslims – otherwise, they could be fought as members of protected groups whose behaviour violates contractual arrangements. They do not offer religious justifications for their behaviour, however, which is crucial in distinguishing them from the remaining groups. 'Apostates', for example, indicate Muslims who turn away from Islam. One may think about particular persons – as, for example, an individual who stands on a platform in the public market, raises a copy of the Qur'an, and says 'Before today, I believed this to be God's speech. I believe this no longer.' One may also think about a group – as, for example, some Arab tribes who refused to send their assigned offerings to the community treasury following the death of the Prophet in 632. In either case, apostates are in violation of a contract – this time, with God, as opposed to the contract of the protected peoples. The Islamic state is responsible to bring them into compliance, or to punish them in a manner proportionate to the offence.

Rebels present a more difficult case. Here, we are to imagine a group of Muslims who are out of compliance with state policy. To illustrate the difficulties of this case, let us consider that the behaviour is akin to that of the Arab tribes who refused payment of assigned offerings. The head of state sends messengers to warn them about noncompliance. Their response is that they consider the ruler's policies unjust and thus unworthy of their allegiance; they cite approved Islamic sources in support of this claim. They are clearly not apostates, because they have not turned from Islam. But they are also not in compliance with the policy of the Islamic state. Or again, consider that the group hides in mountain passes, and comes to the ruler's attention because its members attack merchant caravans which pass through Islamic territory, ostensibly under the protection of the ruler. One of the merchants complains to the ruler, and reports that those who took his goods told him that the ruler's protection was invalid, cited the Qur'an and the example of the Prophet, and warned him that only the protection of a just ruler would guarantee his safety. *Prima facie*, the report indicates that these are not brigands, though their behaviour violates state law.

That the behaviour of rebels constituted a special problem for Islamic political ethics can be ascertained from the plethora of texts addressing the issue. Many of these suggest that armed rebellion against an established ruler is always wrong, and that dissent must be limited to speech and/or passive disobedience.[15] At the same time, we have stories of numerous members of the learned serving time in prison for supporting rebellions, and, more to the point, we have sections of texts by every important scholar of the period discussing rules for the conduct of fighting rebels – rules that indicate both the presumptive right of an established ruler to maintain order, and the limits which the ruler must observe in doing so. While one ought not to speak of these texts as establishing a doctrine of just revolution, their existence at least indicates the creation of a space within which rebel justifications must be heard. Thus fighting against rebels is not described as a matter of punishment for violation of a contract, but as an enterprise limited by the goal of reconciliation.[16] In this regard, the forces representing the Islamic state must abide by a stricter version of the rules of honourable combat than in other cases, while restrictions on rebel forces are somewhat more open.[17]

Finally, we have judgements about fighting connected with 'imposed' war, in which the action of an enemy violates Muslim security. In such cases, the nature of the obligation to fight changes from the 'collective duty' described in connection with wars of opening to an 'individual duty'.[18] An important case, as one might expect, occurs in connection with the crusades, when *al-faranj* (the 'Franks') engage in repeated incursions into Syro-Palestine and take control of *al-quds* (Jerusalem). There are many interesting aspects of this case, but for now, I simply note that the use of 'individual duty' in this case seems *not* to mean that 'every single Muslim is obligated to fight', but rather that leaders controlling other regions in the territory of Islam are obligated to come to the aid of their besieged co-religionists in Syro-Palestine. We are not to think of a *levée en masse* or of a mass uprising, but of recognised magistrates who lend their aid.[19]

The importance of such qualifications will become clear. For now, let me bring this summary of historic precedents to a close by noting that a number of themes come together in the work of Ibn Taymiyya (died 1328.) Ibn Taymiyya's context, like that of jurists working during the crusades, was tumultuous. Patterns of political order were shifting. In 1258 Mongol warriors sacked Baghdad and the Abbasid Caliph fled to Egypt, where he came under the protection of the Mamluk sultan. In one sense, this presented no new problems for Islamic political thought. Since *c*. 950, the Abbasid caliphs turned over political and military power to whichever territorial governor (or sometimes, governors) seemed best able to fulfil the requirements of the state in this regard. In Shari'a reasoning, this was understood as a matter of the Caliph's right to delegate power (hence, the person in question was called *al-sultan*, the 'power'). The Mamluk rulers had held this post for some time; by protecting the Caliph, they preserved the symbol of the unity of Islamic government.

In another sense, however, the circumstances of the Caliph's flight did raise important questions. For the Mongols who sacked Baghdad settled in to rule large portions of territory previously controlled by the Caliph. And, just to make matters more complicated, they converted to Islam. For a scholar like Ibn Taymiyya, this raised important questions regarding the normative basis of Islamic politics. Since the Mongols now claimed to establish Islamic values, they might be seen as representing the embodiment of political justice, even as the Abbasid/Mamluk alliance. In various opinions, and also in a treatise on the Shari'a approach to governance, Ibn Taymiyya addressed these matters. Following his predecessors, Ibn Taymiyya argued that the establishment of a political order embodying Islamic values is obligatory. He did not suppose that this required a unitary order – that is, one can read Ibn Taymiyya as suggesting that there might be a number of political-territorial associations with governments considered legitimate, in that they embodied Shari'a values.

This characteristic of Ibn Taymiyya's reasoning resonates well with the problem posed by the Mongol adoption of Islam. It means, *ipso facto*, that portions of his texts dealing with imposed wars cannot be read as applying to the Mongols. They are no longer 'intruders', but present a claim to embody political justice that must be weighed against that of the Mamluks. As Ibn Taymiyya has it, however, there is something problematic about the Mongol claim. Even though they are now Muslims, and ostensibly establish Islam in a given territory, they are reported to rule by a 'mixed' legal regime. That is, the Mongols not only consult experts in Shari'a reasoning regarding patterns of justice in their state; they consult experts in Mongol customary law. The Shari'a basis of the latter is unclear; it seems it even leads to policies that violate important precedents set in the judgements of the learned. The Mongols are thus apostates, in that they have turned from Islam. And the Mamluk sultan is justified in fighting against them, in terms of forcing the Mongols to comply with the terms of the divine–human contract set by the Mongols' profession of faith.

In this task, the Mamluk rulers are the legitimate representatives of Islamic order. Depending on the nature of the threat posed by the Mongols, they may set policies consistent with the notion that fighting is a collective duty, meaning that they may levy taxes and call for volunteers sufficient to maintain a fighting force, or (if things get bad) they may set policies consistent with the notion that fighting is an individual duty. Here, the idea is that they may call for greater sacrifice, impose military service on individuals, and so on. In either case, their military policies are to reflect the norms of honourable combat, so that women, children, the old and other non-combatants do not become the direct and intentional targets of military attack. The one very interesting qualification Ibn Taymiyya makes in this regard is to say that non-combatants (he mentions women specifically) may sacrifice this protected status if they join the war effort, for example by engaging in propaganda activities against the Islamic forces. I highlight this last by way of contrast with earlier judgements focused on the status of persons as fighters – that is, actually bearing arms.

Modern Developments

Ibn Taymiyya is of interest not only because of the complicated historical context in which he wrote, but also because he is the favourite exemplar of Shari'a reasoning in many contemporary texts. The *Declaration*, for example, speaks of the judgements of the learned, citing al-Qurtubi (died 1273), Ibn Qudama (died 1223), al-Kisai (died 805) and *al-shaykh al-islam*. The last is a title indicating one regarded as a first among equals. The fact that the authors take time to quote from this person's work is a further indication of their respect: 'As for fighting to repel [NB: as I have described it, this is 'imposed' war], it is aimed at defending sanctity and religion, and is by consensus an obligation. Nothing is more sacred than belief except repulsing an enemy which is attacking religion and life.' The quote is from Ibn Taymiyya's book on the Shari'a approach to governance.

Contemporary discussions of armed resistance are filled with references to Ibn Taymiyya and his context. *The Neglected Duty*, described as the 'testament' of those who assassinated Egyptian President Anwar Sadat, connects the great scholar's analysis of the apostasy of the Mongols to Sadat's administration, and argues that fighting such criminals is a duty most Muslims are neglecting (literally, the author describes it as 'hidden'; most don't see their duty, and he and his colleagues want to bring it to light). The testament or memoir of Ayman al-Zawahiri ('bin Ladin's physician') goes to great lengths in arguing that the circumstance of present Muslims is as that of Ibn Taymiyya and his contemporaries, as do the statements of al-Qa'ida spokesman Sulayman Abu Ghayth and of bin Ladin himself. Clearly, Ibn Taymiyya catches the imagination of many involved in contemporary resistance movements.[20]

More generally, one should say that the tradition of Shari'a reasoning about politics is under stress, and has been so since the mid- to late eighteenth centuries.

The various campaigns inspired by the teachings of Muhammad ibn 'abd al-Wahhab (died 1791) and his followers directly challenged the claim of the Ottoman sultanate (or sometimes, caliphate) to embody the Islamic ideal of political justice.[21] The charge, in brief, was that the Ottomans failed to implement Shari'a judgements. The Ottoman state should thus be regarded as fostering 'unbelief' (*kufr*), a category that included hypocrisy, idolatry and apostasy. In the absence of a just polity, the Wahhabiyya claimed the right of a rightly guided vanguard to engage in armed struggle against these expressions of unbelief in order to establish an Islamic state.[22]

Similarly, the example of Shah 'Abd al-'Aziz (died 1824) in the Indian subcontinent is instructive. As British dominance in the subcontinent became clear, Muslims understood that India would no longer be ruled by the Moghul elite, or by any other power dedicated to the establishment of Islamic values. 'Abd al-'Aziz, the scion of a family long recognised for its importance among the learned, issued a Shari'a opinion declaring that India could no longer be regarded as *dar al-Islam*, meaning that the current state of governance should not be viewed as an embodiment of traditional notions of political justice. 'Abd al-'Aziz's judgement was less than clear regarding Muslim response. Some, however, took him to authorise armed resistance, and the series of revolts culminating in the Sepoy Mutiny of 1857 are usually interpreted along these lines.[23] Here one recalls Shari'a precedents: the establishment of an order capable of sustaining justice is obligatory. If one presumes, in a manner consistent with most precedents, that the terms 'just order' and 'state in which an Islamic establishment prevails' are synonymous, then it would seem to follow that the British are invaders, and that fighting against them is an obligation. Further, the nature of the fighting is such that one might consider it as analogous to the historic notion of imposed war, so that the duty to fight is in some way an individual matter. Just how those participating in Muslim uprisings in the first half of the nineteenth century understood this seems unclear, though the popular nature of resistance to the British might suggest something akin to the *levée en masse* or the twentieth-century notion of war fought by a 'people'.

These two cases provide early examples of the ways contemporary Muslims relate justifications of armed resistance to the tradition of Shari'a reasoning. In the Wahhabi-Saudi case, one sees the development of earlier precedents justifying fighting against those who claim to be Muslims, but are somehow in abeyance of their duty. Fighting is justified to bring them into compliance or to punish unbelief, with the overall purpose of restoring just public order. The major difficulty here has to do with the designation of right authority in the sense of *competence de guerre*. All the precedents discussed thus far envision such fighting as a matter internal to an established polity. It is thus clear that the decision to fight rests with public officials, or to put it another way, this decision results from a process of consultation between recognised political and religious leaders. For Muhammad 'Abd al-Wahhab, or later, for a Wahhabi-Saudi coalition to claim the right to bypass or otherwise ignore the Ottomans would seem a violation of the consensus of the learned. There are questions to be answered, to say the least.

In the Indian resistance to the British, one sees the development of precedents relative to 'imposed' war. The logic is simple, in one sense. The British are non-Muslim invaders. They exercise power in ways that render Islamic authorities impotent. This could raise questions of security, but those are not paramount in 'Abd al-'Aziz's opinion. Rather, the issue is whether Muslims can and should live under the protection of a regime that has no intention of maintaining an Islamic establishment. 'Abd al-'Aziz himself does not provide a clear answer to this question. His direct focus is on the question of classification: Is British India to be regarded as an Islamic state (a just political order), or not? Those who organized popular resistance movements in response to 'Abd al-'Aziz's negative answer would seem analogous to the publicists who called on Muslims to fight against the Crusaders in Syro-Palestine, or to Salah al-Din (Saladin) as the leader of an active and armed resistance to *al-faranj*.[24] Again, however, the analogy is imperfect. As indicated above, Shari'a precedents cast the duty to fight in an imposed war as an 'individual' duty. In that context, however, this does not appear to suggest a popular uprising. Rather, it is a call to Muslim leaders in neighbouring territories, or ultimately throughout the empire, to lend their aid – to send fighters, money, and material that will enable Muslims in Syro-Palestine to defend themselves against the crusader advance. Even Salah al-Din was actually a candidate for the designation of Sultan by the Abbasid Caliph. Again, Shari'a precedents appear to presume a resistance organised by publicly established authorities. The notion of a popular resistance requires some additional justification, or so it would seem.

In my view, spokespersons for groups like Egyptian Islamic Jihad, Hamas and al-Qa'ida are best construed as trying to address this problem. That is, they are trying to develop Shari'a justifications for armed resistance in a variety of late twentieth- and early twenty-first-century settings. As such, they are the inheritors of the Wahhabiyya, of the Indian movements inspired by 'Abd al-'Aziz's opinion, and of the numerous other resistance movements marking the landscape of modern Islamic history. In every case, the first issue has been to speak in a way that addresses the question of right authority.[25] Thus *The Neglected Duty* argues in ways reminiscent of earlier precedents dealing with fighting against apostates.[26] It is, the author writes, 'a well-established rule of Islamic Law that the punishment of an apostate will be heavier than the punishment of someone who is by origin an unbeliever ...' (169). An apostate is in breach of a contract with God, and must repent (that is, return to compliance with the terms of the contract) or be killed. If one is speaking of 'group' apostasy, then this judgement (that is, that the apostate must return to compliance or be killed) translates into a justification of armed struggle.

Precedent teaches us that any 'group of people that rebels against any single precept of the clear and established judgements of Islam must be fought ... even if the members of the group pronounce the Islamic Confession of Faith'. (169–70). The author notes standard precedents, for example the fighting authorised by Abu Bakr (died 634), first caliph following the Prophet's death in 632. In this case, Abu Bakr ordered military action against certain Arab tribes who refused to send obligatory offerings to the communal treasury – even though the tribes were very clear regarding their faith in the unity of God and Muhammad's status as prophet. If anyone or any group refuses 'to apply [established precedents] on matters of life and property, or merchandise and commodities of any kind...', they must be fought (170).

Who are the apostates spoken of in the text? 'The Rulers of this age are in apostasy from Islam ...They carry nothing from Islam but their names...' (169). The crime of which established leaders are guilty is 'innovation' (*bid'a*). This means that they are introducing legislation that is not founded in (not only not consistent with, but not derived from) recognised Shari'a sources. They govern by a 'mixed regime' in which laws are derived from European codes and customary law, as well as from Shari'a sources. Leaders who do such things no longer deserve respect. They must be fought. One who is guilty of innovation 'no longer has the qualifications needed in a Leader. To obey such a person is no longer obligatory, and the Muslims have the duty to revolt against him and depose him, to put a just leader in his place when they are able to do so' (191–2).

The argument as conceived supports a right of the Muslims to revolt, in the name of fulfilling the obligation to establish a just political order. In terms of Shari'a precedents, this is a difficult judgement. As noted, there are numerous texts that suggest that, even in a context where a ruler is impious or otherwise unjust, the duty of Muslims is to withhold obedience. But that suggests a rather different mode of action than a popular uprising, particularly one construed in terms of enforcing Shari'a provisions for the punishment of a crime (in this case, apostasy). The author acknowledges that a judgement supportive of popular revolution is difficult, saying that it is wrong in almost every case. The one exception occurs when the ruler 'suddenly becomes an unbeliever' through a 'public display' (191). One is not sure that this argument actually works, that is, that the author has adduced a proof that is convincing, within the framework of Shari'a reasoning. Thus, in what might be considered the author's 'ultimate' appeal, he writes in tones that suggest an emergency situation: the enemy now 'lives right in the middle' of Islamic territory, and 'has got hold of the reins of power, for this enemy is the rulers who have seized the leadership of the Muslims' (200). In such a case, the necessity of fighting against apostates is elevated to the point where 'waging armed struggle against them is an individual duty ... it is thus similar to prayer and fasting' (200). To come back to the title of the treatise, the 'neglect' of the duty to fight is itself a sin, at least of omission.

The argument remains difficult. It is not an impossible argument, however, and it is interesting that, when more established members of the learned class, including the Shaykh al-Azhar himself, responded to *The Neglected Duty*, they did not criticise this argument directly (35–62). Rather, they questioned its prudence: they asked the author and his associates to consider that armed rebellion against the Egyptian state might well lead to widespread violence in which innocent people would be killed. Drawing on historical analogies, the Shaykh al-Azhar explicitly reminded the group of the notorious *khawarij*, who in Islamic history represent the archetypal example of what might be called 'excess of zeal' – they are well-meaning, devoted to justice, but imprudent, and thus end up causing more harm than good. To anticipate a point to which I will return, the al-Azhar critique focuses less on *The Neglected Duty*'s claim that a vanguard has authority to fight than on the question of whether armed resistance will violate the norms of honourable combat.

By contrast with *The Neglected Duty*, the *Charter* of Hamas presents the case for armed resistance as a matter of imposed war.[27] The precedents cited by the authors do not speak about the punishment of apostasy. Rather, the argument proceeds largely on the basis of an analogy with the crusades. The actions of colonial powers in the nineteenth and twentieth centuries are interpreted as picking up where the medieval *al-faranj* left off. In the nineteenth century, missionaries set the stage with an attack on the ideological foundations of Islamic society. Military action followed in the twentieth, as European powers liberated Palestine from the Turks, only to assume control themselves. Struggles between Israelis and Palestinians are the flashpoint of this ongoing clash, with Zionism and the Israeli state seen as a kind of crusader outpost in the midst of historically Islamic territory. Imperialist powers 'support the [Zionist] enemy with all their might, material and human … When Islam is manifest the unbelieving powers unite against it because the Nation of unbelief is one' (22). From this perspective, it did not (and does not) matter that non-Muslims powers were and are often engaged in power struggles among themselves, and with quite different policies regarding the state of Israel. The struggle is between a people that submits its life to God, and one that does not (the nation of 'faith' and the nation of 'unbelief'). The modern-day crusaders (or crusader-Zionist alliance) try to divide and conquer, by 'picking off' (or perhaps one should say, 'buying off') those states, for example Egypt, which ought to take up the cause of defending Islam.

Most directly, the *Charter* conceives armed struggle as resistance to the taking of land entrusted to the Muslim community: 'The Islamic Resistance Movement believes that the land of Palestine is entrusted to the Muslims until the Day of Resurrection. It is not right to give it up in whole or in part. No Arab state … no King or Leader … no organisation, Palestinian or Arab, has such authority …' (11). Fighting is justified, even obligatory, in the light of crusader attempts to take land entrusted to the Muslim community. And, in accord with Shari'a precedents, the duty to fight is construed as an 'individual' obligation.

As we have seen, however, historical precedents vary on the meaning of this idea. The crusader analogy seems not to serve so well as the authors of the *Charter* believe, given that Salah al-Din was actually a publicly recognised authority, and that, more generally, the appeal to fighting as an individual duty in that context appears as a summons to Muslim rulers in neighbouring provinces to come to the aid of their co-religionists in Syro-Palestine. The *Charter* is speaking of a popular resistance movement, in which leadership appears to reside with a group including some members of the learned class (Shaykh Ahmad Yassin and others like him) and

ordinary Muslims able to organise local initiatives. No doubt the presence of
Shaykh Yassin and others lends a certain aura of public authority to the struggle. It
is of interest, however, that the *Charter* does not make mention of this point (for
example, by stipulating that its judgements about the duty to fight are formally
issued by a member or members of the learned class), but rather lays heavy stress on
the notion that the obligation to fight belongs to each individual Muslim: 'There is
no higher peak in nationalism, no greater depth of devotion than this: when an
enemy makes incursions into Muslim territory then struggle and fighting the enemy
becomes an obligation incumbent upon every individual Muslim and Muslimah.
The woman is allowed to go fight without the permission of her husband and the
slave without the permission of his master' (12). In effect, the argument is that the
Muslims are in an emergency situation, in which ordinary lines of authority are
suspended. The justification for armed struggle is created by the incursion of non-
Muslim forces into Islamic territory. It may be that, ideally, the struggle should be
organised and carried out by publicly constituted political leaders. Failing that,
however, the duty to resist falls to each member of the Muslim community, and the
right of authority belongs, or seems to, to anyone able to organise the resistance.
Necessity, Shari'a experts say, 'makes the forbidden things permitted'. If that is too
strong, put it this way: in an emergency situation, a people cannot rely on publicly
constituted leadership. There is a right, even a duty to engage in defence of the life,
liberty and property of Muslims. And that right/duty belongs to or is incumbent
upon anyone who recognises the need, and who has the available means.

Such 'emergency reasoning' seems also to provide the background for the World
Islamic Front *Declaration*.[28] Certainly the language suggests such:

> The Arabian Peninsula has never – since God made it flat, created its desert, and encircled
> it with seas – been stormed by any forces like the crusader armies spreading in it like
> locusts, eating its riches and wiping out its fertile places. All this is happening at a time in
> which nations are attacking Muslims like people fighting over a plate of food. In the light
> of the grave situation and the lack of support, we and you are obliged to discuss current
> events, and we should all agree on how to settle the matter.

Further, the summary presentation of the 'three facts that are known to everyone'
make clear that the authors are speaking in terms reminiscent of imposed war. The
'facts' constitute the basis for an indictment, or perhaps better, a verdict of guilt
against an enemy: 'these crimes and sins committed by the Americans are a clear
declaration of war against God, his messenger, and the Muslims'. The judgement of
the authors follows the logic we have seen before:

> '*ulama*' throughout Islamic history have unanimously agreed that armed struggle is an
> individual duty if the enemy destroys the Muslim countries … The ruling to fight the
> Americans and their allies, civilians and military, is an individual obligation for every
> Muslim who can do it in any country in which it is possible to do it … We call on every
> Muslim who believes in God and wishes to be rewarded to comply with God's order to
> fight the Americans and plunder their money wherever and whenever they find it. We also

call on Muslim *'ulama'*, leaders, youths, and soldiers to launch the raid on the adversary's U.S. troops and the satanically inspired supporters allying with them, and to displace those who are behind them so that they may learn a lesson.

It seems plain that the sense of fighting as an 'individual' duty here is of a popular resistance. In that, it is interesting that the signatories, including Usama bin Ladin, are not recognised members of the learned class, yet consider themselves qualified to issue a formal Shari'a opinion on the duty of Muslims, including the learned. Once again, it appears that necessity establishes both a right and duty of defence, and that directive authority falls to whoever is able to organise resistance. It is instructive on this point to compare the argument of bin Ladin's 1996 *Epistle* with the *Declaration*.[29] In the earlier document, he expresses disappointment in the Saudi family and more generally in the elite who make up the religio-political establishment of the Saudi state. He has not given up hope entirely, however: the *Epistle* calls on the Saudi-Wahhabi political and religious leaders, as well as on unspecified other Muslim leaders, to put aside their differences in the service of a 'collective' or 'communal' duty to resist American designs on Muslim territory. In this text, bin Ladin writes very much in the manner of the eleventh- and twelfth-century publicists who appealed to Salah al-Din and others to do their duty and marshal their resources in defence of Islam. Bin Ladin recognises that it is likely that the Saudi-Wahhabi establishment as a whole will not fulfil this duty, and so goes on to appeal to the 'good' political and religious leaders to assist in organising an armed resistance that will engage in 'lightning-quick' strikes at American targets in the Arabian Peninsula with the aim of convincing the Americans to withdraw their troops. Even that seems difficult, however, since he goes on to say (in this very long treatise) that the corrupt and impotent leadership has managed to kill or imprison many of the best leaders. So leaders from outside the Peninsula, beyond the reach of the Saudi-Wahhabi establishment, should take on the task.

By February, 1998, bin Ladin's al-Qa'ida reached an accord with other groups, particularly a branch of the Egyptian Islamic Jihad movement (see the discussion of *The Neglected Duty*). While the *Declaration* does not speak to the question of current rulers and their apostasy, it simply bypasses them in the service of its overarching cause: justifying a popular and international armed resistance to the United States and its allies. In subsequent statements, most notably following the US-led response to the 11 September 2001 attacks on New York and Washington, bin Ladin noted that it is the privilege of a vanguard chosen by God to organise active resistance to the anti-Muslim forces, and thus to defend Islamic rights. Those who fight, and thus respond to the *Declaration*'s judgement regarding the duty of Muslims, do not need the endorsement of any established religious or political authorities, for they are responding to the call of God: 'And why should you not fight in the cause of God and of those who, being weak, are ill-treated? Men, women, and children, whose cry is "Our Lord, rescue us from this town, whose people are oppressors, and raise for us out of your beneficence one who will help!" (Q.4:75)'

It is interesting that in the cases of the *Charter* of Hamas and the *Declaration*, as of *The Neglected Duty*, Muslim response seems not to focus on rebuttal of the authors' arguments for the authority of a vanguard to fight. It is, of course, true that at the time of the publication of the *Charter* (1988), the Palestinian National Authority was not yet in existence. Even now, that body does not have the same legal standing as the the governments of recognised states. In this context, PNA officials and more generally Palestinian leaders not associated with Hamas or its military wing, Palestinian Islamic Jihad, do not challenge the right of such groups to engage in resistance, as such. They appeal, rather, to prudential considerations along the lines of those articulated by the Shaykh al-Azhar in response to *The Neglected Duty*. Similarly, and perhaps less understandably, discussion of the *Declaration* does not seem to challenge the World Islamic Front on grounds of *competence de guerre*. One might expect established authorities to say that the authors of the *Declaration* and those who follow their directives are in violation of Shari'a precedents, precisely on the grounds that they lack standing: they are not established public authorities.

In general, Shari'a discussion of all the cases mentioned tends to focus less on the claim of authority to engage in resistance and more on arguments about the means appropriate to armed resistance. I have already suggested this with respect to the al-Azhar response to *The Neglected Duty*. The Shaykh al-Azhar's rebuttal to the arguments of that text ask, in effect, where will killing stop? From the standpoint of *The Neglected Duty*, it might seem that anyone participating in the building of the modern Egyptian state – say, by voting or paying taxes – is potentially an apostate. Or at least, many Muslims ignorant of the judgement the author pronounces on their rulers might rise to their defence and suffer death at the hands of the author and his comrades. 'How much blood?' is the al-Azhar question. In this sense, the leading religious authority in the Egyptian (and by some lights in the entire Sunni world) establishment appears to be worried that the means employed will result in damage disproportionate to the evil at which resistance is aimed. To put it another way, those engaged in armed resistance will violate Shari'a precedents establishing norms for honourable combat.

In the case of Hamas, arguments about such matters become clear if we attend to the recent discussion of 'martyrdom operations'. On 19 June 2002 a group of 55 Palestinian leaders issued a joint statement in which they argued that such operations should be stopped. The argument was pragmatic or even consequentialist in nature: that Palestinian youths were sacrificing themselves in actions that had little or no effect on Israel's military capacity, and which also hurt Palestinian attempts to cultivate world opinion. In the end, those advocating such tactics should consider that they are actually helping the most intransigent segment of Israeli opinion (meaning the supporters of Ariel Sharon). On 30 June, 150 Palestinian leaders issued a counter statement arguing that resistance to oppression by any and all means is justified, and that those willing to take action (any action) should be praised.

In the background of this exchange was the extensive debate about Shari'a norms and martyrdom operations that took place during the spring and summer of 2001.[30] The debate began when a prominent Saudi scholar suggested that such operations were without precedent in the history of Islam, and that those participating might best be judged as 'mere' suicides. The prominent scholar and television personality Yusuf al-Qaradhawi responded (as did many others), saying that this argument was incorrect. Those giving their lives in attacks against Israeli oppression are not committing suicide, said al-Qaradhawi. They are sacrificing themselves for the sake of justice, and are therefore martyrs, worthy of praise.

Most of those making public statements agreed. Nevertheless, many wondered about the targeting of such attacks. The use of one's body as a mechanism for delivering explosives to a military target might be justified, especially under conditions of necessity. Nevertheless, the Prophet's orders to fighters are binding, and prohibit direct and intentional attacks on civilian targets. So the Shaykh al-Azhar argued that the self-sacrifice of Palestinians should only be considered praiseworthy if the intention is to kill the enemy's soldiers. Direct and intentional attacks on noncombatants are forbidden, even under conditions of necessity.

Following this opinion from al-Azhar, al-Qaradhawi spoke for the majority when he argued that:

> Israeli society is militaristic in nature. Both men and women serve in the army and can be drafted at any moment … If a child or an elderly person is killed in this type of operation, he or she is not killed on purpose, but by mistake, and as a result of military necessity. Necessity makes the forbidden things permitted.

Clearly, al-Qaradhawi meant to defend martyrdom operations in terms of Shari'a notions of honourable combat. Whether the defence is successful seems open to question. It seems, for example, that al-Qaradhawi is saying that the 'potential combatancy' presented by the fact that all Israelis of a certain age are eligible for military service justifies attacks in public places. If that is in fact his argument, it seems to stretch Shari'a precedents; perhaps that is why al-Qaradhawi ends with the statement about necessity. That is, perhaps he should be understood as arguing that extremity or emergency conditions gives those engaged in resistance more latitude than would otherwise be the case. 'How much latitude?' would then seem an important question, as would a set of questions concerning whether al-Qaradhawi actually means to justify the acts of martyrs, or to excuse those who carry them out, and whether he means to provide justifications or excuses relative to particular circumstances, or for a general practice of martyrdom operations.

Given such reasoning, it is interesting that both Qaradhawi and the Shaykh al-Azhar issued opinions against the al-Qa'ida-sponsored bombings of US embassies in Kenya and Tanzania (in 1998). The Shaykh, for example, said that: 'Any explosion that leads to the death of innocent women and children is a criminal act, carried out only by people who are base cowards and traitors. A rational person with only a small portion of respect and virtue refrains from such operations.' Again, following the 11 September 2001 attacks, Qaradhawi argued that the attacks were to be considered grave sins, because they failed to distinguish between civilian and military targets, and to be condemned in accordance with the Qur'anic dictum that 'whoever kills a human being other than as punishment for manslaughter or acts of sowing corruption in the earth, it shall be as if that person killed all humankind ...'. Noting that he and his associates were strongly opposed to US policy with respect to Israel/Palestine, Qaradhawi nevertheless considered it important to express his judgement that the attacks of 11 September constituted a violation of Shari'a norms. What exactly is the difference between the activities of al-Qa'ida or the World Islamic Front and those sponsored by Hamas, Islamic Jihad, or other Palestinian organisations? I confess that I am not entirely clear about this yet, but would suggest consideration of the following as possible explanations: (1) that this is a difference regarding fighting a 'near enemy' and a 'far-off enemy'; (2) that once one accepts the notion that any man or woman living in Israel and of a certain age should be regarded as contributing to Israel's military readiness and thus as a combatant, one can distinguish targets in Israel from the World Trade Center. With respect to (1), the idea would be that Israeli forces constitute a clear and present military threat in ways that the New York and Washington targets do not. To continue this line of thought for a moment, it is interesting that, so far as I am aware, Qaradhawi, the Shaykh al-Azhar and others did not condemn the bombing of US barracks in Khobar, Saudi Arabia, nor did they condemn the attack on the USS *Cole* off the coast of Yemen. Fighting forces located within historically Islamic territory thus pose a threat in ways that far-off targets do not.[31] With respect to (2), the point would be that the people at the World Trade Center are not immediately eligible for military service in the way that most men and women in Israel are, and thus that it is not possible to speak of the intention of those carrying out the attacks in terms that make military targets primary, and civilian damage secondary. In either case, the explanation must be joined with the obvious point that Qaradhawi and others regard the Palestinian case as special, and do not want to see the justice of that cause mitigated by association with other, less clear cases.

With respect to the *Declaration*, we have a clear judgement that it is not only permitted, but obligatory to strike at Americans (and those allied with them) without distinction between civilian and military targets. One should note here that, prior to 11 September 2001, Usama bin Ladin commented in various interviews that 'indiscriminate' tactics were not only excused, but justified in light of two considerations: the shared guilt of citizens in a democratic state, and the law of reciprocity. With respect to the first, the point is that democracy allows citizens freedom to express opinions contrary to the policies of their government, and to vote the scoundrels out. With respect to the second, it is simply a fact, bin Ladin argued, that in the end you get what you give. Here, he appeals to a kind of law of nature; for him, this law is like gravity – one can try to overcome it, and even seem to for a while, but it expresses the direction of forces that are in the end inexorable. It is clear as well, however, that bin Ladin means the law of reciprocity to function as a moral appeal. Muslim fighters are justified in killing American civilians in so far as US forces kill Muslim civilians. It does not matter to him whether the latter are killed incidentally or accidentally, whether their deaths are actually a violation of just war notions of discrimination or not. The law of reciprocity, almost here interpreted as a gloss on the law of retaliation, allows Muslim fighters to avenge the deaths of Muslim innocents.

We have already seen that such established authorities as the Shaykh al-Azhar and Yusuf al-Qaradhawi dispute the validity of bin Ladin's reasoning. Their criticisms clearly indicate a judgement that the *Declaration* is inconsistent with Shari'a notions of honourable combat. Others, including some who are otherwise quite sympathetic to bin Ladin and his colleagues, share this judgement.

Thus, in July 2002, the Al-Jazeera network broadcast a live interview with three Saudi dissidents.[32] The transcript of the interview/discussion begins with comments about the United States and the war on terror. Needless to say, these men are not particularly supportive of the USA and its efforts in Afghanistan or elsewhere.

The discussion then turns to bin Ladin. The three agree that his popularity with the Saudi people rested, and continues to rest, on his dedication to Islamic ideals. They agree that bin Ladin is a character type the Saudi people find hard to resist. Al-'Awaji says:

> Bin Ladin is perceived to be a man of honor, a man who abstains from the pleasures of this world, a brave man, and a man who believes in his principles and makes sacrifices for them … What the Saudis like best about bin Ladin is his asceticism. When the Saudi compares bin Ladin to any child of wealthy parents, he sees that bin Ladin left behind the pleasures of the hotels for the foxholes of jihad, while others compete among themselves for the wealth and palaces of this world …

In the past, al-'Awaji indicates, especially during the resistance to the Soviet Union's incursions into Afghanistan, this affection was without reservation. But now, the Saudi people have three complaints about bin Ladin:

> First, bin Ladin accuses clerics and rulers of heresy, when he has no proof of this. Second, he is making the Muslim countries an arena for jihad operations. Third, he and those with him target innocent people, and I refer to the innocents on the face of the entire earth, of every religion and color, and in every region.

With respect to the first point, one might think that al-'Awaji and his colleagues (who concurred with his assessment) are questioning bin Ladin's authority. Other statements render that less likely, however. Rather, they disagree with bin Ladin's judgement that the Saudi establishment is irrelevant. They want to hold out the possibility of change. On the second point, they are obviously concerned that the actions of al-Qa'ida will divide the Muslim community.

It is the third point that is of most interest to us. Al-'Awaji's statement is as clear a pronouncement of Shari'a norms about targeting as one will find. Bin Ladin and those associated with him violate the notion of honourable combat. Because of this, they are losing support among the Saudi people, and among Muslims more generally; one would not be wrong, I think, to understand al-'Awaji and his colleagues to say that they *should* lose this support.

The Al-Jazeera transcript should be read in the light of the article published by al-Qa'ida spokesman Sulayman Abu Ghayth one month earlier (that is, in June of 2002). There, Abu Ghayth reiterated bin Ladin's announced principle of reciprocity in support of the judgement that:

> Those killed in the World Trade Center and the Pentagon were no more than a fair exchange for the ones killed in the al-'Amiriya shelter in Iraq, and are but a tiny part of the exchange for those killed in Palestine, Somalia, Sudan, the Philippines, Bosnia, Kashmir, Chechnya, and Afghanistan … We have not reached parity with them. We have the right to kill four million Americans, two million of them children, and to exile twice as many and wound and cripple hundreds of thousands. Furthermore, it is our right to fight them with chemical and biological weapons, so as to afflict them with the fatal maladies that have afflicted the Muslims because of chemical and biological weapons.[33]

The three Saudi scholars, by contrast, appear to argue that even in the midst of armed combat, the norms of honour apply. To reiterate, they are as unstinting in their criticism of the United States as Abu Ghayth or bin Ladin. They hold, however, that the Shari'a requires that armed struggle be conducted according to the directive of the Prophet: Do not mutilate anyone, nor should you kill women, children, or old men.

Following the Al-Jazeera interview, in late September or early October 2002 a prominent leader of Muslim resistance located in Great Britain published a short treatise on the question 'Is Armed Struggle a Legitimate Means for the Establishment of Islamic Government?' It should be noted that the group with which the author, Shaykh 'Umar Bakri Muhammad, is affiliated is well known for its support of Muslim resistance movements, especially in Chechnya. His view, like that of bin Ladin and other authors of the *Declaration*, is that Muslims are under attack around the world.[34]

Here, however, Shaykh Muhammad is interested in discerning the Shari'a concerning the legitimacy of armed struggle. In the familiar manner, he works through textual precedents in order to make the argument, first, that the establishment of just political order is a requirement for Muslims, and really for all human beings. Second, he says that the surest way to accomplish this goal is to establish a state governed by Islamic values. He does not believe that the Shari'a restricts such a state to one pattern of administration. A unified caliphate or single-ruler state is acceptable, so long as there is provision for consultation with the learned; but so is a parliamentary state in which the constitution establishes the Shari'a as the law of the land. Third, he says that once established, such a state has an obligation to extend its influence (and thus the influence of Shari'a) and thus to bring the blessings of justice to the entire world, or at least as large a portion of it as possible. According to Shari'a precedents, this should be done first by preaching, second by diplomacy, and third by fighting, if that should be necessary. This kind of fighting deserves the name of jihad. It is a means authorised by God to secure human happiness. Such fighting is to be governed by Shari'a norms – that is, by notions of honourable combat.

Such a state no longer exists. This is Shaykh Muhammad's fourth point. Since the demise of the Ottomans, no group has arisen to establish the kind of political-territorial association envisioned by Shari'a authorities. This means that there is no authority with competence to engage in the type of fighting deserving of the name jihad. Establishing such a state is essential to the well-being of the Muslims, and of the world as a whole. Muslims should strive for it. But – and this is the fifth point – it cannot be established by jihad, since that name is reserved for fighting conducted under the auspices of an Islamic state. Nor – sixth – can this state be established by fighting, in any case. It must be founded by agreement among the Muslims, and they are not allowed to coerce one another. Consensus must be reached as a matter of reasoned discourse, conducted according to the rules of Shari'a inquiry.

It is not wrong, I think, to read this as a direct rebuttal of statements in bin Ladin's *Epistle* indicating that Muslim forces should drive the USA and its allies, including the Israelis, out of the region, with the aim of establishing a caliphate with its territorial base extending from the Arabian Peninsula to Damascus. In that sense, one might understand Shaykh Muhammad's criticism as directed at the way bin Ladin's language leads to confusion regarding the precise nature of the resisters' *competence de guerre*. As Shaykh Muhammad goes on to argue, however, there is a kind of fighting in which such resisters not only can, but should engage. This (in his seventh point) is to be classified as *qital* ('fighting' or 'killing') in defence of Muslim lives, liberty and property. Shari'a precedents recognise a right of self-defence, he writes. And this right is not only a matter of one's own life, liberty and possessions. It extends to the protection of others. Such fighting is an individual duty, in the sense that any Muslim who is able should come to the aid of co-religionists who are under attack by non-believers. Thus, in Chechnya, Saudis or others who are able should come to the aid of those who suffer. If the Saudi government will support them, fine. If not, there is nothing to stop individuals from coming on their own initiative. The point, in distinction from the *Declaration*, is that the fighting is carefully delimited in its purpose. Further, as Shaykh Muhammad concludes, it is clear that norms of honourable combat are to govern fighters, even in the emergency circumstance suggested by the analogy with self-defence.

From the sayings and actions of the Messenger Muhammad that non-Muslim lives are protected unless they are at war with the Muslims as determined by the foreign policy of an established Muslim state or they are violating the sanctity of Muslim land, honour, or life. Also, much advice has been given by the Messenger Muhammad regarding armed struggle which makes it clear that this duty is pro-life, as opposed to anti-life: rules against killing women and children, the elderly or monks, not targeting trees or livestock, and so on. Hence, although foreign forces occupying Muslim land are legitimate targets and we are obliged to liberate Muslim land from such occupation and to co-operate with each other in this process, and can even target their embassies and military bases, there is no divine evidence for us to fight against Muslims who are part of the regimes in Muslim countries as a method to establish the Islamic state. Rather we urge our Muslim brothers in Islamic movements who are engaged in this violation of Shari'a to look at the evidence and to follow that which is based on certainty. May God guide us all to the best.

Concluding Remarks

The argument does not stop there. In November 2002, bin Ladin, or someone writing in his name, replied to Muslim and non-Muslim critics in a 'Letter to America'.[35] The document reiterated previously stated reasons why bin Ladin believes attacks on civilian as well as military targets are justified in Shari'a terms. First, he writes, the citizens of a democratic state share responsibility for the policies of their government. Second, God 'legislated the permission and the option to take revenge. Thus, if we are attacked, we have the right to return the attack ... whoever has killed our civilians, we have the right to kill theirs.'

Who has the better of the argument, in terms of the practice of Shari'a reasoning? Recalling the form of this type of Islamic practical reasoning (above), one should note that answering such a question is a matter of evaluating the use of precedent. With respect to notions of honourable combat, established precedents are consistent on the matter of restrictions on targeting. Those critical of the judgement advanced in the *Declaration* or in bin Ladin's 'Letter' reflect the plain meaning of such precedents, as do those worried about the conduct of martyrdom operations in the Palestinian struggle. One can, of course, argue that the context of contemporary resistance is sufficiently different from those in which established precedents were crafted. In that sense, an argument like al-Qaradhawi's might be read as suggesting that the Palestinian case has special features (the 'militaristic' nature of Israeli society, and the emergency conditions faced by Palestinians), and thus that those engaged in resistance should be given more latitude than suggested by historic judgements about targeting. The argument of the *Declaration* is more opaque on these matters. I have sometimes been tempted to read it as a sort of 'pure' emergency appeal, along the lines of Michael Walzer's discussion of supreme emergencies, in which the threat of imminent defeat by a sufficiently wicked foe justifies a temporary suspension of the ordinary rules of engagement.[36] Such an interpretation does require adding to the text, however; and bin Ladin's 'Letter' makes no such appeal to emergency, but rather focuses on the shared guilt of citizens in a democratic state and the Islamic version of the *lex talionis*. Noting that established precedents do not authorise such moves, one might well regard the judgement of the *Declaration* as problematic, at least in the sense of failing to provide an adequate argument for the overriding of precedent. With respect to the Shaykh al-Azhar's worries about *The Neglected Duty*, I will only comment that the al-Azhar argument fits better with established precedent. The latter's response is again an appeal to the state of emergency: the lack of any mechanism (other than armed resistance) with which to counter the apostasy of public authorities.

This suggests a return to arguments establishing the legitimacy of armed resistance per se. I've already noted that critiques of the *Declaration* and other documents do not focus on these. Part of the explanation for this lack is surely tied to the oft-cited legitimisation crisis of contemporary Islamic establishments. However, I am more interested in whether or not the arguments justifying armed resistance are successful, that is in terms of the application or extension of established precedents to contemporary contexts. Here, I have outlined two model arguments. One refers to precedents justifying or even requiring punishment of apostasy. The other refers to precedents related to fighting imposed by foreign incursions into Islamic territory. In either case, the arguments are buttressed by the notion that, under certain conditions, fighting becomes an 'individual' rather than a 'collective' duty. I've suggested that this is a way of signalling an extraordinary threat or a judgement that fighting is a response to emergency conditions. By contrast with the notion (in the *Declaration* and elsewhere) that emergency conditions justify an exception to prohibitions on the targeting of noncombatants, the idea that emergency conditions alter ordinary lines of authority seems relatively clear. An enemy is threatening Muslim lives, liberty and property, and anyone who can assist in defending these should do so. I have noted that contemporary arguments stretch this a bit. Historical precedents suppose that the appeal for help is to Muslim rulers whose sphere of influence is outside the region under immediate attack, rather than to individual Muslims. What happens, though, if those rulers do not respond? The idea is that fellow Muslims are in need. If no established ruler will lend a hand, is there nothing to be done?

Advocates of armed resistance are clearly saying that something can be done. In some ways, the problematic of Shari'a reasoning on this point is reminiscent of Quentin Skinner's description of the dynamic of Lutheran and Calvinist discussion of the relative merits of 'private law' and 'constitutional' theories of resistance.[37] In the former, the right of armed resistance to tyranny is an extension of rights to defend one's life, liberty and property. Everyone has such rights, as a private person. In the latter, the right of armed resistance is entrusted to designated public officials – the 'lesser magistrates' described by Calvin in *Institutes* IV.xx. As Skinner describes it, Lutherans and Calvinists alike feared the anarchic consequences of the private law argument. They had no satisfactory response, however, to the question 'Who defends the people against tyranny, if the designated magistrates fail to follow through?'

The answer, according to those Muslims advancing justifications for armed resistance, seems to be 'the people themselves' or, failing that, 'a rightly-guided vanguard.' In terms of precedent, the argument is a stretch, but it is not implausible.

Perhaps the lack of criticism aimed directly at the *competence de guerre* of contemporary resisters is as much a recognition of the strength of resistance arguments as of the legitimisation crisis afflicting Islamic establishments.

In all this discussion, one available line of thought seems to be missing. The omission of appeals to the type of fighting that the learned characterised as rebellion seems odd, to say the least. This may be due to the *prima facie* ways this set of precedents is directed at governmental response to resisters, rather than to the justification of resistance itself. There is an interesting line of development of rules for fighting rebels in certain Shi'i materials, however. In particular, the late Ayatollah Khomeini's lectures on *Islamic Government* suggest that when rulers resort to military force as a means of suppressing a non-violent popular resistance, the rulers themselves become rebels.[38] The class of the learned, understood as the guardians of the peoples' rights (NB Skinner's 'constitutional' theory of resistance!) is then justified in calling the people to arms against the 'ruling rebels'. To take up this argument would extend this already overlong chapter, however, and so I leave it for another day.

Notes

1   All dates are CE, following the convention in religious studies. I don't note the corresponding *hijri* date, which is from the calendar used by Muslims. In addition, let me note that Arabic terms are transliterated without most diacritical markings, the exceptions being '*ayn* and *hamza*'. In this, I follow the practice of the *International Journal of Middle East Studies*. Most Arabic terms are represented in italics. The exceptions are terms very common in English use, such as Shari'a or Qur'an.

2   Hereafter, I shall simply refer to this document as the *Declaration*. The document first appeared, in Arabic, in *al-Quds*, an Arabic-language newspaper published in the United Kingdom, on 23 February 1998. It attracted scholarly and other attention right away; among others, cf. Lewis, Bernard, 'License to Kill: Usama bin Ladin's Declaration of Jihad,' *Foreign Affairs*, Vol. 77, No. 6, November/December 1998, 14–24. As printed in *al-Quds*, the text was signed by five people (see the appended translation, below). The best-known of these is Usama bin Ladin; second is his colleague Ayman al-Zawahiri, the Egyptian physician and activist sometimes referred to as 'bin Ladin's physician'. Cf., among others, Wright, Lawrence, 'The Man Behind Bin Ladin', *New Yorker Magazine*, September 2002, 16.

3   Those interested in examples of these may wish to consult my article 'Ethics' in Esposito, John (ed.) (1995), *The Oxford Encyclopedia of the Modern Islamic World*, New York: Oxford University Press, Vol. 1, 442–6, where each of these types of writing is discussed, and suggestions of exemplary texts in translation advanced.

4   See Khadduri, M. (trans.) (1961), *Islamic Jurisprudence: Shafi'i's Risala*, Baltimore, MD: Johns Hopkins, for this and other references to Shafi'i. The material following is not controversial, so I won't footnote extensively. A convenient summary of the theory connected with Shari'a can be found in Reinhart, Kevin A., 'Islamic Law as Islamic Ethics,' *Journal of Religious Ethics*, Vol. 11, No. 2, 1983, 186–203.

5   I think it would be fair to say that most Shari'a reasoning is committed to some version of ontological voluntarism. Epistemologically, some practitioners are committed to the

necessity of special revelation, others to a view that reason (as an apprehension of 'general' or 'natural' revelation) and special revelation are complementary, and others to a kind of rationalist intuitionism in which special revelation's main purpose is to confirm that God is on the side of a moral law apprehended by reason.

6   Qur'an 2:2. My translation.

7   This is for the Sunni, or what one might call the majoritarian strain of Islam. For the Shi'i or minority view exemplary practice includes not only that of the Prophet, but of the succession of leaders designated by God to provide the Muslim community (and through it, all humanity) with continuous and righteous guidance through the ages. There are other differences in the Shi'i approach to Shari'a reasoning and, more concretely, to the justification of armed force that require special treatment, or at least a longer chapter than I will produce here. The focus of discussion at this point and throughout will be Shari'a reasoning as it pertains to Sunni Islam.

8   The story is found in Bosworth, C. E. (trans.) (1989), *The History of al-Tabari*, Vol. XXX: *The Abbasid Caliphate in Equilibrium*, Albany, NY: State University of New York Press, 125.

9   The authority of precedent in Shari'a reasoning is represented in a number of ways. Historically, those aspiring to join the class of the learned undertook a set course of study at a recognised centre of learning. Those who completed the preliminaries and entered into the study of *fiqh* began with texts reporting the judgements of a particular school of interpretation. Having mastered these, they would be certified to judge cases according to this (one) set of precedents – essentially, they could serve as advisers or judges for those Muslims who (usually by reason of family tradition) preferred a particular school of *fiqh*. Such scholars did not usually render creative or innovative judgements; rather, in response to a question, they simply gave an account of the consensual judgement of the school.

   One could go further as a scholar, however. Suppose that a young person mastered the texts of a number of schools. Sunni Islam recognised four legitimate schools; theoretically, one could master the texts of all four, and thus possess qualifications to render judgements consistent with any of the four. One might even deign to suggest which of the four was best for a particular circumstance. Even at this point one's independence was limited to picking and choosing among standard precedents, however.

   Only a few scholars attained the level of *mujtahid*, indicating their right to issue independent opinions or, to put it another way, to actually set rather than adhere to precedent. For most purposes, then, established consensus or precedent could be regarded as a kind of regulatory norm. In the case of the few, however, the judgements of prior generations are better understood as 'that to which one must respond'. One might depart from precedent, for example, by showing that some circumstance is altered, so that the underlying principle at work in two (analogous) cases yields different conclusions. A very interesting example of this is presented in Mir-Hosseini, Ziba (1999), *Islam and Gender*, Princeton, NJ: Princeton University Press, which analyses contemporary Iranian discussions of historic judgements regarding gender roles. Here one sees very clearly the different ways precedent can work in Shari'a reasoning.

   The role of precedent becomes even more controversial when one considers some of the documents to be discussed later in this essay. This is so because people who, from the historical standpoint, are 'ordinary' or 'lay' Muslims are taking on something of the role of the learned, at least in matters of political ethics. More on this below.

10   The following is a summary of material described in greater detail in my essay 'Islamic Tradition and the Justice of War', in Brekke, T. (ed.), *The Ethics of War in Asia*, forthcoming.

11   Cf. among others, Khadduri, M. (trans.) (1966), *The Islamic Law of Nations: Shaybani's Siyar*, Baltimore, MD: Johns Hopkins Press, where this report of the Prophet's orders is printed at 75–7.

12   For a translation of this report see Hamid Siddiqi, Abdul (trans.) (1981), *Sahih Muslim*, Lahore: S. Muhammad Ashraf, report number 4321. NB: *Sahih Muslim* is one of six standard collections of *ahadith* ('reports') of the exemplary practice of the Prophet.

13   With respect to fire, however, some texts indicate a special reservation, by which fire is the means of the judgement of God. Humans are not to utilise it in their disputes.

14   I use this term in accord with the usual designation for the early Muslim conquests. The idea is that one is removing obstacles to a people's ability to hear the Islamic message.

15   As in the following, reported as a sound *hadith*: '[the Prophet said] "Your best leaders are those whom you like and who like you, on whom you invoke blessings and who invoke blessings on you, and your worst leaders are those whom you hate and who hate you, whom you curse and who curse you." [His companions asked] whether in that event they should not depose such leaders, but the Prophet replied "No, as long as they observe the prayer among you; no, as long as they observe the prayer among you [that is, they do not act so as to disestablish Islamic values]. If anyone has a governor whom he [or she] sees doing anything which is an act of disobedience to God, he [or she] must disapprove of the disobedience, but must never withdraw from obedience"'. Robson, James (trans.) (1963–4), *Mishkat al-Masabih*, Lahore: S. M. Ashraf, with my own emendations of the translation. Texts like this lead many historians to suggest that Islam cannot conceive of a just rebellion, which seems to me not quite right. For a recent study giving great detail on this question, cf. Abou El Fadl, Khaled (2000), *Rebellion and Violence in Islamic Law*, Cambridge: Cambridge University Press.

16   As per Qur'an 49:10: 'Those who believe are brothers. Make things right between brothers who have separated. Consider God, whose mercy you have received.' My translation.

17   See my description in (1993), *Islam and War*, Louisville, NB: Westminster/John Knox, 77–110.

18   Arabic *fard 'ayn*.

19   E. Sivan discusses and translates a most interesting text in this regard in 'La Genèse De La Contre-Croisade: Un Traité Damasquin Du Debut Du XII Siècle,' *Journal Asiatique* 254, 1966, 197–224. The article also includes an edition of the Arabic text.

20   *The Neglected Duty* is the title given in English translation by Johannes J. G. Jansen (New York: Macmillan, 1986). Jansen also provides an account of the publication of the Arabic text, *al-farida al-gha'iba*, which might also be translated as 'the hidden duty'. In brief, the text became widely known when the Shaykh al-Azhar published a refutation of it with the intent of refuting the reasoning of those who had assassinated President Anwar Sadat in October of that year. Parts of this refutation were excerpted in Egyptian newspapers in December 1981. Subsequently, several versions of the militants' *apologia* appeared in various newspapers, and a number of Islamic authorities joined their voices to the Shaykh al-Azhar's criticisms. Jansen's translation includes materials from the criticisms, as well as the militant text.

          Parts of the testament of al-Zawahiri, *Knights Under the Prophet's Banner*, may be read in English translation at <http://www.fas.org/irp/world/para/ayman_bk.htm>. As indicated above, note 2, al-Zawahiri's pilgrimage to radical Islam is conveniently summarised in Lawrence Wright's article in the *New Yorker Magazine*.

21 Ottoman rulers presented themselves as successors to the Abbasids.

22 For a helpful account, see Christine Moss (1981) Helms *The Cohesion of Saudi Arabia*, Baltimore, MD: Johns Hopkins.

23 On 'Abd al-'Aziz and this controversy, see Rizvi, S. A. A. (1982), *Shah 'Abd al-'Aziz: Puritanism, Sectarian Polemics, and Jihad*, Canberra, Australia: Ma'rifat Publishing House. It is worth noting that Hindus as well as Muslims participated in the Sepoy Mutiny; here I am interested in the way 'Abd al-'Aziz's opinion relates to the tradition of Muslim argumentation concerning resistance.

24 For the career of Salah al-Din or 'Saladin', cf., among others, Gibb, H. A. R. (1973), *The Life of Saladin*, Oxford: Clarendon Press.

25 Indeed, one could argue that the more recent cases exemplify an ever-expansive crisis of authority in Islam, particularly since (as mentioned earlier) Shari'a arguments justifying resistance are often from 'ordinary' Muslims (that is, they are not members of the learned class) who lack the credentials historically required for those who would engage in Shari'a reasoning. One can overdo this: in such groups, one usually finds participants from the learned class, as well as ordinary Muslims. But there is something important indicated by this development of ordinary Muslims participating in Shari'a debates.

26 Jansen, Johannes, J. G. (trans.) (1986), *The Neglected Duty: The Creed of Sadat's Assassins and the Resurgence of Islamic Militance in the Middle East*, New York: Macmillan. The book includes responses by the Shaykh al-Azhar and other Egyptian leaders. I discuss this text in *Islam and War*, especially at pages 100–106, though I have slightly changed my understanding of the argument since that book was published (1993). The quotes are all from Jansen's translation. For convenience, I just cite the page number in parentheses.

27 The *Charter* is available in a translation by Maqdsi, M. (Dallas: Islamic Association for Palestine, 1990). I've altered Maqdsi wherever I think the Arabic is obscured by his style. When I quote, I cite the section number (not page number) in parentheses.

28 Since I have attached a translation of the document in the Appendix to this chapter, I will not give citations. Where there are differences between a citation in my narrative and the translation, these are due to my effort to make the sense of the Arabic more clear.

29 The *Epistle* is available at <http://www.washingtonpost.org>. It represents an earlier stage in the development of bin Ladin's programme of opposition to the United States and its 'occupation' of Islamic lands.

30 I describe some of this debate in a popular article on 'Suicide Bombers,' in the *Christian Century* 119/17, 14–27, August 2002, 22–5.

31 As a matter of current interest, this seems important to the logic of the Shaykh al-Azhar's recent opinion justifying resistance to US action in Iraq.

32 The interview was primarily of Shaykh Muhsin al-'Awaji. Now based in the UK, al-'Awaji was at one time the Imam of the Great Mosque at King Saud University in al-Riyadh. Following the Gulf War, he was quite vocal in his opposition to Saudi policy, particularly with respect to the continuing presence of US troops in the Arabian Peninsula, and served time in a Saudi prison. For this interview, he was joined by two other scholars well known for similar positions, and who also served prison terms: Safar al-Hawali and Muhammad al-Khasif. Quotes below are from a translation of portions of the interview available at the website for the Middle East Media Research Institute (<http:www.memri.org>, cf. the series on Saudi Arabia/Jihad and Terrorism Studies, No. 400). Some of the material following reargument among Islamists regarding the

tactics of al-Qaʿida was presented in my Templeton Lecture (October 2003) at the Foreign Policy Research Institute in Philadelphia, PA. Cf. <http://www.fpri.org>.

33 Here I use the translation available at <http://www.memri.org>, Special Dispatch Series No. 388. The article was originally published (in Arabic) under a title that translates as 'In the Shadow of the Lances', at <http://www.alneda.com>.

34 Available at <http://www.almuhajiroun.com>.

35 First published on a website affiliated with al-Qaʿida, the document was translated by sympathetic Muslims in the UK and published in the *Observer*. See <http://www.observer.co.uk/worldview/story/0,111581,845725,00.html>.

36 See Walzer, Michael (ed.) (2000), *Just and Unjust Wars*, 3rd edn, New York: Basic Books, 251–68.

37 Cf. Skinner, Quentin (1978), *The Foundations of Modern Political Thought*, Cambridge: Cambridge University Press, 189–359.

38 Available, among others, in Hamid, Algar (trans. and annot.) (1981), *Islam and Revolution: Writings and Declarations of Imam Khomeini*, Berkeley, CA: Mizan Press.

Appendix to Chapter 4

Jihad Against Jews and Crusaders

World Islamic Front Statement

23 February 1998

Shaykh Usamah Bin-Muhammad Bin-Ladin Ayman al-Zawahiri, amir of the Jihad Group in Egypt Abu-Yasir Rifa'i Ahmad Taha, Egyptian Islamic Group Shaykh Mir Hamzah, secretary of the Jamiat-ul-Ulema-e-Pakistan Fazlur Rahman, amir of the Jihad Movement in Bangladesh.

Praise be to Allah, who revealed the Book, controls the clouds, defeats factionalism, and says in His Book: 'But when the forbidden months are past, then fight and slay the pagans wherever ye find them, seize them, beleaguer them, and lie in wait for them in every stratagem (of war)'; and peace be upon our Prophet, Muhammad Bin-'Abdallah, who said: I have been sent with the sword between my hands to ensure that no one but Allah is worshipped, Allah who put my livelihood under the shadow of my spear and who inflicts humiliation and scorn on those who disobey my orders.

The Arabian Peninsula has never – since Allah made it flat, created its desert, and encircled it with seas – been stormed by any forces like the crusader armies spreading in it like locusts, eating its riches and wiping out its plantations. All this is happening at a time in which nations are attacking Muslims like people fighting over a plate of food. In the light of the grave situation and the lack of support, we and you are obliged to discuss current events, and we should all agree on how to settle the matter.

No one argues today about three facts that are known to everyone; we will list them, in order to remind everyone:

First, for over seven years the United States has been occupying the lands of Islam in the holiest of places, the Arabian Peninsula, plundering its riches, dictating to its rulers, humiliating its people, terrorizing its neighbors, and turning its bases in the Peninsula into a spearhead through which to fight the neighboring Muslim peoples.

If some people have in the past argued about the fact of the occupation, all the people of the Peninsula have now acknowledged it. The best proof of this is the Americans' continuing aggression against the Iraqi people using the Peninsula as a staging post, even though all its rulers are against their territories being used to that end, but they are helpless.

Second, despite the great devastation inflicted on the Iraqi people by the crusader-Zionist alliance, and despite the huge number of those killed, which has exceeded 1 million ... despite all this, the Americans are once against trying to repeat the horrific massacres, as though they are not content with the protracted blockade imposed after the ferocious war or the fragmentation and devastation.

So here they come to annihilate what is left of this people and to humiliate their Muslim neighbors.

Third, if the Americans' aims behind these wars are religious and economic, the aim is also to serve the Jews' petty state and divert attention from its occupation of Jerusalem and murder of Muslims there. The best proof of this is their eagerness to destroy Iraq, the strongest neighboring Arab state, and their endeavor to fragment all the states of the region such as Iraq, Saudi Arabia, Egypt, and Sudan into paper statelets and through their disunion and weakness to guarantee Israel's survival and the continuation of the brutal crusade occupation of the Peninsula.

All these crimes and sins committed by the Americans are a clear declaration of war on Allah, his messenger, and Muslims. And ulema have throughout Islamic history unanimously agreed that the jihad is an individual duty if the enemy destroys the Muslim countries. This was revealed by Imam Bin-Qadamah in 'Al-Mughni', Imam al-Kisa'i in 'Al-Bada'i', al-Qurtubi in his interpretation, and the shaykh of al-Islam in his books, where he said: 'As for the fighting to repulse [an enemy], it is aimed at defending sanctity and religion, and it is a duty as agreed [by the ulema]. Nothing is more sacred than belief except repulsing an enemy who is attacking religion and life.'

On that basis, and in compliance with Allah's order, we issue the following fatwa to all Muslims:

The ruling to kill the Americans and their allies – civilians and military – is an individual duty for every Muslim who can do it in any country in which it is possible to do it, in order to liberate the al-Aqsa Mosque and the holy mosque [Mecca] from their grip, and in order for their armies to move out of all the lands of Islam, defeated and unable to threaten any Muslim. This is in accordance with the words of Almighty Allah, 'and fight the pagans all together as they fight you all together,' and 'fight them until there is no more tumult or oppression, and there prevail justice and faith in Allah'.

This is in addition to the words of Almighty Allah: 'And why should ye not fight in the cause of Allah and of those who, being weak, are ill-treated (and oppressed)? – women and children, whose cry is: "Our Lord, rescue us from this town, whose people are oppressors; and raise for us from thee one who will help!"'

We – with Allah's help – call on every Muslim who believes in Allah and wishes to be rewarded to comply with Allah's order to kill the Americans and plunder their money wherever and whenever they find it. We also call on Muslim ulema, leaders, youths, and soldiers to launch the raid on Satan's US troops and the devil's supporters allying with them, and to displace those who are behind them so that they may learn a lesson.

Almighty Allah said: 'O ye who believe, give your response to Allah and His Apostle, when He calleth you to that which will give you life. And know that Allah cometh between a man and his heart, and that it is He to whom ye shall all be gathered.'

Almighty Allah also says: 'O ye who believe, what is the matter with you, that when ye are asked to go forth in the cause of Allah, ye cling so heavily to the earth! Do ye prefer the life of this world to the hereafter? But little is the comfort of this life, as compared with the hereafter. Unless ye go forth, He will punish you with a grievous penalty, and put others in your place; but Him ye would not harm in the least. For Allah hath power over all things.'

Almighty Allah also says: 'So lose no heart, nor fall into despair. For ye must gain mastery if ye are true in faith.'

Note: There are a number of translations of this document; this one is from the Federation of American Scientists' website, at http://www.fas.org/irp/world/para/docs/980223-fatwa.htm. In my judgement, it corresponds reasonably well to the Arabic original.

Chapter 5

War and Reason in Maimonides and Averroes

Noah Feldman

What happens when Aristotelian rationalism confronts the stringent obligations of holy war in the Jewish and Islamic legal traditions? Maimonides and Averroes are the right figures to consider in confronting this question. Born a decade apart and less than a mile from one another in medieval Muslim Cordoba, they seem never to have met, since the younger, Maimonides, fled the 1148 Almohad invasion of al-Andalus with his family when he was as just a boy of 13, finding refuge in more tolerant Fatimid Egypt. Yet along with Thomas, these two men were the greatest Aristotelians that the medieval world knew, and arguably the greatest of any time.

Had they met, Maimonides and Averroes would have been struck by the degree to which they shared a common basic predicament. Each took his religious tradition as the starting point for constructing a legal order necessary for making sense of the practical world, and each was a highly trained lawyer from a legally accomplished family. Islamic law for Averroes, who served as a royally appointed judge in Cordoba and Seville, and Jewish law for Maimonides, who became the acknowledged world authority on the subject in his lifetime, were coherent, self-sufficient structures of order that had to be taken seriously in their entirety and approached through their own conventional hermeneutic tools. Yet at the same time, both men were committed to Aristotelian metaphysics and the use of Aristotelian practical reason and political philosophy. The resulting engagement between religious law, with its scriptural origins, and rational philosophy, with a particularly Aristotelian flavour, shaped the intellectual lives of both men.[1]

This chapter takes up two instances in which Maimonides and Averroes were each independently called upon to confront the teachings of their respective legal traditions on the topic of holy war, which is to say, in classical Jewish and Islamic law, war that is mandated by Scripture. My claim is that both Maimonides and Averroes used Aristotelian ideas to *rationalise* the harsh demands of the law of obligatory war. By rationalising I mean, literally, infusing the law with reason where it otherwise would have appeared to be simplistic or irrational. This process of rationalisation did not necessarily mitigate the harshness of the calls to mandatory war found in both traditions; but it did affect the interpretation of laws that demanded killing.

Neither Maimonides nor Averroes crudely replaced legal reasoning with philosophical analysis; to do so would have been to betray the internal logic of legal reasoning, which can only rarely accommodate overt encroachment by alternative logical or interpretive structures. Both, instead, drew on philosophical ideas in order to advance original legal interpretations that could none the less be justified from within the norms of law. These two case studies therefore demonstrate a characteristic operation of philosophically oriented legal theory in its engagement with actual legal systems. Legal theory does not circumvent or supersede ordinary legal reasoning; instead, acting much more subtly, it leads the law to new conclusions by routing the familiar modes of legal reasoning through an abstract understanding of how the law ought to develop.

I make no claim of mutual influence here, and suppose that there was none. Yet the juxtaposition of Maimonides and Averroes here is intended to lend support for what are relatively subtle claims about both; to see Aristotle between the lines in either Maimonides or Averroes on the topic of holy war is to see how the other might have similarly thought of law and philosophy as particularly closely connected in the sphere of warfare, the particular expertise of kings. I also intend this essay as a study in the engagement between philosophy and law more broadly, a subject that almost invariably poses the tension between the constraints of positive legal obligation and the philosophical impulse to form correct judgements on the basis of first principles, regardless of context.

Maimonides: Coercion and Philosophical Truth

The Jewish legal tradition that Maimonides sought to re-state in its entirety in his magnum opus, *Mishneh Torah*, was very explicit on the obligation to wage war under certain particular circumstances. The Bible specifically commanded the Israelites on the occasion of their entrance into Canaan that they conquer the land and kill all of its inhabitants, referred to in rabbinic sources as 'the seven peoples (*ammamim*)' who inhabited, according to the biblical texts, most of the land.[2] Furthermore, the Bible mandated total war against the Amalekites, who had ambushed the Israelites on the latters' flight from Egypt.[3] The Book of Samuel recorded the terrifying judgement rendered by God through the Prophet Samuel against Saul, Israel's first king, whose destruction of the Amalekites omitted to kill the Amalekite King Agag and spared the Amalekites' livestock as spoils of war. For these omissions, Saul lost the possibility of dynastic succession, and the crown passed to his armour-bearer and rival, David, instead of his son, Jonathan.[4]

Maimonides took up the subject of war in Jewish law in a section of Mishneh Torah entitled 'the laws of kings and their wars'. The title itself is significant for making war into a royal obligation, rather than some other sort of obligation, whether individual or collective. The initial conquest of Canaan described in the Bible took place under the leadership of Joshua, who, while divinely appointed, was not a king, so there was no biblical necessity to treat the subject of mandatory war and monarchy in tandem. Maimonides assumes, however, that the political functions of war connect it to the royal function, and he draws on the numerous biblical and rabbinic sources that associate the waging of war with royal duty and prerogative in order to join the two topics.

Maimonides devotes the first four chapters of 'the laws of kings and their wars' to delineating the powers and limitations of kings. In Chapter 5 he begins the discussion of war in Jewish law by distinguishing two types: obligatory war (called in Hebrew *milhemet mitzva*, or 'a war of commandment') and voluntary war.[5] The category of obligatory war comprises the biblically mandated war against the 'seven peoples', war against the Amalekites, and war fought in self-defence, to 'save Israel from the hands of an enemy who comes upon them'.[6] Voluntary war, which the king must not take up until he has satisfied the conditions of obligatory war, is war waged at the king's discretion 'against other nations to expand Israel's border and to increase his greatness and reputation'.[7] The distinction between obligatory war and voluntary war was present in the Talmudic sources on which Maimonides relied; as we shall see, Maimonides was to exploit the ambiguity of some legal provisions relating to voluntary war in order to transform the legal concept of obligatory war.

Maimonides goes on in the chapter to report faithfully the affirmative biblical commandment to destroy the seven peoples, an obligation which in theory continues to bind even the individual Jew who might encounter an individual member of one of those peoples.[8] But, following a Talmudic source, Maimonides adds that all trace of these peoples has now disappeared (*kevar 'avad zikhram*). By implication, the obligation to destroy the seven peoples therefore no longer has any practical application, even if it remains on the books.

Yet Maimonides none the less appears to be troubled by the superficially absolute character of the biblical commandment. This appears when, at the start of Chapter 6, he describes the biblically grounded obligation to sue for peace prior to making war. Maimonides cites the biblical verse that imposes this duty: 'When you approach a city to make war upon it, then shall you call upon it for peace.'[9] Although a plausible reading of the biblical texts – adopted by commentators before Maimonides[10] – assumes that the duty to sue for peace does not apply to the seven peoples or the Amalekites, who must be utterly destroyed, Maimonides apparently reads the obligation to apply to all conflict: 'one is not permitted to wage war against any man in the world (*'im adam ba-'olam*) until one calls to him for peace (*korin lo shalom*)'.[11] Maimonides is following a classical rabbinic text here in stating the law; but by not stating that there is an exception for obligatory war, he makes the phrase 'against any man in the world' stand for a universal obligation, and functions to apply the duty to sue for peace to all wars, whether obligatory or voluntary.

Still following a classical rabbinic text, Maimonides goes on to delineate the content of the suit for peace: 'If they submit (*hishlimu*[12]) and accept the seven commandments regarding which the sons of Noah were commanded, then one does not kill even one soul and they shall be taxed (*hare hen la-mas*).' Potential enemies, in other words, are to be presented with a choice. They may avoid war by (1) submitting, (2) accepting seven legal obligations, and (3) paying a tax, or they will be attacked. If this is a voluntary war, Maimonides says a bit later, then an attack will be followed by the killing of all adult males. If it is an obligatory war, not a soul will be left alive.[13]

Maimonides makes it clear that submission, acceptance of the seven legal obligations, and taxation are all three necessary to avoid attack. Of the three, taxation and submission have a clear biblical mandate, which Maimonides cites. Yet Maimonides presents all three as entailed by the universal duty to sue for peace. What, precisely, does Maimonides mean by these three conditions of peace? Where do they come from?

Begin with submission. It appears that Maimonides subtly transforms a familiar Hebrew verb into an Arabic-influenced quasi-neologism. The root sh-l-m corresponds to peace. The associated causative verb form (*hishlimu*) means, in classical Hebrew, 'to make peace'.[14] At first glance, the sentence would seem to be translated best 'if they make peace and accept the seven commandments ...'. Making peace is surely the sense in which the word *hishlimu* was intended in the rabbinic source Maimonides is paraphrasing here. But Maimonides inflects the meaning of this verb with the meaning of the Arabic cognate s-l-m in the cognate causative (fourth) verb form. That word in Arabic is *aslama*, 'to submit'. One who submits is known as a *muslim*. Maimonides makes the word *hishlimu* stand for an independent condition of submission.

The evidence that Maimonides means to use the Hebrew word *hishlimu* as the equivalent of the Arabic word *aslamu*, signifying submission, is that he immediately, in the very next sentence, speaks of acceptance of tax and acceptance of *servitude* as two separate phenomena: 'If they accept the tax but not servitude or if they accept servitude but not the tax, one does not listen to them until they accept both.'[15] Up to this point, Maimonides has not mentioned servitude at all. Unless one realises that Maimonides has delineated an initial obligation of submission, which corresponds to the servitude of which he speaks here, the notion of servitude would have appeared in the text entirely unannounced. But, for Maimonides, servitude has already been introduced in his presentation – in the form of the word *hishlimu*, which he takes to indicate submission.

The nature of the servitude makes the association with submission all the more clear: 'The servitude which they shall accept is that they shall be despised and subordinated (*nivzim u-shefelim le-mata*) and shall not raise their heads to Israel, rather they shall be defeated beneath their hand. They shall not be appointed over Israel [or, over any Israelite] for any matter in the world.'[16] As various scholars have noticed, this definition of servitude has little earlier basis in Jewish law.[17] It does, however, parallel closely the state which Islamic law requires for non-Muslim peoples of the book who wish to live unconverted in Muslim lands. Jews and

Christians under classical Islamic law are entitled to 'protected' (*dhimmi*) status; formally speaking, in this status they must be subordinate to Muslims and may not exercise political authority over them. Protected persons were also obligated under Islamic law to pay a special tax (*jizya*), corresponding neatly to Maimonides' requirement that the enemies of the Israelites must pay a tax as part of the arrangements they reach in order to avoid conquest. Maimonides here both borrows the Islamic legal model of subordinate status for tolerated peoples and turns it on its head by putting Jews on top and others below.

It is poetically perfect that in borrowing and subverting Islamic law's conception of the subordination of tolerated peoples, Maimonides actually uses the very word that Muslims use to describe themselves. Of course '*Islam*' means submission to God, but the verb *aslama* itself just means 'to submit'. In Maimonides' account, it is the people who submit to avoid being killed who are exercising submission. But the use of the verb is no coincidence. Indeed, the other requirement for being tolerated, namely the acceptance of the seven commandments regarding which Noah's sons were commanded, also turns out to bear a striking resemblance to protected status under classical Islamic law – with an Aristotelian twist.

To see the Aristotelian component of Maimonides' transformation of the classical Jewish law of war, we must turn to his stated requirement that conquered peoples who wish to avoid slaughter must accept 'the seven commandments on which Noah's sons were commanded'. These so-called 'Noahide commandments' have an interesting history in Jewish law, and much has been written about them, as well as about Maimonides' treatment of them.[18] Without entering too deeply into that literature, one may still provide a basic précis, without which the use of the seven commandments in the context of the law of war would not be comprehensible.

In the book of Genesis, just after the flood story and God's subsequent covenantal promise not to destroy the world, the text records a series of statements in the form of commands. Rabbinic tradition took these to be commandments permanently binding on all humanity. The Talmud identified seven separate commandments: no idolatry; no cursing of God's name; no unjustified bloodshed; no forbidden sexual liaisons; no theft; mandatory creation of a judicial system; and finally, no eating of any part of a living animal.[19] Talmudic sources further specified that a person who was not a Jew, but wished to live as a citizen in the land of Israel, must accept these seven commandments to be accorded the status of 'resident alien' (*ger toshav*).[20]

Maimonides, of course, accepts the existence of these commandments, as well as the necessity of their adoption by a resident alien. Yet he also transforms both the meaning of those commandments and the scope of the context in which they must be accepted. In short, Maimonides reads the commandments as the necessary infrastructure for the acquisition of philosophically correct beliefs; and he mandates their adoption by all persons who come under Israelite dominion, on pain of death. In the process, he transforms both obligatory war and voluntary war into the pursuit of philosophy by other (coercive!) means. Their purpose is transformed from territorial conquest to the imposition of the minimally necessary beliefs and social institutions capable of giving rise to correct philosophical attainment that is the true purpose of society in Maimonides' (Aristotelian-influenced) conception.

Begin with Maimonides' original, philosophical interpretation of the seven commandments. He writes that at least the first six of these seven commandments could be described as rules 'to which reason inclines' (*ha-da'at note lahem*), thereby suggesting that they have some philosophical content. He furthermore states that these first six were actually commanded to Adam, and merely reiterated to Noah's sons. This view has rabbinic warrant, but more importantly, it is crucial for the view that these commandments are necessary as a matter of reason: if they are indeed necessary, then how could human society have subsisted without them from the time of Adam?

Maimonides further suggests the reasonable character of the seven command-ments by his gloss on a rabbinic tradition stating, in Maimonides' paraphrase, that 'anyone who accepts the seven commandments and takes care to perform them is one of the pious of the nations of the world, and has a share in the world to come.'[21] Maimonides introduces a distinction between 'the pious of the nations of the world', who accept the commandments by reason of biblical authority, and persons who accept the commandments on the basis of reason alone. He explains that the rabbinic passage identifying 'the pious' refers to a person who 'accepts [the seven commandments] and performs them because the Holy One, blessed be he, commanded it in the Torah and told us through Moses that the children of Noah were commanded regarding them'.[22] Piety, in other words, for the non-Jew as for the Jew, consists in obedience on the basis of accepting the Bible as a binding source of law. (Indeed, Maimonides goes out of his way here to insist that what makes the commandments binding is not that God commanded them to Noah's sons, but that they are mandated by the law of Moses.) By contrast, says Maimonides, if a person performs the seven commandments 'out of the force of reason' (*hekhre'a ha-da'at*), then he does not fall into the category of 'resident alien' nor of 'the pious of the nations of world.' Rather, such a person counts as 'one of their wise men'.[23]

The statement that someone who performs the seven commandments out of the force of reason counts as one of the wise non-Jews was sufficiently surprising that copyists mangled it, misreading the Hebrew word for 'but rather' ('*ella*) as the word for 'and not' (*ve-lo*), so that the sentence was made to say that such a person was not one of the pious of the nations of the world *and not* one of their wise men. Yet the correct reading, preserved by a few manuscripts, goes to the very heart of Maimonides' conception of the character of the seven commandments. Put simply, a person of philosophical attainment could accept these laws on the basis of reason alone, without acknowledging the authority of the Bible. It follows that the laws must be capable of being derived from reason.

Maimonides does not undertake to derive these seven commandments from principles of reason, but his probable derivation can be roughly reconstructed. Idolatry is, for Maimonides, the fundamental error of failing to recognise God's existence as the first mover, which is both the first and the ultimate philosophical truth.[24] The laws that govern human society have as their purpose establishment of rules and conditions for the preservation of the physical individual (*tikkun ha-guf*), in order to serve the purpose of attaining true philosophical knowledge (*tikkun ha-nefesh*).[25] Those of the seven commandments necessary for the safe and secure ordering of society might be derived from reason by someone who understood clearly that the purpose of civil law was to produce conditions conducive to the attainment of truth. The 'wise man of the nations of world' who performs the seven commandments of the force of reason is, it would seem, the philosopher, or at least the philosopher who has not been exposed to the Mosaic law, which is the form of law best suited to the inculcation of philosophical truths.

Having suggested that the seven commandments embody the necessary conditions for philosophical attainment, we can then turn to the role that they play in Maimonides' account of war. The most critical point is that Maimonides makes the acceptance of the seven commandments into a condition that must be accepted by the enemy if it is to avoid being slaughtered. This condition arises, as we have seen, both with respect to obligatory war and voluntary war. It has, however, a different effect on the state of the law prior to Maimonides in the respective cases of obligatory war against the seven peoples of Canaan and the Amalekites commanded by the Bible, and the voluntary war which the Bible authorises for the expansion of the borders of Israel and royal glory.

In the case of the former, Maimonides' use of the option of accepting the seven commandments helps to justify Maimonides' remarkable and original view, against the grain of both biblical and rabbinic sources, that the members of the seven peoples of Canaan and the Amalekites need not be slaughtered if they agree to accept the seven commandments, servitude and taxation. On Maimonides' view, it would seem, the peoples who occupied Canaan did not pose a territorial obstacle so much as a philosophical-theological one. The genocidal biblical command to exterminate them absolutely – men, women, children and even cattle – may be properly understood as designed to require them to relinquish their idolatrous views on pain of death. Had they been permitted to continue, the danger that they would influence the Israelites would be very great – indeed, the Pentateuch regularly warns against allowing such influence, while the books of the Prophets depict the idolatrous influence as pervasive and destructive.

In the context of obligatory war, then, Maimonides' position is that the threatened bloodshed is not intended for its own sake, but rather to serve philosophical interests. In a sense, Maimonides' legal view could be described as more lenient than the traditional reading of the biblical verses, according to which the requirement to slaughter the seven peoples and the Amalekites is absolute. After all, Maimonides affords these peoples the opportunity of continuing to live, albeit subject to submission, taxation and the acceptance of new beliefs. But calling Maimonides' view on obligatory war 'lenient' on the ground that it allows the avoidance of slaughter anachronistically misses the point of his interpretation, which is that the legally enforceable threat of total extermination is not pointless or merely territorial-political, but philosophical. It relates, in other words, to the very purpose of human existence, which is the acquisition of correct philosophical beliefs.

The case of voluntary war poses a related, but still more intriguing reinterpretation of the tradition. By making acceptance of the seven commandments a necessary condition of surrender, alongside submission and taxation, Maimonides might appear at first glance to be transforming voluntary war into a species of obligatory war, designed to spread correct philosophical beliefs. But Maimonides does not go quite that far. He does write that one is obligated to enforce acceptance of the seven commandments on pain of death.[26] He does not, however, impose a general obligation of pursuing aggressive war against idolaters wherever they might be found. The duty to enforce acceptance of the seven commandments apparently applies only in places to which the jurisdiction of the Israelite king extends. Maimonides says that 'any idolater who has not accepted the commandments regarding which Noah's sons were commanded must be killed if he is under our hand'.[27] It is not precisely clear what is meant to be the relationship between this statement and his adjoining statement[28] that there is an obligation 'to compel all the citizens of the world (*kol ba'e 'olam*) to accept the commandments regarding which Noah's sons were commanded'. Together they might be read to obligate universal war, but this reading seems unlikely. In any event, when the Israelite king pursues voluntary war, he must require acceptance of the seven commandments as the condition of his enemies' surrender, because the newly conquered territory will now come under his jurisdiction.[29] (It may, in fact, become part of the land of Israel for these purposes, so that the conquered peoples become resident aliens who fall under the duty to accept the seven commandments as a condition of residence.)

Maimonides therefore leaves voluntary war as truly voluntary, in the sense that the king preserves his discretion to use his own practical reason to decide whether or not it is appropriate to seek to expand his borders. To the extent that he comes to rule over new territory, the requirement of the seven commandments mandates that the Israelite king impose the conditions for philosophical attainment there. It could plausibly be argued that this requirement is intended primarily to serve the interests of the Israelites who would now come into contact with the newly conquered people, and not to serve the interests of the conquered themselves. After all, if the concern were to maximise the total number of people living under conditions conducive to philosophical attainment, then the obligation to war should presumably have been more general. Yet Maimonides is ambiguous on this point, perhaps deliberately so. He surely recognises that the royal decision to wage war must be exercised, above all, with prudence. Imposing a duty to fight always and everywhere would be ruinous to the interests of the Israelites; in the end, they are not obligated to extend the basic condition for philosophical attainment everywhere in the world.

Here, the relevant comparison is to the obligation of jihad in Islamic law, by which Maimonides was certainly influenced. Under classical Islamic law, there exists an obligation to fight and kill idolaters.[30] That obligation, however, does not extend in the same form to Jews and Christians, who, as peoples of the book, possess correct monotheistic beliefs and legal systems based on divine revelation. Jews and Christians may be permitted to live in Muslim lands unmolested so long as they accept conditions of political submission and taxation. Maimonides has clearly borrowed his concept of the submission of the conquered from Islamic law; and the requirement of taxation was a parallel, convergent legal development. But Maimonides has also evidently been influenced by Islamic law's distinction between idolaters, who must be extirpated, and tolerated peoples of the book, who may be permitted to live.

The Aristotelian justification that Maimonides invented to justify the differentiation of idolaters from persons who accept the seven commandments resembles structurally the Islamic legal distinction between idolaters and monotheists: both models agree to tolerate persons who accept the unity of God and follow basic legal norms. But Maimonides' distinction is, of course, different in its philosophical character. Classical Islamic law tolerates peoples of the book because they possess divine sanction in the form of divine revelation, which was specifically transmitted to them, even if it has suffered from corruption and been edited and amended by the Qur'an. The toleration of the peoples of the book is therefore essentially religious, and adopted on religious grounds. For Maimonides, however, the basis for tolerating those who accept the seven commandments would seem to be philosophical: although they may accept the commandments on the basis of biblical authority ('the pious'), it is also conceivable that a few among them might accept on the basis of reason ('the wise'). In practice, Maimonides clearly expects that the overwhelming majority of persons who accept the seven commandments will do so on the basis of authority; that is, after all, the basis for most belief among the philosophically uninitiated. But the reason these beliefs are important is ultimately philosophical-rational, rather than dependent on textual-religious authority.

Averroes and the Obligation to Fight the Jihad

As we have seen, Maimonides rationalises both obligatory and voluntary war, yet ducks the question whether the Israelites are obligated to spread the rationally grounded seven laws beyond their borders, or simply to apply them forcibly to all persons within their jurisdiction. For Averroes, however, it was not possible to avoid the crucial question whether the community of the faithful is obligated to spread truth by the sword, because this is a central problem for the law of jihad, obligatory war in the Islamic tradition. As we shall see, Averroes, like Maimonides, relied on Aristotle to rationalise his legal approach to this classical problem in Islamic law.

The question of the general obligation to fight the jihad emerges from a tension between different verses of the Qur'an. Like other scriptures, the Qur'an is susceptible of multiple interpretations, and scholars of Islamic law must exert time and effort in reconciling potentially conflicting passages to begin to determine what the law requires. To make matters more complicated, the text of the Qur'an, by its own testimony, was revealed piecemeal to the Prophet Muhammad over a period of years. Different revelations concerned different particular circumstances. Some passages were meant by God to abrogate earlier passages that were no longer to be applicable – and yet it is not always clear which passages are meant to abrogate others, both because of uncertain context and because the text of the Qur'an is not organised chronologically or along a narrative structure, consisting instead of series of chapters that today are arranged from longest to shortest.

The easiest way to present the different verses that address the obligation to fight is to listen to Averroes' treatment of the subject in the chapter on jihad in his sole legal work.[31] The work proceeds by explaining discordant views of the law, and grounding each of those views in an interpretation of Islamic legal sources; this was one familiar genre of Islamic legal writing. Averroes addresses the issue in the context of a discussion of when the Muslims may call a truce in their war against polytheists. He begins by explaining that there exist two views with respect to the permissibility of concluding a truce with the polytheists:

> The conclusion of truce is considered by some to be permitted from the very outset and without an immediate occasion, provided that the Imam deems it in the interest of the Moslems. Others maintain that it is only allowed when the Moslems are pressed by sheer necessity, such as civil war and the like.[32]

Averroes then explains the controversy by reference to three verses from the Qur'an:

> The controversy about the question whether the conclusion of truce is also allowed without a compulsive reason, is rooted in the fact that the obvious interpretation of [Q 9:5]: 'Slay the polytheists wherever ye find them' and that of [Q 9:29]: 'Fight against those who do not believe in Allah nor in the last day', contradict that of [Q 8:61]: 'If they incline to make peace, incline thou to it, and set thy trust upon Allah.'

In short, two verses seem to make the obligation to fight general. The first, Q 9:5, tells the faithful that when the holy month arrives, they must fight (or kill – the Arabic word, *aqtalu*, is the same) the polytheists 'wherever you shall find them'. The second verse, Q 9:29, speaks of war against the peoples of the book. It commands fighting those of the peoples of the book who deny God and the last day and refuse 'the religion of truth' until 'they submissively pay the poll-tax and are subjected'. This is the verse on which the requirements of the subordinate status of Jews and Christians who accept Islamic dominion are based. (Indeed, it is the very verse to whose legal consequences Maimonides is reacting in his own presentation of the taxation and subordination of those conquered by the Israelites.) A third verse, however, Q 8:61, sounds a more conciliatory note, instructing the faithful that if 'they' (the enemies of God, based on the previous verse) incline towards peace, the Muslims should incline likewise, 'and put your trust in God', who will protect the faithful should the enemies prove treacherous.

Averroes explains the possible legal consequences of these divergent verses:

> Some hold that the verse which commands the Moslems to fight the polytheists until they have been converted or until they pay the poll-tax [Q 9:29] abrogates the Peace-verse [Q 8:61]. Consequently, they maintain that truce is only admissible in cases of necessity. Others are of the opinion that the Peace-verse [Q 8:61] supplements the other two verses and they consider the concluding of truce allowed if the Imam deems it right.[33]

Averroes does not elaborate beyond explaining the rationales for the two views, nor does he prefer one of the views explicitly. None the less, it is clear that the two rationales depend upon different methods of resolving the apparent contradiction between, on the one hand, the two verses which require war against polytheists and peoples of the book respectively (9:5 and 9:29), and, on the other, the so-called 'Peace-verse,' which permits a truce 'if they incline to make peace'. On the view of those who oppose truce except in case of necessity, the existence of contradictory verses may be resolved by the principle that, on occasion, a later revelation to the Prophet may abrogate an earlier one. Hence, they dismiss the Peace-verse as dead letter. On the view of those who permit truce where the imam deems it right, however, the Peace-verse 'supplements the other two verses'.

What does Averroes mean by invoking a supplementary relationship between verses here? Do not the two verses contradict the one? Averroes implies that they may not. He writes that the contradiction exists between 'the obvious interpretation' of the two verses requiring war, and 'that of' the Peace-verse. He leaves room for the possibility that the 'obvious interpretation' need not be adopted. An alternative interpretation would allow for the view that, while the Qur'an indeed requires war against polytheists and peoples of the book, there exist circumstances in which the Peace-verse applies.[34] According to this view, the existence of the Peace-verse constitutes a grant of authority to the imam, the leader of the community of the Muslims, to judge when the verses requiring war apply, and when they do not.

So far, we would seem to be in the presence of a standard dispute in a matter of Islamic law, regarding which Averroes does not indicate which view he prefers. Yet Averroes provides another window into the question in an unlikely place: his discussion of the famous problem of equity in his commentary on the *Nicomachean Ethics*.[35] There, Averroes has set out to illustrate Aristotle's argument in Book V.7 that, when the law speaks generally but a case arises that is not covered by the general statement, it serves the virtue of equity to correct the omission and to rectify the law in accordance with what the legislator would have said had he in fact been present.[36] Although Averroes rarely turns to Islamic law to illustrate a philosophical point, he does so in this instance:

And this will be clear [or, you will clarify this[37]] from the laws laid down on the matter of war in the law of the Muslims, for the command in it regarding war is general, until they uproot and destroy entirely whoever disagrees[38] with them. But regarding this, there are times when peace is more choiceworthy than war. And as for [the fact] that the Muslim public requires this generality, despite the impossibility of destroying and uprooting their enemies entirely, they attain in this great harm; this is ignorance on their part of the intention of the legislator [Hebrew *mekhuvvan ha-toriyyi*], may God watch over him.[39] Therefore it is appropriate to say that peace is preferable to war sometimes.[40]

Averroes intends for the reader of his philosophical commentary to understand the Aristotelian model of equitable rectification by reference to the relationship of the general command of the verses that require war to the practical reality that war is not to be pursued at all times under a correct interpretation of Islamic law. His analysis comes in two parts: a correct statement of Islamic law, and a condemnation of the error of the Muslim public in misapprehending the law.

In first stating that peace is at times preferable to war despite the generality of the verses commanding war, Averroes gives his own ruling on the dispute whose two sides he laid out in his legal treatise: a truce may be concluded at the discretion of the leader of the Muslim community. Peace is sometimes to be preferred to war. It follows that the correct interpretation of the Qur'anic verses was not that the Peace-verse had been abrogated by later revelations calling for war, but that the Peace-verse 'supplements' those other verses.

How does this example from the law of jihad demonstrate Aristotelian equitable rectification? One possibility is a fairly radical reading of what Averroes says in his commentary. Averroes may mean that, regardless of the fact that Qur'anic verses are written generally, equity demands that the leader of the Muslim community not apply those verses when they were not intended to apply. This reading would seem to give the *imam* enormous authority to exercise discretion in applying the law.[41] It also ignores the existence of the Peace-verse, to which Averroes does not directly allude in his Ethics commentary.

A more cautious reading of the passage, informed by the legal discussion we covered above, suggests that Averroes means to apply Aristotelian principles to interpreting the relationship between the different verses. The general verses that call for war are to be understood as supplemented by the Peace-verse. The Peace-verse, properly understood, confers authority on the imam to decide when to pursue a course of peace rather than war. On Averroes' view, this model instantiates Aristotelian equitable rectification: the verses, taken together, confer authority on the imam to act as the legislator would have intended had he been present by choosing, on prudential grounds, whether to fight or not. The general law indeed sets the baseline by recommending war, but the Peace-verse makes the arrangement practically tractable by creating the option of peace.

Averroes makes this clear by his condemnation of the Muslim public for its misunderstanding of the law. The public thinks that the general command of war is always required, despite the impossibility of winning such wars. They harm themselves by fighting when it is not appropriate to do so. This reflects the public's 'ignorance of the intention of the legislator'. The public's ignorance is that they have misunderstood the intention of the Qur'anic text by failing to realise that the Peace-verse supplements the war-verses. The view, mentioned in Averroes' legal treatise, that truce is acceptable only in cases of absolute necessity therefore amounts to a misunderstanding of the philosophical structure of law-making. Wise general laws are constructed with room for equitable rectification when it serves the interests that the law was intended to achieve. Harm to the Muslim community cannot be the purpose of the law of jihad.[42] Aristotelian legal theory is informing Averroes' interpretation of Islamic law.

As we saw in the case of Maimonides, however, it would be mistaken to conclude that Aristotelian thought somehow liberalises Averroes. Aristotle does help Averroes reach the conclusion that peace is sometimes preferable to all-out war, so Aristotelian reasoning does lead to the more lenient of the two positions regarding the obligation of jihad. But notice that even on Averroes' view, the strong implication is that war is appropriate when it serves the interests of the Muslim community. The duty of holy war has not been lifted, but it has been rationalised by an interpretation that avoids requiring self-destructive behaviour from the Muslim community.

Both Averroes and Maimonides, then, in their respective discussions of the law of war, adopted Aristotelian principles to interpret the classical Islamic and Jewish legal sources they had before them. Averroes drew on the notion of equitable rectification to reach the best interpretation of contradictory Qur'anic verses. Maimonides, for his part, shaped his legal analysis on the basis of what he understood to be the purpose of war; and that purpose was, in essence, philosophical. Islamic law provided Maimonides with some valuable parallels for determining specific legal obligations, while philosophy helped explicate the place of war in the hierarchy of ultimate ends.

To the modern or postmodern eye, there is something profoundly disturbing about the idea that war is an instrument of the spread of true belief. Our scepticism – hard-won, at least in historical terms – indeed may make us think that spreading belief is the worst of all possible reasons for war. We may share Maimonides' view (and that of classical Islamic law) that defensive war is justified and indeed obligatory, but we balk at the idea of aggressive or expansive war in pursuit of philosophical goals, no matter how noble. In the final analysis, it may be that neither Maimonides nor Averroes provides us with an ethical guide to thinking about war that seems in any way sufficient as a matter of public reason. Yet the enquiry into the encounter of reason and war is none the less instructive. The exercise of reason may not be the panacea we sometimes imagine it to be.

Acknowledgements

Thanks to Richard Sorabji, Jeannie Suk, Moshe Halbertal and Gidon Rothstein for very helpful comments.

Notes

1 Both also pursued side-lines in medicine, Averroes as an influential writer and Maimonides as court physician to Saladin – and both were therefore interested in and affected by the Aristotelian analogy which compared the statesman to a physician and the exercise of statecraft to the practice of medicine. This further point of contact brought considerations of political theory to bear on the relation between religious law and Greek philosophy in the writings of both. Although neither man was an active politician or, so far as we know, a political counsellor, both knew kings, were profoundly affected by politics in their personal lives, and understood that statecraft, in order to succeed, must be an exercise in practical reason.

2 See, for example, Deuteronomy 7:1–6.

3 Deuteronomy 26:17–19; see also Exodus 17:8–16.

4 First Samuel 15.

5 Hilkhot Melakhim 5:1.

6 Ibid. The biblical source that would make the last of these categories obligatory is less obvious than for the former two, and it may be that Maimonides relies here on the logical force of the notion that the king is obligated to act in the self-defence of the people; he may also have been influenced here by the fact that Islamic law, as we shall see, makes a war fought in self-defence the paradigm case of obligatory holy war.

7 Ibid.

8 Hilkhot Melakhim 5:4.

9 Deuteronomy 20:10.

10 See Sifré, ad loc. ('The Scripture speaks of voluntary war'). For a full accounting of the various commentaries agreeing with this interpretation, see *Lehem Mishne* on Hilkhot Melakhim 6:1.

11 Hilkhot Melakhim 6:1.

12 On this translation, see immediately below.

13 Hilkhot Melakhim 6:4.

14 See, for example, Joshua 10:1: 'and that the residents of Gibeon made peace (*hishlimu*) with the Israelites and were amongst them'.

15 Hilkhot Melakhim 6:1.

16 Ibid.

17 See, for example, Blidstein, Gerlad J., *Ekronot Mediniyyim be-Mishnat shel Ha-Rambam*, Ramat Gan: Bar Ilan University Press, 1983.

18 See, for example, Novak, David (1983), *The Image of the Non-Jew in Judaism: An Historical and Constructive Study of the Noahide Jews*, New York: E. Mellen Press.

19 Babylonian Talmud *Sanhedrin* 56a.

20 Babylonian Talmud *Gittin* 8b; see also Maimonides, Hilkhot Avodat Kokhavim 10:6.

21 Hilkhot Melakhim 9:11.

22 Hilkhot Melakhim 8:11.

23 Ibid.

24 For Maimonides' account of the genealogy of idolatry, see Hilkhot 'Avodat Kokhavim 1:1–2.

25 See, generally, Maimonides, Hilkhot De'ot.

26 Hilkhot Melakhim 8:10.

27 Hilkhot Melakhim 8:9.

28 Hilkhot Melakhim 8:10.

29   As Moshe Halbertal has pointed out to me, the very reason the requirement of
      enforcement of the Noahide law appears in this chapter is that it is an Israelite royal
      duty, not a general duty incumbent on non-Jews themselves wherever they might live,
      as Nahmanides holds.

30   See below for refinement of this formulation.

31   *Bidayat al-mujtahid wa-nihayat al-muqtasid*, translated as Nyazee, Imran Ahsan Khan
      (trans.) (1997), *The Distinguished Jurist's Primer*, Reading, UK: Garnet. The chapter
      on jihad had previously been translated into English in Peters, Rudolph (trans. and
      annot.) (1997), *Jihad in Medieval and Modern Islam: the Chapter on Jihad from
      Averroes' Legal Handbook 'Bidayat al-mudjtahid' and the Treatise 'Koran and
      Fighting' by the late Shaykh al-Azhar, Mahmud, Shaltut*, Leiden: E. J. Brill, 6. I use
      Peters' translations here.

32   *Bidaya, Chapter on Jihad*, Part 6, trans. in Peters, *Jihad in Medieval and Modern Islam*,
      21. Averroes identifies the former view as that of Malik, Shafi'i and Abu Hanifa (the
      founders of three important schools of Islamic legal thought); he does not identify by
      name those who choose the second position. The overwhelming support of the
      authorities for the former view, as well as the anonymity of the dissenters, makes
      Averroes' endorsement obvious.

33   Ibid.

34   One might inquire whether Averroes might not hold that the general precept is peace,
      and war choiceworthy only sometimes. But Averroes writes here that the Peace-verse
      supplements the other two, not vice versa. This suggests that the baseline, as it were, is
      war; truce constitutes the exception to the general. The obligation of jihad is well
      enough established to make it impossible for Averroes to claim jihad as an exceptional
      state.

35   Only a few fragments of the commentary survive in Arabic. The complete commentary
      exists in two independent translations, one into Latin by Hermannus Alemannus,
      completed in 1240 in Toledo and reprinted in various Junctas editions of Averroes'
      works, and one into Hebrew, completed by Samuel ben Judah of Marseilles around
      1322, and existed only in manuscript until recently, when a Hebrew critical edition
      appeared. Berman, Lawrence (ed.) (1999), *Averroes' Middle Commentary on
      Aristotle's Nicomachean Ethics in the Hebrew Version of Samuel Ben Judah*,
      Jerusalem: Israel Academy of Science and Humanities; see also Feldman, Noah (1994),
      'Reading the Nicomachean Ethics with Ibn Rushd', unpublished D.Phil. dissertation,
      Oxford.

36   *Nicomachean Ethics* 1137b, 22–3.

37   The underlying Arabic must surely have been *tbyn*. Samuel vocalises *tubayyinu*;
      Hermann vocalises *tabayyana*. The latter vocalisation seems preferable; Averroes does
      not normally address the reader in the second person in the *EN* commentary.

38   Samuel translates 'whoever fights with them'. Another version of Samuel gives *mi
      she-holek*, 'whoever disagrees'. See Berman, L., review of Rosenthal's *Averroes'
      Commentary on Plato's 'Republic'* in *Oriens*, 21, 1968–9, 439, for the variant. Berman
      does not specify the manuscript source; it may be one of those edited to accord with the
      Latin translation.

39   The formula is omitted in the Latin version, perhaps as a result of Hermann's Christian
      piety, perhaps because Hermann took it to be inessential. It seems highly unlikely that
      Samuel would have added it to a text in which it did not occur; it is not an idiomatic
      Hebrew phrase, and Samuel would have as little reason to pray for the Prophet as would
      Hermann.

40 This is my own translation. It differs in some points from the one offered by Berman in *Oriens*, 21, 1968–9, 439:

> And you can understand this from the laws laid down with respect to war in the law of the Muslims (Latin: *saracenorum*) because the command pertaining to war in it is very general to such a point that they destroy root and branch whoever differs with them. Now there are times in which peace is more to be preferred than war. However, since the Muslim masses make this edict of war generally valid despite the impossibility of destroying their enemies completely (read in the Latin edition 1550: *et cum hoc fuit eis impossibile* with the edition of 1483 and the Hebrew version) great damage has attained them on account of their ignorance of the intention of the Lawgiver, the blessings of God be upon him. It is therefore proper to say that peace is preferable at times to war.

The translation is also quoted in Lerner, R. (1974), *Averroes on Plato's Republic*, Ithaca, NY: Cornell University Press, 69, n. 60.4. The Latin reads:

> Et manifestum est sibi hoc ex foro posito in praecipiendo bella in lege Saracenorum. praeceptum enim bellandi in ea vniuersale est, donec extirpetur radix eorum, qui diuersi sunt ab eis. & sunt hic horae, in quibus eligibilior est pax bello. & quia populus Saracenorum tenuit pro necessario hoc praeceptum vniuersale: et cum hoc fuit possibile extirpare suos inimicos: consecuti sunt damna multa ex hoc. & istud fuit ex ignorantia ipsorum intentionis legislatoris. & propter hoc oportet vt dicatur quod magis quaerenda est pax, quandoque que bellum (Venice, 1562 edn, 1574 edn, 79a–b; 1560 edn, 247b).

Berman questions the text of the printed editions of the Latin in his review of Rosenthal's *Averroes' Commentary on Plato's 'Republic'* in *Oriens*, 21, 1968–9, 439.

41 Al-Farabi confers such discretion on a prophet interpreting the law given by those prophets who have come before, but does not extend the authority to a non-prophet. Najjar, F. (trans.), *The Political Regime*, in Lerner, R. and Mahdi, M. (eds) (1963), *Medieval Political Philosophy*, Ithaca, NY: Cornell University Press, 37. Maimonides' complex discussion of these issues is one I have treated elsewhere, in Feldman, Noah (2004), Aristotelian Equity and Accrctionary Law in Maimonides, in Ben-Menahem, Hanina and Lipshitz, Berachyahu (eds), *On Law and Equity in Maimonidean Jurisprudence: Reading the Guide for the Perplexed*, Jerusalem: Institute for Research in Jewish Law.

42 There is even a general maxim of Islamic law to the effect that the law intends to do no harm. Islam includes 'no injury or malicious damage': *la darara wa-la dirara fi'l-islam*. See Paret, R., '*Istihsan* and *Istislah*', in *Encyclopedia of Islam*, 2nd edn, 256–7.

Chapter 6

The Ethics of War: Judaism

Norman Solomon

*A longer version of this Chapter is due to appear in Torkel Brekke (ed.)
(forthcoming),* The Ethics of War in Asian Civilisations.

Definitions: Sources and How to Read Them

By 'ethics' I mean 'norms of behaviour', whether they are formulated as laws, or as
ethical or moral principles.

'Judaism' is the religion of the Jews, more properly called 'Rabbinic Judaism'. I
shall *not* be offering you 'Old Testament Theology', nor an account of what Jews in
general have said about war. My area of discourse is the Judaism of the rabbis.

Judaism, like Christianity, has deep roots in the Hebrew scriptures ('Old
Testament'), but it interprets those scriptures along lines classically formulated by
the rabbis of the Babylonian Talmud, completed shortly before the rise of Islam.

The Talmud is a reference point, rather than a definitive statement; Judaism has
continued to develop right up to the present. To get some idea of how Judaism
handles the ethics of war, we have to review sources from the earliest scriptures to
rabbinic discussion in contemporary Israel, a period of three thousand years.

The Hebrew Scriptures comprise a collection of books compiled over more than
a millennium. The sections relevant to war describe wars waged by the Israelites
against the Canaanites and other nations; they also encompass the vision that
'nation shall not lift sword unto nation' (Isaiah 2:4; Micah 4:3).

Jewish reading of biblical texts is guided by the Talmud and other works of the
rabbis. For instance, the Bible reports (Genesis 34) that Jacob's sons slaughtered the
inhabitants of Shechem on account of the rape of their sister, Dinah. Are we to
interpret this as a model of righteous zeal, or as a grave aberration? From the Bible
itself, we would not know. Later Jewish tradition, however, regarded the massacre
as a crime, or at best as an act requiring exceptional justification.[1]

Law must be distinguished from narrative. For instance, Deuteronomic
legislation, rightly interpreted, is normative; the behaviour of, for example, King
David, is not, and may indeed be open to criticism in the light of Torah law.

The legislation concerning warfare in Deuteronomy 20 is the starting point for
rabbinic thinking about war, as it was to be among Christians.

In form, it is a 'military oration',[2] concerned with *jus in bello* rather than *jus ad bellum*; it regulates conduct in war, but does not specify conditions under which it is appropriate to engage in war. It distinguishes between (a) the war directly mandated by God against the Canaanites, and (b) other wars. This is something like the distinction made in early modern Europe between religious wars (wars of the Church) and wars of the Prince.[3]

War against the Canaanites is based on the *herem*, or holy ban; it is a war of extermination that knows no bounds (verses 15–18). Justification – a sort of *jus ad bellum* – is offered, on the grounds that these nations might teach Israel 'abominations' and lead them to sin (verse 18).[4] No restraints are indicated.

However, 'normal' war is subject to several restraints:

- The war is to be fought only by those who are courageous, possessing faith in God, and who do not have a commitment such as a new house, vineyard or wife (verses 1–10).
- An offer of peace is to be made to any city which is besieged, conditional on the acceptance of terms of tribute (verses 10, 11).
- Should the city refuse the offer of peace, the males are put to the sword, the females and small children are taken captive, and the city plundered.
- Food trees may not be cut down in prosecution of the siege (verses 19, 20).
- Verses 21:10–14 offer some amelioration of the status of the female captive.

Joshua 11:19 states: 'No city made peace with the Israelites, save the Hivites who lived in Gibeon'; the rabbis infer from this that offers of peace were made to the Canaanites, too.[5]

As to *jus ad bellum*, many biblical passages indicate the need for a *casus belli*, though the Bible does not articulate principles from which we might judge whether a particular cause was justified. If God issued explicit instructions, that would constitute adequate justification. However, God conspicuously does *not* rely on divine fiat alone when he commands the Israelites to conquer the 'promised land', but justifies it with the claims that (a) He has condemned the Canaanites on account of their immorality,[6] and (b) if left, they might 'contaminate' the Israelites.

The Dominican theologian Francisco de Vitoria (1492–1546) supports his 'natural law' arguments against war for religion by a direct appeal to the Hebrew scriptures:

> [E]ven in the Old Testament, where much was done by force of arms, the people of Israel never seized the land of unbelievers either because they were unbelievers or idolaters or because they were guilty of other sins … but because of either a special gift from God or because their enemies had hindered their passage or had attacked them.[7]

Two kings, Saul and Ahab, certainly challenged the ruthlessness of Deuteronomy, and it is unlikely that the war laws of Deuteronomy governed Israelite activities in the biblical period; one scholar has called them the 'radicalism of the writing desk,' a retrojection by authors attempting to bolster the covenantal consciousness of Israel.[8]

The rabbis dared not criticise Deuteronomy, for they regarded it as the direct word of God; rather, they expressed their unease by means of interpretation. They could not exonerate Saul for being remiss in destroying the Amalekites, since the Bible states that he deserved his punishment; but they retold the story in a way that was sympathetic to Saul and expressed their own puzzlement at the command to destroy Amalek:

> 'And he strove[9] in the valley (1 Samuel 15:5).' Rabbi Mani says, 'Concerning the inheritance.'[10] For when the Holy One, blessed be He, said to Saul, 'Go, smite Amalek ...' (15:3) he said, Surely, if the Torah says that if someone kills even one person a calf's neck must be broken,[11] how much more so for all these people, and if the adults have sinned, what about the children! A heavenly voice issued forth and said, 'Do not be over-righteous' (Ecclesiastes 7:16).[12]

The 'heavenly voice' here is put on the defensive; Saul's moral reasoning is made to appear correct.

Rabbinic Readings of Scripture

By the time the Talmud was compiled, Jews had lost political independence; rabbinic discussion of war lacks firm contact with contemporary reality. Their legislation on warfare is essentially an exposition of Deuteronomy 20; it is historical reconstruction or messianic speculation, not the operational law of an actual society.

Changing attitudes to war emerge. Rabbi Eliezer ben Hyrcanus, early in the second century, ruled against his colleagues that a man might adorn himself with weapons on the Sabbath even when not required for defence. To the majority sages, the bearing of arms, though necessary for defence, disgraces the wearer; but Eliezer, a staunch Jewish nationalist, regarded the bearing of arms as honourable.[13]

The rabbis tone down the severity of the plain biblical text of Deuteronomy in three ways, so that it cannot become a general warrant for genocide:

1 They argue, against the plain sense, that offers of peace were to be made even to the Canaanites.

2 They rule, rather impractically, that in wars other than those of the original conquest, if a town was placed under siege an escape route was always to be provided.[14]

3 Joshua ben Ḥananiah, around 100 CE, declared that since 'Sennacherib mixed up all the nations', no one can any longer be identified with the nations of earlier times; hence, the specific laws pertaining to those nations cannot be invoked.[15]

Limitations are set within the text itself, which limits the *ḥerem* ban to the 'seven nations'.[16] But this would leave open the question of identification, and it would be only too easy to categorise a potential enemy as belonging to one or other of the despised nations.

They distinguished three kinds of war:

- *milḥemet ùova* (obligatory war)
- *milḥemet reshut* (optional war)
- pre-emptive, or perhaps preventive war.

Rava said:

> All agree that Joshua's war of conquest was *ḥova* (obligatory) and the expansionist wars of David were *reshut* (optional). But they differ with regard to [the status of] a pre-emptive war intended to prevent idolaters from attacking them.[17]

There is some resonance here with the Roman notion of *bellum justum*, though the rabbinic classification is into obligatory and optional, rather than just and unjust.[18] A defensive war is obligatory (just); a pre-emptive war *might* be.[19]

On the other hand, the 'expansionist wars of David' are seen as more questionable, notwithstanding Psalm 18:48, 'He has subdued nations beneath my feet'.[20] Elsewhere the Talmud insists that the king would need to seek authorisation from the Great Court of 71 justices, as well as divine approval through the oracle[21] of the High Priest, before engaging in such a war[22]. As these institutions have not existed for two thousand years, the definition of 'competent authority' virtually rules out the possibility of non-defensive war; there is no Jewish equivalent to the process by which some seventeenth-century English Puritans declared wars to be 'commanded by God' simply because they were deemed by the leadership to be in conformity with God's will.[23]

The Talmudic distinction between *kibbush yaḥid* (individual conquest) and *kibbush rabim* (public conquest) may indicate the need for popular support in addition to the other requirements.[24]

A clear precedent for the exemption of non-combatant 'clerics' from military service[25] emerges from a consideration of King Asa's gout[26] (1 Kings 15:23): Rava, a fourth-century Babylonian rabbi, speculated that this was a divine punishment because he had conscripted 'disciples of the sages' into his army.[27]

Self-Defence and Proportionality

Defence, including self-defence, is not so much a *right* as a *duty*. The principle of self-defence is derived from Exodus 22:1, understood by the rabbis as referring to a thief who breaks in with intent to kill should he be discovered; *ha-ba l'horg'kha hashkem l'horgo*, 'If someone comes to kill you, kill him first'.

Proportionality follows from Exodus 22:2: 'If the sun has risen on him, there shall be blood-guilt for him …'; as the rabbis express it, 'Does the sun rise only on him? [Surely not. But the verse teaches:] if it is as clear as day to you that he does not come in peace (i.e. that he is ready to kill), kill him, but otherwise not.'[28]

The duty to defend a threatened third party, even at the expense of the life of the aggressor, is derived from the case of the betrothed rape victim (Deuteronomy 22:25–27). Scripture itself compares rape to murder, and implies that if anyone heard the victim cry out he should have defended her, if need be by slaying the rapist. The same would apply to someone intent on murdering another person. But what, asks the Talmud, if the victim could be saved by 'one of his limbs' – that is, without killing him? Then the saviour would himself be guilty of murder if he killed the attacker.[29] This last caveat establishes the principle of proportionality.

These texts are set in the criminal code, not among the laws pertaining to war. Later authorities extrapolate from personal to collective self-defence, that is, war designed to defend society as a whole, or its most cherished values. This is analogous to the way in which Christians such as Ambrose and Augustine argued that 'Christian love' mandated not only personal defence of individual Christians, but military defence of Christian society.[30]

Accepting the 'Yoke of the Nations'

Since the abortive revolts of the late Roman Empire, Jews have reconciled themselves to minority status, and rarely if ever rioted or engaged in open revolt, let alone terrorist acts, against their oppressors. Whether out of conviction or through duress, they have taken to heart Jeremiah's words, 'Seek the peace of the city to which I have exiled you and pray to the Lord for it, for in its peace will you find peace' (Jeremiah 29:7), embodied in the somewhat Hobbesian rabbinic dictum, 'Pray for the welfare of the government, for if not for fear of it one man would swallow the other alive.'[31]

This resigned attitude is expressed in a Midrash which states that Israel swore an oath 'not to rebel against the [oppressing] nations, not to force the End, not to reveal the mysteries [of Torah] to the nations, and not to go up [to the land of Israel] from the diaspora in [military] formation'.[32] This Midrash was cited by anti-Zionist rabbis who opposed the setting up of a secular Jewish state which would have to rely on military force for its defence.[33]

Compassion

After a crushing defeat, Ben-Hadad, King of Syria, sought refuge with the victor Ahab, King of Israel; his advisers had counselled him that Israelite kings were *malkhei ḥesed* 'merciful kings'(1 Kings 20:31). Ahab was reprimanded by the prophet for affording refuge to Ben-Hadad on this occasion, and the consequences were disastrous. More recently, however, the reputation of the Israelite kings for showing compassion has been a source of pride, and has been cited as an indication that even in wartime, compassion should be shown to one's enemies if circumstances are such that it will not undermine the war aim.

Philo of Alexandria, writing early in the first century with an eye to a gentile as well as Jewish readership, refers the provisions for non-Canaanite war in Deuteronomy 20 to those who revolt from an alliance, implying that wars of conquest or aggression are never sanctioned; he stresses the restraint to be shown by Israel in first offering peace. The women are, in any event, to be spared 'as in virtue of their natural weakness they have the privilege of exemption from war service':[34]

> All this shows clearly that the Jewish nation is ready for agreement and friendship with all like-minded nations whose intentions are peaceful, yet is not of the contemptible kind which surrenders through cowardice to wrongful aggression.[35]

In the Middle Ages there were rabbis, for instance the thirteenth-century author of *Sefer ha-Ḥinukh*, who argued (rather like Philo, whose work was unknown to him) that the rationale of less-than-total war against the 'other nations' was to instil compassion, for 'it is fitting for us, the holy seed, to act [with compassion] in all matters, even towards our idolatrous enemies'.[36]

Environment

> When you are at war, and lay siege to a city … do not destroy its trees by taking the axe to them, for they provide you with food … (Deuteronomy 20:19)

In its biblical context, this is a counsel of prudence rather than a principle of conservation; Israelites are enjoined to use only 'non-productive', that is, non fruit-bearing trees, for their siege works. However, rabbinic tradition has applied it generally as a prohibition of waste, and modern Jewish environmentalists have quarried this tradition in support of their pleas for conservation.

It does provide an additional argument against warfare, and raises the question of whether there is some limit to the amount of environmental degradation that might be caused even in pursuit of a just war. Was the defoliation of the forests of Vietnam acceptable even if the war aims were agreed? Irrespective of the human suffering caused, could it ever be acceptable to have recourse to nuclear weapons, seeing that their use would severely damage the environment? The works of Artson and Landes give some indication of the range of Jewish views on these matters; while the duty of conserving nature is universally acknowledged, there is disagreement over how this duty should be balanced against the duty of defence of human life.

Arms Trade

The Mishna ruled: 'One may not sell bears or lions, nor anything that may harm the public, to [gentiles]'.[37] A discussion in the Talmud on whether iron lamps may be sold to gentiles, seeing that the material could be reworked into weapons 'that harm the public', is cut short by the interjection, 'But nowadays that we sell them ...', to which Rav Ashi replies: 'To the Persians, who protect us'.[38] Evidently, Jews felt it appropriate to sell arms to Persians in the fourth century; the remark of the Tosafists that 'It would seem that nowadays we are permitted for the same reason ...' shows that the same business was afoot in thirteenth-century Rhineland. These are among precedents cited by Chaim David Halevi (b. 1925), then Sefardi Chief Rabbi of Tel Aviv/Jaffa, in his responsum, published shortly after the Yom Kippur War of 1973, on whether the sale of arms by Israel to friendly countries is permissible under the halakha.[39]

Although for almost two thousand years Jews were rarely involved as principals in war, they often played a subsidiary role in finance and supply. Isaac Abravanel is said to have loaned 1½ million gold ducats to Ferdinand and Isabella to pursue the war with Granada (1491–2). Jewish immigrants, including refugees from Spain, are said to have introduced significant military technology to their new Ottoman overlords.[40] Jews were very prominent as military contractors in the seventeenth and eighteenth centuries; among the most famous army contractors for pay and supplies in eighteenth-century England were Sir Solomon de Medina, the associate of Marlborough, and Abraham Prado. In such cases, it is impossible to assess the extent to which Jews were acting under duress, or in the perceived interest of their own communities, rather than on the basis of some freely embraced religious principle.

Some Mediaeval Jewish Views

The Qur'an records Muhammad's negotiations and battles with some of the Arabian Jewish tribes, and from Arab sources we learn about the activity of Jewish Berber tribes such as the Aurés, led by the female warrior Kahina Dahiya,[41] which for a time c. 700 successfully resisted the advance of Ḥasan ibn al Nu'man through the Maghreb and into Spain. Literary records are scant for all of these, as for the short-lived Jewish kingdom of Khazaria,[42] and from none of them can we garner information on distinctively Jewish religious thinking about war.

Otherwise, though there are numerous references to Jewish mercenaries throughout the pre-modern period, and occasional references to organised armed defence,[43], Jews were not collectively involved in warfare other than as bystanders and incidental victims. No mainstream Jew was called upon, in a real-life situation, to determine whether to engage in war or how to prosecute it. Nevertheless, there was reflection on earlier sources and on future 'messianic' wars, and a handful of Jewish religious leaders were sufficiently close to political reality to devote serious attention to the ethics of war.

One such was Shmuel (Samuel) ha-Nagid, also known as Ismail ibn Nagrela (993–1055/6), who was vizier to Kings Ḥabbus and Badis of Granada, and a

Hebrew poet and scholar of distinction. He is probably unique among medieval Jews as military commander of a Muslim army.

Samuel nowhere expressly justifies his involvement on behalf of his dissolute master in the internecine wars of Muslim Spain. Presumably, he accepts war as an unfortunate fact of life, and is prepared to discharge his responsibility towards his prince in the interest of protecting his own community. He may even have entertained illusions that he was commencing the messianic wars.[44]

But if his war poems fail to address the moral problems of warfare they certainly address the emotional, spiritual and ritual issues:

> War at the outset is like a beautiful maid
> With whom everyone wishes to flirt
> At the end it is like a despised hag
> Bringing tears and sadness to whomever she meets.[45]

There are prayers before a battle, commitment to the will of God, thanksgiving for victory, a declaration that throughout the battle he has faithfully observed the Sabbath and Festivals – his hint that others were 'less scrupulous'[46] rather suggests that Jewish mercenaries formed part of the forces under his command.[47]

The Yemenite Jewish philosopher Netanel ibn Fayyumi (died *c.* 1165), writing in Arabic, lists jihad amongst the 'external,' or bodily commandments.[48] Perhaps he had picked up the broader Islamic concept of jihad as struggle, effort, readiness to commit totally to God's work, or perhaps he was hinting to Jews that they, too, given the appropriate conditions, have a duty to fight for their faith just as Muslims do; the hint was not taken up by later authorities.

Maimonides

Moses Maimonides (1135/8–1204), or Rambam as he is generally known, compiled in the 1160s a comprehensive Code of Law incorporating a section titled 'The Laws of Kings and their Wars'. He did not aim in this work to formulate an original theory of war, but to articulate the rabbinic tradition. Occasionally, he exceeds his brief; expounding the biblical verse (Deuteronomy 20:8) that lays down that one who is afraid, lacking in courage, should return from the muster (7:15), he writes:

'What man is there that is fearful and faint-hearted?' *This is to be taken at its face value, [of one who] lacks the courage to withstand the rigours of war. Once he engages in the rigours of war he should rely on 'the Hope of Israel' (God), his saviour in times of distress, and know that he is engaging in war for the Unity of the Name. He should take his life in his hands, neither fear nor tremble, not think of his wife or children, but erase their memory and all considerations other than war from his mind ... he bears responsibility for the blood of all Israel, and if he does not win, or fails to exert himself to the utmost, it is as if he spilled the blood of everyone ... he who fights courageously and fearlessly with the sole intention of sanctifying the Divine Name will certainly suffer no harm, but will ... earn the [rewards of the] World to Come.*[49]

This may echo some Islamic interpretations of jihad, but has little connection with Maimonides' rabbinic sources.

Another significant deviation from the rabbinic sources concerns the exemption from warfare of those who devote their life to God. The context is the biblical command that the tribe of Levi, who are designated as teachers, should not be apportioned land or receive the spoils of war.[50] Maimonides, perhaps mindful of the story of King Asa's gout cited above, introduces with the phrase 'it appears to me' three paragraphs that lack support in earlier sources of halakha:

> Why did the tribe of Levi have no right to a share in the Land and spoils of war with their brethren? Because they were singled out to serve God, to teach His upright ways and true judgments to the public ... so they were set apart from the ways of the world, and did not wage war like the rest of Israel nor inherit [the Land] nor acquire rights through physical exertion. But they are the Lord's army ... and He, blessed be He, grants their rights.
>
> And not only the tribe of Levi, but any human being whose spirit and intellect move him to stand before God and to serve and know Him, and who walks uprightly as God has made him, and casts aside the designs of men, is a most holy person; God is his portion for ever and will grant his needs in this world as he granted the Priests and Levites ...[51]

This has been cited by modern Israeli rabbis in justification of the exemption from military service of yeshiva students and others who devote their life to the study of Torah. Since Maimonides pointedly uses the expression *kol ba'é 'olam* (any *human being*) rather than 'any Israelite', he implies that the immunity of clerics and the like on the opposing side is to be respected (provided, of course, that they are non-combatants).

Like his European contemporary Gratian (mid-twelfth century) and later Thomas Aquinas (1225–74), who grant non-combatant immunity only to clerics and bishops,[52] Maimonides grants immunity only to those devoted to the service of God, not to non-combatants in general. The reason for exemption is not that such people do not bear arms, but because they are holy, removed from mortal concerns. So it does not follow that immunity would be granted to other non-combatants such as merchants and peasants listed in the treatise *De Treuga et Pace*[53] proclaimed by Pope Urban II at the Council of Clermont (1095) and incorporated in the canon law under Gregory IX (1227–41).

In a section of his later philosophical work, *A Guide for the Perplexed*, he again summarises the commandments under 14 heads, but omits the commandments relating to kings and war. Elsewhere in the work, in the context of idolatry, he briefly justifies the genocide of the Canaanites:

> Do you not see in the texts of the *Torah*, when it commanded the extermination of the *seven nations* and said *thou shalt save alive nothing that breatheth*, that it immediately follows this by saying: *That they teach you not to do after all their abominations, which they have done unto their gods and so ye sin against the Lord your God?* Thus it says: do not think that this is hard-heartedness or desire for vengeance. It is rather an act required by human opinion, which considers that everyone who deviates from the way of truth[54]

should be put an end to and that all obstacles impeding the achievement of perfection that is the apprehension of Him, may He be exalted, should be interdicted.[55]

This is a doctrine of 'right intent', as it was later characterised by Thomas Aquinas.[56] Maimonides' overall view seems to be that war is a sad fact of life, a consequence of the moral and intellectual failings of human beings; the Torah regulates it, making due allowance for frail human nature, in accordance with divine compassion, which demands the elimination of evil, the source of which is idolatry. Maimonides nowhere suggests that Jews have a duty to go out into the world actively to seek and destroy idolatry.

Naḥmanides

Naḥmanides (1194–1270), or Ramban as he is generally known, was a rabbi and exegete in Catalonia; he completed his *Commentary on the Torah* in Palestine, where he ended his days having fled Spain in the aftermath of the 1263 Disputation in Barcelona.

His comment on Deuteronomy 23:10. 'You shall guard yourself from every evil thing' carries a ring of personal observation:

> Scripture warns [us to be especially careful] at times when sin is common. It is well known that when groups go to war they eat every abominable thing, steal, do violence, and are not ashamed even to commit adultery and other detestable things, so that even the most naturally upright of men is enveloped in violence and anger when setting off to battle against an enemy. Therefore scripture warns, 'You shall guard yourself from every evil thing' … for 'the Lord your God is in the midst of your camp.' (verse 15)

This comment is cited by contemporary Israelis in support of the notion of 'purity of arms' which we shall meet later.

In opposition to Maimonides, Naḥmanides lists 'conquest of the land' among the 613 commandments.[57] His use of the term *kibbush* ('conquest') denotes 'living in', 'settlement', not military conquest.

Late medieval commentators emphasise Jewish commitment to peace. The Spanish theologian and commentator Isaac Arama (*c*. 1420–1494), contends that the Torah's commandment to proclaim peace requires:

> Entreaties and supplications offered in the most conciliatory possible way, in order to turn their hearts … for this follows necessarily from the human wisdom of peace, and the Divine will consent … For if we find that He commanded 'You shall not destroy its tree [that is, that found in the city of the enemy], to lift against it an axe' [Deut. 20:19], all the more so should we take care not to commit damage and destruction to human beings.[58]

Isaac Abravanel (1437–1508) served, in succession, Afonso V of Portugal, Ferdinand and Isabella of Spain (with whom he interceded in vain to revoke the edict expelling the Jews from Spain in 1492), Ferrante I and Alfonso II of Naples, and latterly the Council of Venice; his biblical commentaries incorporate observations relating to the European society of his time and formulating political positions such as his preference for republican government over monarchy.

He comments on Deuteronomy 20:10:

> The offer of peace is desirable for three reasons. (a) It is proper to follow the ways of God , Who does not desire [people's] death and the destruction of the world, but forgives the penitent; (b) peaceful conquest denotes the power and magnanimity of the ruler; (c) the outcome of war is at best uncertain and at worst catastrophic.
>
> Should the offer of peace be rejected, war is justified since it is proper that the more perfect should dominate the less perfect.[59]
>
> The women and children should be spared since they are by nature non-combatants.[60]

Abravanel completed his commentary on Deuteronomy in 1496, well before men such as Vitoria and Suarez rejected the idea of 'holy war' for the sake of religion. Abravanel's position is that in these pre-Messianic times we have to accommodate ourselves to the essentially undesirable phenomena of autocracy and its concomitant, warfare; this being so, both have to be restrained within the limits imposed by Torah.

The Modern Period

Western attitudes to war have undergone four major transformations in the modern period.

1   In reaction to the Wars of Religion, a consensus emerged that wars should not be fought to spread 'true' religion.
2   The Industrial Revolution led to the invention of more effective weapons and communications, and made possible the deployment of large armies over great areas. The new concepts of war were articulated by the nineteenth-century Prussian military strategist Carl von Clausewitz (1780–1831), whose *Vom Krieg* first appeared in 1832/4. War, declared Clausewitz, is 'only a part of political intercourse, therefore by no means an independent thing in itself'.[61]
3   The development of international law from Grotius onwards, and its institutionalisation through the League of Nations and subsequently the United Nations, has established the position that the only permitted wars are defensive wars, including wars for the defence of an injured third party, and arguably also pre-emptive strikes.
4   The principle that all nations have a right to self-government has been accepted, and imperialism has been discredited.

Jews participated in all these developments. In addition, the piecemeal and often tenuous emancipation of Jews in the West from the eighteenth century onwards resulted in three trends specific to Judaism:

1   The traditionalists (eventually known as 'Orthodox') continued to teach on the
     basis of rabbinic texts, though their interpretations were often coloured by the
     ambient culture.
2   Religious reformers stressed the ethical and universal dimension of Jewish
     teaching; this led them to modify or even abandon *halakha* (traditional Jewish
     law) in favour of what they took to be the purely ethical monotheism of the
     prophets.
3   Secularists accorded primacy to 'Jewish culture,' again stressing its ethical
     dimension in contrast to *halakha*. Many of them, rebuffed when they attempted
     to gain acceptance within the new European nations, articulated their own,
     Jewish nationalism, since 1892 termed Zionism. It was this third group who
     until recently dominated Zionism and Israeli society, and who determined the
     doctrine of the Israel Defence Forces.

The recent dynamic of Jewish war ethics has involved all three trends in inter-
reaction against the background of evolving Western political theory.

From Mercenary to Patriot

As Jews in the Western world gained rights as citizens of the countries in which they
lived, they assumed the responsibility of participating in the armed struggles of those
countries, not as mercenaries, but as citizens, or would-be citizens. When Joseph II
introduced conscription of Jews in Austria-Hungary in 1787, many regarded it as a
privilege of citizenship. Less welcome was the Russian Cantonist system, introduced
by Czar Nicholas I in 1827, which conscripted Jewish youths aged from 12 to 25
years into military service; those aged under 18 were sent to special military schools
also attended by the children of soldiers. Alexander II abolished the seizure of Jewish
children for military service, reduced the maximum period of service to 15 years, and
in 1874 enacted a law obliging all Russian citizens to report for military service at the
age of 21, so placing Jews on an equal footing with others.

   Jews fought on both sides in the American Civil War (1861–5) and in the First
World War. In the Second World War, well over a million Jews served in the Allied
armies, almost half a million of them, including more than a hundred generals, in
the Soviet army; over a hundred Jews were awarded the title Hero of the Soviet
Union, 150 000 US Jews saw service in the Korean War, and nearly 30 000 fought
in Vietnam, though Jews were also active in the anti-war movement.

   But how have the *religious* authorities looked on such activity? And how has it
come about that whereas the religious authorities forbade or at least discouraged
active Jewish involvement in international warfare well into modern times, by the
nineteenth century in the West they condoned it, and in the twentieth frequently
encouraged young Jews to volunteer?

   The answer lies in changes in the collective self-perception of Western Jews.
Throughout the Middle Ages, Jews lived in autonomous communities and saw

themselves as a separate nation in exile; with the Emancipation, they learned to look on themselves as citizens of the new European nation-states. Defence became defence of the nation-state, or of civilisation itself, rather than of Jews collectively, and ideas on warfare were strongly influenced by those of the surrounding nations; Clausewitz rather than Maimonides determined Jewish public policy.

Moses Schreiber ('*Ḥatam Sofer*' 1762–1839), who as Orthodox Rabbi of Pressburg (Bratislava) lived in proximity to the seat of Austro-Hungarian government, forbade those under his authority to engage in aggressive war, though conceding that land acquired through war was legitimately retained;[62] he objected to voluntary enlistment.[63]

Naftali Zevi Yehuda Berlin (1817–1893), head of the Yeshiva of Volozhin (Belarus) for some forty years, exerted a powerful influence over the secular as well religious leadership of late nineteenth-century non-hasidic Jewry. In his commentary on the Pentateuch, first published in 1879/80, he argued that despite the universal prohibition of murder, non-Jews 'and even Jews' were permitted to engage in war, since 'this is the way the world was set up'.[64] Possibly he was anxious to set at rest the minds of his students, many of whom would be recruited into the Russian army. He may also have felt it prudent to promote a view which would satisfy the secular (Russian) authorities that Jews were loyal to the regime. His assertion that 'this is the way the world was set up' reads as a sigh of resignation from a man who cannot envisage a purely human, pre-Messianic, progress to universal peace, and who regards war as an unavoidable evil of nature on a par with disease and earthquakes.

Israel Meir Hacohen (1838–1933), better known as the Ḥafetz Ḥaim, was a leading Polish halakhist who combined outstanding spirituality with a reactionary outlook. He published his legal commentary, *Mishna Berura*, between 1894 and 1907, when the more lenient conscription introduced by Alexander II was still in force. He rules that Jews must allow themselves to be conscripted in accordance with the 'law of the land': 'Know that nowadays when nations from beyond our borders come to despoil us we are obliged to confront them with arms, even if [they come only to rob].'[65] Ḥafetz Ḥaim is probably concerned more with Jewish defence ('if we do not play our part the citizens will be angry and kill us' – it was after all a period of pogroms) than with any theory of *jus ad bellum*, but even from this perspective the implication is clear that armed combat is only appropriate for defence.

Menaḥem Zemba (1883–1943) argued that the Torah forbade Jews to engage in aggressive war.[66] Zemba was one of the last Warsaw rabbis to remain in the ghetto after the first wave of extermination. On the eve of the Warsaw Ghetto Uprising, Catholic circles offered their assistance to save the three remaining rabbis of Warsaw, but Zemba declined the offer and died a martyr's death in the ghetto. At a meeting of its surviving leaders on 14 January 1943, he gave rabbinic approval for the uprising, stating:

Of necessity, we must resist the enemy on all fronts … We shall no longer heed his instructions … Sanctification of the Divine Name manifests itself in varied ways. During the First Crusade, at the end of the 11th century, the Halakhah … determined one way of reacting to the distress of the Franco-German Jews, whereas in the middle of the 20th century, during the liquidation of the Jews in Poland, it prompts us to react in an entirely different manner. In the past, during religious persecution, we were required by the law 'to give up our lives even for the least essential practice'. In the present, however, when we are faced by an arch foe, whose unparalleled ruthlessness and program of total annihilation know no bounds, the Halakhah demands that we fight and resist to the very end with unequaled determination and valor for the sake of Sanctification of the Divine Name.[67]

Rabbis and scholars in the West were more strongly influenced than their East European colleagues by Enlightenment culture, and generally more broadly educated. The struggle for emancipation was more successful than in Eastern Europe, though its achievements were insecure; consequently, Western Jews tended to assert to excess their loyalty and their readiness to fulfil civic obligations including military service. Moses Mendelssohn (1729–1786), for instance, in a caustic response to J. D. Michaelis' argument that Jews should not be granted full civic rights since their religion rendered them incapable, *inter alia*, of becoming soldiers, points out that no religion, Christianity included, has the task of making men soldiers. Church and state ought to be rigorously separated,[68] in no way did Jews lag behind others in civic conduct, and they were as committed as anyone to the defence of the fatherland.[69] Mendelssohn was at the time reacting positively to Joseph II's *Toleranzpatent* of 1782.

The Italian Samuel David Luzzatto (1800–1865) states more clearly that the only permissible war is defensive. He comments on Deuteronomy 20:10-11:

> The text does not specify the cause for a permitted war or [say] whether Israel may wage war without cause, merely to despoil and take booty. [But] it seems to me that in the beginning of this section [20:1], in saying 'When you go forth to battle against your enemy,' scripture indicates that we should make war only against our enemies. The term 'enemy' refers only to one who seeks to harm us; so scripture is speaking only of an invader who would enter our territory to take our land and despoil us.[70]

The Slovakian-born, American-trained J. H. Hertz (1872–1946), who from 1913 until his death was Chief Rabbi of the United Hebrew Congregations of the British Empire, preached an intercession sermon, 'Through Darkness to Light', at the Great Synagogue, London, on 1 January 1916:[71]

> None could have foretold that civilized mankind would rush back to savagery with such dreadful fervour …
>
>   The men who fought and died at Gallipoli have not fought and died in vain. They have created new standards of human courage. Their dead lie on the abandoned cliffs, but the memory of all they did and tried to do will never fade …

Is there nothing for which to bless God ... the readiness for unbounded sacrifice, as soon as it was realized that we were confronted by a powerful foe who desired nothing less than England's annihilation. Nobly have also the sons of Anglo-Jewry rallied round England in the hour of her need ... our brethren ... have been admitted to the glorious privilege of fighting for their country ...

With the victory of Great Britain, the old Egyptian idols and heathen ideals – the worship of brute force – will be shattered ... Let us prayerfully resolve that the new order be a better order, rooted in righteousness, broad-based on the liberty of and reverence for each and every nationality, and culminating in a harmony of peoples. Amen.

Hertz, like Luzzatto, was very much a child of the Enlightenment. War is no longer, to him, an issue of Israel versus the world of idolatry, but of enlightened civilization versus barbarism and superstition. With this hermeneutic key he interprets Bible and tradition to allow identification of his Jews with the British – equals civilised, equals Torah-true – cause.

Precisely this hermeneutic enables Jews to rally to the defence of democracy, liberal values and even, for those who think it is justified, the 'war against terrorism'.

The Jewish State

Secularism and Early Zionism

The religious proto-Zionist Rabbi Zevi Hirsch Kalischer (1795–1874), witnessing the armed independence struggles of several European nations, proposed a militarily trained home guard to protect settlements in the Land of Israel,[72] but the early secular Zionists paid little attention to the possibility of war, even defensive. Theodor Herzl, for instance, in his vision of a future Jewish state (not necessarily in Palestine), 'allotted far more space to describing how steam engines were changing the face of the earth than to the topic of the defence of the proposed state'.[73] As their naive slogan 'The land without a people for the people without a land' indicates, they were but dimly aware of the Arab population of Palestine, even though Aḥad Ha-'am, the great proponent of 'cultural Zionism,' who spent some months in Palestine in 1891, had trenchantly pointed out that there were few desolate fields awaiting Jewish cultivation, and that the 'natives' were not uncivilised simpletons, nor would they welcome wholesale Jewish immigration.[74]

Nobody, religious or secular, proposed a military expedition to take Palestine by force.

Two factors, however, impelled some Zionists at the Sixth Zionist Congress (Basle, Switzerland, 1903) to envisage a more proactive military role. Reaction to the Kishinev pogrom of 1903 had stimulated the creation of trained Jewish defence groups in the Pale of Settlement,[75] and there was increasing acceptance of Aḥad Ha-'am's assessment that not only was the land populated, but its population was likely to be hostile towards Jewish settlement. Although the majority demurred, some of the younger delegates including Vladimir Jabotinsky (1880–1940), called for military preparedness. Jabotinsky fought with the Jewish units under Allied command in the First World War, and after the war insisted on the need to maintain the Jewish Legion in Palestine as a guarantee against the outbreak of Arab hostility; this led to the formation in 1920 of the Haganah, later to become the Israel Defence Forces.

These secular developments were anxiously watched by the religious. Abraham Isaac Kook (1865–1935), Ashkenazic Chief Rabbi of pre-state Palestine, urged that Jewish settlement of the land should proceed by peaceful means only.[76] Even a Jewish king, Kook reasoned, would need to consult the High Court before embarking on war, for no war (other than purely defensive) might be pursued against those who observe the Seven Commandments, and if the enemy were idolaters (this would exclude Muslims and Christians), it would still be necessary for the Court to examine their moral condition before declaring the war justified.[77] (For Kook, it was axiomatic that no such Court existed in the present day.) Later, a similar position prohibiting offensive war was taken by the ultra-Orthodox Yeshayahu Karelitz (the *Ḥazon Ish* 1878–1953).[78]

There was, however, an inherent inconsistency in Kook's stance that became evident as time went on. On the one hand, there were those who shared or further developed the irenic aspect of his teaching, and who are represented in Israel today by the religious peace movements. Kook's younger contemporary, Moshe Avigdor Amiel (1883–1946), illustrates this trend. On 25 August 1938,[79] Amiel wrote to the editor of a Jewish journal in Prague. Amiel, who was at that time Chief Rabbi of Tel Aviv, felt that his criticism of the Zionist policy of restraint (see below) had been misunderstood. He makes clear in his letter that what he had objected to was not restraint, but the impression given by the secular Zionists that military restraint was an act of generosity towards the Arabs. Far from it, it was an *absolute* demand of Torah law, for 'Thou shalt not kill' applied irrespective of whether the victim was Arab or Jew, and was the basis of Jewish ethics:

> In my opinion, even if we knew for certain that we could bring about the Final Redemption [by killing Arabs] we should reject such a 'Redemption' with all our strength, and not be redeemed through blood. Moreover, even if we were to apprehend several Arab murderers, if there was the slightest possibility that one of them was innocent we should not touch them, lest the innocent suffer.[80]

On the other hand, Kook's own son, Tzvi Yehuda (1891–1982) focused on his father's irredendist concept of Redemption through return to the Land: '... the establishment of Jewish sovereignty over Eretz Yisrael is a commandment of the Torah'.[81] Tzvi Yehuda demanded that no land within the biblical boundaries of Israel be given up voluntarily once settled by Jews, though he did not advocate aggressive conquest. His followers are found today among the religious in the 'settler' movement.

The Israel Defence Forces

Until the mid-1930s the Zionist leadership in Palestine permitted defensive action only; the policy of *havlaga*, or restraint, was maintained even in the face of the Arab riots of 1920, 1921, 1929 and 1936, and only slightly modified when the British Captain Orde Wingate insisted on the need to take action to prevent further massacres of Jews. It is in the 1930s that the concept of *tohar ha-nesheq* 'purity of arms' emerges, demanding minimum force in the attainment of military objectives, and discrimination between combatants and non-combatants.[82] Despite doubts in the face of indiscriminate terrorism, *åohar ha-nesheq* remains the guiding rule for the Israeli forces.

The concepts of *havlaga* and *åohar ha-nesheq* arise out of:

● the secular, reformist and neo-Orthodox stress on the ethical and moral values of Judaism;
● extrapolation from the *halakha* on personal relationships to that on international relationships; and
● the desire for moral approval, and hence political support, from the world community, combined with the naive belief that military restraint would attain these objectives.

These foundations have sustained a fair degree of consensus among Jews, both religious and secular.

Some extracts from the Israel Defence Forces' (IDF) official Doctrine Statement will amplify these comments.[83]

The IDF Mission is:

● to defend the existence, territorial integrity and sovereignty of the state of Israel; and
● to protect the inhabitants of Israel and to combat all forms of terrorism which threaten the daily life.

Basic Points in the Security Doctrine stem from the notion that 'Israel cannot afford to lose a single war.' The IDF stance is 'defensive on the strategic level, no territorial ambitions'; war should be avoided by political means, but a credible deterrent posture maintained.

At the Operational Level, 'the IDF is subordinate to the directions of the democratic civilian authorities and the laws of the state. Its Basic Values include "Human Dignity – The IDF and its soldiers are obligated to protect human dignity. Every human being is of value regardless of his or her origin, religion, nationality, gender, status or position."'

The values are defined as:

- Human Life – The IDF servicemen and women will act in a judicious and safe manner in all they do, out of recognition of the supreme value of human life. During combat they will endanger themselves and their comrades only to the extent required to carry out their mission.
- Purity of Arms – The IDF servicemen and women will use their weapons and force only for the purpose of their mission, only to the necessary extent and will maintain their humanity even during combat. IDF soldiers will not use their weapons and force to harm human beings who are not combatants or prisoners of war, and will do all in their power to avoid causing harm to their lives, bodies, dignity and property.
- Discipline … IDF soldiers will be meticulous in giving only lawful orders, and shall refrain from obeying blatantly illegal orders.

The IDF Doctrine Statement is not, of course, a religious document. Nevertheless, it commands broad acceptance among the religious, and that is because of the modern reading of traditional sources which, partly through Zionism, has absorbed both secular and universal ethical elements.

Rabbinic Debates in Modern Israel

Israel's need for military defence has generated considerable debate among the religious, and this is reflected in the large number of rabbinic responsa, addressed mainly to individual enquirers, on the conduct of war. Three trends may be discerned:

1　Some of the ultra-Orthodox refuse to serve in the armed forces. This may be because:
   a　they are *de facto* pacifists, believing that God will defend the faithful;
   b　they believe they are 'doing their bit' for the country by praying and studying Torah; or
   c　they are afraid of 'contamination' by the non-Orthodox, in which case they particularly object to the conscription of women.
2　The mainstream Orthodox serve in the regular forces, and consider it their religious duty to defend the land.
3　The Orthodox 'settlers'[84] (not all settlers are Orthodox or even religious, and the majority of Orthodox are not settlers) believe they have a religious duty to maintain a Jewish presence wherever possible throughout the biblical 'Land of Israel,' though few, if any, believe there is a religious duty actively to conquer it.

Shlomo Goren (1917–1994), Ashkenazi Chief Rabbi of Israel from 1972 to 1983, set the tone for Jewish discussion on *jus in bello*:

Human life is undoubtedly a supreme value in Judaism, as expressed both in the *Halacha* and the prophetic ethic. This refers not only to Jews, but to all men created in the image of God.[85]

We see that God has compassion for the life of idolators and finds it difficult to destroy them. Since we are enjoined to imitate the moral qualities of God, we too should not rejoice over the destruction of the enemies of Israel.[86]

The following are typical of the matters discussed in the responsa and allied literature. Naḥmanides listed 'conquest of the land'[87] as a divine commandment. Naḥum Rabbinowitz, presumably targeting the religious 'hawks', writes that this does not afford 'any basis for concluding that war is permitted [in the present era] for the sake of conquest of the Land. What is worse, such a reading entails indifference towards bloodshed. Such indifference undermines the very foundations of society and endangers the entire enterprise of the beginning of our redemption.'[88]

Related to this is the religious status of the Israel-controlled areas of the West Bank, and the question of whether it is permissible to risk life in holding on to them. Chaim David Halevi (born 1925), then Sefardi Chief Rabbi of Tel Aviv/ Jaffa, argued that there was a religious duty to settle in these areas, but not to conquer them by force.[89] He takes issue with some rabbis who had maintained that those territories should be defended at all costs as part of the 'land of Israel', and urges a more pragmatic view on political negotiation.[90]

Several, including the late British Chief Rabbi Lord Jakobovits, have asked, 'Can land be traded for peace?' The land they are talking about is land occupied by Israel as a result of the 1967 war, not land within the internationally recognised borders of Israel. Most, in line with the powerful advocacy of Sefardi Chief Rabbi Ovadya Yosef and Ashkenazi Rabbi Shilo Refael,[91] answered positively; perhaps the planned withdrawal of Israel from Gaza will put the matter to the test.

Is there a prima facie religious duty to serve in the army?[92] If so, does it apply to yeshiva students, who are engaged full-time in the study of Torah?[93] Halevi, like others, addresses these questions; but he also speculates on theological matters. Several of his responsa in the aftermath of the Yom Kippur War of 1973, in which Israel had suffered substantial losses, attempt to reconcile the events with divine providence.[94]

Conclusion

We must now consider how all these traditions and interpretations lead us to address the harsh realities of contemporary international conflict.

Several Jewish religious thinkers, for instance Irving Greenberg among the Orthodox and Marc Ellis among the liberals, have taken the line that Jewish 'empowerment' brings a new responsibility. They exaggerate the degree of Jewish empowerment; Israel is small among the nations of the world, and under constant threat, while the Jewish communities of the United States and other democracies have no power per se, and only limited influence on the world scene.

Nevertheless, the point is well taken; to the extent that people have power, they have responsibility to use it wisely and justly. Unfortunately, this moral stance does not get us very far. It stirs our consciences, but does not advance clear thinking about either *jus ad bellum* or *jus in bello*.

For Jews today, the question of involvement in war arises in two contexts: Israel, and participation in wars of countries of which Jews are citizens. Their religious traditions, as we have seen, afford ample resources to guide them, but must be read within a modern context markedly different from that in which the traditional sources were compiled. Differences include:

- There is general recognition of the principle of national self-rule (that is, imperialism is rejected), though it is not always clear what constitutes a nation.
- At a global level, and in most instances even at the national level, religious pluralism is accepted (that is, individual religious freedom must be guaranteed, and it is not acceptable to impose religion by force).
- International communications are better than ever before, and there is at least a semblance of international law and order independent of religious authority.
- Modern armaments are capable of inflicting large-scale damage, but not of discriminating effectively between combatants and non-combatants.

These differences set the parameters within which a Jewish theologian has to re-evaluate traditional sources. On this basis, they might reasonably conclude:

- Every attempt should be made to settle international disputes by negotiation, not by war nor by the threat of war.
- The only possible just wars are defensive, 'defence' being understood as defence of national territorial integrity and/or the physical safety of citizens. In extreme cases, attempted 'cultural genocide' might afford grounds for defensive war.
- Such wars are not only permissible, but mandatory; in appropriate circumstances there is a duty to assist other nations in their defence.
- The extent to which perceived threat rather than the actual onset of hostilities justifies pre-emptive warfare is a matter for judgement in particular cases. Deterrent (preventive) wars, aiming to stop potential enemies getting to the point at which they might threaten, are less justifiable.
- Territorial or religious expansion does not justify war.

As to the conduct of war:

- Minimum casualties should be inflicted to attain legitimate objectives. This is not the same as minimum force. The threat, or even the use, of maximum force may shorten a conflict and minimise casualties.
- If at all possible, non-combatants should be spared. The difficulty of exercising such discrimination with modern weapons of mass destruction means that it is not always possible to spare non-combatants; but on the other hand, it would be absurd for a country to surrender to an aggressor simply to save the life of one non-combatant hostage.
- If at all possible, there should be no recourse to nuclear, biological and chemical weapons, or other weapons destructive of the environment.
- Hostages should not be taken; prisoners' rights should be respected.

As the phrase 'if at all possible' indicates, there are few if any absolutes in the conduct of war. A document such as the 1949 Geneva Convention IV Relative to the Protection of Civilian Persons in Time of War,[95] and its subsequent Protocols, may attempt to define categories of non-combatants, or may recommend that hospitals be sited as far as possible from military objectives (Article 18), but this is of little help where opposing combatants are targeting hospitals or deliberately siting their own military units in hospitals in order to use the sick as hostages.

Standards can be adopted unilaterally, or set by international agreement, but the moral dilemma arises of whether a party that ignores the standards can be allowed through its perpetration of evil to gain ascendancy over the moral side. Article 7 No. 1 of the 1981 UN Weapons Convention candidly states: 'When one of the parties to a conflict is not bound by an annexed Protocol, the parties bound by this Convention and that annexed Protocol shall remain bound by them in their mutual relations'.[96] But they are not bound by them in their relations with the unbound party.

The legal formulation by no means determines the moral position. However, only a 'party' with overwhelming military superiority can afford to be generous towards an unscrupulous foe.

Other interesting questions remain:

- What constitutes 'competent authority' to declare war? Traditional Judaism, we have seen, requires a Great Court of 71 justices, as well as divine approval through the oracle of the High Priest, for a 'voluntary' war. But as the only allowable wars (in the present world order) are defensive, this unattainable requirement need not be invoked. Is the United Nations the competent authority? In the case of defensive wars, it is unrealistic to expect a country under attack to await authorisation from the UN before defending itself, just as it would be unrealistic to expect a citizen who is about to be mugged to await police authorisation before defending him or herself. That is why

Article 51 of the UN Charter permits self-defence: 'Nothing in the present Charter shall impair the inherent right of individual or collective self-defence if an armed attack occurs against a Member of the United Nations, until the Security Council has taken measures necessary to maintain international peace and security.'[97] The only competent authority is therefore the legitimate national government of the defending state.

- Terrorism is difficult to fit into any of the traditional categories. If it is state-sponsored, or permitted by a host state, it can be classified as an act of war. Alternatively, it could be viewed as a form of hostage-taking.
- The taking of hostages is clearly forbidden by the Jewish sources, since it involves both depriving non-combatants of their freedom, and the credible threat of violence against them. On the other hand, traditional sources seem unanimous that one should not yield to an enemy who *has* taken hostages, even though refusal to concede to the hostage-taker's demands may result in harm to innocent hostages.[98]
- What constitutes 'territorial expansion'? Where there is a territorial dispute between two nations, as between Israelis and Palestinians, what appears to one side as expansion appears to the other side as recovery of the homeland.

Although the religious principles for engagement in and the conduct of war seem clear, their application in practice is hard to determine. The acute questions that arise in modern warfare tend to be about the assessment of particular situations. For instance, if Iraq under Saddam Hussein had posed a serious (how serious?) threat to the security of the United States or any of its allies (including Israel), and if the threat could not be averted by diplomatic means, *jus ad bellum* would have permitted the United States and its allies (including Britain) to wage war against Iraq. What was questionable was not the principle, but the assessment of the situation.

Likewise, if it was clear either that the Israeli assessment of the Palestinian threat was objectively correct, or that Palestinian accounts of Israel's actions and intentions were objectively correct, it would not be hard to know what to do. The doubts arise through the lack of consensus as to salient facts, including the aims of the other side, through subjectivity of judgement, through different perceptions of history, and through the adoption of conflicting value systems.

Again, *jus in bello* demands that non-combatants be spared. But this does not help us to define who is a combatant, nor does it define what degree of sacrifice is necessary to save non-combatants from harm, or what degree of restraint is appropriate to avoid 'collateral damage' when using powerful and indiscriminate weaponry.

In sum, it seems that many exponents of contemporary Judaism read the traditional texts in close conformity with secular ethics and international law. This convergence is hardly surprising in view of the interaction between secular ethics, international law and Jewish texts, including those later than the Bible. A minority of fundamentalist rabbis, however, differ on specific issues rather than general principles, in particular with regard to definition of the borders of Israel and the acceptability of relinquishing control of areas of 'historic' Israel once conquered.

All share the ideal of peace, and so we close with two Jewish texts extolling its virtue. The first is a rabbinic comment on a verse from the 'military oration' of Deuteronomy:

> 'You shall proclaim peace to it'. Great is peace, for even the dead need peace. Great is peace; even in war Israel needs peace. Great is peace, for even those who dwell on high[99] need peace, as it is said, 'He makes peace in His high places' (Job 25:2). Great is peace, for the priestly blessing concludes with it. Moses too loved peace, as it is said, 'And I sent messengers from the desert of Qedemot … [with] words of peace …' (Deuteronomy 2:26)[100]

The second is one of the most famous of prophetic visions:

> And they shall beat their swords into ploughshares,
> And their spears into pruning-hooks
> Nation shall not lift up sword against nation,
> Neither shall they learn war anymore. (Isaiah 2:4; Micah 4:3)

Select Bibliography

Note: Many of the sources on which the article is based are not available in English.

Artson, Bradley Shavit, *Love Peace and Pursue Peace: A Jewish Response to War and Nuclear Annihilation*, New York: United Synagogue of America, 1988.

Benamozegh, Elijah, *Le Crime de la Guerre Dénoncé à l'Humanité*, Paris, 1881.

Bleich, David J., 'Sale of Arms', in *Tradition*, 20, 1982, 358–9.

——, *Contemporary Halakhic Problems*, Vol. II, New York: Ktav, 1983, 159–166 (War and Non-Jews); 169–188 ('The Sanctity of the Liberated Territories'); 189–221 ('Judea and Samaria: Settlement and Return').

——, *Contemporary Halakhic Problems*, Vol. III, New York: Ktav, 1989, 251–292 ('Preemptive War in Jewish Law') and 293–305 ('Of Land, Peace and Divine Command').

Brown, Robert McAfee, Heschel, Abraham and Novak, David, *Vietnam: Crisis of Conscience*, New York: Association Press, 1967.

Collins, John J., 'The Zeal of Phinehas: The Bible and the Legitimation of Violence,' in *Journal of Biblical Literature*, Vol. 122, No. 1, Spring 2003, 3–21.

Cohen-Almagor, Raphael, *The Boundaries of Liberty and Tolerance: The Struggle Against Kahanism in Israel*, Ganesville, FL: University Press of Florida, c. 1994.

Crossroads: Halakha and the Modern World, Jerusalem: Zomet, 5747, 1987. (The volumes of *Crossroads* contain select material based on articles in the Hebrew journal *Teḥumin*.)

Daube, David, *Collaboration with Tyranny in Rabbinic Law*, London: Oxford University Press, 1965.

Gendler, Everett E., 'War and the Jewish Tradition', in Kellner, Menachem (ed.), *Contemporary Jewish Ethics*, New York: HPC, 1978, 189-210.

Goren, Shlomo, 'Combat morality and the Halakha', *Crossroads*, Vol. I, 1987, 211–31.

Greenberg, Irving, 'Judaism and the Dilemmas of War', in *Judaism and World Peace: Focus Viet Nam*, New York: Synagogue Council of America, n.d.

Hertz, J. H., *Sermons, Addresses and Studies*, Vol. 1. London: Soncino Press, 1938.

Inbar, Efraim, 'War in the Jewish Tradition', *Jerusalem Journal of International Relations*, Vol. 9, No. 2, 1987, 83–99.

Jakobovits, I., *Territory for Peace?*, London: Office of the Chief Rabbi, 1990.

Johnson, J. T., *Ideology, Reason and the Limitation of War: Religious and Secular Concepts 1200–1749*, Princeton, NJ: Princeton University Press, 1977.

——, *The Just War Tradition and the Restraint of War*, Princeton, NJ: Princeton University Press, 1981.

Kelsay, J., 'Islam and the Distinction between Combatants and Noncombatants', in Kelsay, J. and Johnson, J. T., *Cross, Crescent, and Sword: The Justification and Limitation of War in Western and Islamic Tradition*, New York: Greenwood, 1990, 197–220.

—— and Johnson J. T. (eds), *Cross, Crescent, and Sword : The Justification and Limitation of War in Western and Islamic Tradition*, New York: Greenwood, 1990.

—— and Johnson, J. T. (eds), *Just War and Jihad: Historical and Theoretical Perspectives on War and Peace in Western and Islamic Traditions*, New York and London: Greenwood, 1991.

Kook, T. Y., *Torat Eretz Yisrael: The Teachings of HaRav Tzvi Yehuda HaCohen Kook*, with commentary by David Samson, Jerusalem: Torat Eretz Yisrael Publication, 1991.

Lamm, Maurice, 'After the War – Another Look at Pacifism and Selective Conscientious Objection', in Kellner, Menachem (ed.), *Contemporary Jewish Ethics*, New York: HPC, 1978, 239–58.

Landes, Daniel (ed.), *Confronting Omnicide: Jewish Reflections on Weapons of Mass Destruction*, Northvale, NJ and London: Jason Aronson, 1991.

Lewis, Bernard, *The Jews of Islam*, Princeton, NJ: Princeton University Press, 1984.

Maimonides, Moses, *The Code of Maimonides (Mishneh Torah) Book 14: The Book of Judges*, NewHaven, CT: Yale University Press, 1949.

——, *The Guide of the Perplexed*, trans Pines, Shlomo, 2 vols, Chicago, IL and London: University of Chicago Press, 1963.

Marx, Tzvi, *Ethics Within the Reality of War*, Jerusalem: Shalom Hartman Institute, n.d. (after 1982).

Nardin, T. (ed.), *The Ethics of War and Peace: Religious and Secular Perspectives*, Princeton, NJ: Princeton University Press, 1996.

Niditch, Susan, *War in the Hebrew Bible: A Study in the Ethics of Violence*, New York and Oxford: Oxford University Press, 1993.

Novak, David, *Law and Theology in Judaism*, New York: KTAV Publishing, 1974, Vol. 1, 125–35.

Peli, Pinchas, 'The possession and use of nuclear weapons in the light of the Torah', *Ecumenical Institute for Theological Research*, 1982–83, 151–62.

Piron, Mordechai, 'War and Peace in Jewish Thought', *Revue Internationale d'Histoire Militaire*, 42. 1979, 16–24.

Ramsey, Paul, *The Just War: Force and Political Responsibility*, New York: Charles Scribner's Sons, 1968.

Ravitsky, Aviezer, *Messianism, Zionism and Jewish Religious Radicalism*. trans Zwirsky, M. and Chipman, J., Chicago, IL: University of Chicago Press, 1996a.

——, 'Prohibited Wars in the Jewish Tradition', in Nardin T. (ed.), *The Ethics of War and Peace: Religious and Secular Perspectives*, Princeton, NJ: Princeton University Press, 1996b, 115–27.

——, 'The Roots of Kahanism', *Jerusalem Quarterly*, 39, 1986, 98–118.

Roberts, Adam and Guelff, Richard (eds), *Documents on the Laws of War*, revised edn, Oxford: Clarendon Press, 1989 (contains a valuable bibliography).

Samson, David and Fishman, Tzvi, *Eretz Yisrael: Lights on Orot: The Teachings of HaRav Avraham Yitzhak HaCohen Kook*, Jeruslaem: Torat Eretz Yisrael Publications, 5756, 1996.

Shapira, Anita, *Land and Power: The Zionist Resort to Force, 1881–1948*, trans Templer, William, Stanford, CT: Stanford University Press, 1999 (reprint of the 1992 Oxford University Press publication).

Shimoni, Gideon, *The Zionist Ideology*, Hanover, MA and London: Brandeis University Press, 1995.

Sinclair, Daniel B., 'Conscientious Objection', *Jewish Law Annual*, Vol. IX, Chur, Switzerland: Harwood Academic, 1988, 262–5 (summarises Israel High Court decision 734/83).

Solomon, Norman, 'Zionism and Religion: The Transformation of an Idea', *Annual of Rabbinic Judaism*, Vol. III, 2000, 145–74.

Vermes, G., *The Complete Dead Sea Scrolls in English*, London: Penguin Press, 1997.

Wald, Marcus, *Jewish Teaching on Peace*, New York: Bloch, 1944.

Walzer, Michael, *Just and Unjust Wars: A Moral Argument with Historical Illustrations*, New York: Basic Books, 1977, 1992.

——, 'War and Peace in the Jewish Tradition', in Nardin, T. (ed.), *The Ethics of War and Peace: Religious and Secular Perspectives*, Princeton, NJ: Princeton University Press, 1996, 95–112.

——, 'The Idea of Holy War in Ancient Israel', *Journal of Religious Ethics*, Vol. 20, No. 2, Fall 1992 (note exchange with Yoder).

Weinberger, Leon J., *Jewish Prince in Moslem Spain: Selected Poems of Samuel Ibn Nagrela*, Birmingham, AL: University of Alabama Press, 1973.

Weinfeld, Moshe, *Deuteronomy and the Deuteronomic School*, Oxford: Clarendon Press, 1972.

Wilcock, Evelyn, *Pacifism and the Jews*, Stroud: Hawthorn Press, 1994.

Notes

1   Goren (1987), 223–6.
2   Weinfeld (1972), 45.
3   On this distinction, see Johnson (1977), 53.
4   Compare Deuteronomy 9:5. Michael Walzer (1992), 215, aptly observes that no biblical author 'undertakes to construct an argument on behalf of the seven Canaanite nations comparable to Abraham's argument on behalf of the Canaanite cities of Sodom and Gomorrah'.
5   Jerusalem Talmud *Shevi'it* 6:1.
6   'For the sin of the Amorites will not be total until then' (Genesis 15:16) is a justification of the Israelite conquest on the grounds that God would not have permitted the Canaanites to be destroyed unless and until their evil justified it.
7   *De Indis*, Sect. II, 16, cited by Johnson (1977), 156–7.
8   Weinfeld (1972) compares Deuteronomy's military orations with those to be found in Herodotus and Thucydides; they are 'literary programmatic creations and do not convey the actual content of speeches delivered in concrete circumstances' (51). He attributes them to the scribes of Josiah's Reform (158 f.).
9   Some English translations have 'lay in wait'.
10 The Hebrew *naḥal* may be translated 'valley' or 'inheritance'; Rabbi Mani interprets the verse as hinting that Saul was troubled about the means by which he was to secure possession of the land for Israel.
11 The allusion is to the atonement ceremony to be performed by representatives of the town nearest to where a slain person was found (Deuteronomy 21:1–9, immediately following the section on war).
12 Babylonian Talmud *Yoma* 22b. *Midrash Rabba* Deuteronomy 5:12 ascribes to Moses the initiative, confirmed and praised by God, to seek peace with Sihon; *Midrash Tehillim* on Psalm 120:7 ascribes a similar initiative to the Messiah.
13 Mishna *Shabbat* 6:4.
14 Rabbi Nathan, in *Sifré* on Numbers 31:7. Perhaps he wants to explain how, despite the annihilation of the Midianites alleged in Numbers, Midianite raids are reported in Judges 6. Meir Simcha Ha-Kohen of Dvinsk (Daugaupils, Latvia) (1843–1926), in his commentary *Meshekh Ḥokhma* (1927), notes that whereas Naḥmanides understands the requirement of an escape route as motivated by compassion, Maimonides regards it as merely tactical.
15 Joshua's example concerned a self-proclaimed 'Ammonite proselyte' who, if not for Joshua's ruling, would have been forbidden to marry a native-born Jewish woman. See Mishna *Yadayim* 4:4.

16   Altogether, ten nations are named in various verses, but they are conventionally referred to as seven.
17   Babylonian Talmud *Sota* 44b.
18   The Puritan Henry Ainsworth, leader of the Separatist congregation in Amsterdam, in his 1627 *Annotations upon the Five Books of Moses* (London: John Bellarmine), leaning upon Maimonides, makes the same distinction. Johnson (1977), footnote p. 131, comments that 'this distinction overrides any that might be attempted between offensive and defensive war'; he is incorrect.
19   Inbar (1987), 86 and note 6 on 98, points to the distinction between pre-emptive and preventive war. He cites *Lehem Mishneh* who interprets Maimonides' expression 'war to enlarge the borders of Israel' (Mishneh Torah, *Melakhim* 5:1) as preventive war, to deter potential aggressors. (Inbar wrongly attributes *Lehem Mishneh* to Joseph Karo; the author was the Salonika-born rabbi Abraham ben Moses di Boton, 1545?–1588.)
20   That the rabbinic tradition is not entirely anti-imperialist is demonstrated by a midrash such as *Targum Sheni* on Esther (probably eighth century) that wildly exaggerates the extent of the dominions of Solomon and Ahab.
21   The Urim and Tumim (Exodus 28:30), the precise nature of which is a matter of debate. The oracular function assumed by the rabbis is hinted at in Ezra 2:62; Nehemiah 7:65.
22   Mishna *Sanhedrin* 1:5.
23   Johnson (1977), 104, and 117 f., especially the section on Alexander Leighton, 125 f.
24   Inbar (1987), 94, refers only to the later comments of Rashi (*Gittin* 8b and *Avoda Zara* 20b) and Maimonides (*Terumot* 1:2) for the consensus requirement.
25   For an example of this application, see *Crossroads* (1987), 199.
26   Other diagnoses are, of course, possible.
27   Babylonian Talmud *Sota* 10a.
28   Babylonian Talmud *Sanhedrin* 72a.
29   Babylonian Talmud *Sanhedrin* 74a.
30   Ambrose, *De Officiis* 1.41.201. Augustine, *Letter* 185 (to Boniface) and *Contra Faustum* 22.74, 78.
31   Mishna *Avot* 3:2. The statement is attributed to Ḥanina the Deputy High Priest (first century CE).
32   Midrash Rabbah on Song of Songs 2:7.
33   Ravitsky (1996a), Appendix, 211–34 'The Impact of the Three Oaths in Jewish History' (some versions have three rather than four oaths), argues that 'the wall placed by the oaths between the people and its land was far higher than the historians suggest'.
34   Philo, *The Special Laws*, 219–23.
35   Ibid, 224.
36   *Sefer ha-Ḥinukh*, No. 527. The work is of unknown authorship, though traditionally ascribed to Aaron ha-Levi of Barcelona (*c.* 1235–1300).
37   Mishna *Avoda Zara* 1:7.
38   Babylonian Talmud *Avoda Zara* 16a.
39   Halevi, Hayyim David (1975/6), *Ase l'kha Rav*, Tel Aviv: author's publication, Vol. 1 No. 19. See also *Shulḥan 'Arukh: Yore De'a* 151 and *Ḥoshen Mishpat* 409. Some more recent responsa are reviewed in Bleich (1982).
40   Lewis (1984), 134–5.
41   The matter is enshrouded in legend, unknown from Jewish sources, and there is doubt as to Kahina's Jewishness. See Hirschberg, in *Tarbiz* (Hebrew), 26, 1956/7, 370–83.

42 The Khazars constituted an independent Turkic nation centred on what is now Southern Ukraine between the seventh and tenth centuries CE. During part of this time, the leading Khazars professed Judaism.

43 Ravitsky (1996), 122, gives references for armed resistance to marauding crusaders in the Rhineland.

44 See his letter informing the Exilarch Hezekiah in Jerusalem of his victory over Seville in 1055, in Leon J. Weinberger (1973), 8, with references.

45 Weinberger (1973), 118.

46 Ibid., 40.

47 The debate as to whether to engage even in defensive warfare on the Sabbath goes back at least to Hasmonean times; the rabbinic view was unambiguously that saving life has priority over Sabbath observance. Among the questions addressed by Ḥisdai Ibn Shaprut to the Jewish Khazar king *c.* 960 was whether war abrogates the Sabbath; Ḥisdai was not in doubt about the law, but interested to know Khazar practice.

48 Levine, D. (ed.), *The Bustan al-Ukul by Natanaël Ibn al-Fayyumi*, with an English translation (1908; repr. 1966), *The Garden of Wisdom*. New York, English 40 Arabic 24.

49 Maimonides, *Mishneh Torah: Melakhim* 7:15. RaDBaZ, who traces Maimonides' rulings to their sources, comments laconically: 'Some of this is in midrashim, and some the Master compiled on the basis of biblical verses.'

50 Numbers 18:20, 23; Deuteronomy 18:1, 2.

51 Maimonides *Mishneh Torah: Shemiṭa v'Yovel* 13:12,13.

52 Aquinas, Thomas, *Summa Theologicæ* 2:2 40:2; *Corpus Juris Canonici: Decretum* Quaest. VIII, Cans. IV, XIX.

53 This treatise, like the 'Peace of God' declared at the Council of Chanoux in 988, is concerned with the sacredness of the lives of Christians, that is with internecine Christian warfare; there is no evidence that immunity was applicable to clergy and non-combatants on idolaters or heretics.

54 The original Arabic is *al-ḥaqq*, which could be a term for God.

55 Maimonides, *Guide* 1:54. The point is made even more briefly in 1:36. The emphases are the translator's (Shlomo Pines); they indicate Hebrew words within the Arabic text.

56 Aquinas, Thomas, *Summa Theologicæ* 2:2 40:1: *requiritur ut sit intentio bellantium recta*. Thomas was acquainted with the *Guide* in Latin translation, and occasionally acknowledges a debt to it, but in this case his model was Gratian (his citation from Augustine is unidentifiable).

57 No. 3 of the supplementary list of Positive Commandments in his Notes on Maimonides' *Sefer ha-Mitzvot*.

58 Arama, *Aqedat Isaac* No. 81 on Numbers, cited by Ravitsky (1996b), 121–2. See also No. 74, and Munk, Eliyahu (trans.) (1986), *Akeydat Yitzchak: The Commentary of Isaac Arama on the Torah* (condensed version), 2 vols. Jerusalem: Rubin, MA, 726 f. and 791 f.

59 'Perfect' here is understood as possessing the true religion: Abravanel appears to offer the same justification for conquest as the Conquistadores themselves!

60 Summary is necessary on account of his prolix style. The Commentary on Deuteronomy has not, so far as I am aware, been translated into English.

61 Book 5, Chapter 6 (Penguin, 402). See also Book 1, Chapter 24 on war as a continuation of policy by other means.

62 Bleich (1983), 165, citing *Ḥatam Sofer: Yoré De'ah* 19.

63 Bleich (1983), 166, citing *Ḥatam Sofer* 6:29.

64 *Ha'ameq Davar* on Genesis 9:5, basing himself on B *Shavu'ot* 35; he makes a similar comment on Deuteronomy 20:8.
65 *Mishna Berura* 329:17.
66 Bleich (1983), 165, citing *Zera' Abraham* 24.
67 *Encyclopaedia Judaica*, s.v. Zemba.
68 This is the theme of Mendelssohn's well-known and frequently translated *Jerusalem*.
69 Mendelssohn, Moses, *Anmerkungen zu des Ritters Michaelis Beurteilung des ersten Theils von Dohn, über die bürgeliche Verbesserung der Juden*, in *Moses Mendelssohns Gesammelte Schriften*, Leipzig 1843, Vol. 3, 365–7.
70 Luzzatto, 157. Walzer (1996), 101, citing this at second hand, unfortunately lacks the final sentence.
71 Hertz (1938), 25–9.
72 According to Shapira (1999), 16, the proposal is in Kalischer's *Derishat Zion* (1862). I have not located it there, and Shapira's footnote cites only Moses Hess's *Rome and Jerusalem*, New York edn, 106.
73 Shapira (1999), 10.
74 Aḥad Ha-'am ('one of the people') was the pseudonym adopted by Asher Hirsch Ginsberg (1856–1927). He composed his essay *Emet me-Erets Israel* (the first of two with that title) on 21 Iyar 5651 (1891) on board ship en route from Jaffa to Odessa, and it was published later that year in the Hebrew journal *Ha-Melits*, 13–24, Sivan 5651.
75 That is, the areas under Russian domination where Jews were permitted to live.
76 Even so, he refused a compromise, acceptable to the secular Zionist leadership, that might have acknowledged Muslim title to the Western Wall. Samson and Fishman (1996), xv–xvi.
77 Ravitsky (1996b), 116, based on Kook, T. Y. (1962–3), *Igrot R'ayah*, Jerusalem: Mosad Harav Kook, Vol. 1, 140.
78 Ravitsky (1996b), 116, based on Karelitz's notes on Maimonides' Code *Melakhim* 5:1 in the Jerusalem 1957 edition.
79 It is dated 25 Ab 5698.
80 The letter (in Hebrew) was republished in *Teḥumin* X, 148.
81 *Torat Erets Yisrael*, 165.
82 See Elliot Dorff's remarks in Landes (1991), 177–9.
83 The extracts are excerpted from the English text on <http://www.idf.il>.
84 'Settlers' does not capture the religious dimension of the Hebrew term *mitnaḥ'lim*, 'those who take possession of a rightful inheritance'.
85 Goren (1987), 211. Goren is at some pains to establish that the correct text of Mishna *Sanhedrin* is 'Therefore man was created singly, to teach us that one who causes the loss of a single life is considered by the Torah as though he has caused the loss of an entire world …' and not as in some copies, 'one who causes the loss of a single *Jewish* life'; his reading has manuscript support.
86 Ibid., 215.
87 We remarked above that he probably meant no more than 'living in'.
88 Rabbinowitz in *Teḥumin*, Vol. 5, 1984, 184, cited by Ravitsky (1996b), 118.
89 Halevi *'Ase l'kha Rav*, Vol. 3, No. 60, 366–7.
90 Ibid., No. 61, and also his *Dat u-Medina*, 49. There is a fuller discussion by Saul Israeli, Halevi and Mordecai Breuer in the Hebrew publication *Af Sha'al*.
91 Their papers were published in 1980 by the religious peace movement, *Oz v'Shalom*, for whom they had been written. They were republished in *Teḥumin*, 10, 5749, 1989.
92 Ibid., No. 58.

93   Halevi, *'Ase l'khla Rav*, Vol. 1, No. 21.

94   Ibid., Nos 7–9.

95   Roberts and Guelff (1989), 271 ff.

96   UN Convention on Prohibitions or Restriction on the Use of Certain Conventional Weapons Which May be Deemed to be Excessively Injurious or to Have Indiscriminate Effects. Roberts and Guelff (1989), 473 ff.

97   Chapter VII Article 51 of the Charter of the United Nations. The text is available on the United Nations website. International lawyers have argued that this permission extends to pre-emptive strikes.

98   Mishna *Terumot* 8:12, and Daube (1965).

99   Angels.

100 *Sifré* Deuteronomy 199.

Chapter 7

Just War in the *Mahābhārata*

Nick Allen

The *Mahābhārata* is a lengthy Indian epic, composed in Sanskrit, the classical language of India. Originally an oral tradition, the epic probably began to be written down around the turn of the eras, growing in length over the course of several centuries. The longest poem in the world, it is often said to be seven to eight times the length of the *Iliad* and *Odyssey* combined. Among much else, it includes the gist of the story contained in the other Sanskrit epic, the *Rāmāyaṇa*. Even today, parts of it are very widely known in India (for example, through comics and TV), and to some extent it constitutes an encyclopaedia of classical Hindu culture. However, being a poem, it is less systematic than an encyclopaedia, and often contains discrepant accounts of particular events or ideas.

Within this vast work, about one third is didactic: contributing nothing to the progress of the plot, it is devoted rather to the exposition of *dharma*. The meaning of *dharma* is notoriously broader than any single-word English translation, though perhaps the best short approximation is 'socio-cosmic order'.[1] The word covers religion, ritual, morality, justice, law, duty – how life and the universe should be, and even in essence are.

As for the main plot of the epic – the matter that is not explicitly didactic – much of it of course focuses on war. Situated right in the middle of the epic, Books 6–10 (out of the total of 18) give us a long account of the great war between the Kauravas and their cousins, the Pandavas, who are helped by the essentially divine Krishna. The war lasts eighteen days and occupies about a quarter of the epic. What comes before Book 6 deals with events leading up to the great war, and what comes after Book 10 (so far as it is not didactic) deals with the aftermath of the great war and with the fate of its survivors.

Let us pick up three of these introductory points. First, the epic can be seen as an encyclopaedia of one of the world's great archaic literate cultures. Second, much of it consists of teachings about social order and morality. Third, the didactic material is interspersed in a long account of a great war. Given these three facts, one might expect from the epic a reasonably coherent doctrine about just war.

Just Warfare

So far as concerns *jus in bello*, rules about battlefield behaviour, the expectation is largely met. What follows is based on 14 passages which state (or occasionally imply) such rules. Some come from didactic sections, but many belong to the main narrative. Most of the references are given by Brockington in his standard work on the Sanskrit epics (1998, 174–5), though I have added 10.5.9 and 12.101.24–6. Some of the rules are stated many times, others only once – a full treatment would include indication of frequency. At the start of Book 6 (1.26–33), a fairly standard list of rules is presented as a formal agreement: Kauravas and Pandavas make a covenant (*samaya*, literally 'together-coming'), and establish the rules (*dharmāḥ*) for the fighting; but the covenant is not alluded to again as such, and the epic seems to regard the rules as well-established norms.

Both in the rules and in the narrative, the focus is on duels between aristocratic opponents who are reasonably well matched. Ideally, then, one member of the warrior estate fights another member of the same estate using similar equipment and techniques – a chariot warrior versus a chariot warrior, and if one fighter uses deceit, so should the other. In general, one should not fight people who are at a disadvantage – those whose accoutrements are or have become deficient, who lack or have lost their armour or chariot, whose weapons are broken, whose bowstring is cut – nor those who are unprepared or unaware of their danger, whose chariot is unyoked, who are asleep, having a meal or grieving, nor those who have laid down their weapons, are retreating, weak, wounded, exhausted or terrified or have left the ranks, nor those who have surrendered, or are doing so, or are suppliants, nor those already engaged in a duel with someone else. Certain general categories are explicitly excluded: women and children, the aged (once), brahmans and ascetics, those from whom one has received food, drivers, transporters, drummers, conch players, foragers, camp-followers, doormen, menials or servants in charge of menials, artisans such as miners, those who are beginning a sacrifice, seeking Deliverance (*mokṣa*) or undertaking a religiously motivated fast to death (*prāya*). A few rules are referred to only in a particular context. In a club fight, one should not strike below the navel, as Bhima does when he fatally wounds Duryodhana in Book 9; and Karna (who has notably high standards of honour) seems to imply that it is dishonourable to discharge the same missile twice (somewhat as a duellist should not fire twice).[2] The mortally wounded Duryodhana deems it dishonourable of Krishna to make Karna waste on Ghatotkaca the non-reusable weapon that he was specially reserving for use against Arjuna (9.60.33) – an objection that may again be based on the rule against third parties intervening in duels.

In reality, the rules get broken, often but not only by the Pandavas: Duryodhana blames Krishna for half a dozen other ignoble acts committed during the battle, and the next book describes the massacre of the sleeping Pandava army (Krishna has taken the Pandava brothers themselves elsewhere). The infringement of the rules by the Pandavas, who generally represent virtue, is a long-standing puzzle in epic studies, and the only solution seems to be to say that there is more to *dharma* than humans and human institutions can comprehend. This should become clearer later, together with the issue of proportionality (the idea that a just war should be fought in such a way as not to constitute a greater evil than the one it is intended to remedy). But let us now turn from *jus in bello* to *jus ad bellum*, the rules governing the outbreak of war.

Conditions for a Just War

In European tradition (I follow Norman, 1995), typical conditions for a just war have concerned the authority of the leader, the justice of the cause, the failure or impossibility of other methods of settling a dispute, and the need for a declaration of war and for a reasonable hope of victory. Of these, the just cause seems most interesting and will provide my main focus, but I first touch on the others. The epic here gives little by way of overt rules or normative discussions, and the poets' attitude has to be inferred from the events themselves and from the actors' reactions.

As regards authority, the case is evenly balanced. The Kaurava leader is in effect Duryodhana, son of Dhritarashtra, while the Pandavas are led by the five sons of Pandu (whence their name), among whom the eldest, Yudhishthira, is the chief. The two fathers are brothers: Dhritarashtra the elder, Pandu the younger. The elder would normally succeed, but since he is born blind, the throne falls to Pandu. When Pandu dies, Yudhishthira is too young to succeed, and the throne reverts to Dhritarashtra, a weak figure who generally gives way to his own son. So both sides have leaders with a claim to royal authority, and it is taken for granted that kings have authority to make war.

Let us turn to the idea that a just war can be undertaken only as a last resort. Here, rights and wrongs are not evenly balanced. The Pandava side make several efforts to reach a compromise, and the Kauravas do not – Duryodhana refuses to concede even a pinprick of territory. The failed attempts to reach a peaceful solution occupy much of Book 5. Envoys travel to and fro between the two parties: Drupada's unnamed priest from Pandavas to Kauravas, the bard Samjaya in the opposite direction, and Krishna again from the Pandavas. When reporting back on his efforts, Krishna uses a recognised list of methods available to deal with conflict (5.148.7–16, Kalyanov, 1979). First he tries peaceful conciliation (*sāman*), hoping for a sense of fraternity to prevail; then he tries splitting their unity of purpose, fomenting internal dissension (*bheda*) by threats and by denigrating Duryodhana; finally he tries bribery (*dāna*).[3] Now that all three have failed, he sees no alternative to the use of force (*daṇḍa*).

After Krishna's mission, one final envoy is sent by the Kauravas, but by now the die is cast and what Uluka delivers is a challenge, not negotiation. War has been in the air since the start of the book, and the challenge seems equivalent to a formal declaration.

The Kauravas outnumber the Pandavas by 11 armies to 7, but the impression is given that both sides can reasonably hope for victory.

A Just Cause?

I come now to the central issue: in what circumstances is it moral for one group of people to take up arms against another? Again, if one looks for overt normative formulations, one is disappointed; just war is not a standard theme for moralising. When I first suspected this, I wondered if I was missing something – easily done in a work of such length, where teachings are widely scattered and by no means well organised. Of course, many passages can be found that treat *ahiṃsā* as a virtue (Sutton, 2000), and the word is often translated 'non-violence', but they mainly concern Vedic animal sacrifice, which is regarded as 'violent'. In my uncertainty, I turned to the 13 essays by Indian writers assembled by Matilal in 1989. Only one essay, Agrawal's on 'Arjuna's moral predicament', even refers to the notion of just war or *dharmayuddha*,[4] and it does so in passing, without making it a focus. As many readers will guess, in referring to Arjuna's predicament, Agrawal has in mind the *Bhagavad Gītā*, about which a few words are needed.

The *Gītā* is, of course, often separated from the rest of the epic, being regarded as the most sacred text of Hinduism. Editions, translations and commentaries abound (for example, van Buitenen, 1981, which I use). It is in fact a short part, less than one sixth, of Book 6, probably an insertion. The two armies are drawn up on day one of the great war, but have not yet engaged. Arjuna, the central Pandava brother, has as his charioteer Krishna, who is no ordinary hero: he is the great god Narayana, who has taken on mortal form. Already in a previous life he was closely linked with Arjuna, but (for reasons unstated) he refuses to shed blood alongside the Pandavas; instead, he gladly acts as their helper and adviser. In Chapter 1 of the *Gītā*, Arjuna asks Krishna to drive into the space between the two armies, and on seeing so many teachers, relatives and friends among his foes, he loses heart. He feels that it would be better to die at once than to commit the sin of killing them. Prompted by Arjuna's questions, Krishna counters his friend's depression. To refuse to fight incurs the charge of cowardice, and anyway his enemies have immortal souls, which will be reborn. Arjuna's duty is to fight, fighting is in his nature (18.59–60), but he should do so with a serene mind, without desiring kingship or the pleasures that will go with it. He should fix his mind on god – that is, on Krishna himself. Arjuna is granted a vision of Krishna as supreme god, and receives much metaphysical/religious instruction – far more than is realistically called for on a battlefield.

So, like most philosophical/theological discourse in India, the *Gītā* is primarily soteriological. It is telling Arjuna how to obtain salvation. It is not exploring the rights and wrongs of the war. As Agrawal implies, it does refer to the war as just (*dharmya* 2.31): if Arjuna dies in such a war he will go to heaven, while if he wins he will enjoy the earth. But Krishna does not address the question of what makes the war *dharmya*.

Perhaps this is natural, since Arjuna's worry is not whether the war is just, but whether he should kill people he knows. Admittedly, he refers to killing them from desire for kingship and its pleasures (*rājyasukhalobha* 1.45), thus implying both that this *is* his motive for fighting and that, although it is morally acceptable as a motive, it is outweighed by the sin of killing close associates. But Krishna ignores the issue of killing close associates, and as for the desire for kingship, he urges that Arjuna should fight without it. Krishna is recommending a middle path between two extremes. The path of complete renunciation of activity *and* that of ordinary passion-driven activity – both are inferior to passionless activity combined with worshipful devotion to god.

Thus Krishna simply assumes that this particular war is just, rather than arguing it, and a fortiori he assumes that some wars can be morally right. He thereby conforms to a cardinal doctrine of Hindu *dharma* ('socio-cosmic order', to recall the short definition), namely the *varṇa* doctrine, which states that society consists of four estates – priest, warrior, wealth-producer and serf. Arjuna belongs by birth to the warrior category (*kṣatriya*), and that is why he must and will fight. As throughout the early Indo-European world, war is taken for granted. As Hopkins put it long ago (1889, 183-4): 'peace is the ultimate goal of a happy kingdom but throughout the epic peace is proposed as an anomaly in life. Constant strife, with insidious citizens and with open foes, must always be carried on … the whole business of the whole warrior caste was fighting.' Moreover, the warrior need not regard fighting negatively, as a burden imposed by his birth. On the contrary, death in battle provides a direct path to heaven, while dying at home in bed from illness is sinful as well as inglorious (for example, 12.98.23–31).

Human Rights and Wrongs of the Kurukshetra War

Since the *Gītā* does not tell us what justifies the Pandavas in fighting this particular war, we must look more closely at the story. The many preconditions and causes of the war are interwoven in a dense nexus, which is not easy to analyse. Epic characters offer different evaluations and emphases, sometimes in dispute with each other, often commenting that *dharma* is subtle (*sūkṣma*), that is, involves fine judgements. The analyst too, whether trying to apply Hindu values or Western ones – or even, in aspiration, culture-free philosophical ones – will often be uncertain how to allocate responsibility and blame. But we need to try.

One approach is to separate the human and divine realms; as Dumézil puts it (1968: index s.v.), we often meet *causalités superposées*. At the human level, we already know the core issue: this is a battle about sovereignty, about succession to the throne. Two generations back from the main warriors, the unitary kingdom was ruled by Vicitravirya. In the parental generation, Dhritarashtra, the elder brother, was at first passed over because he was blind, but when the younger brother Pandu dies, his children are still young, and the throne reverts to the elder brother. Duryodhana is already jealous of and hostile to his cousins: he engineers their dismissal from the capital and tries to have them killed in a fire. But they survive, and on their return are granted half the kingdom, where they set up their own capital and flourish. Duryodhana's jealousy is exacerbated by the grandeur of Yudhishthira's palace and inauguration ceremony. He invites the Pandavas to a crooked gambling match at which Yudhishthira loses everything, including his own freedom and Draupadi, the shared wife of the five brothers. The brothers watch helplessly while Draupadi is humiliated. Eventually, instead of being enslaved, the Pandavas are simply exiled for thirteen years, and on return from this second exile they find their kingdom has been taken back by the Kauravas. It is Duryodhana who blocks any concessions, and a simplistic reading of events, as proposed for instance by the sage Vyasa to Dhritarashtra (11.8.27), blames the whole war on Duryodhana, together with fate.

On the other hand, much responsibility falls on Dhritarashtra himself, the official king, who in other contexts is repeatedly blamed for his weakness and indulgence towards Duryodhana – faults which he in turn blames on fate. But a measure of blame accrues to the Pandavas. Pandu only died young because he disobeyed a prohibition on making love, which itself arose from a hunting accident when by mistake he shot an ascetic; and Yudhishthira, who was a poor gambler, only suffered exile and dispossession because he accepted the invitation to gamble.

The chain of causation, if not of responsibility, can be traced still further back. In the grandparent generation, three half-brothers are involved in the succession. The eldest, Bhisma, takes an oath not to reproduce; Vicitravirya marries two princesses, but dies prematurely without an heir (from overindulgence in sex!), and the third, the ugly Vyasa, sleeps with the two widowed queens, but does so on the urging of his impatient mother Satyavati, before the queens have undergone the recommended one year of preparation. That is why the elder queen Ambika closes her eyes during intercourse and bears the blind Dhritarashtra. All these figures contribute to causing the war, but the disruption to the royal line in fact goes back two further generations: the fisher king selfishly insists to Bhisma that the throne pass to the son of his daughter Satyavati (Vyasa's mother), who marries Bhisma's father Shamtanu. The fisher king is one of Arjuna's great-great-grandfathers, and disappears from the story long before the family splits; one cannot say that he is the original cause of the war, but he is certainly *implicated*. My point is that at the human level, the causal nexus behind the war is intricate, and if we want to say that the Pandava cause is just, it is because in the calculus of justice we normally prioritise proximate causes.

Involvement of Supernaturals

However, all the human deeds and misdeeds appear in a new light when we take account of the supernaturals. We can start with the parentage of the main protagonists. Pandu is reckoned the father of the Pandavas, but his two wives are impregnated not by him, but by gods, of whom he selects the first three. Thus, in order of birth, Yudhishthira is biological son of Dharma (Socio-cosmic Order personified), Bhima is son of Wind (an old Indo-Iranian war god), Arjuna is son of Indra (king of the gods); and the twins are sons of the twin Ashvins, selected by Pandu's second wife. Clearly, if the Pandavas are led by the son of Dharma, they are likely to be fighting a just war, one directed against *adharma*; and the assumption is confirmed when we find that Duryodhana is the incarnation of the evil and destructive demon Kali, while his 99 brothers incarnate equally demonic *rākṣasas*. The argument can be taken further: thus the important Vedic gods Agni and Soma are also incarnated on the Pandava side (in Dhrishtadyumna and Abhimanyu respectively), and above all, Krishna on the Pandava side incarnates Narayana, who is often identified with Vishnu, the assistant of Vedic Indra.[5] Now the central myth of the Vedas – or even, according to some (Sullivan, 1999, 90), of Indian civilisation in general – is the ever-renewed war between the gods led by Indra and their elder brothers, the demons (*devas* versus *asuras* in the terminology of the Brāhmaṇa texts). Accordingly, we often find the Kaurava and Pandava armies compared to demons and gods (for example, 6.20.5).

One should not exaggerate the neatness of the dualism. The first Kaurava general, Bhisma, incarnates Dyaus Pitar (cognate in name with Jupiter and Zeus); his killer Sikhandin on the Pandava side incarnates a *rākṣasa* demon; and the role of Shiva raises complex issues (well discussed by Scheuer, 1982). All the same, as the translations 'god' and 'demon' suggest, it can be assumed that the gods are fighting a just war in defence of *dharma* against demons who represent *adharma*. Thus Duryodhana was hardly a free agent. His very birth condemns him to represent evil, and it makes little sense to blame him.

In coming to earth to continue their eternal struggle with demons, the gods are obeying Brahma himself; Brahma in the epic has the role of Creator, and is the senior active member of the pantheon (1.58.38). The story is that, after a golden age, the demons, defeated by the gods, begin to be born on earth. Violent and oppressive, they multiply to such an extent that the personified Earth goes to Brahma to beg relief. The god undertakes to lighten the complainant's burden, and tells the other gods and supernaturals to incarnate with parts of their being to fight a great war. After a sort of *Theogony*, a list is given of these partial incarnations, first on the Kaurava then on the Pandava side (1.61). Earth later returns to Indra's heaven, recalls the promise made in Brahma's abode, urges speed, and receives Vishnu's reassurance (11.8.20 ff.). In some of the relevant passages (Vielle, 1996, 114–23) the overburdening of the earth is attributed not to demons as such, but simply to overpopulation.[6]

Dumézil emphasises the importance of this theme by entitling his main treatment of the *Mahābhārata* 'La Terre soulagée', and he also makes the fundamental point about the linkage of human and divine levels of causation. Dhritarashtra could have prevented the war by restraining his demonic son and some of his friends; 'he would then apparently have avoided the miseries of war; but in fact he would have been opposing the salvation of the world' (Dumézil, 1968, 169). In other words, although Dhritarashtra's feebleness at first sight seems so blameworthy and contrary to *dharma*, in a larger view it plays its part in supporting socio-cosmic order.

A similar point applies to Krishna. Regarding the man-god's role in Book 5, Amiya Dev writes: 'I have a hunch that at this stage Krishna wants war' (Dev, 1989, 82), and in so far as Krishna is the omniscient god, this must be right. At a human level, Krishna's failed embassy seems a catastrophe that confirms Duryodhana's wickedness, but at a divine level, the failure fits the dharmic plans of Brahma.[7]

In other words, whatever the problems of justice among humans, from the viewpoint of the gods the war is both necessary and just – for it is scarcely thinkable that the gods' response to Earth's complaint should be unjust. But however fascinating this motif may be to comparativists (since it so closely parallels a Greek tradition involving Earth and Zeus), one must not overemphasise it. It does not exhaust the divine level in the causation of the war; indeed, a further dimension seems in some way 'deeper'.

As we have seen in passing, both Vyasa and Dhritarashtra blame the war in whole or part on fate (*daiva*). But as Vassilkov (1999) has argued, the concept of fate or destiny is very close to that of time (*kāla*), which is elaborated, both in the epic and elsewhere, to form a recognised doctrine (*kālavāda*). When Kala is personified, he is often identified with Shiva, and Shiva is god of destruction – albeit sometimes presented as creator no less than destroyer. We need to look at the relevance of this force or deity to the outbreak of the war.

As is well known, Hinduism has a cyclical theory of time, of which the relevant aspect here is the notion of *yugas* (I ignore the higher units and the *manvantaras*). On this theory, the four ages or *yugas* represent a step-wise decline from the first age, one of perfection, to the last, the degenerate *kali yuga*, in which we have the misfortune to live. During the series, *dharma* regularly declines. When in due course the *kali yuga* ends, the universe dissolves into the primal waters (undergoes *pralaya*), only to be recreated anew when the cycle restarts. Now although some epic passages use the imagery of dissolution (for example, Biardeau, 2002, 135), the great war is explicitly located (1.2.9) at the junction between the third and fourth ages; the fourth begins either at the end of the war or at the death of Krishna (Brockington, 1998, 25). This fact can hardly be overlooked since the demon of strife incarnate in Duryodhana is also called Kali, and Duryodhana's maternal uncle, the cheating dicer, incarnates the demon of the previous age. A whole complex of ideas is involved, since the names of the four *yugas* are also the names of the four throws in a game of dice, and Shiva, lord of time and of destruction, himself enjoys dicing.[8]

Although we cannot explore this complex in depth, the notions of time and fate are part of *dharma* in the sense of socio-cosmic order, and we must at least ask how they bear on the idea of a just war. So far as timing is concerned, they clearly relativise the significance of the deeds and motives of individuals, whether human or divine (not to mention the less personal force of demographic growth); whatever the decisions of individuals, the timing of the war accords with the rhythms of the universe. More centrally, the theory of time affects our evaluation of the war. Despite its being a victory for Yudhishthira (who is Dharma incarnate), the outcome is (paradoxically) not a better world, but a worse one: we must now endure the *kali yuga*.

However, we should not end this section with such a bleak, abstract and fatalistic view of the war, since a more theistic view better represents the overall thrust of the epic, as generally perceived. As Krishna says in the *Gītā* (4.7–8), whenever *dharma* languishes and *adharma* grows, he is reborn age after age (*yuge yuge*), to re-establish *dharma*. How to harmonise this statement with the *yuga* doctrine is, like so many internal doctrinal discrepancies, left to the reader, but at least the passage connects the idea of divine incarnation for this particular war with the idea of temporal cycles; no doubt it represents an early stage in the development of the later list of Vishnu's ten avatars. The overall message seems to be that if one worships Krishna and does the duty one is born to, then one need hardly worry over intractable questions of justice.

Coherence of Epic

When I began this chapter, I thought that the epic's view of the *jus ad bellum* was incoherent. On the human level, it was basically a just war against the wicked Duryodhana (even if many others contributed to the situation in which war became inevitable); but once the picture included the gods and the cosmic order, the moral dilemmas of humans paled to insignificance: the blame lay with demons or fate. But my judgement has become more favourable. First, I would now separate off the fatalistic/deterministic dimension: the difficulty of harmonising it with the free-will agency of humans and gods is an enduring philosophical problem, and rather than blaming the epic for not providing a solution, I respect it for including the problem. Second, what I took to be incoherence between the human and divine aspects of the story now seems to me to be recognition of a profound and genuine tension or polarity in the human condition, albeit one that might nowadays be expressed in different language and with different emphases.

As humans, we are still faced (and this will alas continue) by moral judgements on whether a particular war is just; and the judgements we make are still relative to our limited situation and subject to revision in the light of a larger picture. Nowadays, fewer of us ascribe knowledge of this larger picture to omniscient deities, but the idea has not therefore become vacuous. Larger pictures will become available to us (to society) retrospectively, 'in the light of history', when we can see the unforeseen consequences. Such hindsight, be it of historians or lay people, will not, of course, exhibit omniscience or lie beyond revision, but sometimes it will lead to more or less stable judgements (the Second World War may provide an instance). But it is part of the human predicament that the larger picture will never be available in our here-and-now dilemmas, however many resources we pour into intelligence services.

Personally, as a modern Westerner, I regret Krishna's ready acceptance of the warrior's duty to fight (no allowance here for conscientious objectors) and his failure in the *Gītā* to problematise the justice of the cause; but he is right in implying by his silences that when we decide to make war it is never in light of the full picture. A chasm exists between what we know or think we know when choosing to fight, and what we would like to know, what a god would know, and what we *will* know. Arjuna cannot know that the war will mean the death of all save three of the Kaurava warriors and all save seven of those on his own side, or that he will lose not only his combatant nephews and sons but also all foetuses in the wombs of the Pandava wives. The only descendant of the five brothers will be Arjuna's one grandson, Parikshit, and even he is stillborn and has to be resuscitated by Krishna. From the human point of view, the recovery of Pandava sovereignty comes at a cost that is disproportionate, as Yudhishthira certainly feels when it is too late (12.1.13 ff.). Nevertheless, if the epic is taken as a whole, this is a war that has to be fought for the sake of socio-cosmic order, and the tension between these two positions is not a sign of incoherence but a recognition of realities, an expression of the insight of the ancient bards. The epic does not treat the just war as a topic for moral discourse, but it provides plenty of material for reflecting on it.

Acknowledgement

I am grateful to Torkel Brekke and Francis Clooney SJ, who showed me before publication their essays on just war in South Asia.

Bibliography

Agrawal, M. M., 'Arjuna's moral predicament', in Matilal, B. K. (ed.), *Moral Dilemmas in the Mahābhārata*, Delhi: IIAS/Motilal Banarsidass, 1989, 129–42.

Allen, N. J., 'Imra, pentads and catastrophes', *Ollodagos*, Vol. 14, 2000, 278–308.

Biardeau, Madeleine, *Le Mahābhārata*, Paris: Seuil, 2002.

Brockington, John, *The Sanskrit Epics*, Leiden: Brill, 1998.

Dev, Amiya, 'La guerre de Kuruksetra n'aura pas lieu: Udyoga reconsidered', in Matilal, B. K. (ed.), *Moral Dilemmas in the Mahābhārata*, Delhi: IIAS/Motilal Banarsidass, 1989, 77–88.

Dumézil, Georges, *Mythe et epopée*, Tome I, Ie Partie, Paris: Gallimard, 1968.

Ganguli, K. M., *The Mahabharata*, Calcutta: Bharata Press, 1883–96.

Hopkins, E. W., 'The social and military position of the ruling caste in ancient India', *Journal of the American Oriental Society*, Vol. 13, 1889, 57–376.

Kalyanov, V. I., 'On Kṛṣṇa's diplomatics in the Mahābhārata', *Indologica Taurinensia*, Vol. 7, 1979, 299–308.

——, 'On the military code of honour in the *Mahābhārata*', in Joshi, S. D. (ed.), *Amṛtadhārā: Prof. R. N. Dandekar Felicitation Volume*, Delhi: Ajanta, 1984.

Kane, P. V., *History of the Dharmaśāstra*, 2nd edn, Poona: BORI, 1968.

Mahābhārata, Critical Edition by Sukthankar, V. and others, 19 vols, Poona: BORI.

Matilal, B. K. (ed.), *Moral Dilemmas in the Mahābhārata*, Delhi: IIAS/Motilal Banarsidass, 1989.

Norman, R. J., 'War, just', in Honderich, Ted (ed.), *Oxford Companion to Philosophy*, Oxford: Oxford University Press, 1995.

Scheuer, Jacques, *Śiva dans le Mahābhārata*, Paris: PUF, 1982.

Sullivan, Bruce M., *Seer of the Fifth Veda: Kṛṣṇa Dvaipāyana Vyāsa in the Mahābhārata*, Delhi: Motilal Banarsidass, 1999.

Sutton, Nicholas, *Religious Doctrines in the Mahābhārata*, Delhi: Motilal Banarsidass, 2000.

van Buitenen, J. A. B. (trans. and intro.), *The Mahābhārata*, Books 1–5, Chicago, IL: Chicago University Press, 1973–8.

—— (trans. and ed.), *The Bhagavadgītā in the Mahābhārata: Text and Translation*, Chicago, IL: Chicago University Press, 1981.

Vassilkov, Yaroslav, '*Kālavāda* (the doctrine of cyclical time) in the *Mahābhārata* and the concept of heroic didactics', in Brockington, M. and Schreiner, P. (eds), *Composing a Tradition: Concepts, Techniques and Relationships*, Zagreb: Croatian Academy of Arts and Sciences, 1999, 17–33.

Vielle, Christophe, *Le mytho-cycle héroïque dans l'aire indo-européenne*, Tome 1, Louvain: Peeters, 1996.

Notes

1 '*Dharma* is one of those Sanskrit words that defy all attempts at an exact rendering in English or any other tongue.' This is the opening sentence of the 6500-page study by Kane (1968).

2 'Even if I have to slay a hundred Arjunas, I will not shoot the same shaft twice' (8.1104*; the asterisk labels passages excluded from the main text of the Critical Edition – the text used here.) For English translations, see van Buitenen, J. A. B. (1973–8, Critical Edition), and Ganguli (1883–96).

3 The three methods possibly represent the three Dumézilian 'functions', in descending order.

4 This word does not in fact occur in the *Gītā*.

5 The pre-eminence of the incarnation of Narayana relative to those of Dharma, Indra and so on must be explained in terms of the development of Hinduism.

6 This motif needs to be seen as one form of cosmic catastrophe, a theme that is widely found within the Indo-European world, as well as beyond it (Allen, 2000).

7   The first person that Yudhishthira sees in heaven (though it seems that he may not stay there long) is Duryodhana, who has performed his *kṣatriya* duty of dying on the battlefield (18.1.4, 18.3.12).

8   For instance, he is seen dicing in 1.189.14, in a myth where 'our' Indra meets four Indras from previous times.

PART II
CONTEMPORARY PROBLEMS

Chapter 8

The Ethics of Asymmetric War

David Rodin

One of the oldest and most enduring images of war is that of the game of chess. Although chess is clearly an abstraction, it powerfully embodies a conception of a particular type of war, and moreover, it is a conception that has significant moral content. On the chessboard, two equally configured forces, displaying clear and distinguishable uniforms, do battle on a bounded field and in strict accordance with rules that specify how conflict is to commence, how it is to be conducted, and how it is to be terminated.

Chess can be seen as reflecting moral assessments appropriate to war in two ways: first, with its emphasis on equality and reciprocity, chess gives us an image of war as a *fair* fight between two combatants; second, because battle occurs on a clearly demarcated field isolated from all non-combatant elements, it accords with one of the most important elements of our idea of *justice* in war – that soldiers use force only against other combatants, and use due care not to expose non-combatants to risk of harm.

Yet there are forms of war that do not embody the symmetry and equality implicit in the chessboard image of war. It will be the argument of this chapter that when conflict diverges too drastically from the assumptions implicit in the chessboard image of war we experience serious difficulties in interpreting and applying standard judgements of just war theory. In short, when war ceases to be roughly equal and symmetrical, the considerations of justice and fairness, rather than supporting and reinforcing each other in a symbiotic relationship, begin to dangerously diverge.

Asymmetric and Unequal War

It is generally agreed that since the end of the Cold War, important changes have been occurring in the nature of war and military conflict. There are many causes for these changes, and the exact nature and extent of the change is still unclear and highly contested. I would like to indicate one important vector of this change, and to discuss its relevance for our moral assessment of war and in particular the just war theory. The changes I wish to investigate were dramatically highlighted by the terrorist attacks of 11 September 2001 and their aftermath, and can be grouped together under the two closely related concepts of 'asymmetric war' and 'unequal war'.

'Asymmetric war' is a new term for an old set of military practices which have grown dramatically in importance in recent years.[1] The term refers to the use of non-conventional tactics to counter the overwhelming conventional military superiority of an adversary. Kenneth F. McKenzie Jr, writing in the US strategic context, defines asymmetric war as: 'Leveraging inferior tactical or operational strength against American vulnerabilities to achieve disproportionate effect with the aim of undermining American will in order to achieve the asymmetric actor's strategic objectives.'[2]

McKenzie identifies six categories of asymmetric tactic: the use or deployment of (1) chemical weapons; (2) biological weapons, or (3) nuclear weapons (collectively Weapons of Mass Destruction or WMD); (4) information war (for example, the disruption of military or civilian strategic information systems); (5) terrorism (the use of force against non-combatants and their property); (6) alternative operational concepts which may include guerrilla tactics (in which soldiers, often disguised as civilians, do not seek to defend fixed positions, but rather to harass a regular army by conducting surprise attacks), the involvement of non-state actors as parties to combat, the intermingling of military forces and installations with civilian communities and infrastructure, using civilians as human shields, shifting the battle site to complex urban environments that degrade the effectiveness of high-technology weapons, and using primitive weapons and technology in surprising ways.[3]

'Asymmetry' is a strategic term, and though the class of asymmetric actions thus identified may seem diverse, they are bound together by an underlying strategic logic. All seek to obtain a strategic advantage from a position of conventional military weakness by subverting the paradigm of war which has become accepted, particularly in the developed Western countries. This paradigm is partly a military strategic one; it includes, for example, the growing dependence on high-technology weaponry, air power and information systems, the professionalisation of the army, and the focus on sovereign states as the main agents of international politics. But the paradigm which asymmetric war subverts and is parasitic upon is also importantly a moral paradigm. It includes, for example, the reluctance by Western powers to incur significant casualties among their own soldiers or to inflict them on civilians. The tactics of asymmetry also often utilise the 'open' nature of Western societies – the active media and the democratic accountability of leaders. As I shall argue below, tactics of asymmetry are therefore bound together also by certain ethical characteristics.

Although the phenomenon of asymmetric war is not itself new, what is new is the global importance this kind of conflict has assumed in the last decades. The 11 September 2001 attacks on the USA were spectacular examples of asymmetric attack and 'the war against terrorism' which Western powers have been engaged in since then is in essence an asymmetric conflict. The reason for the growing importance of asymmetric conflict is bound up with an observation often neglected by commentators on asymmetric war: namely that asymmetry is, so to speak, itself a symmetrical concept. That is to say, the disparity between the capabilities and tactics of adversaries that defines asymmetric war is constituted as much by the means and capabilities of the conventional power as it is by those of the non-conventional, disruptive actor.

This observation is important for understanding the historical origins of asymmetric conflict. Asymmetric tactics are typically the tactics of weakness, not tactics of choice; they are adopted by those who do not have the military capability to engage their enemy on roughly equal terms in a conventional war. Therefore, one would expect asymmetric conflict to increase during periods of great strategic inequality. We are currently living through a historically unprecedented period of military pre-eminence by a single state, the Unites States of America. It has been estimated that in 2002 the USA accounted for 39 per cent of the world's total military expenditure – a higher proportion even than that of the Roman Empire at the height of its power. If the military expenditure of America's NATO allies is added, the proportion rises to 61 per cent of global military expenditure.[4] Since the demise of the USSR, the USA has no 'peer competitor', a power capable of engaging it on roughly equal terms in a conventional war, nor is it likely that one will emerge for several decades.

This massive differential of power has two implications. The first is that groups that feel that they have a just cause against the USA (or, on a smaller scale, a regionally dominant power such as Russia or Israel) have great incentive to use asymmetric or unconventional means. In many cases, this is the only kind of military recourse available that would not lead directly to a suicidal defeat. To attempt to confront the USA on its own terms or match it in technology would be, in the words of one high-ranking Chinese officer, 'like throwing eggs against rock.'[5]

The second implication is that when conventional wars do occur with the USA or one of its allies, they are likely to be highly unequal. The war in Afghanistan and the two Gulf Wars against Iraq were in many ways conventional wars, in that they were fought between states for control over territory, primarily using conventional military means, but they were highly unequal, by which I mean they displayed a significant disparity in the ability of combatants to achieve their desired strategic outcome. With its vast superiority in air power and high technology weaponry, the USA together with its allies was able to overwhelmingly dominate the battle space and achieve extremely swift victories with little cost to its own forces.[6]

Asymmetric war and unequal war are therefore linked on a number of levels. Inequalities in conventional military power lead historically to the use of asymmetric tactics among the conventionally weak and powerless. Indeed, the tactics of asymmetry are a primary means by which weak states and non-state actors can introduce an element of strategic equality to conflict that would be radically unequal if fought on conventional terms. Thus many of today's most intractable military conflicts display elements of both asymmetry and rough equality, at least in the sense that neither side has the ability to decisively achieve its key military objectives. The Israeli–Palestinian conflict is a case in point, and the current 'war on terrorism' (in reality a conflict between the USA and its allies, and Al-Qa'ida and associated anti-Western paramilitary groups) also seems to possess this feature.

This survey of asymmetric and unequal war is no more than indicative. I hope that it will be sufficient, however, to phrase the ethical question that is to be our concern. Given that asymmetric and unequal war seem to be increasing, and that this mode of conflict is aberrant to the commonly accepted paradigm of war, how are we to assess it from the moral point of view? This question has three important components. First, we must assess the moral acceptability of non-conventional asymmetric tactics. Second, we must identify the morally appropriate response to asymmetric war on the part of the conventional power, and come to a decision as to the limits applicable to a conventionally superior power fighting a massively unequal war. The third task is to assess the adequacy of the norms embodied in the just war theory themselves to the phenomena of asymmetric and unequal war.

The Ethics of Asymmetric Tactics

When faced with the tactics of asymmetry – guerrilla tactics, WMD, terrorism, information war – the reaction of many people will doubtless be one of moral revulsion and horror. The first question we must address, therefore, is the moral status of the non-conventional asymmetric tactics. We must enquire whether our moral reaction to asymmetric war is grounded in appropriate moral considerations, or merely reflects an unfounded prejudice favouring the kind of war which Western armies are constituted to fight and which our societies know they can dominate.

Certainly, from a consequentialist perspective, the distaste for asymmetric tactics is difficult to understand. Historically, asymmetric conflicts have tended to be low-intensity affairs in comparison with conventional wars. Terrorists or non-state actors may strike at relatively unprotected civilian targets, but their capacity to do so is restricted by the often limited means at their disposal.[7] The harm inflicted in the worst terrorist atrocity to date – the 11 September 2001 attacks – is dwarfed by the harms inflicted (on both combatants and civilians) by a typical twentieth-century medium-scale conventional war. Moreover, the wars with the most horrifying costs have historically been conventional and roughly equal conflicts between states. This is because it is states that possess the greatest power and resources for the prosecution of war, and conflicts that are roughly equal tend to be protracted and costly (both factors were at work in history's two most devastating wars: the First and Second World Wars). On the other hand, asymmetric tactics can be remarkably efficient in terms of strategic effectiveness compared with harms inflicted. A classic example of the successful use of asymmetric force was the truck bomb deployed against a US base in Beirut in 1983 (probably at the behest of Syria) which led to a major strategic withdrawal of US forces from Lebanon the following year.

For the consequentialist, then, there is nothing intrinsically wrong with the tactics of asymmetry. The question is simply: do they work, and at what cost? As I have argued elsewhere, however, consequentialism is a poor guide in the ethics of war because of the extreme difficulty of answering these questions in a meaningful way. The causal effects of war are often opaque and indeterminate, and a military act can have wildly unpredictable and unforeseen results.[8] While some asymmetric acts have apparently been very successful, such as the Beirut truck bomb, many asymmetric acts of violence either fail to achieve their strategic objective, or worse still, galvanise the will of the opponent, thereby escalating the cycle of violence and making the (sometimes legitimate) objectives more distant than ever. Many campaigns of terrorism have historically had this effect.

The consequentialist mode of assessment seems most appropriate in retrospect when it is of least use (for we want ethics to function as a guide for future action). Even as a retrospective tool of assessment, consequentialism must be hedged with uncertainties and qualifications because it is often impossible to accurately assess the costs and benefits of military action, and we can only guess at the questions of counterfactual history required to assess the opportunity costs of a given action.

In contrast to consequentialist approaches, the just war theory presents a more deontological set of guidelines for assessing the justice of engaging in war (the *jus ad bellum*) and just means within war (the *jus in bello*). The starting point for this approach is a conception of persons as deserving of moral respect and enjoying certain important personal moral protections. Although the theory was not originally formulated in these terms, it is now most natural for us to think of this idea in terms of human rights. Persons have the right not to be attacked or exposed to excessive risks, and this right can be alienated or lost only on the basis of some relevant feature of the person him or herself. So, for instance, someone who is engaged in harming another may lose the right not to be killed or harmed – thus the right of self-defence, and the vulnerability of combatants in war.[9] But the non-combatants, those who are neither soldiers nor directly involved in combat operations, retain the inviolable status of the right to life. Michael Walzer described this point of view eloquently: 'The theoretical problem is not to describe how immunity is gained, but how it is lost. We are all immune to start with; our right not to be attacked is a feature of normal human relationships.'[10]

The task of assessing asymmetric war in terms of the just war theory is complicated by the fact that asymmetric war embraces a diversity of activities. However, as I have suggested above, the tactics of asymmetry, though operationally diverse, are bound together by a unified strategic conception. From the moral perspective too, they share an underlying set of characteristics which would seem to explain why we find asymmetric war morally problematic.

Each of the asymmetric tactics identified above depends for its effectiveness upon some degree of subversion of the principles of *jus in bello*, and in particular of the principle of non-combatant immunity. The different tactics of asymmetry do this in different ways and to different degrees. Terrorism involves the unjustified harming of non-combatants, and therefore represents an outright violation of non-combatant immunity.[11] The use of weapons of mass destruction by a non-conventional actor is most likely in the context of a terrorist attack against non-combatants. But even a tactical use of weapons of mass destruction against combat troops would, in reality, entail the infliction of large-scale and almost certainly disproportionate harm to non-combatants. Similarly, the most probable targets of information war would be the civilian information systems of developed countries, for example the computer networks underlying the financial, transport and emergency services. These systems are easier to target than the highly secure military systems, and their disruption would cause massive harm to the life and interest of civilians. In all of these cases, the use of asymmetric tactics is *ipso facto* a serious violation of the principles of *jus in bello*, either because it represents the direct targeting of non-combatants, or because the incidental harm to non-combatants is disproportionate to the value of the attack on a legitimate military target.

Many of the so called 'alternative operational conceptions' use and subvert the principle of non-combatant immunity in more subtle ways. These tactics include guerrilla war, in which the fighters hide themselves in the civilian population (in Mao Zedong's memorable phrase, they 'swim like a fish in the sea of people') and often disguise themselves as civilians during attacks. They also include deliberately co-locating military forces and installations with civilian communities, and using civilians as human shields. In each of these cases, combatants illegitimately use non-combatants to hide behind, hoping either to gain for themselves the moral protection accorded to the non-combatants, or to cause their enemy to kill non-combatants, and thereby gain a public relations or 'moral' victory. Indeed, it would not be an exaggeration to say that such tactics operationalise the moral dispositions of the enemy by using the reluctance of the enemy to target civilians as a source of strategic advantage. In doing so, they implicitly expose non-combatants to risk by making it difficult for the enemy to both fight effectively and to respect the principle of non-combatant immunity. Although these tactics do not themselves directly target non-combatants, they fail to give them due care and protection, as demanded by the various legal war conventions and the principles of the just war theory.

Justice Versus Fairness in the Just War Theory

So much seems to follow from applying the well-established just war principles of *jus in bello*. Asymmetric tactics are *prima facie* wrong because they explicitly violate or implicitly subvert *jus in bello*, and in particular the principle of non-combatant immunity.

But one may have doubts about the sufficiency of this answer. Recalling the image of chess, we may observe that as well as justice, fairness is a form of moral assessment relevant to war. In a conflict that is highly unequal – between, for example, a powerful and technologically advanced state and a weak state or non-state actor – how can it be fair to require the overwhelmingly weaker party to abide by the same rules as the stronger? If the weak are required to attack only fully fledged military targets, and to fight in the open wearing identifiable uniforms, then they doom themselves to certain defeat at the hands of the strong. The tactics of asymmetry may be the only way the weak can restore any measure of equality to a conflict.[12] Although asymmetric tactics conflict with principles of justice in that they attack or expose non-combatants to excessive risks, they are justified by a principle of fairness to restore balance in radically unequal conflicts.

Phrased in this way, however, the fairness objection is clearly inadequate. In the game of chess, a fair contest between players is the overriding objective of the rules of the game, and the pieces themselves have no inherent moral value. This is precisely the difference between actual war and war games. In actual war, it is the intrinsic moral value of soldiers and civilians as human beings that is the proper focus of the rules of war. The rules function to protect those who, because of their moral status as non-combatants, are immune from attack, and to minimise the harm inflicted upon those who are combatants. Notions of a 'fair' fight between the two sides, in the sense of a rough equality of capabilities, symmetrically and reciprocally deployed, is at best a secondary and subservient moral principle. At worst, it is an improper importation from the trivial and inappropriate morality of games. In neither case can the rules protecting non-combatants be appropriately traded away to equalise the chances of success among combatants.

But there is more bite to the fairness objection than this reply acknowledges. Wars are undertaken for reasons, and the just war theory is committed to the claim that these reasons are sometimes reasons of justice. The rules of *jus ad bellum* stipulate what constitutes a just cause for war.[13] Imagine, then, the case of a conventionally weak state with a just cause for war against an overwhelmingly superior enemy. If the weak state were to attempt to fight a conventional war, it would be condemned to certain defeat. On the other hand, it may have some chance to prevail in the conflict if it were to use the tactics of asymmetry, but this it may not do because of the principle of non-combatant immunity.

What is morally troubling about this situation is not that the weak party is being denied a fair chance of success according to some notion of fair-play imported from the morality of games. It is rather that the weak party is required by the rules of war to give up something that, on this account, has real moral importance in itself – the effective pursuit of just war aims. The true significance of the fairness objection then is this: if (as the just war theory assumes) war is a morally appropriate remedy to redress certain kinds of injustice, then fairness ought to dictate that it be a remedy open to the weak as well as the strong.[14] Indeed, it is precisely the weak who have most need of the protection provided by the norm of self-defence. An interpretation of the right of self-defence that effectively denied recourse to the weak while ensuring it for the strong would be a perverse interpretation indeed.

When war is fought between roughly equal and symmetrical parties, the two considerations of justice and fairness support and reinforce each other. By requiring both sides to wear clear emblems, to respect the immunity of non-combatants and follow the war convention, the fight is made both 'clean' and also fair. But in radically unequal conflict, the two considerations come apart: the war can either be clean or it can be fair, but it cannot be both. It is precisely because war is not merely a game, but a contest with important moral stakes, that radically unequal conflicts are unfair, and because unfair, also unjust.

Now the argument so far simply identifies a problem, it does not of itself dictate any solution. It does not tell us whether justice or fairness is to be preferred when the two values conflict. The problem itself is a component of the well-known tension between the *jus ad bellum* and *jus in bello* that runs right through the heart of the just war theory. The one set of rules tells us when fighting is morally appropriate and why, indeed, it may be morally valuable and important to fight and to win. The other places constraints on the means of fighting, even though this may impinge on the ability to fight effectively and to win.

The tension between the two considerations may emerge in different ways. It may, for instance, arise as a tension between consequences and rights – as, for instance, when fighting in ways that violate the rights of persons is the only way to avert a morally appalling consequence such as the victory of a deeply evil regime. Alternatively, it may emerge as a tension between collective goods protected by the *jus ad bellum*, such as state sovereignty and collective autonomy, and individual goods of life and security protected by *jus in bello*. The problem that I have drawn attention to in the case of asymmetric and unequal war is somewhat different to these well-known difficulties. The tension here is rather between the rights of non-combatants protected by *jus in bello* and the claim of the *jus ad bellum* to be precisely that – an account of *jus* (justice or right). In all of these three cases, the pivotal question is the extent to which one may trade off the two values implicit in *jus ad bellum* and *jus in bello* against one another.

On standard interpretations of just war theory, the answer is quite simply that one may not. In this sense, at least, the just war theory represents the subordination of *jus ad bellum* to *jus in bello*. This is made absolutely explicit in just war theory, for fighting in accordance with the *jus in bello* is one of the necessary conditions classically identified for war to be *ad bellum* just. In other words: if a war can't be fought justly, then it shouldn't be fought at all.

Those who support the legitimacy of asymmetric tactics would propose the following solution in contrast to the just war theory: relax the rules of *jus in bello* for the weaker side so that they can pursue asymmetric tactics that 'level the playing field' with the strong.[15] This response explicitly trades off the protections of *jus in bello* against the claims of justice represented by *jus ad bellum*.[16]

But neither of these two responses seems adequate. The just war theory response is inadequate because it makes no provision for how the conditions of recourse to war can be understood as consistent with some minimum considerations of fairness in the context of unequal power. It denies recourse to war to precisely those who have most need of its remedy – the weak, the powerless and the oppressed, those who are most exposed to unjust and predatory use of force. It therefore leaves us with an untenable account of how recourse to war could be, in even a minimal sense, consistent with the demands of justice. On the other hand, the argument that simply trades away the rights protected in *jus in bello* to achieve this fair and equal recourse is based on a misunderstanding of what the source of those rights is. If those rights were merely conventional, the agreement of like-minded parties to war to limit the scope of their harmful activities, then it would be possible to argue for this process of trade-off.[17] But I have indicated that this is not the basis for the rules of *jus in bello*. Those rules are, rather, based on deep and foundational beliefs about the moral status of the person, whose function is precisely to ensure that they cannot be traded away in this manner.

Strengthening *Jus in Bello* Norms for the Strong

I want to explore a third response to the problem, which is consistent both with the claim of *jus in bello* to be based on important human rights, and with the requirement that the conditions of recourse to war must accord with minimum requirements of fairness. Rather than relax the requirements of *jus in bello* for the weak, one may rather strengthen those requirements for the strong. Thus instead of allowing the weak party to engage in attacks against non-combatants, and to disguise soldiers as civilians, one may require the strong party to take exceptionally rigorous steps to ensure that they do not harm non-combatants or expose them to risks of incidental harm in the course of military operations.

What would this mean in practice? Clearly, it could not mean that the strong are required to observe the existing norms of *jus in bello* more stringently. For all moral rules implicitly demand a stringent level of compliance, and such an interpretation would in effect mean tolerating a lesser level of compliance for the weak. Instead, to capture the idea of a higher standard for the strong, the existing norms of *jus in bello* must be taken as a non-negotiable baseline, but the strong held accountable to a set of norms, more demanding still.

There are three ways in which we might strengthen the norms applicable to the strong. The first concerns how one draws the distinction between military and civilian objects when assessing potential targets. There are clear examples of military targets (such as military personnel and fighting equipment) and clear examples of civilian objectives that should never be targeted (such as schools and hospitals). But in between these clear cases there is a grey area consisting of ambiguously military targets and the important class of 'dual-use' facilities such as power plants, and television and radio transmissions stations that are used by the military but which also have an important civilian function. Western powers have historically considered dual-use facilities to be legitimate military targets, but a more stringent interpretation of *jus in bello* would place all ambiguous targets and dual-use facilities that have important civilian functions off-limits for attack.[18]

The second way in which norms could be strengthened for the strong concerns the required degree of certainty over the status of a potential target for it to be permissibly attacked. In the recent wars in Iraq, Afghanistan and Kosovo, Western forces have made devastating errors in which civilians have been mistaken for enemy combatants and attacked. A strengthened set of *jus in bello* norms would require certainty or near-certainty as to the status of a proposed target through clear, unambiguous and reliable evidence before authorising any attack.

The third way in which norms could be strengthened for the strong concerns the rules of proportionality. The principle of proportionality specifies the level of collateral harm to civilians that is acceptable in achieving a specific military objective. The legal formulation of proportionality is contained in Protocol 1 to the Geneva Conventions, which states that it is prohibited for soldiers to engage in any attack 'which may be expected to cause incidental loss of civilian life, injury to civilians, damage to civilian objects, or a combination thereof, which would be excessive' in relation to the concrete and direct military advantage anticipated'.[19] But there is an inherent ambiguity as to what it means for harm to civilians to be 'excessive'. A strengthened set of *in bello* norms would require the strong to take exceptionally rigorous steps to ensure that civilians are not placed at risk of collateral harm, and that the quality and habitability of the environment is not degraded. This may require the stronger side to assume risks for its own forces to ensure that they do not expose civilians to avoidable risk of harm.

Although many will see the intuitive appeal of strengthening *jus in bello* standards for the strong, others will think that this argument gets things precisely the wrong way around. They will feel that when a strong state faces a weak opponent that is already using asymmetric tactics and hence is widely violating *jus in bello*, the strong state has less reason, not more, to abide by the norms of *jus in bello*. Underlying this natural thought is the fact that many important rights are implicitly reciprocal in nature – they provide protection for an agent only so long as, and to the extent that, the agent respects the rights of others. The right to be free of physical attack seems to possess precisely this implicit negative reciprocity. Everyone has the right not to be attacked, but if I unjustifiably attack another, this right can be forfeited so that I may justifiably be killed in self-defence. One might argue that if a group violates the norms of *jus in bello* by attacking enemy civilians, then by a similar process of negative reciprocity, it is no longer entitled to protection for its own civilians.

But this argument radically misconceives the role of reciprocity in moral reasoning. An instructive analogy here is a similar military practice that has at times been justified in terms of reciprocity, though which is now rightly repudiated by most philosophical commentators and is prohibited under international law: the practice of reprisal.[20] A reprisal is an act contrary to the laws of war (typically, the killing of prisoners, or attacks upon civilians) that is performed in direct response to a similar act by the enemy, and with a view to deterring the enemy from undertaking such acts in the future. The practice of reprisal is often defended through a reciprocity argument similar to that given above, but the argument is fallacious.

A reciprocity account of rights guarantees to each individual the protection of rights just so long as they do not violate the rights of others. But the innocent victims of reprisal have not violated anyone's rights, and therefore retain full rights against being harmed for the purposes of deterrence. Reprisal is a case of punishing the innocent to deter the guilty. As such, it is reciprocal action directed at the wrong subjects, which is to say it is not reciprocal action in the morally relevant sense at all. Precisely the same analysis is applicable to the harming of civilians belonging to a group that has engaged in violations of *jus in bello*. If they are really non-combatants, then it is not the civilians who have violated the rules of war. These civilians therefore retain full rights and protection from being attacked or exposed to harm.

A second objection to my proposal questions whether it could ever be effective. The case that is of most concern to us is that in which a weak group with a just cause faces conflict with an unjust and overwhelmingly stronger opponent. But if the strong party has already violated *jus ad bellum*, why should we suppose that they will abide by the norms of *jus in bello*, let alone the strengthened norms that I am proposing? I think this concern can be met. To begin with, unjust combatants do sometimes fight in accordance with the *jus in bello*. The desert campaigns of the Nazi General Erwin Rommel are often cited as an example. If a strengthened set of rules for the strong became a generally accepted part of the *jus in bello*, there is no reason to think that they wouldn't sometimes be respected even by unjust combatants.

Moreover, it is a mistake to think that the combatants themselves are the only audience to whom the rules of war are addressed. The rules of war function in a complex and multi-faceted way. Even if a state or its military have ignored the rules of war, those rules still fulfil many important functions. For example, they guide public debate among citizens who must decide how they will respond to the actions of their state by voting or potentially engaging in protest or civil disobedience. Similarly, the rules can provide guidance for the international community that has various remedies at its disposal, including public criticism and the imposition of sanctions against a state that violates the rules of war. Finally, in case of violation, the rules may function to determine what compensation the victims of unjust force are entitled to and what level of punishment the perpetrators may deserve.

The above objection lends itself, however, to reformulation in a way that is more difficult to rebut. The point concerns what could motivate compliance with a strengthened standard of *jus in bello* for the strong. Recall that providing the weak with some minimally effective recourse to the remedy of war has moral value if we suppose that the weak do, or at least may, have a just cause. But if the strong are prepared to fight, one must charitably grant that they believe their own cause to be just. In which case, what could motivate their assumption of additional *in bello* burdens? If they really believe they are fighting for a just cause, why should they undertake to observe strengthened restrictions that will implicitly afford their opponents an advantage? This is a difficult question that demands a complex and subtle response.

I think that part of the response has to do with the exceptional prominence in warfare of illusion and moral self-deception. The great majority of combatants in war will always believe, often sincerely, that their own cause is just. There are powerful reasons why this should be so. War is a dangerous and difficult activity that always has significant moral costs. It would be extraordinary if persons with a modicum of moral sensibility could undertake it without believing that they had a just cause to do so. And yet if one looks dispassionately at the historical record of wars, including those undertaken by our own nation, one sees that a very large proportion fail (often disastrously) the test of *jus ad bellum*. Thus morally reflective combatants may believe honestly and sincerely that they have a just cause for war, and yet from an objective perspective they must recognise that there is a significant risk that they will be in error in this judgement. The problem is greatly compounded by the fact that there is no genuinely impartial and objective mechanism for determining the justice of a war independently.[21]

Moreover, one must recognise that the risks of fighting an unjust war under the illusion of justice are not symmetrically distributed between weak and strong actors. The temptations of recourse to unjust war are greater for the strong than for the weak. Because they are rich, the strong can more easily absorb the material costs of war. Because their defences are strong, there is little risk that they will be forced to fight on their own soil, with all the hardship and devastation this entails. Because the strong have professional armies, their broader society is substantially insulated from the experience of war. Rank-and-file soldiers are often drawn from the poorest classes of society, and the prospect of a return to universal conscription in countries such as the United Kingdom and the United States is remote.

For the weak, the situation is very different. A militarily weak society must bear the costs and hardships of war much more directly. The fighting will likely take place on or near their territory. Because weak communities are often also poor, they do not have surpluses to fall back on when land is despoiled or working-age men are compelled to leave their community to fight. For such communities, war will often mean hardship at best, famine and starvation at worst. For all of these reasons, there is a much greater temptation for the strong to engage in discretionary 'wars of choice', which are presumptively more dubious from a moral point of view than defensive 'wars of necessity'.[22]

If one accepts this line of reasoning – that parties to war will almost always believe their own cause to be just, yet that they will very often be mistaken in this judgement, and that the risks of fighting an unjust war in error are very much greater for the strong than for the weak – then one can understand why it may be rational for strong combatants to believe that their own cause is just while at the same time recognising the moral value of not excluding the weak from minimally effective recourse to the remedy of war. The reasoning will stem from a second-order (objective) recognition that first-order judgements concerning the justice of one's own cause are frail and highly fallible. Moreover, it is this objective viewpoint that must take precedence when we are considering the most appropriate formulation of the rules of war. If, from an objective viewpoint, strong states are more likely to engage in unjust 'wars or choice', wars which the strong, moreover, possess the overwhelming capability to win, then it is reasonable that the laws of war place higher *jus in bello* demands on the strong. The function of these strengthened demands is twofold: first, to provide the weak with a minimally effective recourse to the remedy of war, and second, to protect the inalienable rights of non-combatants not to be targeted and of combatants and non-combatants not to be exposed to excessive risk of harm in war.[23]

A final consideration, which is independent of the fairness argument I have been developing, is that the strong may have an obligation to abide by a strengthened standard of *in bello* norms in part because *they can*. Pentagon and UK Ministry of Defence spokespeople never tire of telling us of the laser-guided precision munitions and astonishing intelligence-gathering capabilities at their disposal.[24] Because Western powers have capabilities not possessed by weaker groups that enable them to achieve military objectives with lower levels of collateral harm to civilians, it does not seem unreasonable to require them to do so. Just as 'ought implies can', there are perhaps circumstances in which 'can implies ought'.

Conclusion

The proposition that the strong should be subject to more stringent *jus in bello* requirements than the weak in radically unequal and asymmetric conflicts is intended to be a novel and provocative suggestion. Yet it would seem that powerful Western states already recognise this differential burden, at least to some extent. Western military leaders are acutely aware that the strategic success of a military mission can be jeopardised by a breach of the rules of war reported in the world media, and that Western forces will implicitly be judged by a higher standard to those of other states.

Yet the record is mixed. Strong powers such as the United States and the United Kingdom employ many policies that endanger rather than protect civilians. They often use tactics and weapons designed to shelter their own troops from harm, but which impose avoidable risks upon enemy non-combatants. Thus in Kosovo, Afghanistan and Iraq, tremendous reliance was placed on air power either as a substitute for, or to reduce the dependence upon, the use of allied troops for difficult and dangerous ground operations. Even with the tremendous advances that have been made in targeting accuracy, aerial bombardment causes great devastation among non-combatants. There is evidence that in Kosovo, an explicit decision was made to bomb from higher altitudes that compromised targeting accuracy but sheltered allied airmen from residual Serb air defences.[25] Similarly, the USA and the

UK are prominent users of land mines and cluster munitions that can maim and kill civilians and render land useless for many years after their deployment. On weapons of mass destruction too, our nations show a poor example. The international community is rightly concerned to take steps to prevent the proliferation of WMD to states such as Iraq, Iran and North Korea. But if possessing such indiscriminate weapons by relatively weak and insecure states is wrong, how much more so must it be for strong and secure states such as the USA and the UK to possess them?

What I am suggesting, therefore, is an interpretation of the *jus in bello* that starts from a baseline of protection for non-combatants and soldiers, but makes the duty of care incrementally higher for those combatants that possess overwhelming superiority of force. This proposal would go some way to addressing both the problems identified in this paper. It would give proper protection to the basic rights of persons to be free from harm and attack, and it would also address to some degree the radical inequality and unfairness implicit in current interpretations of the *jus ad bellum*. By restoring some measure of balance in this way, it may even reduce one of the motivations for adopting asymmetric techniques in the first place.

Notes

1   The first use of the term appears to have been in the 1997 *US Quadrennial Defense Review Report*.
2   McKenzie, Kenneth F. (2000), *The Revenge of the Melians: Asymmetric Threats and the next QDR*, Institute for National Strategic Studies, National Defense University, McNair Paper 62, p. 2.
3   Ibid., Ch. 2. For a discussion of the ethics of terrorism and how this term should be defined, see Rodin, David, 'Terrorism Without Intention', *Ethics*, Vol. 114, July 2004, 752–71.
4   Data Source: International Institute of Strategic Studies (2003), *The Military Balance 2003–2004*, Oxford: Oxford University Press.
5   Interview with Senior Colonel Qiau Liang, quoted in McKenzie, *The Revenge of the Melians*, Ch. 2.
6   Of course, after initial victories in Iraq and Afghanistan, the USA and its allies found themselves in a very different and much more challenging strategic situation. After the 2003 war against Iraq, they have faced a non-conventional and asymmetric conflict, which they have found much more difficult to control.
7   Clearly, the destructive capacity of terrorist groups would increase dramatically if they ever succeeded in obtaining and using WMD.
8   See Rodin, David (2002), *War and Self-defense*, Oxford: Oxford University Press, 2002, 10 ff.
9   Of course, the case of self-defence and the status of combatants are not entirely comparable. For aggressors in a case of self-defence lose their right to life because they are engaged in an unjust attack. But in the case of soldiers at war, one side may be fighting a just war, and hence presumably their use of force is not unjust in the way that a culpable aggressor's is. It is therefore not immediately apparent what accounts for their loss of the right not to be killed in combat. See on this McMahan, Jeff, 'Innocence, Self-

defense and Killing in War', *The Journal of Political Philosophy*, Vol. 2, No. 3, 1994, 193–221, and McMahan, Jeff, 'The Ethics of Killing in War', *Ethics*, July 2004, 693–733.

10 Walzer, Michael (1977), *Just and Unjust Wars*, 1977: Basic Books, 145 n.

11 I have elsewhere argued that terrorism need not be restricted to acts that deliberately target non-combatants. If military force is used in a way that is reckless or negligent and thereby causes harm to non-combatants, this may count morally as terrorism. Thus some so-called 'collateral damage' to non-combatants from bombing raids, may be acts of terrorism even though the death of non-combatants was not intended either as a means or as an end in itself. See Rodin, 'Terrorism Without Intention', 752–71.

12 Of course, the likely effectiveness of such tactics must be critically examined. It has historically often been the case that the use of such tactics has had a very minimal or even counter-productive strategic effect.

13 According to modern interpretations of just war theory and international law, just cause is effectively limited to self-defence against a prior act of aggression. See the Charter of the United Nations, Article 2.4, and Article 51.

14 Of course, as Kant pointed out, since war is a trial of strength, it can never guarantee success to the just party. War is not a mechanism for determining justice, as some early Christian writers had supposed. At best, recourse to war provides a chance for the vindication of justice. But in massively unequal war, there is not even the chance of vindication.

15 Saul Smilansky considers (though ultimately rejects) what he takes to be a widely held moral view that there exists an 'anti-oppression exception' to the principle of non-combatant immunity. This exception states that weak forces are permitted to engage in terrorist attacks against non-combatants if it is necessary in combating oppressive regimes. (Smilansky, Saul, 'Terrorism, Justification, and Illusion', *Ethics*, Vol. 114, July 2004, 790–805, at 791).

16 This proposal stands in a long tradition of arguments that seek in some measure to challenge the independence of *jus in bello* from *jus ad bellum* implicit in just war theory. Michael Walzer famously argued that in cases of what he called 'supreme emergency', the rule of non-combatant immunity could be violated. The example he gives is of the bombing of German cities during the early stages of the Second World War, when England had no other military recourse with which to strike at its uniquely evil enemy. Walzer's argument is an example of 'threshold deontology', where rules are seen as having deontological force up to a point, but may be overridden in exceptional cases where there would otherwise be horrendous moral costs. See Walzer, *Just and Unjust Wars*, Ch. 16.

17 See Mavrodes, George I., 'Convention and the Morality of War', in Beitz, Charles et al. (eds) (1993), *International Ethics*, Princeton University Press, for an account of the laws of war of this kind.

18 See Shue, Henry and Wippman, David, 'Limiting Attacks on Dual-use Facilities Performing Indispensable Civilian Functions', *Cornell International Law Journal*, Vol. 35, 2002, 559–79.

19 Protocol Additional to the Geneva Conventions of 12 August 1949, and relating to the Protection of Victims of International Armed Conflicts (Protocol 1), Article 51 (5)(b) and Article 57 (2)(b).

20 See Protocol Additional to the Geneva Conventions of 12 August 1949, and relating to the Protection of Victims of International Armed Conflicts (Protocol 1), Article 20. On reprisal generally, see Walzer, *Just and Unjust Wars*, Ch 13.

21 The Security Council is the closest we have to an independent mechanism, but given the veto power wielded by the permanent members, it can hardly be described as impartial and objective.

22 This reasoning contrasts strikingly with the famous 'democratic peace argument' first made by Kant in *Perpetual Peace* (Kant, I., *Perpetual Peace: A Philosophical Sketch*, in Reiss, H. (ed.) (1970), *Kant's Political Philosophy*, Cambridge University Press, 99–102). According to Kant, republics (what today we would call representative democracies) are less likely to engage in spurious wars because the general public who must bear the costs of war have a say in the decision to go to war, unlike in authoritarian regimes. But as I have suggested here, it is arguable that today this dynamic is to a significant degree reversed. The publics of advanced Western democracies have to a remarkable degree insulated themselves from the costs of war. On the other hand, it should not be denied that there are countervailing forces that work against the prosecution of unjust wars within a democracy. For example, strong traditions of openness and freedom of speech mean that spurious reasons for war are often exposed as such – although, as the case of the 2003 war in Iraq has shown, tragically this often does not happen until it is too late.

23 It is the requirement of objectivity that explains why the amendment to the laws of war I am proposing must be phrased in terms of strengthened obligations for the *strong*, rather than for the *unjust*. Why? If the phenomenon of moral self-deception in war is as widespread as I am suggesting, then a rule which specified higher levels of obligations for the unjust would be unlikely to be adhered to by combatants in real conflicts. This is because, as we have seen, almost no combatants go to war believing their own cause to be unjust. Moreover, parties to conflict would be unlikely to assume obligations which implicitly self-incriminate them for the prosecution of an unjust war.

24 Although all are now aware of the limits of military intelligence.

25 See Luttwak, Edward, 'Give War a Chance', *Foreign Affairs*, Vol. 78, No. 4, July/August 1999, 36–44, at 40–41.

Chapter 9

Preventive War and the Killing of the Innocent

Jeff McMahan

The 'Bush Doctrine'

The United Nations Charter prohibits states to use force against other states except in 'individual or collective self-defence if an armed attack occurs'.[1] In the past, it may have seemed reasonable to insist that permissible defence must await the actual occurrence of an armed attack. Because war is usually disastrous for all concerned and to be avoided if at all possible, and because successful defence has often been at least *possible* against a military attack, it may not be imprudent for a state threatened with attack by another state to make every effort to avoid war by diplomatic means and thus to defer military action until its adversary actually strikes the first blow. It is also possible to *deter* the attack by threatening the potential aggressor both with military defeat and with the destruction, if war occurs, of assets that the aggressor values – for example, in the case of a tyrannical regime, military assets on which it depends for control of its own population.

But terrorist threats that many states now face cannot be dealt with in these traditional ways. Traditional forms of military defence are ineffective, indeed irrelevant, in confronting threats from small bands of terrorists operating covertly, often within the cities of those they hope to intimidate and coerce. And because terrorists often operate independently of targetable military or political centres and usually are not representative of any clearly identifiable or delimited group, they are not easily deterred by threats of reprisal, retaliation, or destruction of valued assets. Thus, where terrorist threats are concerned, deterrence is difficult, and once 'an armed attack occurs', it is already too late for 'individual or collective self-defence'.

Concerns similar to these were expressed in a speech given by George W. Bush at West Point in June 2002. On that occasion, Bush asserted that 'the war on terrorism will not be won on the defensive. We must take the battle to the enemy ... and confront the worse threats before they emerge.'[2] The Bush administration's rejection of UN doctrine was stated even more explicitly in its National Security Strategy, issued in September 2002:

> Given the goals of rogue states and terrorists, the United States can no longer solely rely on a reactive posture as we have in the past. The inability to deter a potential attacker, the

immediacy of today's threats, and the magnitude of potential harm that could be caused by our adversaries' choice of weapons, do not permit that option. We cannot let our enemies strike first. ... For centuries, international law recognized that nations need not suffer from an attack before they can lawfully take action to defend themselves against forces that present an imminent danger of attack. Legal scholars and international jurists often conditioned the legitimacy of preemption on the existence of an imminent threat – most often a visible mobilization of armies, navies, and air forces preparing to attack. ... We must adapt the concept of imminent threat to the capabilities and objectives of today's adversaries. Rogue states and terrorists do not seek to attack us using conventional means. They know such attacks would fail. Instead, they rely on acts of terror and, potentially, the use of weapons of mass destruction – weapons that can be easily concealed, delivered covertly, and used without warning. ... The greater the threat, the greater the risk of inaction – and the more compelling the case for taking anticipatory action to defend ourselves, even if uncertainty remains as to the time and place of the enemy's attack. To forestall or prevent such hostile acts by our adversaries, the United States will, if necessary, act preemptively.[3]

The doctrine advanced in this document – which has become known as the 'Bush doctrine' – was soon acted on in March 2003, when the USA launched its second war against Iraq, this time explicitly claiming self-defence as a justification.

The National Security Strategy states that legal scholars have 'often' made the legitimacy of pre-emption conditional on the presence of an *imminent* threat, thereby implying that legal scholars have sometimes accepted that pre-emptive attack can be legitimate even in the absence of an imminent threat. But this is a distortion, both factually and conceptually. The debate in contemporary international law concerns whether even an imminent threat justifies the resort to force. For many legal scholars take the implication of Article 51 of the UN Charter at face value, and therefore contend that pre-emption is never legitimate.

To see how the administration's claim involves conceptual distortion, we must note some familiar distinctions. The use of force to repel an attack *in progress* is *defence, simpliciter*: no qualifier is required. Defence is *self*-defence when the agent that repels the attack is also its target, and *other*-defence when the agent is a third party acting to repel an attack against another. The use of force to prevent an *imminent* attack is *pre-emptive defence*. And the use of force to prevent a perceived future threat that is not imminent is *preventive defence*. A war initiated in preventive defence is a *preventive war*.

As noted, the dispute in international law is about whether pre-emptive defence can be justified. It is uncontroversial that preventive war is illegal. It is unsurprising, therefore, that the authors of the National Security Strategy present themselves as 'adapting' the notion of imminence to contemporary conditions, thereby enabling themselves to declare that the USA will 'act pre-emptively' to threats of attack that are uncertain 'as to ... time and place'. They are, in short, asserting a right to preventive defence under cover of the less contentious category of pre-emption. As the legal scholar Kimberly Kessler Ferzan rightly observes, they are not revising the notion of imminence, but instead repudiating its significance.[4] This emerged quite clearly in a speech given by Vice President Cheney in October 2003 in defence of the second Iraq war. Cheney observed with scorn that 'some claim we should not have acted because the threat from Saddam Hussein was not imminent. Since when have terrorists and tyrants announced their intentions, politely putting us on notice before they strike?'[5] This concedes the obvious point that Iraq posed no imminent threat to the USA, but treats that fact as irrelevant.

Jus ad Bellum

While the legal status of preventive war is at present uncontroversial, it remains an open question whether preventive war can ever be justified *morally*. My concern in this chapter is to explore that moral question. My argument will be rather dialectical in structure, moving back and forth on the question of whether preventive war can be just. The conclusion I reach is that while preventive war can in principle be just, it is subject to extremely stringent moral constraints that make it only very rarely justifiable in practice. The arguments will appeal at key points to parallels with preventive defence by one individual against another, or by a group of individuals against others within the same society.

Many people feel intuitively that preventive war would be morally justified if the following three conditions were to obtain:

1   There is compelling evidence that a certain state or organisation *will* unjustly attack us at some point in the future.
2   It is possible to eliminate the threat now, but would be impossible to defend ourselves against it when the attack would occur – *or*, even if it would be possible to defend ourselves later, our efforts then would be significantly less effective or more costly, or both.
3   Peaceful means of addressing the threat have proved (or promise to be) ineffective.

In considering whether it could be permissible to conduct a preventive attack (that is, launch a preventive war) in these conditions, most contemporary moralists have recourse to the traditional theory of the just war – in particular, the part of the theory that governs the resort to war (the doctrine of *jus ad bellum*). The first and principal question that just war theory poses is whether the prevention of future aggression can be a just cause for war: a just cause being an aim of a *type* that is capable of justifying an activity – war – that involves killing and destruction on an enormous scale. The one aim that, except among pacifists, is universally recognised as a just cause for war is self-defence against armed aggression. So one crucial question is whether preventive war can count as an instance of self-defence within the terms of just war theory. In other words, does preventive defence share the features that make defence against an actual attack a just cause for war?

There is good reason to think that just war theory should recognise the prevention of future unjust aggression as an instance of self-defence, and thus as a just cause for war. The reason is that there is a clear sense in which *all* defence is preventive. One can defend oneself only against *future* harm. There is no defence against harm that one has already suffered or that one is already suffering. One can, of course, defend oneself against the *continuation* of harm that is being caused by an attack in progress, but it is still only harm that one *will* otherwise suffer that one can defend oneself against. Any harm that has already occurred or is occurring *now* is a *fait accompli*. It seems, indeed, a conceptual truth that successful defence consists in *preventing* harm from occurring.

If, however, genuine instances of the prevention of future aggression count as self-defence in the relevant sense, why have most moral and legal theorists insisted that for the use of force to be justified, there must be an actual attack in progress, or at least an imminent threat of attack? It is noteworthy that this insistence is not confined to the use of force by states, but applies also to defensive force by individuals. In the law, while a threat of imminent attack may justify an individual's resort to force in self-defence, there is no right to use force to prevent attacks that are not imminent. There have, for example, been various cases in which a woman with a history of being severely beaten by her husband has reasonably believed that her life would soon have been at grave risk from him unless she killed him in his sleep. When such women have acted on that belief, they have been denied a justification of self-defence, even when the court has conceded that their belief was reasonable.[6] In order to be legally entitled to that justification, they would have had to wait until they were actually attacked, or at least until an attack was imminent – even if at that point defence might not have been possible.

What, then, is the significance of an actual or imminent attack? The obvious answer is that an actual attack provides compelling evidence that there is a very high probability that the attacker will inflict unjust harm, or further unjust harm, unless stopped; and, though an imminent threat of attack offers weaker evidence and a somewhat lower probability of future harm, it is nevertheless above the threshold for meeting the burden of evidence. According to this view, the objection to preventive war within the theory of the just war is not that there is no just cause, but that, in the absence of an actual or imminent attack, there is insufficient evidence to establish a high enough probability of attack or harm to make the resort to war necessary and proportionate. When a perceived threat is still speculative, it is difficult to know or to demonstrate that war is necessary to avert it; and because the magnitude of the threat has to be discounted for probability, it is also difficult to establish that the resort to war could be proportionate.

These considerations, however, cannot ground a sharp moral distinction between self-defence against an actual or imminent attack, and preventive defence. For even an attack in progress does not make it certain that the victim will suffer harm in the absence of defensive action. For the sake of illustration, let us focus on cases at the individual level. Even a person who is in the process of attacking you may be incompetent as an attacker, or may suddenly repent, or be incapacitated by vertigo or the unexpected but excruciating pain of a kidney stone. Your risk of harm from an attack could be higher even in a case in which there was no actual or even imminent attack. Here, for example, is a hypothetical case in which the expected harm (the magnitude of the harm times the probability) to you from a future attack is very high in the absence of preventive defence.

The Paralysis Case

You have a condition similar to Guillain-Barré Syndrome that will, in about a week's time, cause you gradually to become fully though temporarily paralysed. Your long time enemy, whom you have suspected of being criminally insane, learns of your predicament and tells you, with a mad, malicious gleam in his eye, that he intends to kill you while you are incapacitated. Soon afterwards, you overhear him confiding his scheme to a confederate, and, on searching his house, you find diary entries in which his plans are meticulously worked out and in which he notes that he will not be deterred by – indeed, that he is even self-destructively motivated by – the high probability that he will afterwards be captured and punished. Foolishly neglecting to take the diary, you go to the police, but they, on interviewing your enemy, who was once a practising psychiatrist, become persuaded by him that you are suffering from paranoid delusions as a side-effect of your condition. There is, moreover, nowhere for you to go: there is only one hospital that has the life support systems necessary to keep you alive during the period of total paralysis.

Let us assume that, for whatever reason, there are no other options, such as hiring a bodyguard, so that preventive killing seems genuinely necessary to defend your life from an unjust threat. If so, it seems intuitively that killing your enemy would be justified.

One reason that individual preventive defence is not a justification in the law is that in domestic society, the police and the penal system are supposed to render it unnecessary. If you have reason to fear an unjust attack in the future, you should seek protection by the police or the courts. Although they too are forbidden to engage in preventive defence on your behalf, they may seek to deter or to restrain in certain ways the person or people who threaten you, and may also make preparation for your defence should the need arise. *Pre-emptive* defence, by contrast, may be legitimate precisely because the imminence of the threat precludes the operation of these established mechanisms of social protection. But in the Paralysis Case, those mechanisms have failed for reasons other than insufficient time.

Another reason why the law prohibits individual preventive defence is that it is always possible that the potential attacker will repent or change his mind. The law may seek to extend maximal respect for individual autonomy by allowing every opportunity for a change of heart. But, as I noted earlier, the possibility of such a change is present as well in the case of an imminent attack, and even in the case of an attack in progress. The difference is one of probability, which normally varies with the temporal proximity of the threatened harm. But, in principle, the probability of harm from a non-imminent threat could be greater than that from an imminent attack or an attack in progress, and certainly, as I noted earlier, the *expected harm*, which is a function of the magnitude of the harm and the probability of its occurrence, may be greater from a non-imminent threat than from either an imminent threat or an attack in progress.

It seems, in summary, that there can be a strong case, in a restricted range of circumstances, for the moral permissibility of individual preventive defence. And it seems reasonable to suppose that the same kind of case can be made for preventive war when relevantly analogous conditions obtain in relations between states, or between a state and a terrorist organisation. The case may be very hard to make, but that will be because there may yet be ways of addressing the threat other than resorting to war, or because the probability of future attack is insufficiently high or the evidence insufficiently strong. In the language of just war theory, the principal constraints on preventive war may seem to have more to do with the requirements of necessity and proportionality than with the requirement of just cause.

Consistency and Consequences

There are, of course, additional objections to preventive war. One is that the justifications for preventive war as they are actually asserted tend to be overly permissive in their implications. For example, when the Bush administration sought to justify the second war against Iraq as a war of self-defence (as well as an instance of humanitarian intervention and an enforcement of an earlier UN resolution), it appealed primarily to three claims: that Iraq possessed weapons of mass destruction, that it had a recent history of aggressive war, and that it had indulged in bellicose rhetoric directed against the USA. But, as critics immediately observed, all of these claims were also true, *mutatis mutandis*, of the USA itself, with the Bush administration particularly noisy in issuing threats against Iraq, Iran and North Korea. But no one in the administration would have conceded that any of those states had a right to attack the USA in preventive self-defence. So the challenge is to formulate conditions in which preventive war is permissible that, when applied universally, have implications that one can accept.[7]

One response that is open to the Bush administration is to claim that preventive war is justifiable only when a state must defend itself against a threat of *unjust* attack. It could then be argued that whereas Iraq, Iran and North Korea pose (or, in the case of Iraq, posed) a threat of unjust aggression, whatever threats the USA might pose are not unjust or aggressive, but 'reactive' (to borrow the term used by the authors of the National Security Strategy).

It is clearly right that, if preventive war can ever be justified, it can only be in response to an *unjust* threat. But this cannot help the Bush administration to evade a charge of inconsistency, for there are a great many states that have been victims of unjust American intervention (Cuba, Chile, Guatemala), American military aggression (Vietnam, Laos, Cambodia), American terrorism (Libya) and

American-sponsored terrorism (Nicaragua, El Salvador) in recent decades. Nevertheless, the pious notion that the USA never poses an unjust threat does point to a second obvious objection to preventive war, which arises from the fact that Americans are not alone in thinking that whatever threats they face must be unjust, while any threats they pose must be just. For most citizens of most countries cherish the same patriotic delusions about their own country. And this means that, even if we could identify a plausible doctrine of preventive war that would specify the precise conditions in which such a war could be justified, the doctrine would be bound to be regularly misapplied. Acknowledgement of the permissibility of preventive war would, in practice, as Michael Walzer has argued, be likely to encourage the initiation of wars wrongly believed or claimed to be necessary for national self-defence.[8]

There are thus objections to preventive war that focus on considerations of consistency and consequences. Although in principle states may occasionally have compelling evidence that a future attack is sufficiently probable to make preventive war both necessary and proportionate, in practice it is likely that states would appeal for justification to criteria they could not rationally universalise and that a general acceptance of the permissibility of preventive war would encourage unnecessary wars or even provide a cover for wars of aggression.

Justice

While these considerations are important, they seem to leave out something significant. Thus far I have been assuming that the significance of present aggression is merely evidentiary, and therefore that preventive war can be genuinely defensive and that the prevention of future aggression comes within the scope of self-defence as a just cause for war. I have been assuming, in short, that preventive war can in principle be *just*. But there are objections to that assumption. The fundamental problem with defences of preventive war, such as that given in the National Security Strategy, that focus on the concerns of the state that perceives a need for preventive action is that they omit any mention of what the target of preventive action must have done to make it morally *liable* to military attack, so that it would not be *wronged* by the use of force against it. If those attacked are not liable to attack but are innocent in the relevant sense, preventive war may be prudentially rational, but may not be *just*.

It may be helpful in understanding what is at issue here to consider a parallel with punishment.[9] One major justification for punishment – perhaps the most widely accepted and least controversial justification – is that punishment protects innocent people from further harm by the criminal. One of the major functions of imprisonment, for example, is to keep criminals away from other people, where they are unable to cause further harm. One function of punishment, in other words, is preventive defence.

Suppose we were to decide that preventive social defence is the *only* legitimate aim of punishment. Suppose, that is, that we were to become convinced that the other rationales for punishment – those concerned with retribution, deterrence, reform and so on – are mistaken. Punishment, in our view, would then be entirely a matter of preventive defence. But it could still be rational to retain our insistence that punishment is *just* only when applied to those who have actually committed a crime. For it could be held that only by committing an actual offence can people become morally *liable* to punishment, even when the sole aim of punishing people would be to protect society from them in the future.

It is not merely coincidental that the same administration that has claimed a right to conduct preventive wars is also working to undermine the traditional prohibition of preventive detention. Yet the sense that preventive detention is unjust remains pervasive. It is true, of course, that the law lets certain instances of preventive action in through the back door even in the absence of a genuinely harmful offence. It does this by declaring that certain forms of preparation to commit a crime are themselves crimes. Thus conspiracy to commit a certain crime may itself be a crime. But even the conspiracy laws are confirmation of rather than counter-examples to the claim that certain specific forms of wrongful *action* are necessary for liability to punishment. The justification for punishment in any given instance – even when the sole aim of punishment is preventive defence – has to include more than just evidence that a future offence is likely. In insisting that there must be an actual offence, we reveal a concern with more than just the evidentiary significance of the criminal act.

Suppose that there were certain forms of evidence of future criminal action that were statistically *more* reliable than actual instances of criminal behaviour. In the *Future Killer Case*, for example:

> we discover a rare combination of genes whose possessors have a greater than ninety-nine percent probability of becoming serial killers, even after they have been subjected to the most effective forms of psychiatric and pharmaceutical therapy. This gene combination is identified in a child of five who has been brought in for testing by his parents because he already shows a morbid fascination with serial killers, torments animals, bullies his playmates, keeps a collection of animal bones, and so on. Yet so far he has committed no actual criminal offense.

Would it be permissible to lock this child up for the remainder of his life in order to prevent him from later killing innocent people?[10]

Some people, perhaps many, will reluctantly concede that this case is an exception. They will accept that it could be permissible to keep the child away from others if that were the least harmful way we could effectively protect ourselves from the child's predictable tendency to kill people. Those who take this view would, of course, be reluctant to accept that to lock the child away would be an instance of *punishment* – even if, as we are imagining, the sole function of punishment is preventive defence. They might instead regard the forced sequestering of the child as a case of restraining the dangerously insane. But suppose the child is fully rational, and indeed unusually clever, which makes him all the more dangerous. It is not obvious that a powerful disposition to kill people is necessarily a manifestation of mental illness. So perhaps it would be better to view preventive action taken against the child as a lifelong *quarantine*.

But notice that our concern with the labelling of the action reflects an implicit recognition that there are two general forms of justification for forcibly keeping a dangerous person away from other people: one that focuses on the overwhelming necessity of protecting innocent people, and another that appeals to the claim that the person has done something that makes him morally liable to preventive action. The justification for subjecting a person to quarantine is normally of the former sort, while the justification for anything we are willing to call punishment must be of the latter. If we reject retributivism, the relevant form of liability will not be *desert*, but the insistence on some form of liability reflects our sense that anything describable as *punishment* must be held to standards of justice, and not merely, as in the case of quarantine, to standards of utility.

If, therefore, we were to accept that it would be permissible forcibly to keep the child away from other people, we would have to concede that our treatment of the child would be in an important sense unjust. It would wrong the child by inflicting on him a grave and enduring harm to which he had done nothing to make himself liable, and it would do this as a means of protecting or reducing risks to *other* people. The child would be innocent in the relevant sense; he would, as some would say, have done nothing to lose those rights he has by virtue of being a person. (I will, at any rate, *assume* that locking the child away would harm him. It could be argued, however, that locking him away would actually be best for him, even if it would in a sense be against his interests. If he were my child, I would want what would be best for him. I would want, *for his sake*, that he not become a murderer. Even putting aside the interests of his potential victims, I would want him to be locked away.)

When a person commits an actual offence, the constraint against harming him or restricting his liberty is weakened or removed by his own action. This is what is implied by the claim that he makes himself liable to preventive action. In the Future Killer Case, by contrast, the constraint remains in place but (*if* it is permissible, all things considered, to quarantine the child) is *overridden* by the necessity of protecting the innocent. (Considerations of proportionality still apply, of course; thus, while it is perhaps permissible to quarantine the child, it would not be permissible to kill him, even if killing him promised a higher probability of preventing him from ever killing anyone. If we were to change the case by stipulating that the *only* effective way to prevent the child from killing innocent people was to kill him, then killing might be proportionate.)

Because our action would be unjust to the child, we would owe him forms of compensation that would not be owed to those whom we had imprisoned because they had committed an actual offence. We would, perhaps, be obliged to go to considerable lengths to make the child's life as normal and happy as possible.

Preventive war raises the same issue of justice that is raised by preventive action taken against a person who is extremely dangerous but has nevertheless committed no actual offence. For it seems that to wage preventive war is to attack those who are innocent in the relevant sense – that is, who have done nothing to make themselves morally liable to attack.

According to the traditional theory of the just war, what makes a person non-innocent, or morally liable to attack in war, is *actively posing a threat to others*. This is how traditional just war theory can assert an equivalence between the category of the non-innocent and the category of combatants. Combatants are non-innocent because they are by definition engaged in actively posing a threat to others, while non-combatants are innocent because they do not pose such a threat. Preventive war is therefore ruled out by traditional just war theory because those against whom it would have to be waged do not actively pose a threat. If they did, the war would not be preventive. Preventive war, in other words, cannot be waged against those whom the traditional theory of the just war recognises as legitimate targets. Thus Michael Walzer, the most eminent contemporary theorist in the just war tradition, contends that if we go to war in response to 'hostility [that] is prospective and imaginary ... it will always be a charge against us that we have made war upon soldiers who were themselves engaged in entirely legitimate (non-threatening) activities'.[11]

For reasons I will not rehearse here, I reject the traditional theory's criterion of liability.[12] I believe that the criterion of liability to attack in war is moral responsibility for an unjust threat, or, more generally, for any grievance that provides a just cause for war. According to this view, the objection to preventive war is that it is waged against those who are not, at least as yet, responsible for an unjust threat or other grievance that provides a just cause for war.

Stated in more general terms, the central objection to preventive war is that it is necessarily *indiscriminate* – that is, it is war waged in the absence of legitimate targets. And the absence of legitimate targets seems to imply the absence of a just cause. If there are no threateners, there cannot be a threat. And, unless there can be acts by states for which no one is responsible at all, there can be no just cause if there is no one who is *responsible* for a grievance that provides a just cause. Thus, if it is right that preventive war, of its nature, targets those who have as yet done nothing to make themselves liable to attack, it follows, contrary to what I suggested at the end of the section on *jus ad bellum* above, that prevention of future aggression cannot be a just cause for war.

It may seem, therefore, that if there is a justification for preventive war, it must be sought outside the domain of just war theory. It must appeal, for example, to considerations of consequences. Perhaps preventive war can occasionally be justified in a way that parallels the justification for quarantining the boy with a genetic disposition to kill people. On this view, although preventive war would violate a constraint against attacking and killing soldiers and others who had done nothing to make themselves into legitimate targets, the constraint would be overridden by the necessity of protecting ourselves from predictable aggression by the state these people serve. (There is, however, this difference from the case of the boy: that many of those attacked in the course of preventive war might not have been involved in any way in later aggression, even if that aggression would in fact have occurred in the absence of preventive war. Among the various reasons why this is so is that there is a high rate of turnover among personnel in the military.)

If it is right that the justification for preventive war requires overriding the constraint against deliberately attacking the innocent in order to avert harms that are as yet speculative or hypothetical, then the burden of justification must be exceedingly stringent. There are comparatively few forms of evidence, other than the occurrence of actual aggression, that are sufficient to establish a probability of future aggression high enough to warrant overriding the constraint against launching a military assault against innocent people. This is especially clear when we also take into account the effect that an instance of preventive war, and the efforts to legitimise it, might have in weakening respect for the principles and conventions that constrain the resort to war.

Liability and Risk

The case against preventive war is strong. I have presented arguments that purport to show that preventive war is opposed by considerations of justice, and, in many if not most cases, by considerations of consequences as well. Yet I think we should reconsider the claim that preventive war is necessarily indiscriminate, and therefore unjust. The argument for that claim appealed to an analogy with the Future Killer Case. And many cases at the international level may indeed be relevantly analogous to that. But there are other cases at the individual level in which preventive defence seems justified and does *not* seem to be unjust – cases in which it does *not* seem that the constraint against attacking the innocent holds, but is overridden by considerations of consequences. For, in these cases, the individual attacked in preventive defence is not innocent in the relevant sense.

The 'relevant sense' is, however, not the sense of traditional just war theory. Because in just war theory the criterion of liability to attack is actively posing a threat to others, it is simply not possible for that theory to acknowledge the permissibility of any instance of preventive war. I believe that this is one of the traditional theory's many shortcomings. For there *are*, at least in principle and probably in practice, conditions in which preventive war would be just and perhaps even morally required. Because the traditional theory of the just war cannot recognise this, I believe we should reject the theory's criterion of liability – which would, in effect, be to reject the theory.

I will distinguish three types of case in which preventive attack may be just, beginning with the type in which the liability of the person attacked is most obvious, and concluding with the type in which it is most contentious. My initial examples will be of preventive defence at the individual level, but in at least the first two cases I will suggest that there can be parallels at the international level.

Case Type 1

In some cases of individual preventive defence, the potential attacker commits an initial offence that is not itself an actual attack, but offers compelling evidence that there is a high probability that he will attack in the future. Consider, for example, those battered women for whom preventive defence seems necessary because retreat (that is, simply fleeing the threatening situation) is effectively impossible because their husbands have credibly threatened to track them down and kill them if they leave. Some legal theorists have argued that these women are entitled to a justification of self-defence even if an attack is not imminent, because there is an *ongoing* offence – namely, kidnapping or hostage-holding – that itself justifies a lethal defensive response.[13] On this view, the threat of future attack is no part of the justification for defensive violence at the time.

The idea that defensive killing may be justified by the captivity alone seems to me to be right, though it is only part of the truth. In some cases of this sort, the captivity may be sufficiently harmful or wrongful to justify self-defensive killing on its own. But this is not true in all such cases. Imagine a variant in which in two days' time the husband will be shipped overseas for a year's tour of military duty. Suppose he has a history of jealous rages that culminate in extreme violence, that he is currently consumed by the delusion that his wife will be unfaithful while he is away, that he is continuously drunk and increasingly menacing and verbally abusive (he has threatened to beat her if she tries to leave the house), but has not yet actually attacked her. The woman's captivity can last only two days. Yet, although there is no imminent threat, she reasonably believes that her life is seriously at risk.

Killing her husband would be a disproportionate response to the threat of being held captive for only two days. So the captivity alone is insufficient to justify killing. Yet I believe she could be justified in killing her husband while he sleeps. For killing *is* a proportionate response to the combined threats of continued captivity and death; therefore, the non-imminent threat to her life contributes to the justification for her act of killing, which would be an act of preventive defence as well as an act of liberation. (In cases in which a woman's captivity is indefinite and thus sufficient on its own to justify killing, the justification for killing is *overdetermined*: killing is justified both to end the captivity and, independently, to avert the threat to her life.)

The husband's actual offence of holding his wife captive triggers her right of preventive defence. The initial offence makes him *liable* to defensive action, and the two threats he poses – the immediate threat to continue to hold her captive and the non-imminent threat to kill her – combine in gravity to make killing him a *proportionate* response.

Of course, not just any offence would be sufficient to trigger a right of preventive defence. The initial offence must be of the right sort. If, in the intervals between his fits of rage, the husband were entering false claims on his income tax returns, that bit of wrongdoing would not be the right sort of offence to make him liable to preventive defence. The kind of offence that *would* be sufficient to make the husband liable to preventive defence must be one that can in principle justify defensive action and that establishes the husband's *responsibility* now for a risk, or an increased risk, of an unjust attack by him in the future. In the clearest case in which a present offence establishes liability to preventive defence, the future threat is, in effect, inherent in the present offence, in that the future attack would be part of the same threatening sequence as the present offence, which therefore provides evidence for and makes a causal contribution to the potential future attack. In the case of the battered wife, the husband's holding her captive itself puts her at greatly increased risk of a lethal attack by him in the future. It makes a causal contribution to his ability to kill her in the future, and provides evidence for the lethal threat he in fact poses.

Note that what I have offered is a characterisation of the connection between an initial offence and a threat of future attack that is sufficient to make a person liable to preventive defence. I suspect that what I have suggested as a sufficient condition of liability to preventive defence may be a necessary condition as well. But some may find it too stringent. I leave it an open question whether there might be a weaker connection that would be sufficient for liability to preventive defence.

The parallel at the international level is that a country may be liable to preventive attack or preventive war by virtue of having committed an offence that is itself of a *kind* that can provide a just cause for war *and* that creates or increases the risk that the country will in the future conduct an unjust attack. The initial offence makes the country liable to preventive defence because it makes that country responsible for wrongfully imposing a risk of unjust attack on its potential victims. It may well be that the initial offence is not on its own sufficiently grave to make the resort to war a proportionate response. But war may be proportionate to the combination of the initial offence and the threat of future aggression.

Suppose, for example, that in 2003 Iraq had possessed a formidable arsenal of weapons of mass destruction (WMD), as the Bush administration falsely claimed it did. Its possession of those weapons would have been wrongful; it would have been a violation of the ceasefire agreement that ended the Gulf War in 1991, and an act of defiance of the legitimate authority of the UN. Such an offence could arguably have been a just cause for renewed war against Iraq, though it is implausible to suppose that war would have been a necessary or proportionate response to the violation of the ceasefire agreement, considered on its own. Iraq's wrongful possession of WMD might, however, have also triggered a right of preventive defence on the part of those countries that the weapons would have put at risk. The possession of illicit weapons would have been an offence of the right type to establish Iraq's liability to preventive action, for the existence of the weapons would have been a causal condition of, as well as serious evidence for, a threat of future unjust aggression by Iraq. But there were, of course, no such weapons; nor was there any good reason to suppose they existed.[14]

Another actual case to which this form of reasoning might have been applied – and with greater plausibility than in the case of the Iraq War – is actually a case of pre-emptive rather than preventive war: namely, the Six Day War of 1967.[15] It is at least arguable that Egypt's closing of the Straits of Tiran, an international waterway, to Israeli shipping was a belligerent act that violated Israel's rights and therefore provided a just cause for war. Although war would not have been a proportionate response to that act alone, it could be argued that that act made Egypt liable to pre-emptive attack by virtue of its causal and evidential connection with a threat of future unjust attack by Egypt. And war may well have been a proportionate response to the blockade *together* with the threat of future attack.

Case Type 2

A second type of case in which preventive defence may be permissible in relations between individuals is that covered by the conspiracy laws. In the Paralysis Case, for example, your enemy has carefully planned his strategy for killing you, recording the details in his diary. He has engaged in action that is the initial phase of a planned sequence of co-ordinated acts intended to culminate in his killing you. Not only does this action provide compelling evidence that there is a high probability that he will attack you in the future, but it also, and at least equally importantly, constitutes a basis for holding him liable to preventive defence. The Paralysis Case, in short, is relevantly different from the Future Killer Case, in which the child has done nothing to make himself liable to preventive action.

It is, moreover, easy to imagine analogues of the Paralysis Case at the international level – cases in which intelligence reveals an enemy's strategic planning for a surprise attack that can be averted by preventive action, but against which there can be no effective defence if it is allowed to occur. One actual case that approximates this description is Israel's destruction of Iraq's Osirak nuclear reactor in 1981. Although Iraq claimed that the reactor was being built to generate electricity, this was implausible given that Iraq's vast oil reserves offered a cheaper source of electrical power for the indefinite future. Moreover, after Iran had unsuccessfully attempted to destroy the reactor in September of 1980, shortly after the beginning of the Iran–Iraq War, an official newspaper in Baghdad had stated that 'the Iranian people should not fear the Iraqi nuclear reactor which is not intended to be used against Iran, but against the Zionist enemy'.[16] While Israel had no reason to fear a particular attack at a specific time or for a specific reason, it did have reason to fear that Iraq, which, unlike various other Arab states, had refused to sign the armistice agreements in 1949 and therefore remained officially in a state of war with Israel, would at some point use nuclear weapons against it, potentially annihilating both the state and its inhabitants. Iraq's subsequent firing of missiles into Israeli population centres during the Gulf War, in which Israel was not a participant, offers retrospective confirmation of the rationality of Israel's fear. Because the reactor was soon to become active, after which it could not have been attacked without a catastrophic release of radioactive materials, Israel reasonably believed that if it did not act immediately, it would have lost its only realistic chance to eliminate this threat to its own continued existence. It attacked the reactor on a Sunday, when French engineers who were building the plant were absent, thereby destroying it without causing casualties. It is, indeed, an important feature of this example that there were no illegitimate human targets and thus no attacks, whether intended or unintended, on the innocent. Although this preventive attack (which, though technically an act of war, did not progress to full-scale war) was clearly illegal and was universally condemned at the time, a very strong case can be made that it was an instance of legitimate prevention.

Case Type 3

I turn now to the third kind of case in which preventive defence at the individual level may not be unjust. Suppose that, in a variant of the Paralysis Case, your enemy has formulated no plans; he has done nothing other than to form the intention to kill you once you are paralysed. But, as with so many fictional villains, he wants not merely to kill you, but to prove to you that he can *defeat* you. He therefore wants you to know that you are being defeated; so he notifies you of his intention, and you are certain that he is not bluffing. In this case, there is no attack, no immediate threat of attack, no preparatory action that initiates a threatening sequence, no actual offence or wrongful action of any sort. All your enemy does is to form the intention to kill you at a time when you will be utterly defenceless.

Intuitively, there seems to be sufficient justification for preventive defence in this case – even for preventive killing if killing your enemy is the only way you can reliably prevent him from later killing you. But the justification does not seem to be merely a matter of consequences or self-preference. This does not seem to be a case in which the constraint against killing the innocent is overridden by a claim of necessity. Your enemy is not innocent in what must be the relevant sense. Although he does not pose a threat – at least in the sense deemed necessary for liability by just war theory – and although he is not responsible for any act that establishes an unjust threat to you, he cannot be considered innocent: that is, he cannot be regarded as retaining his full moral immunity to attack. But if this is right, it seems that merely forming or having certain intentions can be a sufficient basis for moral liability to attack.

Many will contend that we can evade this latter claim by recognising that even in this case your enemy *does* something to threaten you: he communicates his intention to kill you. This is precisely what we mean by one sense of 'threaten': to issue a threat. But one can threaten in this sense without posing a threat (when one's threat is a bluff), and it is posing a threat that is considered necessary for liability by just war theory. (I believe, by contrast, that bluffs, too, may be a basis for liability, but that is another topic.[17]) I believe that in this variant of the Paralysis Case, your enemy's act of *revealing* his intention adds nothing of moral significance to his merely *having* it, other than providing evidence of its existence. The significance of his revealing his intention, in short, is merely evidential.

I believe, therefore, that the mere formation and retention of a certain intention – both of which are *mental* acts – can be a sufficient basis for moral liability to preventive action. This should not be an altogether surprising or mysterious claim, since mental acts and mental states are considered crucially relevant to responsibility and liability, both in the law and in commonsense morality. It is, however, an unorthodox claim, at least in domestic and international law, where intention alone is not a basis of criminal liability, and in mainstream just war theory, where an actual attack or imminent threat of attack is necessary for liability to defensive force. (In Catholic moral theory, which is the principal historical source of just war theory, the formation or possession of certain intentions can be morally wrong independently of any action that may issue from them. But I am unaware of any endorsement by Catholic theorists of the idea that the formation or possession of a wrongful intention can itself make a person non-innocent in the relevant sense – that is, liable to defensive force.) The claim, suggested by the modified Paralysis Case, that intention alone can be a basis for liability to preventive defence, challenges the orthodox assumption that some kind of act – an overt act, not just a mental act – is necessary for a person to be non-innocent, or morally liable to defensive force.

In the previous section on justice, I asserted that the criterion for liability to force or violence in war is responsibility for an unjust threat or for some other grievance that provides a just cause for war. But the conclusion I have drawn from the modified Paralysis Case seems doubtfully compatible with that claim. For what can someone who as yet has done nothing more than to form an intention to conduct an unjust attack in the future be responsible *for*?

The answer is that your enemy in the modified Paralysis Case is morally responsible for a threat to your life. This is a weaker sense of 'threat' than that recognised by traditional just war theory, which understands 'posing a threat' as, in effect, equivalent to 'being a combatant' or having combatant status. It is clear, however, that your enemy's forming the intention to kill you significantly affects the objective probability of your being unjustly killed in the near future. So what your enemy is morally responsible for *now* is your being at greatly increased *risk* of being unjustly killed (by him) in the near future. You therefore face an unavoidable choice imposed on you by his mental act: either you must kill him now, or you must remain exposed to a high risk of his wrongfully killing you. Because your enemy is morally responsible for the existence of this state of affairs, it can be permissible, as a matter of justice, to kill him to eliminate the risk of his killing you, provided that the risk is sufficiently high to make killing a proportionate response.

Perhaps surprisingly, then, reflection on the three foregoing types of case seems to re-establish the suggestion I made at the end of the section on *jus ad bellum*, but challenged in the section on justice, that the fundamental objection to preventive defence and, by implication, preventive war is not that it necessarily targets the innocent, but that, in practice, matters of evidence and probability are virtually never such that the effort at justification can succeed. For example, because intentions are private and not directly accessible to others, the evidence for the presence of a wrongful intention in another person is *always* fallible and contentious, and is *almost always* insufficiently conclusive to provide an adequate basis for preventive action. If we possessed an *intentionometer* that would infallibly detect other people's intentions and gauge their strength, the moral and legal status of preventive defence would be profoundly different.

These epistemological and evidential problems are greatly exacerbated when we move from relations between individuals to relations between states, nations or other collectives. In our cases involving individuals – the Future Killer Case and the two variants of the Paralysis Case – there are various quite reliable forms of evidence of future attack: evidence of a powerful genetic predisposition, overheard conversations, diary entries, overt threats uttered by a person whose character is well understood. In all three cases, the apparent threat is posed by a single individual whose future action can be predicted with reasonable confidence on the basis of these sorts of evidence. In the case of states, by contrast, there are usually numerous individuals in positions of power and authority whose values, goals, interests and intentions may conflict. And each is likely to be subject to potentially conflicting pressures and constraints from a variety of different institutions and constituencies. In these conditions, how reliable can even the best forms of evidence be in predicting outcomes that will be determined by the complex interactions of so many forces? To answer this question, look back at last year's newspapers, or even last month's, and calculate the ratio of correct to incorrect predictions about the behaviour of states. The results will not be very encouraging to the belief that evidence of future aggression can be sufficiently compelling to justify action so grave as the initiation of war.

The Liability of Unmobilised Military Personnel

I will conclude by noting one further difference between preventive defence by one individual against another and preventive war. I have conceded that the former can in principle be discriminate, even in the absence of any overt offence by the target. It is possible, though not likely, that an individual may be liable to preventive action and that others can know this, even when the individual is not yet guilty of any overt wrongful action. In practice, however, the risk is high that what seems to the agent to be preventive defence will not in fact be defensive at all – because the person attacked did not in fact pose a threat, at least not of the kind perceived – so that the attack will be objectively unjust. In the case of preventive war, there is a further problem. Not only is there a grave risk of misperception or other error, but even when a future threat is correctly perceived, it may be impossible to target those, or only those, who are morally responsible for the risks that ostensibly justify preventive action. For when unjust aggression is only at the planning stage, those who would later *implement* the plans – the military personnel who would do the actual fighting, launch the weapons and so on – may have done nothing to increase the risks to others relative to what those risks were before the plans for aggression were conceived. They might not as yet even have knowledge of the plans. Yet these are the people who would have to be targeted in a preventive war. For the planners – usually political leaders and high-ranking military officers – are not normally feasible or, for reasons of a pragmatic nature, suitable targets for preventive military attack. (An attack on a country's political leadership would be likely to be counterproductive and would also threaten to undermine respect for the useful convention prohibiting political assassination.) Most of the people who would be targeted in a preventive war would, therefore, have a moral status analogous to that of the boy with a genetic predisposition to murder. They would be people who would be likely to participate in an unjust attack in the future, but who would as yet have done nothing – not even form a wrongful intention – to make themselves liable to attack. And, as I noted earlier, there would be some of whom it would not even be true that they would have later participated in the aggression. So many, or even most, of the people targeted would be, as Walzer says, people engaged in wholly legitimate activities.

Thus, while preventive war could in principle be discriminate and therefore not unjust, *in practice* it is far more likely than preventive defence at the individual level to require deliberate attacks on people known to be innocent in the sense that they have done nothing to make themselves liable to attack. In practice, therefore, the considerations favouring preventive war will have to be sufficiently strong to override the constraint against intentionally attacking the innocent in order for preventive war to be justified. If this is right, my earlier claim still stands: the presumption against the permissibility of preventive war is, in practice, extremely strong. And since, for reasons given earlier, considerations of consequences usually oppose rather than favour preventive war, it follows that the burden of justification can rarely be met.

This conclusion might be challenged by seeking to extend the grounds for liability to attack even further. It might be argued that the military personnel who would be attacked in a preventive war are liable to attack by virtue of its being true of them that they will engage in unjust aggression if ordered to by their superiors.

The problem with this suggestion arises from the fact that *liability* to attack is necessarily a consequence (though not a causal consequence) of a person's having *done* something, even if the action is only mental (as in the modified Paralysis Case). So the challenge is to identify something that such people have *done* that makes them liable. It could, perhaps, be suggested that most of them will, as part of what is involved in being in the military, have formed – forgive the jargon – a dispositional, conditional, wrongful intention: that is, they will have made themselves disposed to participate in any war, whether just or unjust, that they are ordered to participate in. But the idea that persons make themselves liable to preventive attack *now* simply by virtue of being disposed to obey an order to act unjustly is clearly far too permissive. Virtually all soldiers at all times have been strongly disposed to obey orders to go to war irrespective of whether the war has been just or unjust. Indeed, as Stanley Milgram's experiments in the 1960s showed, most *people* are strongly disposed to obey an order to inflict unjust harm on others, provided that the order is issued by someone they perceive to be a legitimate authority.[18] We should not conclude that most people are therefore liable to preventive defence.

A more promising defence of preventive war appeals to the claim that by voluntarily enlisting in the military, even those soldiers who are presently unmobilised have acted in a way that conditionally commits them to obey orders to participate in a future unjust attack. This act, it might be argued, is sufficient to make them liable now, *if* there will in fact be such an attack unless it is forestalled by preventive action.

This view has considerable plausibility. The prior action of these unmobilised soldiers cannot, of course, make them responsible for an unjust threat when in fact there *is* no threat; but as soon as their government begins to plan an unjust attack or unjust war, a threat arises to which the soldiers' prior voluntary act of enlisting now makes a substantial contribution. By having enlisted, they now share responsibility for the unjust threat their country poses, even if they are at present entirely unaware of their government's plans.

Let us assume for the sake of argument that this is true, and that merely by enlisting, soldiers can in principle be liable to preventive attack. This leaves open the status of those who were conscripted. It can, of course, be argued that even by allowing themselves to be conscripted, they share in the responsibility for any unjust threat their government poses. There is, again, some plausibility to this, but it also helps to bring out the fact that responsibility is a matter of degree. Conscripts who have no idea that their government is planning to initiate an unjust war surely bear very little responsibility for the threat their country poses to the potential victims of their government's planned action. If the degree of a person's liability varies with the degree of his responsibility, then unmobilised conscripted soldiers bear only a very low degree of liability to attack. What this means in practice is that the proportionality requirement with respect to a preventive attack against them must be very stringent indeed.

There is, moreover, a further question about the status of those in the military, whether enlisted personnel or conscripts, who will have left the military by the time that any planned unjust action by their country would occur. It is hard to see how they could be responsible now for a potential attack in which they would have no part.

Even, therefore, if we grant the controversial assumption that unmobilised soldiers may be liable to attack simply by virtue of having become part of the military, it still seems that preventive war inevitably involves intended attacks both on people whose degree of liability to attack is very low and on those who bear no liability at all and thus are innocent in the relevant sense. If the assumption is false, most of those attacked in a preventive war will be innocent. In order for the moral constraint against deliberately attacking the innocent to be overridden, the consequences of failing to go to war would, when considered impartially, have to be disastrous. If my earlier claim that considerations of consequences generally oppose rather than favour preventive war is correct, the burden of justification for preventive war will in practice be very difficult – though not impossible– to meet.

Acknowledgements

I am deeply grateful for extremely perceptive written comments on this paper by Larry Alexander, Thomas Hurka, David Rodin and Alec Walen. I have also benefited from discussions with audiences at Lund University, the Swedish Collegium for Advanced Study in Uppsala, Pomona College and Canisius College.

Notes

1   See Articles 2(4) and 51.
2   Quoted in Singer, Peter (2004), *The President of Good and Evil: The Ethics of George W. Bush*, New York: E. P. Dutton, 179.
3   'The National Security Strategy of the United States of America' <http://www. whitehouse.gov/nsc/nss.pdf>, 15. It is unclear what the authors could be referring to, other than Pearl Harbor, in suggesting that in the past the USA has relied on a 'reactive posture' in its use of force against other states.
4   Ferzan, Kimberly Kessler, 'Defending Imminence: From Battered Women to Iraq', *Arizona Law Review*, Vol. 46, 213, 2004, 215.
5   'Cheney Lashes Out at Critics of Policy on Iraq', *New York Times*, 11 October 2003.
6   See Ferzan, 'Defending Imminence' Section II.C, and the many references cited there.
7   David Luban argues convincingly that this argument is not as straightforward as it may seem, for the presumption of equality among persons that underlies the insistence that moral principles apply universally does not obviously hold among states. See his 'Preventive War', *Philosophy and Public Affairs*, Vol. 32, 2004, 241–2.
8   Walzer, Michael (1977), *Just and Unjust Wars*, Harmondsworth: Penguin, 77.
9   Some theorists in the just war tradition have explicitly characterised justified warfare as a form of punishment, and have accordingly held that even pre-emptive war is impermissible. Francisco De Vitoria, for example, wrote in 1539 that 'a prince cannot have greater authority over foreigners than he has over his own subjects; but he may not draw the sword against his own subjects unless they have done some wrong; therefore he cannot do so against foreigners except in the same circumstances'. Vitoria therefore concluded that 'the sole and only just cause for waging war is when harm has been inflicted'. To wage war in the absence of a prior injury would be to make war against the innocent, and 'to kill the innocent is prohibited by natural law'; Vitoria, Francisco De,

'On the Law of War', in Pagden, Anthony and Lawrence, Jeremy (eds) (1991), *Political Writings*, Cambridge University Press, 303–4. In my view, whether punishment can be a just cause for war depends on what comes within the scope of the concept of punishment. While many writers have insisted that punishment and self-defence are wholly distinct and do not overlap, I believe that the central aims of punishment are essentially defensive, and that the best justification for punishment appeals to the same principles that govern the morality of self-defence. In this belief I have been greatly influenced by the work on punishment by Daniel Farrell. For a representative example of this important work, see his 'The Justification of Deterrent Violence,' *Ethics*, Vol. 100, 1990, 301–17.

10 The general question is raised, but not answered, by Joyce Carol Oates in her fascinating essay on serial killers. She asks: 'Should these "damaged" individuals [that is, serial killers] be detected … and their condition diagnosed before they kill, how exactly would they be treated? … Every commentator I have ever read on the subject … makes the point that the serial killer is virtually impossible to "reform" … Short of locking these "damaged" people up permanently, or implanting electrodes in their brains, it is difficult to imagine what can be done to prevent them from killing, in a democratic society in which civil liberties are honored. Can, and should, *the potential for violence* be, in effect, punished'? Oates, '"I Had No Other Thrill or Happiness": The Literature of Serial Killers', Oates, Joyce Carol (1999), *Where I've Been, and Where I'm Going: Essays, Reviews, and Prose*, New York: Plume, 249, emphasis in the original. In an earlier novel, Oates' narrator refers to 'murderers yet to commit their sins': Oates, Joyce Carol (1984), *Mysteries of Winterthurn*, New York: E. P. Dutton, 380.

11 Walzer, *Just and Unjust Wars*, 80. I take it that his description of a threat as 'imaginary' implies only that it has so far not materialised, not that it is a mere figment.

12 See McMahan, Jeff, 'The Ethics of Killing in War', *Ethics*, Vol. 114, 2004, Sections VI–VIII.

13 See, for example, Ferzan, 'Defending Imminence', 254.

14 For a moral analysis of the Iraq War, see McMahan, Jeff (2004), 'Unjust War in Iraq', *The Pelican Record*, Corpus Christi College, Oxford. This paper may also be found at <http://webapp.utexas.edu/blogs/bleiter/archives/002121.html> or may be obtained from the author by request. Bush has subsequently begun to appeal to a basically consequentialist defence of the Iraq war. On various occasions during the election campaign, he has taken the same line: 'Knowing what I know today, I would have made the same decision. The world is safer with Saddam in a prison cell', Sanger, David E., 'A Doctrine Under Pressure: Pre-emption Is Redefined', *New York Times*, 11 October 2004. Again, there are problems in universalising this argument. There are many people of whom it is true that the world would be safer if they were in prison, but that is no justification for imprisoning them.

15 For a brief discussion, see Walzer, *Just and Unjust Wars*, 82–5. I am grateful to Thomas Hurka for pointing out to me that this case is susceptible to an analysis that parallels that which I have given of the case of the battered wife.

16 My account of the Osirak raid draws on that given by David Mellow in his doctoral dissertation, 'A Critique of Just War Theory', University of Calgary, 2003, which in turn is based primarily on reports in the *New York Times* in the days following the attack. The quotation is from that source. My conclusions agree with Mellow's.

17 Suppose X unjustifiably issues a credible threat against Y but is in fact bluffing. Y, reasonably believing X's threat to be genuine and therefore reasonably anticipating an imminent unjust attack, begins to take defensive action against X. X now faces an

unavoidable choice: either harm Y in self-defence, or allow himself to be harmed. I believe that even if Y is not justified in posing a threat to X but is merely excused, it is nevertheless X who bears primary responsibility for the fact that either X or Y must be harmed. Because of this, X is not permitted to act in self-defence (unless, perhaps, Y's defensive action is disproportionate to the threat he reasonably perceives). X is liable to suffer those harms made likely by his own wrongful action. (If Y's action is wrongful – though excused – because he in fact faced no real threat, it is possible that X might be permitted to force him to share the harm made inevitable by their combined wrongful action. But the greater share of the harm should still go to X because of his greater responsibility.)

18   Milgram, Stanley (1983), *Obedience to Authority*, New York: HarperCollins.

Chapter 10

War, Humanitarian Intervention and Human Rights

Richard Norman

The most fundamental of the traditional conditions for a just war is that it should be fought in a just cause. That is very vague. What counts as a 'just cause'? Augustine wrote:

> The real evils in war are love of violence, revengeful cruelty, fierce and implacable enmity, wild resistance, and the lust of power, and such like; and it is generally to punish these things, when force is required to inflict the punishment, that, in obedience to God or some lawful authority, good men undertake wars …[1]

If punishment for lust of power is to count as a just cause, that looks dangerously like a justification for a war of all against all. The interpretation of 'just cause' within the 'just war' tradition has increasingly come to be confined to the idea of *defence*. The only just wars are wars of defence, and the only injustice which war can right is the crime of aggression.[2]

More recently still, however, there have been moves, both in theory and in practice, to widen the ethical justification for war by including so-called wars of 'humanitarian intervention'. The latter phrase is typically spelled out in terms of the idea of 'human rights'. Wars are held to be justifiable if waged against countries which fail to uphold the human rights of their own citizens. NATO's military intervention in Kosovo in 1999, preceded by the bombing of Serbia, was undertaken on the grounds that Serbia's policy of 'ethnic cleansing' was systematically violating the human rights of the Kosovar Albanians. America's wars against Afghanistan in 2001 and Iraq in 2003 were ostensibly part of a 'war on terrorism', and, in the case of Iraq, an attempt to eliminate that country's supposed weapons of mass destruction, but when those attempted justifications looked too thin, the human rights of Afghans and Iraqis were also invoked.

The purpose of this chapter is to criticise the idea of 'humanitarian intervention' as a justification for war. I begin with a sceptical discussion of human rights. The scepticism is not unmitigated. The concept of human rights has a significant role to play in moral discourse. My discussion of it is followed by a matching scepticism about the rights of states, which cannot, I argue, found a strong notion of state sovereignty and non-intervention. Interference in the affairs of other states in the name of human rights can therefore, in principle, be justified. What cannot be justified, I argue, are *wars* of humanitarian intervention. Such wars are themselves likely to violate human rights, they are not an effective way of promoting human rights, and they undermine the possibility of an international order.

Human Rights

I begin, then, with some sceptical reflections on the concept of 'human rights'. I shall briefly cover some well-trodden ground. The point of doing so will be not to say anything new, but to look at the implications for the idea of military intervention in the name of 'human rights'.

A distinguishing feature of human rights is that they are supposed to be *pre-institutional*. They are rights which all human beings are supposed to possess, just by virtue of their status as human beings, independently of and prior to the institutional rules of specific organised societies or communities. The idea of *institutional* rights is unproblematic. As a member of the University, I have the right to borrow a certain number of books from the library, for a certain specified period of time. The right is unproblematic in the sense that my possession of it can be established simply by consulting the rules of the University of which I am a member. And to describe it as a *right* is simply to say that the University guarantees to me my entitlement to borrow the books. The concept of a 'right', in other words, here gets its specific sense from its place in a vocabulary of rules, membership, authority and entitlements.

That immediately brings us to the first problem with the idea of pre-institutional 'human' rights. When an organisation such as Amnesty International criticises the government of a particular country for violating, say, the rights of political prisoners not to be tortured, or not to be held in prison without trial, it will not be impressed with the response that the institutions and laws of the country in question recognise no such right. That is precisely what is wrong with those institutions, it will say. That is why they violate human rights. The problem now, however, is how we can meaningfully use the vocabulary of 'rights' to articulate such criticism, since we have now detached the term from the vocabulary which gives it its distinctive meaning. It may be 'wrong' that governments should treat their citizens in this way, and it would undoubtedly be a good thing if they treated them better, if they did recognise rights not to be tortured or imprisoned without trial. But it is one thing to say that it would be a good thing if people had such rights, and it is quite another thing to say that people already have them in some pre-institutional sense. This is what led Bentham to his famous criticism of the idea of 'natural rights' as 'nonsense'.[3] In the absence of guarantees backed by institutional sanctions, he said, talk of 'rights' makes no sense. It may be a good thing if people have certain rights, but it is misleading to equate the claim that people ought to have those rights with the claim that they already have them at some 'natural', pre-institutional level.

In proportion to the want of happiness resulting from the want of rights, a reason exists for wishing that there were such things as rights. But reasons for wishing that there were such things as rights are not rights – a reason for wishing that a certain right were established, is not that right – want is not supply, hunger is not bread.[4]

The difficulty of giving a clear and distinctive sense to the language of rights outside the appropriate institutional context is closely linked to the second problem – that 'human rights' are epistemologically indeterminate. In other words, there is no clear and agreed way of establishing what rights human beings have. Notoriously, every historical declaration of human rights gives a different list, and this is no accident. With institutional rights, there is no problem. We can establish what rights a person has by consulting the rules of the institution, and ascertaining the person's status in relation to the institution. If he or she is a member, and the rules ascribe these rights to members, then he/she has these rights. But how do we establish whether human rights are correctly listed as 'life, liberty and the pursuit of happiness' (according to the United States Declaration of Independence), or as 'liberty, property, security and resistance to oppression' (according to the French Declaration of the Rights of Man and Citizen), or as the 13 rights recognised in the European Convention on Human Rights, or as the more than thirty rights recognised in the United Nations Declaration of Human Rights?

My point here is not a completely general one about the difficulty of establishing any moral or political claim. There are distinctions and contrasts to be made within that category. We have at least some idea of how to establish what the fundamental *needs* and *interests* of human beings are. We know that the most fundamental interest of any human being is that of continuing to live, since that is a precondition of any other interests. We know that the basic biological needs of any human being include food, health, clothing and shelter, since without these, one's very existence is imperilled. We know that human beings need education, and need certain kinds of social freedoms, since without them they cannot act effectively or make effective choices about how they want to live. There is plenty of room for disagreements here about the relative importance of different needs and interests, but at least we know what we are talking about. But what do we mean when we add that human beings have a *right* to these things, and what would be the proper way to establish whether such a claim was true? It is not at all clear.

Despite the difficulties, I do not want to conclude that we should abandon the language of human rights. Apart from anything else, such a proposal would be a vain opposition to what seems to have become an irresistible tide. Its spread and its success demonstrates that the language serves an important purpose. It serves, I suggest, as a political instrument, appealing to some kind of consensus as a basis for criticism of particular states, institutions and practices. That leads me to certain proposals for how we should understand it.

First, we should understand the language of human rights as *stipulative* rather than as *descriptive*. It has no determinate meaning outside particular declarations or conventions. Those declarations and conventions, therefore, do not record the preexistence of the rights which they list. They create such rights; they do not discover them. It makes no sense to ask 'What are the human rights which all human beings naturally possess?' The appropriate question is: 'What rights *ought* we to ascribe to all human beings?' What is required is a *decision*. Again, I do not want to present this, as some philosophers have done, as a claim about *all* value judgements. The point is precisely the contrast. There are values which are discovered, not invented. In the light of an understanding of what human beings are like, and of the kinds of relations in which they stand to one another, we can arrive at truths about what makes for a good human life and how human beings ought to live. The claims that we make to that effect can have a kind of objectivity. But declarations of human rights are not like that.

This brings me to my second suggestion: ascriptions of human rights are *derivative*, not *foundational*. There are no self-evident human rights, and when we ascribe certain basic rights to all human beings, we are not recording some objective fact of the matter about whether human beings do indeed have such rights, but our stipulative declarations can be more or less rational to the extent that we derive them from more fundamental value judgements.

Declarations of human rights can usefully be thought of, I suggest, as stipulations of the basic conditions which any society must meet in order to claim legitimacy. Different societies may be better or worse than one another in all sorts of ways, but if they fail to meet certain minimum standards, if they fail to guarantee to their members the satisfaction of certain basic requirements, then they cannot reasonably claim the allegiance of their members. These basic conditions are of two kinds, corresponding to what have standardly been distinguished as negative and positive rights. First, there are certain kinds of treatment to which no human being should be subjected. There are fundamental moral constraints on what anyone can permissibly do to another human being, even if such actions might yield substantial benefits to others. These constraints are articulated by stipulating such human rights as the right not to be killed, or tortured, or enslaved. They derive from more fundamental judgements of a recognisably Kantian kind about not treating any human being solely as a means to an end, as a thing rather than as a person. Second, there are certain basic needs common to all human beings, and a society which fails to enable its members to meet those needs has forfeited their allegiance. To these basic needs there correspond positive human rights, such as the right to sustenance and a basic standard of living, the right to basic standards of health care, the right to a level of education sufficient to enable one to take an active part in the life and culture of one's society, and the right to at least some degree of political participation in the government of the country.

From this perspective, I suggest, we can not only see the point of declarations of human rights, but also understand why there are radical differences in the lists of rights occurring in such declarations. I have referred to the distinction between negative and positive rights. This distinction is controversial, and some have argued that the only human rights which can meaningfully count as such are negative rights. The European Convention on Human Rights, drawn up in 1950 and now incorporated into British law, is almost entirely confined to negative rights. The United Nations Universal Declaration of Human Rights, on the other hand, includes not only negative but positive rights. Such differences reflect familiar political disagreements about the proper function of social and political institutions, about whether they should be directed at meeting shared human needs through collective action, or whether their proper function is simply to create and protect the space in which individuals can act for themselves to meet their needs. Those political disagreements are bound to give rise to disagreements about the scope and extent of human rights. That is not to say that the latter disagreements are irresolvable, but simply that attempted answers to them are bound to derive from more fundamental moral and political views.

Take, for instance, the example of one of the more contentious human rights listed in the United Nations Declaration: 'Everyone has the right to rest and leisure, including reasonable limitation of working hours and periodic holidays with pay.'[5] It makes no sense to ask: 'Do people *really* have such a right?' The only intelligible question to ask is: 'Is it useful to stipulate this as a human right?' And that can be answered only by considering how important the need for leisure is, as compared with other human needs, and how realistic and helpful it is to set this up as, in the words of the Declaration, 'a common standard of achievement for all peoples and all nations'. Note also that different answers would be appropriate in different historical epochs and conditions. It would make no sense to talk of a universal human right to paid holidays in a feudal society. On the other hand, in a society where most people's subsistence is derived from wage labour, the right to leisure, guaranteed through paid holidays, may be an absolutely fundamental requirement for any decent human existence.

We are now in a position to note in a preliminary way some implications for the idea of military intervention to uphold human rights. On the one hand, if declarations of human rights do indeed identify 'a common standard ... for ... all nations', then they could in principle justify some kind of intervention by the international community in the affairs of individual nations which fail to meet such standards. If, as I suggested, such nations have lost their legitimacy, they cannot claim immunity from outside interference. On the other hand, the account which I have offered so far already identifies a clear problem with appealing to human rights to justify intervention. Such rights are contested. There are no clearly demarcated boundaries to the range of human rights. There is therefore no sharp divide between situations where human rights are at stake and those where they are not, and the appeal to human rights does not provide any clear criterion for when intervention might be justified. It is true that some human rights are incontestably more fundamental than others. A regime which engaged in genocide against sections of its own population would, by any reckoning, be violating fundamental human rights. Consider, however, the assertion that intervention, whether military or of some other form, would be justified to remove a regime which does not allow free democratic elections, or which imposes severe restrictions on political debate and freedom of expression. It is, I think, reasonable to ask someone who makes that assertion whether they would also advocate intervention in a country which violates basic human rights by, for instance, failing to provide elementary education for all its children. The answer could go either way, and I am not suggesting that it has to be arbitrary. On the contrary, there is plenty of scope for rational argument about which of these alleged rights might be the more fundamental, and which of them it might be more important for outsiders to try to promote. My point is simply that the answer is not obvious, and hence even if there is agreement in principle that intervention to uphold human rights might be justifiable, there is unlikely to be any clear consensus on what the practical implications of that principle might be.

The Rights of States

So far I have been looking at the status of the idea of human rights – that is, the rights of individuals – and have suggested that there is a degree of indeterminacy in the idea which should prompt at least an initial scepticism about interfering in other societies to promote the human rights of their members. I turn now to the idea of states' rights, since this is also clearly relevant to the question of intervention. The standard objection in principle to intervention, and especially military intervention, in the affairs of other states is that this would be a violation of sovereignty. It is an objection to intervention in general, because the sovereignty of a state consists in its exclusive jurisdiction within its own territory. It is an objection to military intervention in particular, because such intervention would be a case of military *aggression*, an attack on or invasion of a sovereign state. The idea of sovereignty is typically expressed in the vocabulary of rights, that states have rights of sovereignty and territorial integrity, analogous to the rights of individuals, which should not be violated. Should we ascribe rights of this kind to states?

There are some very general questions here about whether we can coherently talk at all about collective entities having rights, but I do not want to engage in the argument at that level of generality. I want to look at what specific reasons there might be for ascribing rights to states, of a kind which could give substance to the idea of state sovereignty. Now, having suggested that declarations of human rights are essentially stipulative rather than descriptive, it would be possible at this point simply to say that it is up to us to decide whether we want to be similarly stipulative about states' rights, and that if we do decide to ascribe rights to states, that stipulative ascription is self-authenticating and cannot be criticised as any kind of mistake. If we want to say that states have rights, then they have them. Something like that broad approach is indeed what I will endorse at the end of this paper. However, as it stands, it would be too simple. I have emphasised that ascriptions of human rights, though stipulative, are not just arbitrary. They are backed by strong moral beliefs about the constraints on how any human being should be treated, and about the fundamental needs which give any human being a claim on others. If we want to ascribe rights to states, therefore, we need good reasons, derived from other more fundamental values, for doing so.

One obvious approach would be to derive the rights of states from the rights of individuals.[6] An instance of that approach is social contract theory. In its classic version, the idea is that individuals are endowed with basic human rights, but that in a state of nature they would encounter difficulties in protecting those rights, and that they therefore agreed to accept limits to the exercise of their rights, and to give them up in part to the state in return for the state's protection of their rights.

There are familiar problems with any such version of contract theory. There never was, nor could be, a 'state of nature', and there never has been any social contract made by individuals to set up a state. However, even if we could give some sense to the idea of a *hypothetical* contract as a possible model for the relations between individuals and the state, it would not do the job that is required of it in the present context. At most, it could justify the authority of the state *internally*. It could not justify the rights of states *in relation to one another*. It could possibly establish the obligation of citizens to obey the law and accept the authority of the state, on the grounds that they have implicitly contracted to do so by accepting the benefits provided by the state, and have thereby relinquished certain of their individual rights. This might justify a limited notion of sovereignty as the state's monopoly on the exercise of force *within* the community. What this classical version of contract theory cannot do is establish obligations on the part of other states to respect the sovereignty and rights of the state. It cannot justify the idea of sovereignty in its *external* dimension. And that is what would be needed to underpin a principled objection to military intervention.

Walzer uses the idea of a 'contract' in a rather different way:

> Over a long period of time, shared experiences and cooperative activity of many different kinds shape a common life. 'Contract' is a metaphor for a process of association and mutuality, the on-going character of which the state claims to protect against external encroachment.[7]

Talk of a 'contract' here refers not to a process whereby individuals hand over some of their rights to the state, but to the process through which, as Walzer puts it, individuals 'shape a common life'. This 'common life' is what Walzer also refers to as the life of a 'political community', and there is an important distinction to be made between the *political community* and the *state* which protects it. On this picture, the role of the state is to create and defend the space within which a political community can carry on its own life, run its own affairs and work out its own destiny without outside interference. It is important for a political community to shape its own common life, and that includes making its own mistakes and dealing with its own problems. Even if the human rights of individuals are violated within that community, this is a matter for the community to deal with internally. Outsiders 'don't know enough about its history, and they have no direct experience, and can form no concrete judgments, of the conflicts and harmonies, the historical choices and cultural affinities, the loyalties and resentments, that underlie it'.[8] It is a 'morally necessary presumption' that 'there exists a certain "fit" between the community and its government'. The state's rights of territorial integrity and political sovereignty therefore derive from its role in protecting the life of a self-determining political community.

The trouble with this picture is that it assumes *too close* a fit between the community and the state. What counts as a 'political community'? If we simply define 'political' as that dimension of life which is represented by the state, then of course the political community and the state will trivially match one another. On any other, wider definition of 'political', however, there are many different political communities at many different levels, both narrower than and wider than the nation state. Whether we choose to call them 'political' is not the important question. What matters is that there are many and diverse communities in which people share a common life and in which they deliberate and make decisions together about how that shared life should go. Once we recognise this obvious fact, the distinction between political communities and other kinds of communities becomes more blurred and less significant. Communitarian theorists are right to emphasise that community membership is integral to the identity of individuals and is essential for any meaningful and fulfilling human life. However, the communities which are identity-conferring for any particular individual will be multifarious. They may include one's family, workplace, profession, religion or belief-community, and many different kinds of cultural or intellectual community, or a community with which one shares leisure interests or sporting activities. My nationality, my membership of a nation-state, is just one identity-conferring community allegiance, not necessarily the most important, and certainly not the only important one. Some more convincing argument is therefore needed to justify the claim that there is just one community, the nation-state, which should be immune to outside interference and can legitimately be defended by military action, and to justify the attribution of special rights to states as contrasted with other kinds of communities. A strong notion of sovereignty cannot be established simply by appeal to the idea of the common life of a political community.

That is not the end of the argument. I will suggest shortly that there may well be more pragmatic reasons for attaching importance to the political sovereignty of nation-states, and that these may underpin a pragmatic case for ruling out military intervention which purports to be 'humanitarian', and for treating defence against aggression as the only acceptable moral justification for military action. At this point I am simply arguing that such a position cannot be sustained by any strong theory of states' rights. If the status of human rights is problematic, that of states' rights is even more so.

Intervention

If no strong theory of states' rights and state sovereignty can be sustained, I conclude that there is no objection *in principle* to interference in the political affairs of other states and other communities. This will become clearer if we set aside for the moment the specific question of the rights and wrongs of *military* intervention. If we do so, it is easier to see that a general principle of non-interference is not very plausible. Moreover, despite the caution I have advocated about employing the vocabulary of human rights, that vocabulary may often present itself as an appropriate one in which to articulate the reasons for interference. The language of human rights has been increasingly used by various campaigning groups and non-governmental organisations which seek to intervene in and thereby influence the political affairs of other countries, and a consideration of such examples will help to bring out the intuitive implausibility of a general principle of non-interference.

I mentioned previously the work of Amnesty International. It is a classic example of an organisation which sees its task as being to intervene in the internal politics of other states in the name of human rights. It campaigns, for instance, against the torture of prisoners, against the imprisonment of political dissidents, and against the use of the death penalty. Undoubtedly the governments which it criticises are likely to respond that such campaigning is an illegitimate interference in the affairs of another country. It may be true that critics from outside have to take special care to get their facts right, and may not always be in a good position to know, from a distance, whether a prisoner is a political dissident or an ordinary criminal, but there is no good basis for any general presumption that outsiders are in no position to judge because they have no direct experience of or involvement in the political traditions and practices of the country. Certainly, no general theory of states' rights can plausibly justify any claim that such interference is a violation of a state's right to political sovereignty.

Consider, as another example, the campaigning of the anti-apartheid movement over many years, in the end successfully, against the policy of apartheid in South Africa. As far as I know, no one ever advocated military intervention from outside to overthrow apartheid, but the campaign brought various kinds of pressure to bear on the apartheid regime, particularly in the form of sanctions and boycotts. Spokespersons for the South African government objected that this was an interference in the internal affairs of South Africa, and indeed it was. It was a deliberate attempt by outsiders to intervene in defence of the human rights of the majority of the population. Far from lacking knowledge of what was going on, outside campaigners against apartheid may well have had a better idea of its true character than many white South Africans corralled in their privileged localities and with strong motives for self-deception about the treatment of the black population. Here was a case of outside intervention, in the name of human rights, which it would be difficult to criticise.

A third example: there has been widespread opposition to the export of weapons to other countries, especially in cases where it is likely that the weapons would be used for purposes of internal repression and the violation of human rights, and in 2002 the British government introduced tougher legislation to restricts arms sales. Oxfam and other organisations lobbied for the inclusion in the legislation of a 'sustainable development' clause which would prohibit the sale of weapons to developing countries if their purchase of them was deemed a waste of resources which would be better spent on essential services such as education and health care. That would obviously be an intrusion into overseas governments' own decisions about how to spend national resources. It is perhaps a slightly more controversial example than the previous two, but I see no reason why such intrusion should not be justified if governments are failing their own people in this way. The example also takes us back to earlier questions about the range of human rights, and whether these include positive rights to things such as food and health and education. It can be argued that if we should not sell arms to governments which will use them to intimidate and repress their own citizens, we should by the same token not sell arms to governments which, by spending money in this way, neglect their people's basic needs. Whether we call these latter concerns matters of human rights does not, in this case, seem to me to be a question of any great importance.

My final example is again a little more controversial. It is the case of female genital mutilation, also referred to as 'clitoridectomy' and 'female circumcision'. This is a widely established traditional practice in many countries, especially in Africa. It is also seen by many as a violation of women's basic human rights.[9] The rights in question may be variously identified as women's right to control their own bodies, including their own sexual lives, or more generally, the rights to autonomy or to dignity. If it is, however, a traditional practice of the communities in which it is found, are outsiders entitled to intervene with the intention of preventing it and banning it? Here, we need to distinguish between the entitlement to intervene, and the manner in which it might be done. Simply to blunder in and attempt to uproot long-established traditions would be both insensitive and likely to fail. Those who campaign against female genital mutilation typically recognise the need to work with those in the local community who are themselves opposed to the practice, and indeed may themselves have been victims of it. And this (like the example of opposition to apartheid) reminds us again that 'communities' are not monolithic and do not have sharp boundaries. A national community will also include diverse sub-communities, and what may be described from one point of view as interference in the larger community may also be describable as working with one sub-community against another.

I have not argued for the practical conclusions which I assume in my various examples. I rely simply on their intuitive appeal to dislodge the idea that there is anything inherently unacceptable about 'intervention' as such. What is problematic is not intervention in general, or 'humanitarian' intervention, but *military* intervention.[10] It is to this that I now turn.

Military Intervention

I want to argue first that war, and especially modern methods of warfare, are activities singularly ill-suited to the upholding of human rights. I have discussed the difficulty of clearly demarcating what are to count as human rights, but by any reckoning, the most fundamental and least controversial of all candidates is the right to life. It goes without saying that the relation between war and the right to life is problematic. War kills. The standard way of attempting to reconcile the waging of war with respect for the right to life involves making a morally significant distinction between combatants and non-combatants. Combatants, it is said, just in virtue of being combatants, have lost the right to life which they would possess in civil life, and may legitimately be killed, whereas non-combatants retain that right in full, and the deliberate killing of civilians in war is therefore morally prohibited. I want to suggest that both those lines of thought, as typically applied to modern warfare, incorporate a diminished conception of human rights.

First, then, how can it be the case that combatants, just by being combatants, have lost their right to life? Note first that this is indeed what has to be claimed. It is not enough that the soldier on the battlefield who is being attacked by an enemy combatant has the right to kill the attacker. War as it is waged in the modern world cannot be morally justified unless it is accepted that combatants in general, whatever they are doing and regardless of whether they are actually fighting or threatening anyone, are legitimate targets. How can that be? The standard model intended to justify this idea is the self-defence analogy. In the case of individual self-defence, the attacker A, by threatening B's life, has thereby lost his own right to life, and B may justifiably kill A to defend his life. In other words, the reason why killing A is held not to be an impermissible violation of his right to life is that A himself is violating or threatening to violate someone else's rights. There are clear disanalogies between this and killing in war. As I have just noted, the killing of military combatants is standardly held to be acceptable in situations which go well beyond that of defence against immediate threats to life. More specifically, a military intervention intended to uphold human rights is bound to involve the widespread killing of combatants who have not themselves violated or threatened to violate human rights. Some members of the armed forces may themselves have engaged in the torture of prisoners or the assassination of political opponents or the repression of dissent, but it is unlikely that most of them, especially in a conscript army, will be responsible for such activities. Now of course the general question of whether and how the killing of combatants in war can be morally justified is a large and fundamental question which I cannot hope to discuss properly here. The one thing I am claiming is that any plausible attempt at a justification, whether of killing combatants in war in general or in a war of humanitarian intervention in particular, will have to work with a much weaker notion of the right to life than is accepted in any other area of human activity.

The same goes for the idea of non-combatant immunity. This is supposed to embody the principle that those who are not directly participating in the war retain in full their right to life and may not permissibly be killed or made the target of military actions. In practice, as we know, wars purportedly fought to uphold human rights may well involve civilian casualties on a large scale. These are typically referred to, in contemporary military language, as 'collateral damage'. Such a description invokes something like the traditional moral principle of 'double effect'; the taking of civilian lives is said to be justifiable if it is an unintended side-effect of military action, rather than directly intended.

I do not necessarily want to reject the principle of double effect. It does seem to me to have a limited plausibility in a restricted range of cases. Suppose, for instance, that a local health authority decides to close the accident and emergency unit in one hospital and expand that in another, and suppose they have correctly calculated that though some people requiring emergency medical treatment will now be further from the A&E unit and will die as a result, more lives will be saved overall. Despite the loss of some lives, most of us would see such an action as justified and as significantly different from a case of deliberately killing some innocent people in order to save the lives of others. The loss of some lives is quite properly describable as an unintended and unavoidable, though foreseen, side-effect. Notice that the action is subject to a strict requirement of proportionality: it will save more lives overall, and the price to be paid is not disproportional. I think that most people's intuitions about this case also take account of the fact that the deaths which occur, and which would not have occurred if the decision had not be made, are not actively brought about. The case is one of failing to save lives rather than of actively killing, and this helps to support our perception of the deaths as genuinely 'side-effects'.

The killing of civilians as so-called 'collateral damage' in a war is likely to be very different. Consider the case of bombing political buildings, communications centres, television stations, power stations and bridges in urban areas, knowing that substantial numbers of civilians will be killed. It may be true that the civilian deaths are unintended. Nevertheless, it is straining the sense of the phrase to describe them as 'side-effects'. They are actively brought about, and are too directly linked to the character of the intended actions to be regarded as simply incidental. Now it is, of course, possible to engage in humanitarian military intervention which does not involve the bombing of populated areas, and which does not involve the killing of significant numbers of non-combatants. However, the kinds of weaponry and the kinds of military strategy employed by those governments which talk most loudly about 'humanitarian intervention' are more than likely to involve civilian casualties. What is more, the numbers of civilians actually killed in military operations such as the bombings of Serbia, Afghanistan and Iraq, in each case running into thousands, raise serious questions about whether the requirement of proportionality has been met.

As with my previous point, I leave open large questions here about the ethics of war in general. I confine myself again to the modest claim that when it comes to killing in war, much weaker standards of human rights are liable to be applied. Therefore, we need to be much more cautious about *military* intervention in the name of human rights than about other kinds of intervention.

It may be said that though military action is in itself liable to violate and override human rights, this is the price that has to be paid for protecting and promoting human rights in the long term. Such a position is what has been called a 'utilitarianism of rights': the overriding of some people's rights can be justified if this is the course of action likely to bring about the most extensive promotion of human rights in the long run. That is indeed the language which we have sometimes heard from politicians and other advocates of military intervention in recent years.

Notice first that to see rights in this way is to abandon what many writers have seen as one of the distinctive features of rights. I have said that one important category of human rights consists of those fundamental moral constraints which set limits to what one may permissibly do to a human being for any end, however desirable the anticipated consequences. You cannot, for instance, kill innocent people to save the lives of others. Rights cannot be traded in that kind of way. The point is sometimes put by referring to the *separateness* of individual persons. If one person's rights are sacrificed to promote the rights of others, there is no overall collective entity whose rights are maximised. There are only individuals, some of whom have had their rights violated, and others of whom have had their rights promoted. The rights that have been promoted cannot compensate the other individuals for the loss of their rights. This is most conspicuously the case with the right to life. There are only individual lives, and if some people are killed to promote the rights of others, this is in a precise sense an irretrievable loss.

There is also more to be said about a utilitarianism of rights from a practical point of view. Military intervention in the name of human rights may not only enshrine a distortion of the idea of rights. It may also be, quite simply, a bad way of promoting rights, one which is especially liable to fail. Military intervention is essentially *coercive*. Its intention is to threaten death or injury against those who will not comply. The aim of military intervention may be to set up new civil structures of an open and democratic kind based on respect for everyone's rights. The problem is the difficulty of marking a clear cut-off between the military coercion and the rights-respecting structures which it is supposed to install. If the rights-respecting institutions and practices were to some extent present already and can be revived or restored, the transition may be feasible. However, the more repressive the previous institutions were, the more difficult it will be to replace them with new habits and practices of respect for rights. These cannot just be imported and imposed. Rights-respecting institutional practices have to be built up over a period of time, they require mutual trust and an atmosphere of openness and tolerance which cannot be created overnight. A military invasion, in contrast, is bound to be followed by a period of military occupation. If the occupying forces are the principal authority maintaining order, and if there is no tradition of civil institutions embodying respect for rights, a spiral of decline is all too likely. The military forces have to institute a coercive rough justice in order to maintain order, the coercion and the apparent lack of respect for rights provokes resentment and reaction, the occupying forces have to become more coercive, the resistance becomes stronger, and so on. We have seen this before, and (at the time of writing) we are seeing it again now.

These are contingent causal claims about the efficacy of military action as a means of promoting human rights, rather than claims about the intrinsic nature of military action. Both kinds of claims converge, I suggest, on the following practical conclusion. Military intervention cannot, from outside, impose rights-respecting practices on a community. All it can do is to protect such political practices, where they are already in existence or coming into existence, against threats to them. A classic example is the military intervention in East Timor. In August 1999, the people of East Timor voted overwhelmingly, in a poll conducted under United Nations auspices, for independence from Indonesia. The pro-integration militias, with support from some elements in the Indonesian security forces, then began a campaign of intimidation with the aim of preventing the implementation of the decision. The United Nations Security Council authorised the deployment of a multinational military force to restore peace and security in East Timor. Indonesia agreed to accept this, and troops were deployed under a command structure headed by the Australians. By October, they had been able to establish a UN Transitional Administration to take over from Indonesia and oversee the transition to independence, and that process has now been completed. This, then, was intervention to protect rights-respecting practices, not to impose them. As such, it was able to succeed, and to do so without requiring activities which themselves violated human rights. Crucially, although it was intervention employing military forces, it was not a war.

I want to return finally to the relevance of my earlier argument about the indeterminacy of human rights. The range of basic human rights, I argued, is essentially contested. That does not mean that views about what are to count as human rights are arbitrary. The range is rationally contested. Nevertheless, a consensus is difficult to come by, and probably unattainable. Some candidates for basic human rights are less controversial than others, but disagreements about what is included will reflect deep differences about the nature of human society and the relation between individual and collective action. The important implication of this for my present argument is that a principle of military intervention in the name of human rights cannot function as an agreed basis for an international order.

Some politicians, including UK Prime Minister Tony Blair, have talked about a 'New World Order' based on the idea of human rights and on the use of military intervention to establish and maintain such an order. Because of the indeterminacy of rights, I do not believe that this is possible. It is a recipe for international disorder. Even nations committed in good faith to the idea of human rights are bound to disagree about what this requires. In practice, as we know, bad faith is all too apparent. The more the principle of military intervention to uphold human rights gains currency, the more individual nations will use it to intervene in pursuit of their own interests, while rationalising their actions in the language of human rights.

I have been critical of the use of 'contract' theory to illuminate the status of human rights, but one area where the idea of a contract does have application is at the international level. Any international order has to be based on agreement, and the agreement has to be not an agreement between individuals, but between nation-states. Locke's version of the social contract, though untenable as an account of the relation between the natural rights of individuals and the foundation of civil society, provides quite a good model for the relation between states and an international order. According to Locke, in the state of nature men have rights to their lives, liberties and estates, all of which Locke subsumes under the right to preserve their property. They are also bound by the law of nature to respect one another's rights, and to punish those who transgress such rights. The defect of the state of nature is that the imposition of such punishment is left to the judgement of individuals, who both lack the power to enforce it effectively, and are also inclined to be biased in their judgements:

> For though the law of nature be plain and intelligible to all rational creatures; yet men being biassed by their interest, as well as ignorant for want of studying it, are not apt to allow of it as a law binding to them in the application of it to their particular cases … Every one in that state being both judge and executioner in the law of nature, men being partial to themselves, passion and revenge is very apt to carry them too far, and with too much heat, in their own cases; as well as negligence, and unconcernedness, to make them too remiss in other men's.[11]

It is to remedy this defect that people contract to set up a civil authority whose principal aim is to protect them in the enjoyment of their rights to their property.

Locke's subsuming of all individual human rights under the right to property is far too simplistic, but there may be a plausible analogue when it comes to the establishment of an international order to protect the rights of states. Individual governments seeking to uphold human rights are liable to be 'biassed by their interest', in some cases they are liable to be 'carried too far' by 'passion and revenge', and in other cases they are liable to be 'too remiss' because of 'negligence and unconcernedness'. The use of military force to punish violations of rights is therefore likely to be selective and inconsistent. If each government makes its own decisions about when to use military force to uphold human rights, international society is liable to degenerate into a condition of permanent war. This can be prevented only by the establishment of an international order based on the agreement of all states, and the one plausible basis for that agreement is the principle that each state has jurisdiction over its own internal affairs. This version of the right of states to sovereignty is the international analogue of Locke's right of property. In the real world in which we live, that international contract between states is the Charter of the United Nations, which enshrines a commitment to 'promoting and encouraging respect for human rights', but which prohibits states from using military force except in individual or collective self-defence against an armed attack, and which confines the use of military force by the United Nations itself to the maintenance or restoration of international peace and security.[12] All states which are parties to that contract agree to an international order 'based on respect for the principle of equal rights and self determination of peoples', and agree to 'refrain in their international relations from the threat or use of force against the territorial integrity or political independence of any state'.[13] If all states adhered to that principle, and employed military force only in self-defence, there would be no war. In contrast, an international order which allowed states to use military force in order to uphold human rights in other states would be a recipe for war without end.

I argued earlier that it is not possible to defend a theory of states' rights, derived from the human rights of individuals, which would underpin a strong principle of sovereignty. I argued accordingly that there is no objection in principle to interference in the internal affairs of states with the aim of protecting or promoting the human rights of their members. What I have argued against is the use of *military* intervention to that end. My final argument is for a pragmatic principle of sovereignty which would rule out such military intervention. And the pragmatic case for it is that it is the only feasible basis for an international order based on agreement.

Notes

1   Augustine, *Against Faustus* 22, 74, in Beck, Robert N. and Orr, John B. (trans.) (1970), *Ethical Choice*, New York and London: Free Press, 368.
2   The classic modern presentation of this position is Walzer, Michael (1977), *Just and Unjust Wars*, Harmondsworth: Penguin.
3   Bentham is regularly misquoted as saying that the idea of natural rights is 'nonsense on stilts'. What he actually said is: '*Natural rights* is simple nonsense: natural and imprescriptible rights, rhetorical nonsense, – nonsense upon stilts' (*Anarchical Fallacies: An Examination of the Declaration of Rights*, Article II). In other words, to claim not just that human beings have natural rights, but that nothing could deprive human beings of those rights or justify contravening them, is to elevate the nonsensical idea to a higher and more dangerous level.
4   Ibid.
5   Article 24 of the United Nations Universal Declaration of Human Rights.
6   'The rights ... [of] territorial integrity and political sovereignty ... belong to states, but they derive ultimately from the rights of individuals': Walzer, Michael (1977), *Just and Unjust Wars*, 53.
7   Ibid., 54.
8   Walzer, Michael, 'The Moral Standing of States: A Response to Four Critics', in Beitz, Charles R., Cohen, Marshall, Scanlon, Thomas and Simmons, A. John (eds) (1985), *International Ethics*, Princeton University Press, 220.
9   See, for instance, Nussbaum, Martha (1999), 'Judging Other Cultures: The Case of Genital Mutilation', in *Sex and Social Justice*, New York and Oxford: Oxford University Press; and Marzano, Maria Michela, 'Universalism and Cultural Specificity: Female Circumcision, Intrinsic Dignity and Human Rights', in Moseley, Alexander and Norman, Richard (eds) (2002), *Human Rights and Military Intervention*, Aldershot: Ashgate.
10 On this, I agree with Anthony Ellis, 'War, Revolution, and Humanitarian Intervention', in Jokic, Aleksander (ed.) (2003), *Humanitarian Intervention*, Toronto: Broadview

Press, 17. Similar positions are taken by Dower, Nigel, 'Violent Intervention – An Oxymoron?', and by Paul Robinson, 'Humanitarian Intervention and the Logic of War', both in Moseley and Norman (eds), *Human Rights and Military Intervention*. I have learned much from all three.

11   Locke, John (1689), *Second Treatise of Government*, Ch. IX, paras 124 and 125.
12   See, for example, Articles 1 and 2, and 39–51.
13   Article 1.2 and Article 2.4.

Chapter 11

Culture, the Enemy and the Moral Restraint of War

Anthony Coates

I presented an earlier version of this essay at a conference in Alexandria in December 2002 at the invitation of the Averroes and Enlightenment International Association.

In 1864, the Civil War in America took a decisive turn. Avoiding a confrontation with Confederate forces, the Unionist General William Tecumseh Sherman mounted a sustained attack on the infrastructure of the South, commencing with the sack of Atlanta. From there he marched his army south and east to Savannah on the Atlantic coast, and then northwards through the Carolinas, devastating the land as he went. His strategy provoked moral outrage among opponents wedded to ideals of chivalry and civilised warfare. Sherman answered his critics robustly, justifying his strategy by an appeal to the internal necessities of war itself: 'If the people raise a howl against my barbarity and cruelty', he wrote, 'I will answer that war is war' (Sherman, 1961, 104). When the Mayor of Atlanta protested at the inhuman treatment of women and children, Sherman replied: 'War is cruelty, and you cannot refine it … You might as well appeal against the thunderstorm as against these terrible hardships of war' (Sherman, 1961, 121–2).

The view of war that Sherman famously articulated is commonly (though perhaps misleadingly) referred to as 'realism'. A realist, in the sense employed here, regards the '*ethics* of war' as a self-contradictory notion. Just war and actual war are poles apart. The attempt to subject war to moral limitation is doomed from the outset (though limitations of a non-moral, pragmatic kind are another matter). War has its own logic and dynamic that conflict with morality. War is simply not amenable to sustained moral determination, and any attempt to subordinate it, consistently, to morality is bound to fail. From this perspective, an unbridgeable divide exists between war as it is and war as the moralist would like it to be or imagines it to be. The deliberations of moral philosophers, including just war theorists, bear little relation to the harsh realities of war.

The problem, however, is not seen to end there, and the realist is far from indifferent to what is seen as a misplaced moral intrusion into the business of war. 'In such dangerous things as war', wrote Clausewitz, 'the errors which proceed from a spirit of benevolence are the worst' (von Clausewitz, 1982, 102). Although the attempt to apply morality to war is bound to fail, it is not without significant effect. Of course, the actual effect of applying morality to the alien business of war is not the effect intended by most moralists, namely the moderation of war. On the contrary, by disrupting the normal processes of war, the application of morality ends up making matters much worse. Without Sherman's 'unethical' strategy, the military stalemate in the Civil War would have continued, adding very considerably to the already horrendous costs of the war. For the realist, morality is an unwarranted *and* dangerous intrusion into war.

The realist's distrust of morality is, in part, well founded. The application of morality to war often does lead to the escalation of war. It is this that accounts for the deep suspicions harboured by many critics of the idea of the just war. Carl Schmitt, for example, argued that the inherent tendency of all just wars is towards total war, turning a limited 'enemy' into an absolute 'foe'. It is true that the justificatory and empowering effect of a war conceived as just has often been more prominent than its more authentic restraining and inhibiting influence.[1] The moral triumphalism exhibited by some just warriors has led to the enthusiastic embrace of war and its immoderate prosecution. In this guise, just war is closer to militarism than it is to any tradition of limited warfare. However, what this demonstrates is not the futility, or inefficacy, of morality, but on the contrary, its savage power, its ability (albeit in distorted form) to determine the shape of war. To regard war, as Sherman appears to have regarded it, as a natural phenomenon (like the thunderstorm), with its own inner necessity against which morality is powerless, is greatly to misconceive the reality of war. The 'necessity' to which appeal is made *against* morality is, in fact, always a cultural and moral necessity. As contemporary military historians are at pains to demonstrate, 'Culture is a prime determinant of war' (Keegan, 1993, 387). War is not a natural necessity, driven by its own internal and unchanging logic, but a cultural *and* normative reality, for if culture is a prime determinant of war, then so too is morality.[2] Any view of war that neglects this cultural and moral dimension must be radically deficient.

The importance of acknowledging the essential role played in war by the moral culture of war applies just as much to the moral theorist as it does to the military practitioner. The tendency of realists to overlook that culture is matched by those moral philosophers of war for whom the ethics of war consists exclusively in the articulation and application of abstract moral principles and concepts. Realist scepticism about such an unworldly, non-experiential, form of ethical enquiry seems more than justified. More thought needs to be given in moral theory itself to the question of the feasibility of principles. In particular, attention should be focused not just on the moral principles of war but on the moral psychology that those principles presuppose.

Ways need to be found of empowering belligerents to conduct war justly and of inhibiting the unjust conduct of war. The reality of war leaves little room for the moral athleticism of individual belligerents that some versions of the ethics of war imply (the realist is right about that). The just (or unjust) warrior is never a self-made man. Recognition of the collective nature of moral agency, of the intimate connection that exists between the moral agent and the moral community to which he belongs, is essential. To bring the psychology of war to the fore is to bring the culture of war to the fore. The moral habits and dispositions that belligerents bring to war are formed in and through the moral cultures or communities to which they belong. Acquiring the capacity to conduct war justly is as much a social and cultural achievement as it is an individual one. To regard the just conduct of war as more 'ethical' than 'moral', in other words, more a matter of shared moral habits, prejudices and dispositions (formed in and by moral communities and cultures) than a matter of independent reasoning and soul-searching, is greatly to improve its prospects.

A key element of the moral culture of any war is the concept of the enemy. War (including a just war) is inconceivable without *some* image, or concept, of the enemy. It is the presence of the enemy that gives meaning and justification to war. 'War follows from enmity', wrote Carl Schmitt. 'War has its own strategic, tactical, and other rules and points of view, but they all presuppose that the political decision has already been made as to who the enemy is' (Schmitt, 1996, 34). The concept of the enemy is fundamental to the moral assessment of war: 'The basic aim of a nation at war in establishing an image of the enemy is to distinguish as sharply as possible the act of killing from the act of murder' (Gray, 1970, 131–2). However, we need to be wary of thinking of war and the image of the enemy that informs it in an abstract and uniform way. Rather, both must be seen for the cultural and contingent phenomena that they are. The image of the enemy – like war itself – can change from one culture (and one time) to another. Indeed, even within the same culture (and the same time), diverse images of the enemy are discernible. These different images exert a powerful influence on war, largely determining its ethical purpose and direction.

In the Second World War, Germany fought the war in Europe on two main fronts and in two starkly contrasting ways.[3] Its conduct of the war in the west was (with some very notable exceptions) in accordance with the rules and conventions of war. Thus, the immunity of captured POWs was generally respected and their conditions of imprisonment were such that the vast majority of allied prisoners survived the war. Similarly, acts of looting, rape and murder committed by the German soldiery against the civilian populations of the occupied western territories were often subjected to military law and punished by military tribunals.

In the east, the treatment of captured soldiers and of the civilian population was very different. Extermination squads operated behind the advancing German army. Those prisoners who were not killed immediately were forced into hard labour that ended, more often than not, in death from exhaustion and starvation, so that out of a total of 5 million Soviet prisoners 3½ million did not survive capture by the German army.[4] The civilian populations of the occupied territories in the east fared no better. Not only did criminal acts against them go unpunished, but such acts were positively encouraged and systematically led. According to a directive issued by the

commander of Panzer Group 4: 'The war against the Soviet Union … is the old struggle of the Germans against the Slavs, the defence of European culture against the Muscovite-Asiatic flood, the warding off of Jewish Bolshevism. This struggle must have as its aim the demolition of present Russia and must therefore be conducted with unprecedented severity. Both the planning and the execution of every battle must be dictated by an iron will to bring about a merciless, total annihilation of the enemy' (cited in Bartov, 1991, 129).

The grossly uneven treatment of Germany's western and eastern adversaries had its roots in the contrasting images of the enemy cultivated by the racist ideology of National Socialism, with which the units of the Wehrmacht (products of the Hitler Youth) had been indoctrinated. According to the principles of that ideology, Germany was confronted on the Western Front by an enemy whose fundamental equality it could acknowledge, an enemy with whom it shared a common (or closely related) racial and cultural identity. The enemy in the east, on the other hand, was seen to belong to a quite different category. The Slavs (like the Jews, with whom they were forever associated in National Socialist thinking) were sub-humans, *Untermenschen*, destined either for annihilation or, at best, to act as slave labour for their Aryan masters.

Different enemies required different wars. The war in the west was seen as a limited war, a war fought with limited means for limited (political) ends. Against its western adversary, Germany might welcome the prospect of a negotiated peace. With such an enemy, an act of accommodation was both conceivable and tolerable. However, no thoughts of compromise could be entertained towards the eastern foe. This *Weltanschauungkrieg* ('Battle of ideologies') was war of a very different kind. It was the kind of war that Clausewitz termed 'absolute', the kind of war in which the 'political point of view vanishes completely' and only 'war of life and death from pure hatred' remains. This war was 'existential', a total war, fought either for survival or for extinction, a war that could never lead to a negotiated peace, a war that must end either in victory or in defeat. It was the kind of war that Schmitt described as 'necessarily unusually intense and inhuman because, by transcending the limits of the political framework, it simultaneously degrades the enemy into moral and other categories and is forced to make of him a monster that must not only be defeated but also utterly destroyed' (Schmitt, 1996, 36).

After attending a meeting of high-ranking officers with Hitler to plan Operation Barbarossa, Halder (one of Hitler's Generals) made the following entry in his diary: 'Struggle of two ideologies … We must abandon the viewpoint of soldierly comradeship. The Communist is no comrade before and no comrade afterwards. What is involved is a struggle of annihilation … This fight will be very different from the fight in the West. In the East harshness is kindness toward the future. The leaders must demand of themselves the sacrifice of overcoming their scruples' (quoted in Fest, 1974, 649). As Halder implies, the moral test in the east was the reverse of the moral convention that prevailed in the west. Comradeship between adversaries (a key assumption of civilised warfare) was replaced by total hostility or enmity. Atrocities became the moral, and not just the empirical, norm (as they must in a war that is conceived as a war of annihilation). Perversely, the merciless conduct of the war in the east had a *moral* source and inspiration. The systematic cruelty was guided by a strong sense of moral duty and reinforced by a deliberate ethic of 'harshness'. That ethic transformed great crimes into virtues, encouraging its followers to take pride in their ability to triumph over feelings of moral inhibition and revulsion.

It was not some inner necessity of war, but the moral culture of Nazi Germany that made the difference between the war in the west and the war in the east. War is always a reflection of its moral culture. The concept of the 'enemy' is a key part of that culture. Different concepts engender different wars. Whether or not war remains limited, or truly just, depends to a very great extent on the concept of the enemy belligerents bring with them to war. The phenomenon is as old as war itself. One of the earliest reflections on it occurs in Plato's *Republic*. The logic of enmity is laid bare in Book V (470–71), where Plato draws a fundamental distinction between two very different kinds of conflict – 'discord' and 'war'. The first refers to the '*internal*' (or civil) wars of Greek against Greek, the second to '*external*' wars between Greek and Barbarian.

'Discord' is a limited form of warfare between enemies who are (in Plato's words) 'by nature friends'. It is an anomalous and aberrant condition that contradicts the normal state of affairs. Between such enemies, peace, not war, is the norm, so much so that, even in conflict, the primacy of peace is maintained. In discord, adversaries retain the desire for peace in their hearts and do not mean to go on fighting for ever: 'they quarrel as those who intend some day to be reconciled'. With future reconciliation in mind, they moderate their conduct of the war. They limit its severity and destructive force. They conduct it proportionately, that is, economically. They respect the immunity of non-combatants. 'They will not devastate Hellas', Socrates declares, 'nor will they burn houses, nor ever suppose that the whole population of a city – men, women, and children – are equally their enemies, for they know that the guilt of a war is always confined to a few persons and that the many are their friends' (471.a). The aims of this war are always limited. As a result, conflict is readily ended: 'enmity will only last until the many innocent sufferers have compelled the guilty few to give satisfaction' (471.b). Such war ends not with the annihilation of the enemy, but with the attainment of specific redress and the restoration of peaceful relations.

'Discord' is limited war between enemies who are by nature friends, who, for all their differences, still form one community. It is this vestigial sense of community, or friendship, that inhibits war-making and that encourages its moderation. Very different considerations apply to war between Greek and Barbarian. About this 'external' war, Plato is relatively silent, though this is a silence that speaks volumes. 'War', we are meant to conclude, is everything that 'discord' is not. Since 'war' is a conflict between those who are 'by nature enemies', it must be limitless. There is nothing aberrant about this form of war. For such total enemies war, not peace, is the norm. Even when they are not fighting, they continue to exist in a permanent state of war. Between them, a standing cause of war exists – a cause that owes nothing to specific threats made or injuries received, but one that is rooted in the perception of the enemy's fundamental Otherness. Total enmity engenders total war. In 'war', the limits that apply to 'discord' fall away. Here belligerents *do* 'suppose that the whole population of a city – men, women, and children – are equally their enemies'. In 'war' all are numbered among the 'guilty'. 'War' is terminable not by any specific act of redress, but only through the elimination of the threat that the very existence of the Other represents. In short, annihilation is the inherent tendency of 'war'.

The twin distinction of enmity and war has exerted a powerful and lasting influence on European and world history. Instances of the distinction at work are legion. Often it has determined the choice of weaponry as well as the choice of strategy. In 1139, for example, the Lateran Council of the Catholic Church sanctioned the use of the crossbow (a weapon regarded then with the kind of fear and moral repugnance that weapons of mass destruction now provoke) against infidels, but not against fellow Christians. Similarly, in the nineteenth century, the soft-nosed dum-dum bullet, designed not just to penetrate the body but to tear it apart, was developed (by the British in India) for use in colonial wars, but not in European ones. The distinction was even given legal backing. According to the historian V. G. Kiernan: 'The Hague Convention [of 1899] banned the bullet from civilized warfare, but left it to be used against wild animals or wild men' (Kiernan, 1998, 157). The prevailing view among the colonial powers was that 'war against savages cannot be carried out according to acknowledged rules but to common sense' (Kiernan, 1998, 154).

Throughout the history of warfare, classification as an 'external' enemy in Plato's sense, that is, as the Other, has had dire consequences for those concerned. For example, the medieval crusade against the western Slavs by the Teutonic Knights was a war with a mission, a clash of civilisations, a war fought to vindicate Christianity against its pagan rival and cultural antithesis. Of that war, one historian has written: 'The warfare along the Baltic was about as near to total war as medieval man could get – a war of atrocity and counter-atrocity in which no quarter was given … [C]learly, [the author concludes] war against the "other" took on a quite different and extreme form compared to that fought *within* western Europe, where it only rarely reached this level of bitterness' (France, 1999, 203). The conclusion seems premature. Not all the wars fought within western Europe remained 'internal' and, therefore, limited. 'External' wars, wars against the Other, could and did occur. Divisions – first religious, then ideological – created absolute enmities within Europe itself. Thus, of the religious wars of the sixteenth and seventeenth centuries between Catholic and Protestant, Westlake wrote, '[they were] the most terrible in which the beast in man ever broke loose' (quoted in Morgenthau, 1973, 241), and the same could be said of the secular and ideological wars that were to follow.

In the Second World War, it was not just Germany that fought the war on two different fronts and in two utterly contrasting ways. The application of a differential ethic of war was evident elsewhere. The conduct of US soldiers in the European theatre of war contrasted starkly with their conduct of war in the Pacific. In Europe, German soldiers were treated, on the whole, in accordance with the laws and conventions of war. In the Pacific, however, captured Japanese soldiers were regularly killed and their bodies mutilated.[5] Similarly, in Europe the USAAF (unlike its British counterpart, the RAF) employed a strategy of precision bombing of military targets that was at odds with its strategy of fire bombing and, ultimately, atomic bombing, of Japanese cities. At war's end, the American commander, General Curtis LeMay, reflected, almost wistfully: 'We had two or three weeks of work left on the cities … Another six months and Japan would have been beaten back into the Dark Ages' (Duus, 1988, Vol. VI, 381).

This uneven treatment of the enemy was no doubt, in part, a response to the attack on Pearl Harbor and to the ferocity and fanaticism with which the Japanese themselves conducted the war. It may also have owed something to the cultural and racial attitudes that were widespread at that time in American society and in the American military community. E. B. Sledge, a retired biology professor and a veteran of the Pacific War, recalled, in an interview about his war experiences, how '[o]ur attitude to the Japanese was different than the one we had toward the Germans'. As he explained: 'I have heard many guys who fought in Europe who said the Germans were damn good soldiers. We hated the hell of having to fight 'em. When they surrendered, they were guys just like us. With the Japanese it wasn't that way. … At Okinawa, we took about five prisoners. We had orders not to kill the wounded, to try to take prisoners … but the feeling was strong … Our drill instructor at boot camp would tell us, "You're not going to Europe, you're going to the Pacific. Don't hesitate to fight the Japs dirty"' (Terkel, 1984, 61–2).

The key to the uneven conduct of the war lay, at least in part, in the conflicting American perceptions of the enemy: 'The Germans … were guys just like us … [but] with the Japanese it wasn't that way.' In one case the enemy was seen as an equal with a common identity, in the other case the enemy was seen as different and inferior, even perhaps subhuman (a view reciprocated by the Japanese). Against the Germans, the recognition of equality and community generated respect and fair treatment. Against the Japanese, the assumption of radical difference and inequality released moral inhibitions, so that, at its worst, the war was in danger of degenerating into a war of extermination. The Japanese, unlike the Germans, were the Other, and were treated accordingly. Their Otherness made them not just an 'enemy' but an object of intense fear and loathing.

From this perspective, then, war always appears as a cultural and normative reality, not as an independent and autonomous activity governed by its own inexorable laws. For good or ill (all too often for ill), battle and values go together. When cruelties (atrocities) occur, they do so not in spite of values (as realism might incline us to believe), but, rather, on account of values. Total war is value-laden

war. It is a war that finds its source and inspiration in a *moral* vision of the world, however perverse. There is no escape from values in war. Belligerents do not (and cannot) inhabit some amoral world. That being so, the aim of an ethics of war must be to ensure that the values that determine battle – the values that make up the moral culture of war – promote the moral restraint of war, not its barbarisation.

It has been argued that among the cultural variables that determine when and how wars are fought, perhaps the most important is the concept of the enemy. A distinction has emerged between two main ways of thinking about the enemy: one that inhibits war-making, and one that exacerbates it. The key to limited war, it seems, is the vestigial sense of community that adversaries may retain even in the midst of conflict. What is at work in such circumstances is a way of thinking (and feeling – this is not a merely cognitive or rational response) about the enemy that does not place the enemy beyond the moral pale. The enemy remains part of a moral community that unites potential and even actual belligerents. The ethical conduct of war depends on this fundamental sense of solidarity among belligerents. In short, what is at work here is a *limited* concept of the enemy. The enemy is never an enemy in totality. The enemy is never the Other. It is this limited concept that informs and sustains traditional just war thinking. It seems that without it, there can be no moral restraint of war.

One of the most prominent features of early just war thinking is its conceptual economy. Classical just war theorists, like Augustine or Thomas Aquinas, identified few just war principles compared with their modern counterparts. Aquinas identified three: legitimate authority, just cause, and right intention. The later elaboration of principles reflects changes in the moral culture and a growing concern among moral theorists with the formulation and application of moral rules. The economy of principle in Augustine and Aquinas seems to have owed much to the importance they attached to one principle in particular: *right intention*. Their treatment of it bears upon the central theme of this chapter.

To call *right intention* a principle is, perhaps, to do it less than justice. What it stood for was not some abstract rule (as it has tended to become in many modern formulations of the principle), but rather a certain moral character (comprising habits, attitudes, sentiments and prejudices) that disposed belligerents to limit both their recourse to war and their conduct of war. As such, right intention was seen as the key to a just war. It was right intention that *enabled* belligerents to fulfil the manifold requirements of a just war. In this way, the rules of war were made dependent upon the virtues of war. The moral psychology of the just warrior was not taken for granted. What did tend to be taken for granted were the principles themselves (particularly the principles of what later came to be called *jus in bello*). The reason for this seems clear. With *right intention* in place, the other criteria could take care of themselves. In its absence, no amount of moral deliberation could prevent a descent into the moral abyss of war.

Right intention stood for the moral powers or capacities that a just recourse to war and a just conduct of war required, capacities (or virtues) that could be acquired in the first place only within moral cultures and communities of the appropriate kind. The preponderant modern emphasis on the moral self-sufficiency of rational agents stands in marked contrast to this traditional emphasis on the key role played by the community in the moral life of the individual. It was not by unaided reason, but by drawing on the resources of the moral community (through the transmission of shared values, the instilling of moral norms, the formation of moral habits and dispositions) that the individual became morally empowered. Later theorists disagreed. Johnson cites the case of Vattel, who thought that the *rationalisation* of war would lead to its humanisation. From this rationalist perspective, 'When disposition no longer plays a part in war, then our enemy remains a human being like us' (Johnson, 1975, 250–51). The malign effects of an unjust disposition and culture are very evident, but not all moral dispositions are unjust, and neither are the moral cultures or communities that sustain them. What the just war requires is a just disposition and culture (not rationalisation).

What moral disposition did *right intention* entail? In part, it was understood negatively, demanding the overcoming and exclusion of an unjust but all too common disposition to war. Traditionally, the idea of a just war started from a moral presumption *against* war, a presumption rooted in the perception of the great evil of war – its physical evil, but also its potential, and all too actual, moral evil. The question with which Aquinas prefaces his discussion of just war ('Is warfare always sinful?') is indicative of the moral anxiety about war that he shared with his predecessor and mentor, Augustine. The problem they both addressed is the real and abiding one, namely that the just war (in its true or authentic form) runs counter to deeply ingrained attitudes to war. Unjust wars are rife, and so is the disposition that activates them, a disposition that Augustine alludes to in the following sentence (cited by Aquinas): 'The real evils in war are the love of violence, revengeful cruelty, fierce and implacable enmity, wild resistance, and the lust for power' (*Reply to Faustus*, XXII, 74). The moral tragedy is that far from suppressing these evils, as it is intended to do, the 'just' war sometimes ends up giving vent to them.

'The love of violence' or the lust for war – not all wars are fought reluctantly for instrumental, or external, purposes. For some belligerents (especially 'just' ones), war acquires an intrinsic value. Belligerents such as these are (in Walzer's phrase) 'happy warriors', enthusiasts for war, who find both personal and communal fulfilment in war itself. From their perspective, the evil of war is transformed into a good. The moral presumption against war is replaced by a moral presumption in favour of war. There is a good to be had in war itself that is not achievable elsewhere. The act of violence – the killing of the enemy – becomes a redemptive act, both for the individual perpetrator and for the community on whose behalf he acts. War is no longer the instrument of last resort but a matter of first and positive preference.

'Fierce and implacable enmity' – the concept of the enemy need not (in an authentically just war must not) imply enmity or hatred, yet the hatred of the enemy in a war that is conceived as just may well become 'fierce and implacable' as a

result. Such hatred is not simply a matter of spontaneous feelings aroused by the experience of war itself, and in particular, by the extreme threat to self-preservation which the enemy may pose. It is systematic and anterior to war itself. What is at issue here is a culture of hatred that predisposes belligerents both to resort to war and to conduct war mercilessly. This hatred is a 'public' hatred. It is the response of those who feel themselves (collectively) to be 'by nature enemies'. The enemy is dehumanised or, worse still, demonised. The enemy is the Other, the complete antithesis of the collective self, the embodiment of absolute evil.[6] As a result, moral inhibitions fall away. Far from feeling inhibited, belligerents become disposed (empowered by their cultures and moral communities) to mistreat an enemy so conceived. Perversely, what they have learnt is an *ethic* of harshness. The destruction of the enemy has become a moral duty.

'The lust for power' – in an unjust war force is used, not in response to some specific injury or to right some specific wrong, but to dominate the enemy. In its most extreme and comprehensive form, it is used to vindicate a world-view, to establish the dominion of a particular race, religion, class, nation or culture. The subordination of war to such an aim has a disastrous effect on the justice of war. Just recourse (*jus ad bellum*), just conduct (*jus in bello*) and just peace (*jus ad pacem*) are all thoroughly undermined by this lustful and domineering disposition. It abolishes the moral threshold of war that is *jus ad bellum* by providing a standing cause for war (the defeat of the Other), a cause so elevated (so 'just') in its conception that any war, no matter how destructive, is bound to seem proportionate or worth fighting. It abolishes, just as decisively, the *jus in bello* constraints of proportionality and discrimination. In a war fought with such comprehensive aims, the idea of the excessive, or disproportionate, use of force makes no sense, while the principle of discrimination is engulfed by a concept of the enemy that embraces military and civilian alike. In this counter-value warfare, the reasons for targeting *non*-combatants are at least as compelling as those for targeting combatants.[7] The prospects of a just peace (*jus ad pacem*) in such a war are non-existent. The lust for power, or domination, excludes the basic moral recognition of the enemy that a just peace entails. The acknowledgement that the enemy has rights and interests (in peace, let alone in war) is alien to this domineering spirit. Such a war cannot end in a negotiated peace (that would count as a betrayal), but only in outright victory and defeat.

It must be acknowledged that the just war itself remains acutely vulnerable to this unjust disposition. The infusion of war with a moral purpose, its subordination to justice, is not without risk. Schmitt's fear (one that he shares with many realists) that a just war leads to total enmity and total war is not groundless. An excess of morality may be more dangerous and more harmful than any moral deficit. In war, it seems, there is always more to fear from the moral zealot than there is from the moral sceptic. Recognising and countering this unjust disposition, this inflated perversion of the just war, is a key part of the just war project, the realisation of which depends on the progressive elimination of assumptions of natural enmity from the prevailing culture of war.

The negative task is essential, but what positive moral disposition does the just war presuppose? Augustine's just war ethic includes the startling claim that war does not dispense with the universal law of charity. On the contrary, the just warrior must retain a 'loving' disposition towards the enemy.[8] The idea that war can be conducted charitably may seem hopelessly utopian, even nonsensical,[9] but what meaning might be given to 'charity' in the harsh, often brutal, context of war?

Fundamentally, it might stand for the sustained recognition of the moral equality and worth of the enemy. From this moral perspective, war is the anomaly. No belligerents are 'enemies by nature', since no enemy is beyond the moral pale. The enemy is not the Other. There is no standing cause for war. The natural state among enemies is one of peace, not war. This awareness of a moral community that transcends divisions and that endures in war secures the just limits of enmity. Enmity in war does not annul membership of that community, nor does it annul the rights that accompany membership. As a result, both the recourse to war and the conduct of war are moderated.

The key to the moderation of recourse to war (*jus ad bellum*) is the manner in which *just cause* is understood. In unjust 'just' wars, the cause is understood absolutely and unilaterally. From this warped perspective, an absolute divide exists between the forces of Good and Evil. Justice is all on one side, and injustice on the other. This clear moral demarcation releases a moral energy and enthusiasm for war that compromises its moral limitation. So understood, *just cause* undermines the other principles of just recourse. In effect, this single criterion is allowed to monopolise the question of just recourse. Such an understanding ill accords with the idea of the moral community of humankind. From that standpoint, just cause is best understood comparatively or bilaterally. Justice and injustice are seen to be shared. The injustices committed by the enemy are not allowed to obscure his moral worth, while the pursuit of justice does not blind the injured party to his own injustices and moral failings. Recognition of the 'mixed' nature of justice tempers the moral ardour of the just warrior and allows other criteria of just recourse, like *last resort*, to come into play (the prospects of a negotiated settlement that stops short of war being greatly improved by the mutual recognition that comparative justice requires).

The moral recognition of the enemy that the idea of a just war entails exerts, too, a moderating influence on the conduct of war (*jus in bello*). The value placed on the life of the enemy inclines belligerents to employ force proportionately and temperately, desisting from the use of excess force and the infliction of unnecessary suffering. It encourages belligerents to uphold the right to immunity from attack of all non-combatants, including soldiers who have been disarmed. 'Charity' in this unsentimental and robust sense does not seem alien to the business of war. The acceptance of surrender, for example, could be regarded as a manifestation of the 'charitable' or 'loving' conduct of war. To accept surrender is often a risky act that exposes the soldier to increased danger. Readiness to take that risk may be indicative of the value attached to the life of the enemy. It implies a fundamental recognition of the enemy, a respect for the enemy's right to life, of his limited enmity.

'Charity' disposes just belligerents to value peace above war at all times (even in the midst of war). 'Peace should be the object of your desire', wrote Augustine. 'War should be waged only as a necessity … For peace is not sought in order to the kindling of war, but war is waged in order that peace may be obtained. Therefore, even in waging war, cherish the spirit of the peace-maker' (quoted in Deane, 1963, 159). The 'spirit of the peacemaker' manifests itself in a reluctance to resort to war and, in the event of war, in a concern to minimise its destructive force. It involves the acceptance of the enemy as a moral equal and a bearer of rights and legitimate interests. It has as its overriding aim a just and lasting peace that ends in reconciliation rather than victory and defeat. War is fought in a way that accords with that aim. The goal of the just war is not the unilateral triumph of a particular state, but the restoration of community among enemies, a restoration that secures justice for all concerned.

The image of war that just war theory upholds is akin to Plato's 'discord' without its exclusivity. The problem with Plato's distinction between 'discord' and 'war' is that it reinforces (by endorsing) unjust enmity. It leaves the idea and the reality of the Other intact. It accepts that 'war' (total war) is the appropriate response to the Other. Plato employs a concept of limited war ('discord'), but he applies it partisanly. It is not understood, as it needs to be understood, universally. The community that underpins 'discord' is drawn too narrowly. It is because Greeks regard non-Greeks as their inferiors (as Barbarians) that unlimited war may be waged against them. What is needed is a concept of community that embraces Barbarian as well as Greek, that is truly universal.

The Other must be overcome not by its destruction, but by its incorporation into the moral community of humankind. 'The mitigation of war', wrote Westlake, 'must depend on the parties to it feeling that they belong to a larger whole than their respective tribes or states, a whole in which the enemy too is comprised, so that duties arising out of that larger citizenship are owed even to him' (quoted in Morgenthau, 1973, 259). In a just war enmity is always limited. The key to the moral restraint of war is the recognition of a fundamental bond that unites adversaries even in the midst of war. Conversely, what unleashes the full horror of war is the assumption of absolute enmity by one or both belligerents.

Bibliography

Augustine, St, *The City of God*, ed. and trans. Dyson, R. W., Cambridge: Cambridge University Press, 1998.
——, 'Reply to Faustus', ed. Dods, M., *The Works of Aurelius Augustine*, Vol V, Edinburgh: T&T Clark, 1872.
Bartov, O., *The Eastern Front 1941–45: German Troops and the Barbarisation of Warfare*, London: Macmillan, 1985.
——, *Hitler's Army*, New York and Oxford: Oxford University Press, 1991.

Beevor, A., *Berlin: The Downfall 1945*, London: Penguin, 2002.

Coates, A. J., *The Ethics of War*, Manchester: Manchester University Press, 1997.

——, 'Just War', in Bellamy, R. and Mason, A. (eds), *Political Concepts*, Manchester: Manchester University Press, 2003.

Deane, H. A., *The Political and Social Ideas of St Augustine*, New York: Columbia University Press, 1963.

Dower, J. W., *War Without Mercy*, New York: Random House, 1987.

Duus, P. (ed.), *The Cambridge History of Japan*, Vol VI, Cambridge: Cambridge University Press, 1988.

Feifer, G., *Tennozan*, New York: Ticknor & Fields, 1992.

Fest, J. C., *Hitler*, London: Weidenfeld and Nicolson, 1974.

France, J., *Western Warfare in the Age of the Crusades 1000–1300*, London: UCL Press, 1999.

Gray, J. Glenn, *The Warriors,* Lincoln, NB: University of Nebraska Press, 1970.

Hanson, V. D., *Why The West Has Won*, London: Faber & Faber, 2001.

Johnson, J. T., *Ideology, Reason and the Restraint of War*, Princeton: Princeton University Press, 1975.

Jowett, B. (ed. and trans.), *The Dialogues of Plato*, 4th edn, 4 vols, Oxford: Clarendon Press, 1953.

Keegan, J., *A History of Warfare*, London: Hutchinson, 1993.

Kiernan, V. G., *Colonial Empires and Armies 1815–1960*, Stroud: Sutton, 1998.

Morgenthau, H. J., *Politics Among Nations,* 5th edn, New York: Alfred A. Knopf, 1973.

Rieber, R. W. (ed.) (1991), *The Psychology of War and Peace: The Image of the Enemy*, New York: Plenum Press, 1991.

Schmitt, C., *The Concept of the Political*, trans. Schwab, G., Chicago: University of Chicago Press, 1996.

Sherman, W. T., *From Atlanta to the Sea*, London: The Folio Society, 1961.

Sledge, E. B., *With the Old Breed*, Oxford: Oxford University Press, 1990.

Stephenson, W. R., *Christian Love and Just War*, Macon, GA: Mercier University Press, 1987.

Terkel, S., *'The Good War': An Oral History of World War II* , New York: New Press, 1984.

Thomas, W., *The Ethics of Destruction*, Ithaca, NY: Cornell University Press, 2001.

von Clausewitz, C., *On War*, London: Penguin, 1982.

Walzer, M., *Just and Unjust Wars*, New York: Basic Books, 2000.

Notes

1 For further discussion of the two concepts, see Coates (2003).
2 Cf. Walzer (2000), Chs. 1 and 2; Thomas (2001), Chs 1 and 2.
3 See Bartov (1991).

4   Red Army units liberating a POW camp in eastern Germany in 1945 were outraged by the contrasting fates of the prisoners in the camp: 'The appearance of the Americans, British and French inmates was healthy. … Prisoners from the Western Allied countries did not have to work, they were allowed to play football and they received food parcels from the Red Cross. Meanwhile, in the other part of the camp, "17,000 Soviet prisoners had been killed or died from starvation or illness … Healthy prisoners were made to dig trenches, the weak ones were killed or buried alive"' (Beevor, 2002, 85).

5   Cf. Sledge (1990), Dower (1987).

6   From a psychological viewpoint, the identification of the enemy is often seen as 'a process of self-inflation … the inflated self wants to know only its virtues; its vices … form the raw material for projections onto the image of the enemy'. Rieber, Robert W. and Kelly, Robert J., 'Substance and Shadow: Images of the Enemy', in Rieber, R. W. (ed.) (1991), *The Psychology of War and Peace: The Image of the Enemy*, New York: Plenum Press.

7   This conceptual revision is often reinforced by considerations of military weakness and utility. This is clearly the case with international terrorism, where the gross military inferiority of the terrorist can make the targeting of non-combatants appear a military as well as a moral necessity. Terrorism is the 'war of the weak'.

8   Cf. Johnson (1975), 41; see also Deane (1963), Stephenson (1987).

9   Schmitt claims that the Christian tradition did not apply the law of charity to the case of war, arguing that 'in the private sphere only does it make sense to love one's enemy': Schmitt (1966), 29.

Chapter 12

Application of Just War Criteria in the Period 1959–89

Richard Harries

It is sometimes suggested that the just war tradition is outmoded: that the scale and conditions of modern warfare are so different from what pertained in the past that traditional criteria can no longer be applied. I believe that view to be totally mistaken. The criteria are as applicable and relevant today as they have ever been, as Professor Richard Sorabji has emphasised in Chapter 1: but they have to be thought through in ways which take into account both the realities of modern warfare and the context in which they are to be applied. I will be considering two contexts in particular, the armed liberation struggles of the 1960s and the nuclear standoff from about 1959 to 1989.[1] I am not primarily concerned with the validity of the judgements that will be made in the discussion. These are still arguable. What I will be trying to show is that just war criteria can – and I would say must – be applied even in very different circumstances to those which prevailed when they were first formulated and developed, but that this involves a serious effort to take into account the implications of those different circumstances. Just war criteria cannot be applied in a mechanical, wooden way. They require sensitivity to the actual context in which their use is sought.[2]

The 1960s, for those who lived through that period, were heady years. Marxism, particularly that associated with the early Marx, was an intellectual force arousing both antagonism and sympathy. Liberation struggles were taking place in Africa and other parts of the world. In Central America, these were associated with a fierce anti-Americanism which coincided with worldwide protests against the American involvement in Vietnam. Student protest was a feature of the times in a way it is difficult to envisage now, and, in 1968 when students barricaded the streets of Paris, academics from British universities went to join them. Inevitably, all this was reflected in the Church life of the time which is my main concern. Christian–Marxist dialogue was a stimulating intellectual pursuit, bringing together not only left-wing Christians from the West, but Christian theologians living under the rule of the USSR. Some Christians professed to be both Marxist and Christian, among them the Slant group of Catholics, which included Father Laurence Bright, a former nuclear scientist turned Dominican, and Terry Eagleton, still very much in evidence. More significant were the Liberation theologians of South America and the movements of the poor with which they sought to identify and influence. The later papal encyclical on Liberation Theology, while sympathetic to the plight of the poor and calling for justice, was critical of the way these theologians had taken on board so many of the assumptions of Marxism, and it is certainly true that they did take much from a Marxist analysis of what was happening in their societies, and had tried to relate this to the teaching of Jesus about the poor. The World Council of Churches, the central body for Protestant churches, appeared to be more sympathetic to these liberation struggles, as expressed, for example, by the financial support they gave to some of them through their Programme to Combat Racism.

A symbolic figure of the time was Camillo Torres, the son of a well-off doctor in Bogota who entered the priesthood because he thought it was the profession in which he could be most useful socially.[3] He qualified as a sociologist and lectured at Colombia University, gradually becoming more socially aware and politically active. As the prospect of achieving social reform by peaceful means seemed to diminish, he joined a guerrilla band in the mountains, and was killed in a skirmish with government forces in 1966. Torres said that 'The duty of every Catholic is to be a revolutionary', and he agreed with Che Guevara that 'The duty of every revolutionary is to make the revolution.' In short, as he put it, 'The Catholic who is not a revolutionary is living in mortal sin.' Camillo Torres was the best-known Christian revolutionary, but he was not alone in his support for those who resorted to armed force in order to change oppressive regimes. As one experienced observer of the scene commented at the time: 'Nowadays a radical clergy is something one takes for granted. Most governments look nervously over their shoulders at their priests.'

Even if one has a fundamental sympathy for the perspective of these liberation theologians and their desire for solidarity with the poor, it has to be pointed out that there was a crucial element lacking in their approach. They tended to move straight from theology to political action. If there was some analysis of a Marxist kind, there was very little, if any, political or ethical reflection. Torres, for example, argued that the only effective and far-reaching way to make the love of all people a reality was to make revolution. But love simply ensures that you have a desire to help others at the forefront of the mind. It does not answer the question of what might be the most effective form of help, nor does it of itself settle the difficult questions that nearly always have to be answered when there are conflicting values and principles, for example between order and justice, or between the desire to help the poor to a better life and the need to avoid violence if at all possible.

This lack of proper intermediate stages between theology and action went with a surprising failure to refer to the Christian tradition of thought on what we might call 'just revolution'. For there is a tradition of just revolution, if for obvious reasons not such a well developed one as just war thinking, of which it is a particular stream. I will look at that tradition and suggest that the traditional criteria, if brought to bear in a way that takes into account the special features of a liberation struggle, can offer guidance in making judgements about the morality of the use of force in revolutionary situations.

The first criterion that must be met before there can be any resort to armed force is that there should be lawful authority. This would seem to rule out, in principle, any attempt to overthrow a government by violent means, for are they not the lawful authority? This is what the majority of Christians have always assumed, appealing to Paul's teaching in his letter to the Romans that earthly rulers are always to be obeyed. In Anglicanism, this view was reinforced by the doctrine of the divine right of kings. The seventeenth-century Anglican divine Robert Sanderson was fairly typical when he wrote: 'To take up arms offensive or defensive against a lawful sovereign cannot be done by any man, at any time, in any case, upon any colour or pretension whatsoever.'[4] There is, however, more to be said than that.

First, as Helmut Thielicke argued, Romans 13 is not the only passage in the New Testament that guides our attitude to government.[5] There is Revelation 13. This, in his view, describes a state that has become demonic, when it has usurped to itself the authority that belongs to God and to God alone. When that occurs, it has ceased to be the state of Romans 13 to which we owe obedience. Thielicke had in mind Hitler's Germany and Soviet Communism as he radically questioned Lutheranism's traditional loyalty to the state, however tyrannical. His argument is an important one, which needs always to be borne in mind; nevertheless, it does not necessarily fit those governments in Latin America, which while manifestly unjust, were not demonic in Thielicke's sense.

There is, however, another approach. Chairman Mao said that power grows out of the barrel of a gun. But as Hannah Arendt pointed out, for power to be gained or retained, it is necessary to have at least the consent of those who hold the guns.[6] In the last resort, government depends on consent, not necessarily the consent of all the people all the time, but at least enough to be able to wield the instruments of coercion.

A dramatic example of the importance of consent was provided by the overthrow of the Shah of Persia. Outwardly, he had all the panoply of power, a large army and a secret police. But in reality, the people had withdrawn their consent. The Shah seemed to be the legitimate authority, but in fact his authority had been withdrawn. No less important, however, was that the people had transferred their consent to an alternative authority in the form of Ayatollah Khomeini. There was an alternative government in the making. This is crucial from the standpoint of what makes for a just revolution from a Christian perspective.

John of Salisbury in the twelfth century argued that as a good ruler was in the image of God, so a tyrant was in the image of the devil and could be struck down by anyone at any time.[7] Thomas Aquinas rejected this view. He maintained that action to depose a ruler must be undertaken by public authority. It may not be clear in a particular situation what might constitute public authority, particularly if the leading statesmen have been exiled or imprisoned and the major institutions neutralised.[8] Nevertheless, the point is clear. The Christian tradition rules out anarchic violence, or any resort to force against a government, unless there is some prospect of an alternative government. The same point was made by Calvin from a rather different theological perspective. He allowed that when a ruler was oppressing his people, then the 'lesser magistrates', senior people and bodies in the state, 'corresponding to the tribunes of old' could act to depose the ruler.[9]

It can therefore be argued that the condition of lawful authority can be met, even when the use of force is directed against a government, if the people have, despite appearances to the contrary, withdrawn their consent and if there is the prospect of an alternative government to which they have at least implicitly transferred their allegiance. People may wish to disagree with or qualify that argument, but my point is that just war criteria are applicable even in the extreme case of apparently going against lawful authority, as with an attempt to overthrow a government.

The second condition, just cause, applies to revolutionary situations in a way very comparable to that of war. It is not enough that there is tyranny. The tyranny must be long-standing and intolerable. Every means of trying to achieve change by peaceful means must first have been tried and found to fail. This is the theme of both Aquinas and Calvinists in the sixteenth century.

The third principle, that of proportion, or ensuring that evils unleashed by resort to force do not outweigh the evils already in existence, is, for understandable reasons, interpreted in this tradition in a way that urges extreme caution before any attempt is made to overthrow a government by force. Aquinas points out that actions against unjust rulers often fail and lead to even greater repression, and that there is always the danger of a new tyranny replacing the old. Then there is always the likelihood of chaos and anarchy. So, as he wrote, attempting to overthrow a tyrant does not count as sin 'Except perhaps in the case that it is accompanied by such disorder that the community suffers greater harm from the consequent disturbance than it would from a continuance of the former rule.'[10] – In short, a very precise statement of the principle in question. The same considerations are brought into focus by both Suarez and Calvinist writers who point out that the medicine may be worse than the disease. This point reiterates the concern of Christian writers who have at least some sympathy with the possibility of a just revolution that this must be made in the name of a better order, not just for more justice. This is a theme of the American ethicist Paul Ramsay, for example.[11]

The fourth criterion states that there must be a reasonable chance of success. This, as writers in the tradition point out, is a logical extension of the previous one, for unless there is a reasonable chance, more evil than good will inevitably result. Here, it is vital to ask what might count as success in a revolutionary struggle. Some commentators looking at the very limited military force available to guerrilla groups have concluded that they have no chance of achieving victory. For example, one well-known Catholic commentator wrote in 1972 about the liberation movements in Portuguese Africa, 'On the evidence of the last decade they have no reasonable prospect of success at all',[12] and concluded that because this condition could not be met, their struggle was not morally legitimate. Yet, only two years later, in 1974, the Portuguese empire in Africa collapsed and these same liberation movements triumphed. The fact is that the aim of liberation movements is not to win great military victories, which they cannot do. Their purpose is to stay in existence long enough, and to be enough of a military nuisance, until the political victory is won. Whether that political victory is won will depend on the extent of the injustice of the regime and the support which the liberation movement enjoys from the population as a whole.[13] So, in making a judgement about whether there is a reasonable chance of success, it is these factors that have to be weighed more than the military force available.

The just war tradition consists not just of *jus ad bellum* but *jus in bello*. The fundamental principle in this category is that those people not directly contributing to the war must never be the direct object of attack. Some people have judged revolutionary movements inevitably immoral because, so they maintain, they inevitably depend upon directly attacking civilians. If this were indeed the case, then some would say that the possibility of such a thing as a just revolution would be ruled out in principle. Those involved in such actions would always be referred to as 'terrorists' rather than 'freedom fighters'. But is it the case that terrorism is inevitable? An analysis of liberation struggles shows that while terrorism has certainly been part of some of them, some of the time, the majority, even the IRA, have attempted to distinguish between military and civilian targets, aiming for the most part to go for the former. Many have made a distinction between sabotage and terrorism, and certainly the more far-sighted have realised that the success of their struggle depends on having the people on their side, and therefore that terrorism cannot achieve this in the long run. It is important to remember, however, that if the cause is not just in the first place, in other words if the criteria of *jus ad bellum* are not met, then all actions by the offending party in the ensuing conflict are immoral. Thus it would be argued that because the IRA had an opportunity to change government by peaceful means, they had no moral case for resort to violence. Hence all their actions, whether directed at military targets or not, were immoral. That said, it is also important to stress the importance of *jus in bello* in its own right, because there can very often be a major disagreement about whether the cause is just or not. Whether the cause is just or not, the requirements of *jus in bello* still have to be met.

All these criteria merit much further discussion, particularly the last. But the object here is to draw two conclusions. First, in relation to those who argue that attempts to overthrow government by resort to armed force can never be justified on Christian principles, I argue that this is not true, either historically or on the basis of contemporary ethical analysis. Second, in relation to those who instinctively identify with liberation movements and who tend to move straight from theology to action, I argue that for there to be a justified resort to force, certain conditions must be met. From these two conclusions, I would reiterate the theme with which I started, namely that the just war criteria are of continuing relevance and application, provided that proper attention is given to the context in which they are applied and the nature of the struggle engaged in. I have tried to show in relation to what is at first sight a very unpromising field for their application, namely revolutionary struggle, that they can be of use, provided, in this case, we carefully examine the nature of political authority on the one hand, and what counts as success on the other.

I now want to look at the application of just war criteria in the debate on nuclear deterrence during the period 1959–89. During the Second World War, Bishop Bell had condemned the Allied policy of obliteration bombing, and the American Jesuit, Father John Ford had condemned not only this, but the dropping of atomic bombs on Japanese cities. Nevertheless, the real debate about the morality of such actions in the light of just war principles only really got going in the 1960s.[14] The United States and United Kingdom found themselves developing nuclear weapons in response to what was felt to be a threat posed by the Soviet Union, and during the 1950s there were protests about this, notably by CND. Nevertheless, it was only in the 1960s that the debate became refined with both those opposed to a policy of nuclear deterrence and those in favour turning quite explicitly to the just war tradition, and indeed that tradition becoming much more prominent through historical work being done on it.[15] Apart from the awesome seriousness of the issue, it was also an intellectually challenging subject, with just war principles being thought through and refined in new ways. One of the reasons the subject combined reality and intellectual challenge was because it engaged strategists, political theorists and international relations specialists along with philosophers and theologians in a realm of common discourse loosely provided by the struggle to relate traditional moral considerations to the control of power.[16]

Although, as writers at the time pointed out, deterrence has been a feature of the relationship between states throughout recorded history, the deterrent effect of nuclear weapons was something dramatically new. Such was the destructive power of these new weapons that for the first time in history, it could not conceivably have been in the interest of one power to go to war with another nuclear state. The threatened destruction of a nuclear response would outweigh any possible gain, and the nuclear stalemate became entrenched through the development of submarines able to stay undetected, under water, for months on end, thus assuring an absolutely secure second strike capacity. This mutually assured destruction was the big new fact of the time, in the shadow of which every other aspect of the discussion on the use of force took place.

Some took the view that because this system was essentially stable, and that in fact a nuclear stalemate had emerged, this was all that, from a moral point of view, mattered. Nuclear catastrophe, and not only that, but even a conventional war between nuclear powers, was essentially ruled out. If the overriding consideration was to prevent war, then no more questions needed to be asked. Others, however, took the view that the effectiveness of nuclear deterrence depended on a judgement by the enemy that such weapons could and would be used; and this in turn depended on a readiness by NATO actually to use such weapons. From a moral point of view, therefore, the question whether there were situations in which they could be used was crucial. This in turn depended on whether such use would conform to the traditional criteria of discrimination and proportion. It is this latter position with which I am mainly concerned: namely, the one which believes that a morally justifiable policy of nuclear deterrence crucially depends on the possibility of a morally licit use of nuclear weapons under some circumstances, however restricted, and however unlikely it is judged that such a use might prove necessary.[17]

I begin with the principle of discrimination, sometimes called non-combatant immunity.[18] The phrase 'non-combatant immunity', however, is not quite accurate, for in certain circumstances non-combatants can be the direct object of attack. A distinction can be made, for example, between munitions workers and a baker. A baker, even if his bread is eaten by members of the armed forces, is in fact baking for people as such. In contrast, munitions workers are directly contributing to the war effort: that is the crucial distinction which makes it wrong to bomb a baker, even if some of the bread is eaten by soldiers, but other conditions being met, legitimate to bomb an arms factory. It will be clear from this that the term 'civilian' is also too imprecise. The principle of discrimination says that those not directly contributing to the war effort must not be the direct object of attack. This principle came very much to the fore in the debates over nuclear weapons from the 1960s onwards. It had to be held against two opposing arguments. There were those who argued that ever since the time of Napoleon, we have to think in terms of 'The nation in arms'. The whole nation is, on this view, a legitimate target. Advocates of the just war tradition refused to accept this. They argued, for example, that there is a clear difference between children playing in the school playground and people manning a command and control centre; and even if, say, a granny knitting socks for the troops is filled with more hate for the enemy than soldiers in the front line, she does not pose a threat as they do. She cannot therefore be regarded as a legitimate target. The other category of people who rejected the principle of discrimination were some of the philosophically minded who took a consciously consequentialist position about what makes an action right or wrong. For such people, there was no difference, morally, between civilian deaths brought about by direct attacks on civilian targets and civilian deaths that occurred as a result of an attack on a military target. Any consequence that was foreseen was intended, and it was an assessment of the consequences alone that weighed morally. In contrast to this, defenders of the just war tradition argued that certain actions are intrinsically wrong, among them deliberately killing people not directly contributing to the war effort. Clearly, this debate raises philosophical issues of great complexity that have been long discussed and which cannot be considered here. The point is that these issues became very prominent at the time as part of just war thinking, resulting in a re-examination of the notion of 'intention' and a revival of the concept of double effect, which previously had been mainly associated with Roman Catholic thinking about saving the life of a mother with an ectopic pregnancy. From a theological point of view, it was argued that the prime purpose in using armed force is not in fact to kill the enemy, but to render that enemy harmless. When they are harmless, as is the case with prisoners of war, they cannot be hurt. Deliberately killing a prisoner of war, or a civilian not directly aiding the war effort, does in fact amount to murder. Paul Ramsey, who was so influential in these debates, grounded the principle of discrimination in the love ethic of St Augustine, arguing that the same love which takes to arms to protect the innocent on one's own side throws a protecting cover round the innocent, that is the harmless on the enemy's side. The result of these debates was the emergence of a clear category of nuclear pacifist: people who certainly did not regard themselves as pacifists, but who believed that any use of nuclear weapons would violate the central principle of Christian thinking on war, namely that which seeks to discriminate between those who threaten harm and those who don't. They found themselves arguing with equal passion against pacifists on the one hand and advocates of the use of nuclear weapons on the other. As the distinguished philosopher Elizabeth Anscombe put it:

> Now pacifism teaches people to make no distinction between the shedding of innocent blood and the shedding of any human blood and in this way pacifism has corrupted enormous numbers of people who will not act according to its tenets. They become convinced that a number of things are wicked which are not; hence, seeing no way of avoiding 'wickedness', they set no limits to it.[19]

Those who stood within the just war tradition and wished to support, in however qualified a way, a policy of nuclear deterrence had to show that not every use of nuclear weapons would be indiscriminate. The task, never easy, did, however, become more theoretically possible with a change in nuclear strategy in 1967 from 'massive retaliation', to use the shorthand of the time, to one of 'flexible response', which envisaged a mix of conventional forces and battlefield nuclear weapons, with the possibility, but not the certainty, of escalation to ever more horrendous weaponry.[20] The case for a morally licit use of nuclear weapons faced a number of difficulties: for example, the inevitable secrecy of British targeting policy; the powerful deterrent effect of letting the enemy think that weapons might be targeted on cities, together with the implication of a great deal of discussion and publicity that they were in fact so targeted, and the sometimes somewhat unreal speculation which posited nuclear strikes of a highly discriminate, as well as proportionate kind – sometimes referred to disparagingly as the 'fleet at sea scenario'. All this said, attempts were made to formulate a targeting policy that was discriminate, notably by Michael Quinlan (now Sir Michael), who was not only Under Secretary for State at the Ministry of Defence at a crucial time in these debates, but is a Catholic very much concerned that British defence policy could be morally defended. It is no exaggeration to say that his was the crucial influence amongst a whole range of Christian thinkers who were also concerned with these dilemmas.[21]

The other principle, closely linked to the previous one, is that of proportion. This was first formulated within the Christian tradition in a formal way by Aquinas in his discussion of attempts to overthrow tyrannies by force, already referred to earlier, and was asserted by both Francisco de Vitoria and Suarez. During the nuclear debate, it was asserted by many that any use of nuclear weapons would inevitably be disproportionate, and certainly films which pictured the total devastation of whole cities brought this message home, as did the campaigning of CND. The paradox here is that the more horrifying the scenes which were put before the public, the more the message that it could not possibly be in the interest of any state to go to war against a nuclear power was reinforced. But this made it harder for those who wished to reconcile some use of nuclear weapons with just war criteria in order to give a moral grounding to the policy of deterrence. Those who wished to do this had to persuade on two points. First, they had to show that there was some use of nuclear weapons which was not only discriminate, as already discussed, but proportionate. This was done not just by positing the use of battlefield weapons, but also by highlighting the unique threat which, it was believed by many, was posed by the Soviet Union at the time. This debate became sloganised in terms of whether or not it was better to be red than dead: that is, it was not just the scale of damage which might be inflicted that was taken into account, but the value system of the two superpowers, and the belief that the Soviet Union, based upon the big lie of Marxist-Leninist ideology, would be uniquely corrupting of the human spirit and all that it meant to be human. The other point that had to be shown was that even if a limited use of nuclear weapons could be envisaged, that was not in itself disproportionate, and it would not inevitably escalate to a use that would be disproportionate. The argument against this was that escalation was not inevitable, and that, in any case, it would be morally wrong to allow the fear of escalation to prevent one taking proper steps to deter a potential aggressor. Allowing this to happen would in fact mean handing the international order over to the side prepared to pose the biggest threat. The final nuclear strategy which was arrived at, that of flexible response with the possibility of raising the stakes at a number of points, did result in having a number of options that could be used from a moral point of view while keeping the deterrent threat high because of the possibility, but not the inevitability, of escalation to more horrendous levels of nuclear exchange. People might be deterred by the thought of a conflict escalating in such a way that millions of civilians would be killed as a result of collateral damage from direct attacks on military targets. But a policy of deterrence based in part upon such a prospect was not, it was argued, intrinsically immoral. It was a wanted effect of unintended, unwanted collateral damage occurring as a result of a direct attack on a legitimate target. Here, then, we have another example, whatever judgement one makes about such nuclear policy at the time, of traditional just war criteria being brought to bear in a radically new context and having to take into account possibilities such as escalation in a way that had never been necessary to the same extent in conventional warfare.

Closely related to the principle of proportion in Christian thinking on war has been the possibility of success. We saw earlier that in the case of guerrilla warfare, it was necessary to ask what actually counted as success in a potentially revolutionary context. Similarly, in the debates over the threatened use of nuclear weapons, it was necessary to ask what counted as success. Here again, there is a radically different answer from that which was given in relation to conventional war. Clearly, the major rationale of threatening the use of nuclear weapons was to ensure that any war, not just nuclear war, between the major powers was averted. Under the nuclear umbrella, there could be many proxy wars in different parts of the globe, and it meant having to accept a major injustice, namely the continuing occupation of eastern European countries by the Soviet Union. So the success of mutually assured destruction was not unqualified. It spawned some evils and meant accepting others, because there was no other alternative. Nevertheless, in terms of just war criteria, what counted as success was whether or not deterrence held, whether it was fundamentally stable or not. In the judgement of many at the time, though not members of CND, deterrence was fundamentally stable. There was a nuclear stalemate because, to repeat a point made before, for the first time in human history it could not conceivably have been in the interest of one superpower to go to war with another.

One interesting and somewhat unexpected result of this emphasis on the necessity of deterrence and the crucial importance of its robustness was the way that most thoughtful British strategists opposed President Reagan's Star Wars initiative. It was argued first of all that no shield of anti-ballistic missiles, whether placed on the ground or in the sky, could destroy all incoming missiles, and it was only necessary for a few to get through to bring about utter devastation. Second, because of the uncertainty caused by whether or not a shield against incoming missiles would be effective, this might tempt a hostile power to launch a pre-emptive strike to try to ensure that the enemy missiles were destroyed before they were launched. In short, a radical element of instability would be introduced into what had until then been regarded by such thinkers as a very stable, robust system of mutual deterrence. That argument may or may not be so compelling now when we are not dealing with the mutual deterrence of two superpowers but of alleged 'rogue states' against one superpower, but at the time it certainly convinced many thoughtful strategists. As never before in human history, deterrence was the name of the game. All was focused on the necessity of making it work, of mutual deterrence continuing to hold, and this provided a different context in which just war criteria had to be thought through and applied.

Notes

1   The year of the breaking down of the Berlin Wall, 1989, is an obvious terminus point for the end of the Cold War. I have chosen 1959 as a starting point for my consideration because it was only about then that the just war tradition started to come more sharply into focus for thinking about the ethics involved.

2   I argued for this in relation to liberation struggles in a short book: Harries, Richard (1982), *Should a Christian Support Guerrillas?*, Lutterworth, Surrey: Lutterworth Press. Because of restrictions on the number of pages and the desire of the publishers to make the book as accessible as possible, I was not able to include footnotes or an index

or indeed another chapter I had written. But it was, so far as I know, the first and perhaps the only book to rehabilitate the just revolution tradition and apply it in a contemporary context.

3 Gerassi, John (ed.) (1971), *Revolutionary Priest*, London: Jonathan Cape.

4 Sanderson, Robert, Sermon 9, July 1639 and Sermon 12, July 1640 in Jacobson, W. (ed.) (1854), *Works of Robert Sanderson*, Oxford University Press, Vol. 1, 246 and 298.

5 Thielicke, Helmut (1969), *Theological Ethics*, Philadelphia, PA: Fortress, Vol 2, politics, Ch 19.

6 Arendt, Hannah (1970), *On Violence*, Harmondsworth: Allen Lane, Penguin Press, 43 ff.

7 Dickinson, John (1963), *The Statesman's Book of John of Salisbury: Selections from Policraticus*, New York: Russell and Russell.

8 Aquinas, Thomas, *Summa Theologica*, 2:2, 42, 2.

9 Calvin, *Institutes of the Christian Religion*, Book 4, 20.

10 Aquinas, Thomas, *Summa Theologica*, 2:2, 42, 2.

11 Ramsay, Paul (1961), *War and the Christian Conscience*, Durham, NC: Duke University Press, Ch. 6, and 'The Just Revolution', *World View*, October 1973.

12 Eppstein, John (1971), *Does God Say Kill?*, London: Tom Stacey.

13 Tabor, Robert (1970), *The War of the Flee*, London: Paladin.

14 Father Ford's essay was reprinted in 1961, and it was from that point its influence was felt. 'The Morality of Obliteration Bombing' was reprinted in *War and Morality*, ed. Wasserstrom, Richard A., Belmont, CA: Wadsworth.

15 Tooke, Joan D. (1965), *The Just War in Aquinas and Grotius*, London: SPCK; Russell, Frederick H. (1975), *The Just War in the Middle Ages*, Cambridge University Press; Johnson, James Turner (1975), *Ideology, Reason, and the Limitation of War: Religious and Secular Concepts, 1200–1740*, Princeton University Press; Johnson, James Turner (1981), *Just War Tradition and the Restraint of War: A Moral and Historical Inquiry*, Princeton University Press.

16 James Turner Johnson, as already cited a historian in the just war tradition, applied it to modern warfare in Johnson, James Turner (1984), *Can Modern War be Just?*, New Haven, CT: Yale University Press. William V. O'Brien was a Roman Catholic academic lawyer with a wide range of interests in the field who produced O'Brien, William V. (1967), *Nuclear War, Deterrence and Morality*, Westminster, MD: Newman Press, and (1981), *The Conduct of Just and Limited War*, New York: Praeger, from his positions at Georgetown University, Washington. Paul Ramsey, a Methodist ethicist, wrote Ramsey, Paul (1967), *War and the Christian Conscience: How Shall Modern War be Conducted Justly?*, Princeton University Press, and (1968), *The Just War: Force and Political Responsibility*, New York: Charles Scriveners. Michael Walzer, Professor of Government at Harvard, wrote Walzer, Michael, *Just and Unjust Wars: A Moral Argument with Historical Illustrations*, Basic Books (1977) in the USA and Allen Lane (1978), in the UK, and also traversing the same ground from a primarily secular perspective were Osgood, Robert E. and Tucker, Robert W. (1967), *Force, Order and Justice*, Baltimore, MD: Johns Hopkins Press, and also Tucker, Robert W. (1967), *The Just War: A Study in Contemporary American Doctrine*, Johns Hopkins Press.

17 In addition to the writers quoted above who took variously nuanced positions on this issue but using a common realm of discourse, there were philosophers like Kenny, Anthony (1985), *The Logic of Deterrence*, London: Firethorn, who did not think there was such a morally licit use, and therefore who would be judged a nuclear pacifist. In a

similar category would be Stein, Walter (ed.) (1961), *Nuclear Weapons and Christian Conscience*, London: Merlin, and the Catholic academics John Finnis, an academic laywer, Joseph M. Boyle, a philosopher, and Germain Grisez, a Christian ethicist who produced (1987), *Nuclear Deterrence, Morality and Realism*, Oxford: Clarendon, again taking a nuclear pacifist position. A similar position was taken by Oliver O'Donovan in *Peace and Certainty: A Theological Essay on Deterrence*, Grand Rapids, MI: Eerdmans, 1989.

18   When I was lecturing in Christian Doctrine and Ethics at Wells Theological College from 1969–1972, I began doctoral research under Professor Dunstan of King's College London on the principles of discrimination and proportion in the just war tradition. In addition to historical work on people like Francisco de Vitoria, Aquinas and Grotius, the primary educative tool in applying or trying to apply these principles to the contemporary context was probably provided by the writings of Paul Ramsey, already cited. When I became Dean of King's College London in 1982, there was an ideal context for carrying this work forward. The principal of King's was Neil Cameron, later Lord Cameron, a former Chief of the Defence Staff. It had a distinguished Department of War Studies which had recently appointed a Lecturer in the Ethics of War. This resulted in Paskins, Barry and Dockrill, Michael (1979), *The Ethics of War*, London: Duckworth, and a variety of essays from different points of view by members of staff at King's College London in Harries, Richard (ed.) (1982), *What Hope in an Armed World?*, Basingstoke: Pickering and Inglis. King's was particularly well situated, being close to the Ministry of Defence and a variety of think tanks concerned with the use of force. In addition, I was member of a number of groups, including the Council for Arms Control, founded in 1981, which brought together people who on the whole were prepared to defend a policy of nuclear deterrence, but who were desperately anxious to work for significant cuts in arms. Then there was the Pembroke Group, which brought together service chaplains, together with members of the Ministry of Defence, philosophers and theologians, the Council on Christian Approaches to Defence and Disarmament (CCADD), the umbrella body for Christians of a variety of views who are all concerned with the morality of the use of force and which was the main specifically Christian think tank, and Shalom, which sought to provide an alternative Christian perspective to the Campaign for Nuclear Disarmament, providing, among other things, some material for use in schools. Membership of these groups to some extent overlapped. They included people who were deeply committed to humanitarian issues, such as Alan Booth, the Chairman of Shalom, who had once been director of Oxfam, and Leonard Cheshire. What united them was a recognition that in the world as we have it, force must sometimes be faced with force, even nuclear force, but that this had to be done in relation to established moral categories. From these people came such writings as Goodwin, Geoffrey (ed.), (1982), *Ethics and Nuclear Deterrence*, London: Croom Helm (on behalf of CCADD); McCall, Malcolm and Ramsbotham, Oliver (eds) (1990), *Morality and Deterrence in the 21st Century*, London: Brassey's; O'Connor Howe, Josephine (ed.) (1984), *Armed Peace: A Search for World Security*, London: Macmillan (for the Council for Arms Control).

My own contributions in the period included 'Power, Coercion and Morality', in Bridger, Francis (ed.) (1983), *The Cross and the Bomb: Christian Ethics in the Nuclear Debate*, London: Mowbray; 'Conventional Killing or Nuclear Stalemate?', in Martin, David and Mullen, Peter (eds) (1983), *Unholy Warfare: The Church and the Bomb*, Oxford: Blackwell, and 'The Strange Mercy of Deterrence', in Gladwin, John (ed.) (1985), *Dropping the Bomb: The Church and the Bomb Debate*, London: Hodder and

Stoughton, I chaired a working party of the Board for Social Responsibility of the General Synod, Church of England, which produced in 1988, *Peacemaking in a Nuclear Age*, London: Church House Publishing. See also my book, Harries, Richard (1986), *Christianity and War in the Nuclear Age*, London: Mowbray.

19   Elizabeth Anscombe, 'War and Murder', in Stein Walter (ed.) (1961), *Nuclear Weapons and Christian Conscience*, London: Merlin Press, 56. The essay is also reprinted in Wasserstrom, Richard, A. (ed.) (1970), *War and Morality*, Belmont, CA: Wadsworth.

20   Sir Michael Quinlan has written that people sometimes used MAD, the acronym for Mutual Assured Destruction, 'as though it were an alternative description of the strategy of "massive retaliation" – that is a strategy envisaging a general all-out nuclear assault as the only or best option in the face of aggression. Nato's strategy was never in truth quite that crude, but I accept that "massive retaliation" is an established shorthand for the strategy that preceded the 1967 adoption of flexible response. But MAD went side by side with flexible response in the minds of McNamara and Healey, for MAD was in their view (and in mine) an underlying factor which policy had to take account; it was not itself a policy. It referred to the irremovable reality that either side had the physical capability ultimately to obliterate the other. Flexible response was a concept that sought, under the shadow of that reality, to devise options for lesser action that would just conceivably be rational, and therefore credible in deterrence' (personal letter to the author, 1 August 2003).

21   It is difficult to exaggerate the role of Michael Quinlan, both as an architect of British defence policy and as a morally based strategic thinker about the possibility of a nuclear option. He was a member of a number of the groups indicated above, and his intellectual influence was decisive among those sympathetic to the idea of a morally grounded policy of nuclear deterrence. What Michael Quinlan himself could write at the time was, of course, extremely limited because of the nature of his official position. However, a couple of articles by him did appear: 'Nuclear Weapons: The Basic Issues', *The Ampleforth Journal*, Autumn 1986; 'The Ethics of Nuclear Deterrence', *Theological Studies*, Vol, 48, No. 1, March 1987. See also Sir Michael Quinlan's letter to *The Tablet* 15 August 1981. In addition, Fisher, David (1985), *Morality and the Bomb*, London: Croom Helm, came from his provenance. Michael Quinlan is a good example of how far people who justified a policy of nuclear deterrence at the time were from being right-wing ideologues, or indeed ideologues of any kind. For, using the same just war criteria, he was one of the most outspoken critics of the second Gulf War.

Chapter 13

Britain's Wars Since 1945

Michael Quinlan

For those guided by the just war tradition, the first serious challenge in British history after 1945 was that posed by the 1956 Suez episode. (Few would have seen difficulty about participation in the international intervention against North Korea's 1950 attack on South Korea, and internal security operations like those in Malaya were not wars in the normal sense.) The Suez adventure was questionable against more than one of the classical criteria, including just and proportionate cause. But although at its launching there was much controversy about its wisdom and propriety, this was not framed in just war terms and did not especially engage ethicists, for example in the Churches. That may have reflected the outlook of the times, barely a decade after the patriotic solidarity of the Second World War. In addition, because the adventure was conceived in such a closed, even clandestine, way, its credentials were not widely or fully tested beforehand; its duration was brief; and it had few subsequent defenders to sustain debate.

Just war reasoning bore on other debates following the Second World War. Ethical criticism of the 1940–45 Bomber Command campaign against German cities had been voiced in the UK even during the war, but official and other histories revived argument, and this helped to renew awareness of just war concepts. Britain was, however, spared the tensions of involvement in Vietnam, and the prime stimulus to reflection on whether or how just war theory should influence current decision-making was possession of nuclear weapons and planning for their possible use. The morality of government policy was vigorously contested, and the ethical debate became more salient in the UK than in the United States or France, the other two Western countries with nuclear armouries.

This chapter does not seek to review that debate. But some policy-makers derived from it two themes that bore upon later issues. The first was awareness that just war doctrine was not merely an interesting historical construct irrelevant to the modern security world transformed by the nuclear revolution, but flowed from disciplined thinking, tested over many centuries, about the interplay between moral values and the realities of a conflict-ridden world. Elements of it were deeply embedded in Western consciousness, and indeed in international law, and it could not be ignored. The complementary theme however was that the doctrine was not a fixed deposit from revealed scripture or the like; if the realities changed, the doctrine or its application might have to evolve. In short, there was a presumption of abiding by the just war criteria, alongside a readiness to adapt their interpretation if necessary to keep them relevant to the modern world.

In the years following the Suez fiasco, UK forces were continually drawn into operations of various kinds, but there was no clear-cut war until the recovery of the Falkland Islands in 1982. Little public opinion in the UK regarded this as problematic in just war terms. There was a long-running dispute with Argentina about the islands and the Argentine case was not vacuous, but it was unconscionable that forcible annexation should settle the matter. Just cause for reversing the Argentine invasion was accordingly clear. A few commentators questioned proportionate cause – were these remote and thinly populated islands worth a war? – but there were reasonable answers to that, including the unpleasantness of the Argentine regime, the strong preference of the islanders for the *status quo*, and the wider national and international damage likely if such an annexation were allowed to stand. There were for a time questions about last resort; but diplomatic endeavours continued long enough to demonstrate the implausibility of hopes that anything less than force would end the Argentine occupation. And once the war started, problems over *jus in bello* scarcely arose save in the overblown controversy about the sinking of the Argentine cruiser *General Belgrano*.

Britain's next involvement in war came with the 1991 expulsion of Iraq's forces from Kuwait. The justice and sufficiency of the cause could scarcely be in question; the seizure of one UN member by another was plainly intolerable. The main *ad bellum* debate related to 'last resort': had diplomacy been given enough chance before the UN-approved coalition went to war? There was misgiving about this within the United States Senate; the vote on military action was close-run, with individuals as weighty as Senator Sam Nunn among the 'Noes'. In retrospect, it is hard to doubt the judgement reached by mid-January 1991, that there was no prospect of negotiating Saddam out of Kuwait. That did, however, focus attention on two aspects of 'last resort'.

The first concerns the meaning of 'last'. It cannot be purely temporal – it must in some degree mean 'least to be preferred'. It would be unreasonable to demand that every conceivable non-military instrument must have been exhaustively tested irrespective of judgement about efficacy. The coalition could not be expected, for example, to spend six months on a trial of dropping exhortatory leaflets on Baghdad.

The second aspect is that in conflict settings time is rarely neutral. As it passes, options with their consequences will often change, becoming narrower, more difficult, more costly in several ways, or not available at all. The early application of force may do more good and less harm than delay until the situation has grown worse, as in the mid-1990s in former Yugoslavia. Such considerations had a double relevance in the 1991 Gulf setting. First, the longer expulsion was deferred, the more harm Saddam Hussein could do in Kuwait. Second, large military forces cannot indefinitely be held inactive far from home in awkward conditions without some loss of morale, readiness, efficiency and sustainability. That had been a factor in the 1982 Falklands affair, with the tightly stretched UK task force poised at sea and the South Atlantic winter looming. In the Kuwait instance, once there had been in autumn 1990 the major surge in US theatre deployment to a level too high to be refreshed by *roulement*, the clock was inevitably ticking. Such effects are not just a matter of military convenience; they can bear upon the success prospects and the costs of eventual combat; and they are scarcely ever symmetrical between the parties to the dispute. They are therefore a legitimate element of just war assessment.

The prime questions for *jus in bello* evaluation of the 1991 war concerned discrimination. What was it legitimate to target during the coalition's air campaign in preparation for the land offensive? The campaign hit Iraqi communications, fuel supplies and other infrastructure serving not only Saddam's forces but also the civilian population. Considerable suffering to non-combatants resulted. (Mistakes like striking a bunker housing many civilians were a different matter, not resulting from deliberate policy.) The campaign concept was legitimate, since commanders genuinely judged – whether they were proved right is another question, but operational decisions have to be made looking forward, not back – that hitting these facilities would damage Iraqi military capability, whose swift collapse could not be foreseen or counted upon. As often happens, the criteria of discrimination and proportionality almost merged: given that the coalition wished to achieve a military effect, not hit the general population, was the harm to the population out of proportion to the military benefit sought? The coalition's massive resources meant that eventual victory was in no material doubt, so that strikes on infrastructure were not essential to securing it; but it was legitimate to seek ways of reducing the duration and the all-round costs of the conflict. Proportionality could properly be weighed – and was weighed – in those terms.

Overall, there seems no great difficulty in regarding the 1991 war as passing just war scrutiny. Indeed, some criticisms later directed at its conduct relate to actions taken – or not taken – on grounds that were essentially if not explicitly of a just war character. Coalition forces did not press on to Baghdad, because that would have exceeded the right authority of the Security Council mandate; and they did not continue to destroy retreating and near-defenceless Iraqi forces because that would have been unnecessary and disproportionate to the objective of liberating Kuwait.

The next large operational test engaging British forces was the 1999 Kosovo episode, where NATO mounted a campaign of air strikes (with, eventually, the threat of ground intervention in the background) to help halt and reverse the Serbian expulsion of the Albanian majority. Just cause and sufficient cause for military intervention were in little doubt. The Milosevic regime was causing an immediate humanitarian disaster. Aside from widespread torture, murder and home-destruction, a six-figure number of people had already been driven out before NATO bombing started. The expulsions then accelerated dramatically; but the promptness and scale of the acceleration, and its consistency with what had gone before, showed that this was a faster implementation of intentions already formed, not a new policy provoked by the bombing. In addition, the expulsion was propelling hundreds of thousands of destitute refugees into neighbouring countries which had their own severe problems of poverty, instability and ethnic tension. UN Secretary General Kofi Annan had already asked in 1998: 'How can we *not* conclude that this crisis is indeed a threat to *international* [he emphasised "international"] peace and security?'

Nor was there much doubt about 'last resort'. There was a long history of diplomatic striving to make Milosevic desist, and by early 1999 no objective observer could have expected the mischief to be ended in that way. Once more, time was not neutral with the expulsions continuing.

The most awkward *ad bellum* issue over Kosovo concerned right authority. There was no Security Council agreement to the action beforehand (though there was near-endorsement afterwards). The key NATO countries judged that both Russia and China might well veto any adequate resolution, that almost certainly one or other would, and that to try for a resolution and fail would be politically and legally worse than not trying at all. No element of this judgement is beyond dispute, but in the round it was widely seen as defensible. The decision to go ahead with military action rested on three implied premises: first, that the problem was massive and urgent, so that failure to tackle it swiftly would be insupportable; second, that the feared vetoes would be unreasonable, resting upon concerns other than the merits of the issue; third, that the international consensus for action was broad, deep and germane enough in regional terms – the great majority of European states accepted it – to confer collective legitimacy. These considerations constituted a reasonable case that there was sufficient authority; but the issue is not easy, and more recent events have underlined that in this area the application of classical doctrine is still in flux.

Two *in bello* questions arose over how NATO conducted the conflict. One concerned what it was legitimate to target; the other concerned proportion between risk to one's own side and collateral risk to innocent bystanders on the other. The first of these issues was similar to that in the 1991 Gulf War – was it right to target bridges, electricity stations, industrial installations and the like? – but the problem was now more awkward. In the Gulf, the effect on civilians was genuinely incidental; in the Kosovo operation, it seemed in some degree part of the objective. Even if Milosevic regarded the well-being of his armed forces as a critical concern, they were difficult to hit, with no formed enemy on the ground to compel them to concentrate openly and so present vulnerable targets. It was therefore hard to impose on him by this route a penalty painful enough to help make him change his mind – the ultimate objective. Attacks on wider infrastructure appear to have been undertaken partly to make life uncomfortable for (though not to kill) the general population, and so undermine domestic tolerance of the Milosevic regime. Such a concept does not fit easily with traditional just war rules, but the Kosovo task – an international operation to prevent a tyrant from expelling his own people – was highly unusual. Action like this, where no better option for pressure seemed available and where the Serbian population had some power to influence the leader (as their eventual removal of him showed) is not necessarily contrary to the ethos of just war doctrine. It is fair to ask critics what else they would have counselled NATO to do – short, perhaps, of ground invasion, with all its uncertainties and costs – to make Milosevic desist. Just war thinking has an underlying theme of pragmatism – that is a crucial element of its merit and strength – so that 'What is the alternative?' is always a proper question.

This issue in Kosovo does, however, suggest – as also did later problems about Iraq – that international reflection is needed on whether clearer and more systematic concepts ought to be developed to guide the use of military force when the requirement is for coercion to change political behaviour rather than for the imposition of classical defeat.

The other *in bello* issue about Kosovo concerned proportionate risk. No one on the NATO side was lost in combat in the entire two-and-a-half months of the operation. But modern war is not a game in which combatants should give adversaries a sporting chance. If a commander can so conduct operations that, without infringing other moral rules, none of his own side is lost, it is not merely his right but his duty to do so. The question whether there would have been even fewer mistakes in target identification or strike accuracy if coalition aircraft had flown lower, within reach of anti-aircraft fire, turns on complex technical factors; but it is not self-evident that the answer, with modern systems, is necessarily 'Yes', or that being avoidably vulnerable improves care and steadiness of aim.

After the Kosovo operation, the next UK-involving event classifiable as a war was the US-dominated action in Afghanistan in the autumn of 2001 to extirpate al-Qa'ida and unseat the Taleban regime that had partnered it by shelter and support. UK participation was on a small scale, and the justice of the cause was indisputable in the wake of the massive outrage of 11 September 2001 and the risk that the partnership would repeat such acts. A few critics queried the *in bello* legitimacy of some of the US air operations in respect of discrimination or proportionality; but discussion is not attempted here.

The United Kingdom was, however, massively engaged, politically and militarily, in the 2003 war to oust Saddam Hussein's regime from Iraq. Thorough commentary on how that episode should be rated in the just war calculus would need more space than this chapter can command; but the following paragraphs suggest some aspects that may have relevance beyond the event itself.

The first concerns motivations. It is hard to avoid the suspicion that a determined group at and near the centre of the US Administration saw the war as fulfilling their ambition to begin remoulding the Middle East into a political form better suiting their perception of US and global interests. Their declared desire for action to remove Saddam as a key step in the remoulding long pre-dated 11 September 2001; the main import of that event in relation to Iraq may have been to create a public mood ripe to be harnessed. In parallel, it is conjectured in the UK that for Mr Blair's government, the determinant was less Saddam's diverse iniquities – the justifications emphasised from among these shifted as time passed – than the importance of standing alongside the United States. But even if these diagnoses are correct and the motives so portrayed thought insufficient to justify war, that does not close off the *ad bellum* analysis. In most large collective enterprises a wide mix of motivations can be found, and inappropriate impulsions can still lead to doing the right thing. The crucial question is whether legitimate grounds existed for the grave action of starting war, even if those grounds were not everywhere the prime influences upon decision-makers.

The next aspect concerns consequences. Much post-conflict commentary argues that the world, the region and Iraq are better off than if the action had not been taken. The jury will remain out for a considerable time on aspects of that claim; but even if it be accepted, that does not alone legitimise the invasion by just war standards. A reasonable prior judgement that going to war will leave things better than they would otherwise be is a necessary condition, but not a sufficient one; the *ad bellum* criteria are not simply consequentialist. Questions about the Iraq war arise against at least four of these: just cause, sufficient and proportionate cause, right authority and last resort.

Several candidate reasons were offered at one time or another as just cause: for example, that Saddam intolerably oppressed his own people; that through the combination of possessing 'weapons of mass destruction' (WMD) and having links to terrorists, he posed a threat to the homeland of the United States (and other Western countries); that he posed a threat to others in his own region; that his defiance of the Security Council over WMD possession, in breach of the direct bargain with the Council that limited his 1991 defeat, could not be left uncorrected. Much could be said about each of the justifications suggested; but those of particular interest for the evolution of just war concepts are the appalling character of Saddam's internal regime, and threat to the US homeland.

The appallingness had long been manifest, and its termination is greatly to be welcomed. What is debatable is whether it was proper ground for a war costing many lives. The Kosovo episode and the widespread recognition that outside countries should have sought to stop the massacres in Rwanda in 1994 illustrate a powerful case for swift and forceful intervention to halt massive humanitarian catastrophes. But for all Saddam's crimes in the past, nothing like that had been happening or was in prospect in Iraq in 2003. Perhaps the global community ought to be ready, for common humanity, to intervene by force to remove brutally oppressive rulers; but that is not an accepted concept in current international law or custom. It seems both objectionable in principle and dangerous in practice that what was effectively the decision of a single power, not the international community or any regionally relevant subset of it, should establish a major new rule *and* judge which regimes should be regarded as sufficiently awful *and* determine what action should then be taken.

The concept of action to ward off a grave, concrete and imminent threat is not difficult to accept. It is often acknowledged that Israel was entitled to strike first in

1967 against neighbours hostile to her existence and plainly engaged in menacing preparations. But the Iraq case does not fit that template. It is a stretch of language to describe the invasion as pre-emptive – it was, at best, precautionary. The potential coupling of WMD with virulent and suicidal international terrorism creates a new possibility of, at the extreme, terrible character; but that does not exempt decision-makers from weighing probabilities realistically against costs. The feared eventuality combined several propositions:

- that Saddam had a substantial WMD armoury;
- that he was an active supporter and provider for an effective international terrorist group;
- that he would give such a group WMD;
- that the terrorists would succeed in using WMD against the US homeland; and
- that this would cause deaths on a massive scale, not just that of, say, the 1995 Tokyo subway episode.

None of these propositions could be conclusively disproved. Human affairs cannot, however, be managed to a standard of zero risk. The combination of all the propositions – which was what the 'US homeland threat' justification for so drastic a step as regime-changing invasion would require – was little supported by evidence, and of notably low probability. By contrast, the probability that the course taken to remove or narrow this conjectured risk would entail heavy costs – especially for people outside the United States, above all the Iraqi people – was high, indeed certain. The coalition partners have proved unwilling to provide any estimate of how many Iraqis, military and civilian, died in the conflict and its aftermath, but the total seems likely to be in five figures (and reasonable estimation beforehand cannot have assumed less, especially given the belief that Saddam had chemical and biological weapons). To label a government a 'rogue' regime, however justifiably, does not erase the rights of its subjects as human beings; and the duty of a national leader to protect his citizens does not confer a right to inflict heavy and near-certain penalties upon others to ward off an uncertain risk to his own, unless that risk can fairly be judged of both massive scale and high probability. Looking back, many might be less ready now than the Security Council (including Mr Reagan's US administration) was in 1981 to condemn the preventive raid by Israel that destroyed Iraq's Osirak nuclear reactor; but that did not cost many thousands of lives.

The above discussion concerns whether the argument of legitimate pre-emption satisfied, in the circumstances of Iraq, the test of proportionality *ad bellum*. Issues of similar logical pattern arose also under the *in bello* heading. Modern technology gives advanced countries, especially the United States, weapon systems able to hit targets with great precision and effect. But hitting what is aimed at is only half of the task. The other half is aiming at the right thing. Technology and intelligence can help, but cannot guarantee success. Good training and fire discipline also help, but still deal with only part of the problem. The bigger part is often-unavoidable uncertainty, and the resultant difficulty of balancing risks and costs amid imperfect knowledge – most evidently, the risk that if one fires, one may kill innocents or even one's own side, against the risk that if one holds fire, one's own side may suffer, one's own comrades be killed.

This problem often arises in urgent and stressful circumstances. No formulaic prescription is possible. But there needs to be an honest recognition of risks on both sides of the balance, and an honest attempt to weigh probabilities in situations where only probabilities are available. One has a special duty to one's own side, but it cannot override everything else. That approaching vehicle may be carrying a suicide bomber, not just frightened and disoriented civilians. Do I fire if I reckon the chances are fifty-fifty? One in ten? One in a hundred, or a thousand? Somewhere along that spectrum there must be a cross-over point – a moral duty thereafter to shoulder some risk rather than load it all onto others. Reports from Iraq have prompted unease about whether this attitude to ambiguous situations is accepted everywhere. In future, some of the hardest questions about *jus in bello,* at least for Western powers, may centre upon how far it is legitimate to use technological or other superiority to reduce risk to our own side where there is a trade-off between that risk and the risk of doing more harm than we wish, or ought to wish, to others.

Whether there was 'sufficient and proportionate' cause to warrant the remarkable step of starting a full-scale war depends partly on which of the candidate reasons is regarded as providing just cause. If it be judged, with some commentators including this writer, that only the upholding of UN authority is solidly sustainable, it is questionable whether so extreme a step was justified. Other options could have been explored for using force, once credible non-military courses had been exhausted, to establish that defiance of the UN entails painful costs. The US administration never encouraged discussion on such lines; regime-changing invasion was the only option presented.

The issue of right authority also turns partly upon what basis of just cause is recognised. If it be serious threat to the US homeland, the right of self-defence by a sovereign government could ultimately suffice. All the other candidate reasons, however, needed international authority of an up-to-date specificity that was not achieved. The limitations of the Security Council system did not justify proceeding to action – especially if that were to be explained primarily as upholding the Council's authority – with which majorities both of the Council membership as a whole and of the Permanent Five were not content.

Finally, the action was questionable against the criterion of last resort. As noted earlier, interpretation of last resort must take into account that time is often not neutral. But even if one accepts, despite what has subsequently become clear, that the coalition countries sincerely believed that a significant Iraqi WMD armoury existed, there was little ground for judging that Saddam's prevarication about it created dangers severe and urgent enough to justify imposing US and UK belief that the inspection route was exhausted or vacuous over the contrary judgement of the inspectors themselves and most of the rest of the Security Council.

The difficult aftermath of the conflict poses fresh questions, not hitherto prominent in the classical doctrine, bearing upon post-war concerns. It is increasingly recognised, as an aspect of *jus in bello*, that the use of weapons such as anti-personnel landmines and cluster bombs should weigh effects upon the subsequent social, economic and environmental well-being of defeated adversaries. But there is an issue also in a wider framework – a case for recognising something like a *jus post bellum*. 'Right intention' is already one of the classical *ad bellum* criteria, and in logic the test of proportionality calls for likely after-effects to be honestly weighed. Should readiness to accept post-conflict responsibilities – often costly, wide-ranging and long-lasting, as Western countries have found in former Yugoslavia – be recognised as virtually an additional criterion? At this writing, the United States and its coalition partners seem, to their credit, to be shouldering such responsibilities in Iraq; but it is at best questionable whether the prospect was adequately considered and prepared for beforehand. It is plain that the Pentagon authorities who insisted on having the decisive role in planning and executing the management of post-war Iraq gravely underestimated the difficulties, despite copious warnings; the 'political transformation' theory of the case for war perhaps could not admit the severity of the risks.

The Iraq enterprise fails key just war tests. But some of its aspects and of the arguments offered in its defence raise important questions about whether, and if so how, the doctrine or its application needs to evolve further.

Index